THE MAKING OF TANGANYIKA

1 Julius Nyerere

THE MAKING OF
TANGANYIKA

By

JUDITH LISTOWEL

LONDON HOUSE & MAXWELL

New York

Published in Great Britain by
Chatto and Windus Ltd
42 William IV Street
London W.C.2

Library of Congress Catalog
card number: 65-23574

TO
Mwalimu Julius Nyerere
AND
Sir Richard Turnbull

Contents

PART IV: THE NATIONALIST TRIUMPH

POSTSCRIPT

I am deeply indebted to B.O.A.C. for the great courtesy shown to me throughout my visits to East Africa. The B.O.A.C. staff readily helped me to solve whatever travel problems I had during my tours.

Illustrations

Glossary of Swahili Terms

SWAHILI is the fourth most widely spoken language in Africa. It is the *lingua franca* of Black Africa, the Africa south of the Sahara Desert, of which Tanganyika forms a part.

Swahili has a complicated grammar. To simplify matters, I have used only the root name in all tribal references: Hehe, Ngoni, Nyamwezi. These three are the great fighting tribes of Tanganyika, to whom must be added the Masai.

The tribes mentioned in the text in alphabetical order are:

Bennaa who live in the Njombe-Ulanga District of the Southern Highlands

Bisa around Rowuma river in the South Region (now extinct)

Chagga on the slopes of Mount Kilimanjaro in the Moshi District of the Northern Region

Galla in Kenya

Gogo in the Dodoma-Manyoni and Mpwapwa Districts of the Central Province

Ha between Lakes Tanganyika and Victoria in the Western Lake Region

Haya in the Bukoba District of the West Lake Region

Hehe in the Iringa District of the Southern Highlands

Herrero in South West Africa

Hottentot in South West Africa

Ikemba in the area of the Pangani Rapids of the Southern Region

Ikuzu in the Musoma District of the Lake Region

Iraqw in the Mbulu District of the Western Region

Kikuyu in the centre of Kenya

Kilwa in the Iringa District of the Southern Region

Kindole in the Iringa District of the Southern Region

Kurya in the North Mara District of the Western Lake Region

Kutu in the Morogoro District of the Eastern Region

Luguru around Morogoro in the Eastern Region

xiii

Makonde around Mindi, Mtwara and Newala in the Southern Region

Masai in a wedge of country stretching from the Equator to the Central Railway of Tanganyika

Matumbi around Kilwa and in the Matumbi Mountains of the Southern Region

Msovero between Dodoma and Kilosa in the Central Region

Ngindo in the Kilwa, Nachingwea and Ulanga Districts of the Southern Region

Ngoni in the Songea-Ulanga Districts of the Southern Region

Nguruimi in the Musoma District of the West Lake Region

Nyamwezi in the Kahama-Nzega District of the Western Region

Nyanja in the Southern Province of Malawi

Nyaturu in the Singida District of the Central Region

Pare in the Pare Mountains of the Tanga Region

Sambara in the Lushoto-Tanga District of the Tanga Region

Segu in the Ranga District of the Tanga Region

Somali in Somalia, Ethiopia and Kenya

Sukuma in Sukumaland in the Lake Regions

Ukerewe in Ukerewe Island in Lake Victoria

Yao in the Masasi-Tunduru Districts of the Southern Region

Zanaki in the Musoma District of the Western Lake Region

Zaramo in the Bagamoyo and Kisarawe Districts of the Eastern Region.

*　　　*　　　*

Also for the sake of simplification, I have referred throughout the text to the British administrative officials as Provincial Commissioners, District Commissioners and District Officers, although prior to 1926 they had different names.

I have made great efforts to avoid foreign words, but the following Swahili words, in alphabetical order, I had to retain:

Afriti an Arab word which occurs in the Khoran, meaning the equivalent of Satan and his imps; devil

Akida headman, trustee, leader, commander. Originally akidas were appointed by the Sultan of Zanzibar; in German days they were appointed by the German authorities and were often regarded as their stooges

Askari soldier, policeman, guard, armed attendant, any African in uniform working for an established authority, African, European or Arab

Baraza the old Arab leaders used to hold their courts on the verandah because it was the coolest part of the house, from this is derived the word baraza. It now applies to all kinds of meetings, a place of public audience, council, African court of justice

Bibi lady, woman, 'my lady'

Boma fortified or protected place, fort, enclosure for cattle or sheep, centre of district administration, district headquarters.

Bwana Monsieur, mister, sir, esquire

Chui leopard

Damu blood

Duma cheetah

Effendi Sudenese title, meaning African non-commissioned officer, African officer in a European unit

Fitina jealousy, rivalry, vendetta, intrigue, quarrel, false witness, malicious mischief-making

Hongo tribute, toll levied by chiefs on travellers

Hongo-Hongo powerful ghost

Impi Zulu regiment, later Ngoni regiment

Jando African bush education, initiation rites

Jumbe village headman

Kanga brightly coloured cotton square in which Tanganyika women wrap themselves

Katika preposition with a very wide meaning; among or at; verb: to be bent, to be broken in two

Kiboko hippopotamus; whip made of hippopotamus hide

Kimulungu powerful ghost

Kiongozi guide, leader, also name of Roman Catholic magazine

Kugoma passive resistance, general strike

Kwa heri good-bye

Liwali equivalent of mayor, or chairman of an urban council

Maji water

Malongo long grass

Mdaa Euclea Fruticosa, common tree in the low country and the coastal belt; its root provides a brown or khaki dye

Mganga (plural *waganga*) African native doctor, or man skilled in local medicine, including charms and spells

Mkono arm or hand

Mwalimu teacher

Mwami Bahima word, but now also used in Swahili, meaning ruler

Ngurumu rumbling or roaring, thunder

Porojo wild, senseless talk

Rondavel round mud and wattle hut; South African expression

Rugaruga messenger or un-uniformed askari; in 1906–7 name given to bands of men from tribes which had not fought in the *Maji-Maji* uprising, but who roamed and looted during its aftermath

Safari journey

Sauti sounds made by men, animals, birds or musical instruments; voice

Shamba plot of cultivated land; farm

Shauri to-do, affair, quarrel, case

Simba lion

Uhuru freedom

Ukonga to make a noise with a drum; in a wider sense to dance to the sound of a drum

Twiga giraffe

Wadachi dachi is the debasement of the word Deutsch, German, 'wa' the syllable meaning plural. Wadachi was the word used to refer to Germans until the First World War. After 1914 they were called Wajuremani

Wazee old men, elders.

Introduction

I FLEW into Dar-es-Salaam on October 18, 1961.

As I stepped on to the burning tarmac, an African chauffeur handed me a letter. Marion, Lady Chesham, a European member of the Tanganyika Parliament whom I had come to visit, could not meet me because a crisis had blown up in the National Assembly. She wrote: 'I have to stay, Julius has said he will resign, anything may happen. Come straight to the National Assembly, I have a seat for you in the gallery. Keep your fingers crossed. . . .'

I was bound for Karimjee Hall, a fine modern building in the Arab style, which the wealthy Karimjee family had donated to Dar-es-Salaam for its City Hall. The Legislature was borrowing it for its sessions until there were funds for a new Parliament. As my car drove along a road lined with dusty palm trees, overhead the sky hung vast and cloudless. In the town, the crowds were evidence in themselves of the racialist problem that beset Julius Nyerere: there were Asians and Europeans, but the predominant mass of the people were black Africans.

When I arrived the gallery, crammed with visitors, was a furnace. On the floor of the House an African member was violently attacking the Front Bench. He spoke in English: until Tanganyika became a Republic, English was the language for all parliamentary proceedings. He was speaking on the Citizenship White Paper, which offered equal opportunity of taking up citizenship to all Tanganyikans, regardless of race, religion, colour or sex. He said bluntly that Europeans and Asians, to whom he referred as foreigners, should not be given equal citizenship rights with Africans so easily. Even if born in the country, even if their parents and grandparents had been born there, he wanted them because of their white or parchment skins to be put on probation for seven years or to be examined by a committee.

'We have to formulate our own rules of citizenship, Sir. And if government is considering this, again I think it very, very fair that, as a result of all this, on the day of Independence all the foreigners on that Front Bench must resign!' He shouted this,

pointing a finger at the one Asian and two European Ministers in
Nyerere's cabinet. 'Because we cannot be governed by foreigners!
Therefore they must resign! Resign!'

He did not suggest getting rid of all Europeans and Asians, yet
the racialist principle was paraded openly. Some excited members
clapped approval. The question was: how many felt this way?
Would there be a majority for the non-racial principles announced
by Julius Nyerere? When I had met the Prime Minister in London
he had talked as though, in Tanganyika, democracy would defeat
racialism and blind nationalism.

Nyerere rose to reply. In a voice cold with suppressed anger, he
told the racialists what damage they were doing. They were be-
traying the work of the party they had built up together, the
Tanganyika African National Union (Tanu), whose democratic
principles they had sworn to uphold. 'Some people behave like
little Hitlers, drunk with atmosphere, talking rubbish.' He was
having none of this rubbish. Anger giving way to eloquence, he
reiterated his democratic faith and ended: 'This evening we will
have a free vote. Vote according to your consciences. If the decision goes against us, the Government will resign.'

There was a sudden silence as the issue was thus presented as a
stark choice between democracy and racialism. Aged thirty-nine,
with only six weeks to go before the independence to which he had
led his people, Nyerere was staking his political future on the outcome of this debate.

I walked slowly down the stairs, dazed with impressions and
exhausted by my journey. Lady Chesham was waiting for me. In
the Chamber her appeal for a continuation of the work by all
Tanganyikans had met with warm response. As members were
dispersing for lunch, she had gone from one to another.

'I've got the Europeans to agree not to vote on the racialist
issue,' she told me as we drove away. 'This must be a purely
African decision. The Asians will see the point too. . . .'

The House reconvened at 6 p.m. In contrast to the morning
session, there were no explosions; one racialist spoke, but he was
merely a dutiful henchman, saying his piece because he had promised someone to do so.

Julius Nyerere knew that during the adjournment the majority
of Members, who locally supported the principles of Tanu, had
been at work. From his corner on the Front Bench, he listened

watchfully as the Mayor of Dar-es-Salaam, Sheik Amri Abedi,[1] M.P. for Kigoma, made a splendid speech in reply. Sheik Abedi used both wit and ridicule. He had the House grinning broadly as the five rebels squirmed in their self-imposed black *apartheid*. Tension broke and dissolved in laughter. This was a particularly striking speech as Sheik Abedi is an individualist who does not always follow the Tanu line.

By seven o'clock all members had returned to the House and in the gallery every seat was filled.

The debate petered out quietly. Members straightened up in their seats, looking towards the Speaker. Slowly, Abdulkarim Karimjee rose from his chair and solemnly announced: 'I will now put the question in terms of the motion. Those in favour say aye . . .'

The relief at being able to shout after a day of almost unbearable strain showed in the tremendous roar of 'aye'.

For a second time, the Speaker rose: 'Those against it say no . . .' Five despairing voices shrieked: 'No . . .' There was no need for a division.[2]

Everyone agreed that this had been a vindication of Julius Nyerere's trust in his people and his principles. He had defeated the racialists, symbols of a small submerged opposition. He had defeated them in Parliament, by moral courage and leadership.

Lying in bed that night I realised that I had witnessed a historic event—an African legislature wrestling with Africa's most challenging problem—racialism. My tired brain reflected on what had made the Tanganyikans what they are today.

It is the purpose of this book to try and answer that question, to trace the story of the Tanganyikans from the days of the Dark Continent, through the period of foreign domination, German colony, Mandate and Trust Territory, to the fulfilment of national independence. By a rational examination of the past, the present and the future, the Tanganyikans can, perhaps, be understood as they rightly deserve to be.

[1] Died in October, 1964.
[2] The five black racialists were: Christopher Tumbo, Aron Msindai, Saidi Mtaki, John Mwakangale, Richard Wambura.

PART I
THE DARK CONTINENT,
THE RECENT PAST

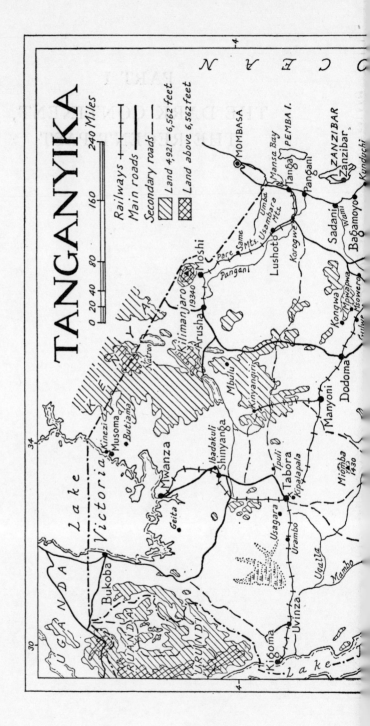

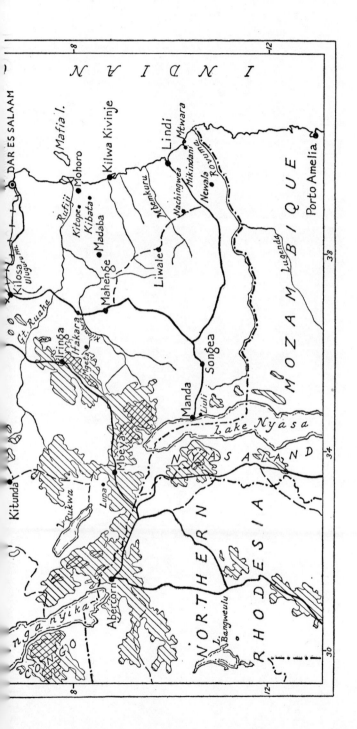

CHAPTER 1

Backcloth to Slavery

THE heritage of Tanganyika is the heritage of Africa. Until the second half of the nineteenth century, that great land mass was called Darkest Africa, and the western world knew practically nothing about it.

The black continent is bisected by the vast equatorial forest, dividing it north from south, east from west. Everything about it is on the grand scale; its colours brighter than any in Europe or America; its skyline larger and ever luminous. Its sunsets are double: near the Equator, the sunset in the west is reflected in the east, and is sometimes surrounded by green clouds. Hot, harsh, hazardous, Africa is yet a continent of flaming beauty and utterly demanding.

For thousands of years this geographical heart of Africa beat in mysterious isolation. The tribes had no written language and little is known of their history. Yet they must have had great rulers, perhaps even great dynasties. Further south, the ruins of Zimbabwe, in what is now Southern Rhodesia, bear testimony to an African culture of a thousand years ago, about which much has yet to be learnt. One thing is certain: Africans claim that, once upon a time, they belonged to a powerful chain of empires, stretching from the west to the east, and that sometime in the future, they will again play a mighty role.

Racially, most Tanganyikans stem from the great nation of Bantu-speaking peoples, about whom we have a good measure of information. Between five thousand and ten thousand years ago these black-skinned, fuzzy-haired, thick-lipped nomads are said to have trekked into Africa from Asia. Then, starting at some undefined date in the thousand years preceding our era, a wave of Hamitic people of Caucasian stock worked their way up the Nile valley, bringing with them their cattle, their traditions and their particular social organisation. Some came southwards on the western side of Ethiopia, others followed the route between Ethiopia and the Red Sea; many of them took part, either from the east or from the west, in the great Hamitic invasion of Ethiopia of the seventeenth century. Both Kenya and Uganda can show

5

populations of mixed Hamitic and Bantu blood, but Tanganyika, apart from the Masai, is a world of Bantu-speaking people, strangely unaffected by the great migrations that have so strongly influenced the history and development of the other two countries.

To trace the history of any tribe in Tanganyika is almost impossible. African tribal history has been passed on by word of mouth from one generation to the next. Legendary events change according to the loyalty of the narrator. Only in rare cases do we have impartial witnesses.

In the nineteenth century, when Europeans first penetrated to the African interior, they found in Buganda, to the north-west of modern Tanganyika, a feudal society similar to the societies of medieval Europe. The king, the Kabaka, was elected from among the previous king's sons; his power and political organisation would have seemed familiar to the Plantagenet rulers of England.

In the 1840s, high up in the lush Usambara Mountains, which run from the coast near Tanga north-west towards Kilimanjaro, reigned the great king, Kimweri. The first missionary to go to Tanganyika, the German Johann Ludwig Krapf, visited him at Wuga, his capital, where he ruled over a quarter of a million subjects. Each district had a governor, often a son of the king, who had to send a representative to the royal court to advise Kimweri in affairs of state. A water furrow, which he built from irrigation taxation, stretches over some twenty miles and is still used. Unfortunately Kimweri's descendants lacked his gifts. Soon after his death in 1860 his domain was broken up into seven chiefdoms.

In many respects the Tanganyikans' ancestors were sealed off from the outside world, but they lived in touch with the coast of East Africa. From the coast came the foreign influences that shaped the future.

Thousands of years ago, driven by the monsoon, Phoenician and Assyrian ships came to this coast. Thanks to the same benevolent wind, Jews, Arabs and Hindus came also. They were traders in search of slaves and elephant tusks, those two commodities—black and white ivory—the demand for which has been Africa's misery. China also prized African ivory, but at this stage it did not trade with East Africa directly.

The seventh century A.D. brought Islam. When Mohamed died in 632 the United Arab tribes set out with the simple purpose of conquering the world. They captured the whole of North Africa

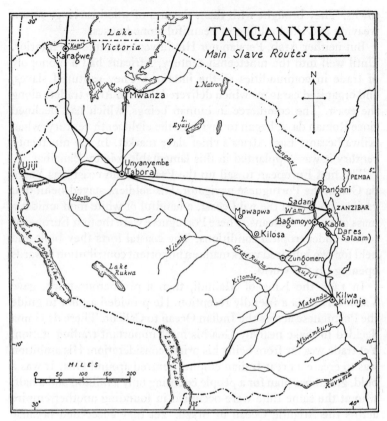

and spilled into Spain, half of which they held down for seven hundred years. But quarrels within the Arab Empire forced defeated leaders to seek sanctuary abroad and some found it along the East African coast. Two well known exiles were Suleiman and Said, both former rulers of Oman. The two settled on the Lamu Peninsula and applied themselves to the highly profitable business of slave-hunting. Many Arabs followed their example, founding slave centres along the coast as far south as Mombasa. They intermarried with coastal Africans and the Swahili people are the fruit of these unions.

About the year A.D. 1000 there was political upheaval in southern Persia. The losers fled to Africa's east coast, developing Mombasa, Pemba, Kilwa and Johanna in the Comoro Isles into fortified towns. They brought with them the arts of wood carving, cotton weaving and the building of beautiful stone houses.

But neither Arab, Persian nor Hindu ventured into the interior. Until well into the nineteenth century, Africans had a monopoly of trade in commodities of the interior.[1] They captured slaves, and organised caravans which delivered them to Arab traders along the coast. The commerce in human beings, which had declined since Roman days, began to revive in the eighteenth century, when Kilwa became East Africa's chief slave market. In the nineteenth century it was supplanted in this lamentable role by Zanzibar.

The first European to sail up the East African coast was Vasco da Gama, the Portuguese navigator. His soldiers stayed behind at various points on the wild coast, a handful of white men amidst a mass of savage Africans. These Portuguese were the first Europeans to live under tropical conditions. The coastal forts they built and held for two hundred years made an important contribution towards opening up the world.

In 1490 the King of Malindi, then a prosperous town, gave Vasco da Gama a friendly reception. He provided a pilot to guide the Portuguese across the Indian Ocean to Calicut. There da Gama decided to make near-by Goa his most important trading station. Yet trade was far from being his prime consideration. His ambition was to create a great Indian empire, centred around Goa. It was a bold, grandiose plan for a people counting only a million and a half, who at the same time were occupied in founding another empire across the Atlantic Ocean in Brazil. Yet they succeeded because they kept a permanent fleet in the Indian Ocean, victualled by three great fortresses: Socotra, an island in the Red Sea, Ormuz at the mouth of the Persian Gulf, and Malacca at the western end of the China Trade. In their turn these strong points depended on supplies from Africa's east coast.

The Portuguese secured their East African bases in nine years by demanding tribute from all Arab settlements. If this was not forthcoming, they destroyed. Eventually Mozambique became, and remains to this day, the centre of their East African possessions. Its future is uncertain. At the end of 1961 Nehru expelled

---

[1] Kilwa, an important trading centre on the coast, was an exception to this. Its rulers controlled the gold supplies which originated in the Kingdom of Monomopata in the interior of what are today Zambia and Portuguese East Africa.

the Portuguese from Goa and Vasco da Gama's four and a half centuries old dream was dissolved.

The Portuguese occupation of the East African coast was a unique interlude of non-racialism. These early invaders had no colour prejudice and treated African men with arrogance or respect, merely according to whether they considered them weak or strong. Because they were greedy and cruel after the fashion of the sixteenth century, the Africans named them *afriti*, devils. They tried to cut out all Arab and Swahili middlemen and trade with the Africans direct. Filling their warehouses with calico, beads and alcohol, they waited for Africans to bring them the slaves and ivory upon which their commerce was based. They waited in vain and although they crippled Arab trade, which never recovered its world-wide contacts, they failed to attract its profits.

The Portuguese introduced manioc, maize, groundnuts and pineapple, since then East Africa's staple foods. They also brought bullfighting to Pemba, the island opposite Tanga, where in a modified form it is still to be seen. The Africans imitated the Portuguese, who dealt with them on their own level, fell in love with African girls and set up homes with them.

When in 1512 the Portuguese garrison of Kilwa was ordered to abandon the city, a number of soldiers preferred to stay with their wives and children, moving far into the interior, slave-raiding and elephant hunting on their own. Their first settlement inland was at Mufindi, where they were joined by other Portuguese from Mozambique, who had also married African girls. A few years later, Lisbon sent three expeditions inland to search for the gold-mines of Monomopata. They never found them, but heat and disease crippled over a thousand Portuguese, who had to be left behind where they fell ill. Cared for by local Africans, many recovered and married those who had nursed them.

Three clans of the Hehe, one of the great fighting tribes of Tanganyika, lay claim to Portuguese ancestry. Father Michele Musso,[2] of the Consolata Fathers' Mission at Tosamaganga in the Southern Highlands, has collected and examined the Hehe legends. In his view, these claims have some foundation in fact.

One of these clans, the Bennaa, believe that they are descended from a Portuguese nobleman, allegedly called Bennaes. This may

[2] Father Musso's book, *Masimulizi ya Uhehe*, will be published by the Kipalapala Printing Press in Swahili.

be a distortion of the name of Bernanos. They have practices which may have sprung from certain Christian rites. When a Bennaa bush doctor mixes his medicinal powders with water, he does so by dropping the powder into the water while leading his hand in the sign of the cross.

The Kilwa, who take their name from the town from which they migrated inland about a century after the other Hehe clans, brought with them iron axes and ladles made of one piece with their handles. Their implements were far superior to any the other Hehe clans possessed.

The Kindole are not only proud of their noble origin, but claim to belong to a European Royal family.

A further indication of Hehe contacts with Portuguese civilisation is their gynaecological knowledge. The great-grandfather of the present Hehe paramount chief, Adam Sapi, had a son born by caesarian section immaculately performed in a mud hut. According to Hehe legend, they have acquired this skill from a surgeon among the Portuguese officers and transmitted it to their descendants.

Finally, physical appearance. Some members of the 'Portuguese' clans have European type features and crania; golden-brown skins, fair hair and clear eyes with golden irises. Unlike other Africans, they have hairy arms, legs and chests. They seem to possess gifts of leadership and organisation, and an intelligence above that of the average Hehe.

Great as was the Portuguese influence, it must be remembered that Lisbon regarded the East African bases as mere stopping places on the way to India. Gradually the Arabs learnt to use firearms and by 1690 had recaptured the last coastal posts; but by then the once flourishing settlements had diminished into decaying towns remote from the main shipping lanes. Their only political link was with the Imam of Muscat, Zanzibar's overlord.

The waning influence of Portugal was overtaken in 1804 by an event a thousand miles from Lake Victoria, and the fate of the Africans in Tanganyika took a new turn.

In that year a youth aged fifteen, called Seyyid Said, murdered his rival and became Imam of Muscat. With British help, he defeated the Jawami pirates who, based on the Persian Gulf, had for long raided both Muscat and British East India shipping. Then the young man turned to deal with his second enemy, the warlike

Wahabi tribe of the desert. Meanwhile Napoleon had been beaten at Waterloo and the Imam no longer feared the French. He sailed confidently for East Africa, where he was recognised by the British as rightful ruler. He introduced the cultivation of cloves to Zanzibar, developed the town's natural harbour and played an important part in ensuring that the flow of trade from the interior was to Zanzibar's advantage. Like his predecessors, Seyyid Said had no imperial dreams, only commercial ambitions, which meant, predominantly, the slave trade furthered by the dispatch of regular caravans to the interior. By 1832 he had so lost his heart to Zanzibar that he decided to transfer his court and capital there, stimulating the sleepy little town into becoming East Africa's commercial and political centre and the biggest slave market of the east.

During the first twenty or thirty years of the nineteenth century, trade inland was dominated by the Kamba in the north, the Nyamwezi in the centre of what is today Tanganyika, and by the Yao and the Bisa in the south. In addition to slaves, these four tribes provided the Arabs with copper from the Kingdom of Katanga, with grain from the Lake Nyasa region; they also dealt in frankincense, palm oil, rhinoceros horn, cinnamon and ambergris. Their caravans roused the curiosity (and the greed) of the Swahili and the Arabs, who from 1825 or so onwards were pushing inland with their own caravans. By 1850 large parts of East Africa were under the Arab slavers' sway, with the result that the interior and the coast became more closely joined. For the first time, events on the coast began to affect the tribes of the interior.

The grief and damage caused by slave-raiders was prodigious, and was to reach a peak during the third quarter of the nineteenth century. The most heavily trodden slave routes of East Africa ran through Tanganyika; from Pangani, Sadani and Bagamoyo on the coast, through Zungomero to Unyanyembe–later called Tabora–to Ujiji on Lake Tanganyika. In 1857 Sir Richard Burton, the famous explorer, wrote:

Zungomero is the great *bandari* or centre of traffic in the eastern, as are Unyanyembe and Ujiji in the middle and the western regions. Lying upon the main trunk-road, it must be traversed by the main up-and-down-caravans, and during the travelling season, between June and April, large bodies of some thousand men pass through it every week. Kilwa formerly sent caravans to it. (*Lake Regions of Central Africa* Vol. I, p. 95.)

From Unyanyembe, the northern route passed through Karagwe, one fork following the Nile to Khartoum, the other ending in Buganda. Yet another sad trail set out from Kilwa to Lake Nyasa, then branching into Nyasaland and Mozambique. The main slave depots were on the island of Kasenge, at Ujiji, Unyanyembe and Zungomero; from here slaves for export were driven to the coast by Arab and Swahili merchants. Pitiful slave markets were held at Unyanyembe, Pangani, Kilwa and the biggest of all, Zanzibar.

It has been calculated that ten persons were killed for every slave delivered safe at Zanzibar. (C. Vivian, Question 25, 1871 Committee.) It is on record that during the nineteenth century, fifteen thousand slaves—men, women and children—were sold in Zanzibar alone each year, representing well over a hundred thousand dead. The multiplication is staggering.

Other African countries were desolated by slave-raids, but none as terribly as Tanganyika. From West Africa millions of natives were taken, packed tight in the suffocating holds of bedraggled slavers, to the American mainland and to the Islands of the Caribbean. But there was one difference. In East Africa the profits of this shameful business poured into Arab and Indian pockets; in West Africa they enriched Europeans. Whatever complaints Tanganyikans may have against Germans or Britons or Greeks, profiteering from human cargoes does not figure among them.

The raiders normally bribed aggressive tribes to procure slaves. If these failed to deliver the goods, then the slave caravans did their own raiding. Dr Livingstone has described a burnt-down village, without one living soul left. Others have written of the long, pathetic lines of slaves, yoked together, carrying on their heads elephant tusks, bundles of cloth, beads and grain—with raiders' escorts marching beside them with 'ready whip for the weary and ready sword for those who could march no more'.[3]

During the nineteenth century England alone campaigned for the abolition of the slave trade. At home this had been achieved by 1807. Twenty-five years later, in 1832, slavery itself became illegal. But the British people wished to see all slavery removed from the face of the earth. Pressed by a powerful public opinion, the English

---

[3] *An Introduction to the History of East Africa* by Z. A. Marsh and G. Kingsworth, p. 30, Cambridge University Press.

Government worked for abolition wherever their authority was strong enough to achieve this end.

One such place was Zanzibar. In 1822 England induced the Sultan, the same Seyyid Said, to sign the Moresby Treaty, which forbade all trading in slaves between the subjects of the ruler of Oman and the subjects of any Christian power. British naval vessels were authorised to seize Arab ships violating the terms of the agreement. Conscious of British sea power, the Sultan did his best to comply, but the Arab traders, facing financial ruin, did not. They soon discovered that three or four cruisers could not effectively patrol the vast Indian Ocean.

In 1845 Seyyid Said was compelled to sign the Hamerton Treaty, which banned the slave trade everywhere except between the island and the mainland. By the time of his death eleven years later, slavery had been much restricted, though it was still legal. Thanks to constant English agitation and, in the last resort, to the threat of a naval blockade, Seyyid Said's son signed in 1873 a treaty making all slave trade illegal. The Zanzibar slave market was closed and an Anglican church built over the whipping post. In January, 1964, descendants of the African slaves deposed Seyyid Said's great-grandson and forced him to flee from Zanzibar.

The abolition of the slave trade, a British achievement, was of the greatest possible benefit to Tanganyika. It stopped the drain on manpower before the tribes were so much weakened as to lose their identities.

The last word concerning this tragic part of Tanganyika's heritage comes from the greatest of British colonial administrators, Lord Lugard. He wrote in 1893:

Our horror-stricken outcries in Europe against the unspeakable atrocities of the 'Arab' slave-raiders ill becomes us when we look back at the history of the past and recall the fact that for two and a half centuries we ourselves stained our hands with this traffic and pocketed the gold which was the price of human blood. We have a duty of expiation to perform towards the African. (*The Rise Of Our East African Empire*, by Captain F. D. Lugard, p. 27.)

B

CHAPTER 2

The Invaders Arrive

FROM the 1870s on, the story of the Tanganyika people was enacted for all to see.

When national consciousness first stirred in what was then German East Africa, blows, reprisals, humiliations and defeats rained on the tribes. In the face of overwhelming odds, they had no chance of winning; but the indomitable spirit of great chieftains was the first manifestation of national sentiment on which Tanganyika's unity is being built today.

This heritage came into being through three anti-German uprisings. It was cast in the mould of a tragedy in three acts.

The curtain went up on Act One in 1884, when three young Germans landed at Sadani. They were led by a man called Carl Peters, aged twenty-eight. He had founded the Society for German Colonisation with the chauvinistic purpose of acquiring as big a chunk of East Africa as possible.

Disguised as mechanics, using false names and travelling third class, Peters and his two friends passed through Zanzibar unrecognised. He was no Siegfried. Of medium height, dark, with a long nose, scraggy neck and mobile Adam's apple, he wore pince-nez with a golden chain. He had a bushy moustache over a large, narrow-lipped mouth.

The trio canoed up the Wami river to Usagara, where Peters induced a dozen chiefs to sign away their territories. His treaties of 'Eternal Friendship' read like this:

'Mangunga, Sultan of Msovero in Usagara, offers all his territory with all its civil and public appurtenances, to Dr Carl Peters as the representative of the Society of German Colonisation, for the exclusive and universal utilisation of German colonisers . . . for all time.'

Illiterate African chiefs understood neither what they were signing, nor that they were lightheartedly disposing of territories which the Sultan of Zanzibar would certainly have claimed as being part of his dominions.

When Peters returned to Germany, Bismarck upheld these worthless treaties, for they fitted into his European policy. To help

14

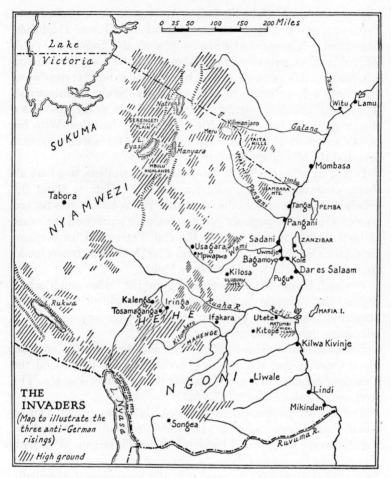

0 25 50   100   150   200 *Miles*

Lake
Victoria

SUKUMA

Tabora

NYAMWEZI

L. Rukwa

Natron

SERENGETI
PLAIN

L.
Eyasi

L.
Manyara

MBULU
HIGHLANDS

Kilimanjaro

Meru

TAITA
HILLS

USAMBARA
MTS.

Pangani

Witu   Lamu

Galana

Mombasa

Tanga   PEMBA

Pangani

Sadani

ZANZIBAR

Usagara
Mpwapwa

Wami

Uwmdje

Bagamoyo   Kole

Kilosa

ULUGURU
MTS.

Pugu

Dar es Salaam

Kalenga
Tosamaganga

Iringa

HEHE

Ifakara

Ruaha R.

Utete

Kitope

MATUMBI
HIGH-
LANDS

MAFIA I.

Kilwa Kivinje

Kilombero

MAHENGE

NGONI

Liwale

Lindi

LIVINGSTONE MTS.

L. Nyasa

Songea

Mikindani

Ruvuma R.

THE
INVADERS
(Map to illustrate the
three anti-German
risings)
//// High ground

the French to forget the humiliating defeat of Sedan, he had
backed their colonial expansion. He ranged himself beside them in
Egypt the more readily because of his annoyance with Britain.
Taking advantage of the British Foreign Secretary's dilatoriness,
Bismarck claimed parts of south and west Africa. Then on
February 27, 1885, he made the Kaiser sign a Bill placing the areas
gained by Peters in East Africa under his imperial protection.

The indignation of Sultan Barghash can be imagined. Without
anyone in Zanzibar being the wiser, Peters had laid hands on the
most valuable territories opposite his capital and bestriding his

vital caravan route to the Big Lakes. At the same time, on the Lamu Peninsula, two of Peters' rivals, Clemens and Gustav Denhardt, negotiated a 'Covenant of Friendship' with the 'Sultan of Witu'. This old ruffian, who chose to call himself Simba (lion), had offered a haven to runaway slaves, rebels, bandits and exiles. He developed them into a force which became known as 'Simba's Janissaries'. They fought with desperate courage, for even death was better than a return to the masters from whom they had fled. With his outlaw followers Simba became the scourge of the northern coastal area and the ally of the Denhardts.

Peters and the Denhardt brothers, propagandists and liars all three, exchanged insults, accusations and 'revelations about the criminal inhumanities' of the other side.[1] Each faction was backed by rich German newspaper proprietors, who publicised the cause of their respective protégés. In the end, Peters and his German East Africa Society won hands down. The Denhardts, facing bankruptcy, had to sell their interests in Lamu.

England, beset with problems in Egypt, the Sudan and Turkey, showed little interest in East Africa. When told of Carl Peters' activities, Gladstone's comment was: 'If Germany becomes a colonising power, God speed her.'

Bismarck sent a naval squadron and an ultimatum to Zanzibar. He demanded that the Sultan either accept the Peters and the Denhardt treaties, or have his island blown out of the sea. The wretched Barghash had no choice.

The British public was uninformed and uninterested. Only a handful of eccentrics, who had made geography their hobby, speculated on what would happen if Peters linked up Witu with Tanganyika by way of Uganda, thereby encircling British East Africa. Confronted by this real risk, the Government eventually organised an international commission to define the frontiers of the Sultan's mainland possessions.

While German and French representatives wrangled as to whether Barghash controlled a ten or a forty mile coastal strip, the British representative, a certain Captain Herbert Kitchener, later to become Field-Marshal, took a hand. He reported that, in order to defend British communications with the East and to neutralise the German harbour of Dar-es-Salaam, a strong point on Africa's east coast was essential. He pointed to Mombasa

[1] *Deutschland-Zanzibar-Ostafrika*, by Fritz Ferdinand Müller, pp. 294–309.

as the terminus of a railway line which could penetrate to the interior.

Then came another diplomatic alignment among the European powers. The British and French Commissioners were instructed to accept the German proposals, limiting the Sultan's rights to a narrow coastal strip and to the islands of Pemba and Mafia. Meanwhile Britain retained Mombasa, although the Admiralty did not judge it worth fortifying.

East Africa was thus divided into British and German spheres of influence. The mainland between the Tana and the Umba rivers was to become Kenya; that between the Umba and the Rovuma, Tanganyika; the Imperial British East Africa Company should develop the former, the German East Africa Company the latter. Both received from the Sultan concessions to administer, in his name and under his flag, their respective areas for half a century.

In this way Tanganyika became German East Africa.

No one thought of enquiring how the Africans felt; not even the foreign traders were consulted. While the British made no changes in their protected territories, the Germans set about applying Carl Peters' harsh colonisation methods. As a result, they were rapidly faced with a rebellion, headed by a fiery half-caste chief, called Bushiri-bin-Salim-el-Harthi. A strange mixture of brigand and man of honour, the red-bearded Bushiri had already defied the Sultan over slave-raiding. Now he was exultant. He had a cause, war against the foreign infidel invaders.

Under his flamboyant leadership the revolt flared up and down the coast and caused excitement far inland. The reason was threefold. The Concession granted by the Sultan to the Germans included the levying of customs and the control of customs posts. As for many years the tribes had been tacitly allowed to collect *hongo* (tribute) on goods passing through their territories, the new arrangement enraged the local chiefs.

Simultaneously German merchants set out to break the Arab trading monopoly. Since slaving caravans and their profits had soared as the Sultan's prestige had declined, the announcement that slaving must stop dismayed the Arab traders.

Finally the Sultan agreed that the Germans should hoist their imperial flag alongside his. This set the spark to faggots already piled high.

In August, 1888, when the German East Africa Company tried

to move into Tanganyika, Arabs, Indians and a number of African tribal leaders concluded an overnight alliance.

The Arabs were determined to defend their trading monopoly. The Indians, East Africa's moneylenders, were determined to prevent Arab traders (most of whom owed them money) from going bankrupt. Secretly they provided arms and ammunition. The more far-sighted among the African chiefs had come to realise what the Peters treaties of 'Eternal Friendship' meant and how the *Wadachi* differed from Arab and Asian visitors. For the first time there was talk of hurling the invaders into the sea.

This opportunist alliance was largely due to Mkwawa, chief of the Hehe. Although he lived some two hundred miles from the coast, he had an instinctive grasp of political problems. Bushiri, the cruel slave-raider, was of little use to him, but he realised that if the Arab rising succeeded in expelling the invaders from the coast, the hinterland would be safe. If Bushiri failed, Mkwawa foresaw that a clash between the invaders and the Hehe was inevitable.

The rebellion first flamed at Pangani, where the local head of the German East Africa Company forbade the landing of a large consignment of munitions. The people joined in the rioting, capturing the Company's staff. A few days later they were rescued by Zanzibari troops, but the majority of the soldiers went over to the rebels.

The fighting spread to Tanga, to Bagamoyo, to Dar-es-Salaam, to Lindi, to Kilwa, to Mikindani. The German flag could only be hoisted after these towns had been bombarded by German cruisers. Plantations were abandoned before the advancing rebels, and even British Indian subjects were forced to seek refuge in Zanzibar. British warships had to help in maintaining order on the mainland. At last the Company appealed to Berlin for help.

Anticipating this development, Bismarck had negotiated an agreement with England and Portugal to blockade the Tanganyikan coast against the import of war material and the export of slaves. The slaves were to have paid for the war material. The *Reichstag* voted two million marks for 'the suppression of slavery and the protection of German interests in East Africa'. Lieutenant Hermann von Wissmann, a traveller and explorer of high reputation, was sent out as *Reichskomissar* to crush the uprising.

Meanwhile in Tanganyika the rebels refused to grant landing permission to a party of Arab soldiers, accompanied by Bishop Charles A. Smythies, whose purpose was to escort British missionaries from the Usambara Mountains to the coast. When the Bishop ordered the soldiers to stand firm in face of a hostile reception, Bushiri personally dragged him from the hands of the agitated mob which had surrounded him the moment he stepped ashore. Next day Bushiri accompanied the Bishop on his way and later gave his protection to the missionaries, who reached Zanzibar safely.

At this point two officials of the German East Africa Company persuaded Bushiri to enter into an armistice with a view to concluding a peace treaty. The Arab behaved with dignity and a settlement *could* have been worked out, but when von Wissmann arrived he denounced these proceedings and at once resumed hostilities. Bushiri believed he had been tricked into giving the Germans time to build up their forces. This in fact was not so. The Company officials knew nothing of von Wissmann's instructions from Berlin.

Infuriated by the German betrayal, Bushiri became a bitter and implacable foe with no shred of chivalry left. This episode roused strong anti-European feeling and led to the martyrdom of two members of the Protestant London Mission Society and three of the Roman Catholic Benedictine Mission of Pugu.

At Bagamoyo, von Wissmann's first pitched battle against Bushiri ended inconclusively, with the Arab entrenching himself near Kaule. African peasants, in spite of their abject poverty, had provided food and sustenance for his eight hundred followers. Equipped with modern weapons, von Wissmann stormed the camp with some fifty men, but Bushiri lived to fight another day.

The second leader of the uprising was the Segu chief, Bana Heri, who had surrounded himself with trenches between Sadani and Uwindje. On June 6, 1889, after four cruisers had bombarded the camp, von Wissmann took it. Uwindje fell the same day but Bana Heri had slipped away. In the next weeks, by hard fighting, von Wissmann conquered and fortified Bagamoyo, Pangani and Tanga. With the German superiority of arms, the ultimate outcome was never in doubt.

Meanwhile Bushiri, with six thousand Matumbi tribesmen, marched north and gave battle in the Kingali valley. Although he inflicted considerable losses on the invaders, they carried the day. Fleeing with a few supporters, Bushiri roamed the country at large until December, when he was betrayed by one of his own kind. A German detachment came upon him, starving and half-naked in a hut. Led to Pangani in chains, he was publicly hanged on December 9, 1889.

But Bana Heri, undaunted and supported by Hehe tribesmen, kept the uprising going in the interior. Only at the end of December did the Germans find his astonishingly well fortified camp. Von Wissmann attacked with all the forces at his command, including five cannon. It fell after tough resistance on January 4, 1890.

After two more defeats, Bana Heri capitulated. Von Wissmann spared his life and four years later the Segu chief organised another unsuccessful rising. He bore a charmed existence and died peacefully in Zanzibar years later.

Von Wissmann's problems were not solved by Bushiri's execution and Bana Heri's surrender. The southern coastal strip held out stubbornly and the German cruiser *Carola* had to wreak terror by bombardment before the insurgents were defeated at Kilwa and Lindi. By the end of May, 1891, nearly three years after the resistance had begun, Tanganyika was safely in German hands.

The Arab-led uprising had revealed many interesting facts. While the London Government would not lend the Imperial British East Africa Company a single soldier, rifle, cartridge or field-gun, the German East Africa Company was amply provided with troops, officers, and modern arms. In the face of the German invaders, even the detested Arab slave-raiders received support from Africans. Von Wissmann could neither bribe nor cajole a single tribe to side with him; nor could he play off missionary against missionary. Fortunately for Tanganyika, their interest was in God and not in politics.

Act One of the Tanganyika story was over, but a seed had been sown which was to bear fruit in the years of tribulation, lasting until 1907.

*   *   *

Meanwhile Carl Peters was busy in the north, as a handful of Englishmen with geographical knowledge had predicted. He aimed at forming a continuous belt of German territory, linking an enlarged Witu to Tanganyika by way of Uganda. Thus the British area would be encircled and cut off both from the Indian Ocean and from the important line of communications with the Nile.

The first part of this plan, when he laid claims to the British

occupied areas around Witu, was so blatant that it failed. Thereafter, he set out to grab the hitherto undefined area west of the
British sphere of influence. His ostensible excuse for leading an
expedition into Uganda was to rescue Emin Pasha, an able soldier
of fortune of German birth, whose province, Equatoria, was
threatened by the Mahdist revolt. This sounded a plausible reason,
but in fact two expeditions were already on their way. Henry
Stanley, coming up from the Congo, got there first and took Emin
to Zanzibar. Sir Frederick Jackson, who set out from Zanzibar on
behalf of the British East Africa Company, heard that Emin was
safe and, having strict orders not to enter Uganda, refused to help
Kabaka Mwanga. The Kabaka had asked for his support against
the Arab Party, then threatening to take over his country. Instead,
Jackson went off to shoot elephant on Mount Elgon, hoping that
the ivory would pay for his expedition.

While Jackson was trying to replenish the coffers of the British
Company, Peters arrived well supplied with money. Calmly he
searched Jackson's base camp, read all his letters, including those
from Mwanga requesting help. This was indeed a stroke of luck;
Peters rushed to the Buganda capital and offered the Kabaka
everything Jackson had felt unable to promise. Although by then
the Arab Party had been defeated, Mwanga signed the treaty the
German put before him.

Peters was jubilant. This time he had done it. The British sphere
was encircled and Germany was at last supreme in East Africa.
It was a bright jewel for the Kaiser's crown. Peters moved on to
Tanganyika, collecting treaties on the way, hoping to depart for
Berlin, there to receive congratulations from Bismarck's successor,
Chancellor Georg Leo von Caprivi, and an accolade from the
Emperor.

But in Bagamoyo he had the shock of his life. He there first
learnt of the Heligoland Treaty which recognised the territory he
thought he had acquired for Germany as a British sphere of influence. In his book, *New Light on Dark Africa*, he admitted that
his feelings were so strong that he had to withdraw to a private
room to regain his composure.

Caprivi did not discard the Peters plan easily. Had he not been
afraid of a French, or a Russian, attack and of a Franco-Russian
alliance, he need not have courted England's friendship. But now
he had to gain her good-will and he agreed to her demands. These

*

were: a protectorate over Zanzibar, (the German residents there outnumbered all other Europeans six to one); the British sphere of influence to include Uganda and the source of the Nile; the removal of all Germans from Witu in the north.

In exchange, and on payment of £200,000 by way of compensation, Caprivi secured the ten-mile strip of Tanganyika's coast that had, up to that time, been recognised as a part of the Sultan's dominions. (The British, it will be remembered, tried to save money and to avoid the stigma of aggrandisement by 'renting' that part of the ten-mile strip that lay in their sphere of influence; they accepted it as being under the Sultan's sovereignty and paid him £11,000 a year for the use of it.) From Britain, Caprivi obtained the island of Heligoland in the North Sea. Carl Peters, who did not consider Heligoland to be a valuable naval base, exclaimed bitterly: 'Fancy sacrificing two African kingdoms for a bathtub in the North Sea . . .'

In 1891 the Kaiser's Government took over the work of the German East Africa Company and appointed Carl Peters as Imperial High Commissioner for the Kilimanjaro District. By then his scandalous methods were so well known that several German settlers raised their voices and the Social Democrats protested loudly in the *Reichstag*. Not only was Peters incredibly cruel, but he also kept a harem. Woe betide any woman who tried to escape. One succeeded. Somehow he lured her back and then had her flogged to death. A young African secretly visited his sweetheart whom Peters had kidnapped. Peters first had him castrated, and then hanged. It is small wonder that Africans still remember him as *Mkono-wa-damu*—'the man with the bloodstained hands'.

Eventually he was indicted by a German judge 'for excessive cruelty to Africans'. But such was his influence that it took five years to dismiss him from the German colonial service 'for misuse of official power'. In 1906 he was restored to his previous rank. He died in 1918, his dreams of Germany's greatness as a colonial power shattered. In 1934 Adolf Hitler rehabilitated him to short-lived glory as a 'model, though stern, colonial administrator'. The Führer issued a series of propaganda stamps in his honour.

CHAPTER 3

Mkwawa's Anti-German War

ACT TWO in this period of Tanganyika's story is dominated by one man: Mkwawa, chief of the Hehe.

His war against the Germans had a Sophoclean simplicity: all the principals were true to their character and moved, logically and inexorably, towards their predestined goals. It is a tale so stark that Africans tell it as the Greeks used to tell their epic tales.

To the rhythm of beating drums, the traditional song runs: 'Mkwawa was a big man, tall and heavily built, with the neck of a bull and the muscles of a lion. His daughter, Fatuma, is his image. Only Mkwawa was taller, much, much taller. . . .'

His intelligence, will-power and courage matched his physical attributes. Without them, he could not have survived, for he had to fight from childhood on, first for his own position, then for that of his people, the Hehe tribesmen. Their example inspired other tribes to struggle against the German invaders.

Mkwawa had a remarkable father, Munyigumba. About the middle of the nineteenth century, he became chief of the Muyinga clan,[1] living in the Southern Highlands. Munyigumba had great, constructive ideas. He began by adding peacefully to his lands, becoming more powerful than other chiefs. Then he scrapped the old system of loose alliances between related clans, appointed instead to every region a leader (in Kihehe called *Munzaliga*) with wide political and military powers. Each *Munzaliga* had to report to him and to carry out his personal instructions. Munyigumba's domain thus achieved a unified character as a hundred clans merged into a single tribe.

Munyigumba also laid the foundations of a trained army, based on the hierarchy of rank and strict discipline. Anyone studying Munyigumba's record will be wary of the notion that Africans, because illiterate, were necessarily simple people.

Like all autocratic innovators, Munyigumba was a hard taskmaster. After his death in 1879, those whom he had antagonised forced his son and heir, Mkwawa, to flee for his life. A relation

[1] An African clan is a very large family within a tribe. *Muyinga* means in Kihehe the wanderer.

23

offered him sanctuary, but within two years the subchiefs, loyal to Munyigumba's memory, brought him back. With the talent of one born to rule, Mkwawa established his authority and, like his father, earned the loyalty of the Hehe men. Having secured his chiefdom, he set about completing the political and military pattern devised by his father.

In the following year, 1882, he felt strong enough to start his military campaigns: their purpose was to win over all tribes whom he regarded as natural allies and to subdue those which were potential enemies.

First, he took on the Nyamwezi; then he turned against the Ngoni, whom he not only beat in open combat but forced, by scorched earth tactics, to retreat into a swampy area where hundreds died of starvation. Eventually peace was negotiated and as a pledge of good faith Chaburuma, the Ngoni Sultan, married his daughter Ilagala to the victor. Mkwawa's harshness to the Ngoni was to prove expensive seven years later.

At this time the Masai, the tall, aristocratic warriors who believe that the whole world's cattle belongs to them, were harrassing two Hehe clans, the Tegeta and the Mgunda. Mkwawa sent a clever subchief to help them; this man trained a small army, worked out a plan of attack and routed the Masai. But a few months later the Masai again broke into Hehe territory. This time the defence was commanded by a woman, Mtage, Mkwawa's sister. The final engagement was so fierce that all warriors of both sides were killed. Mtage and the women camp followers were the only survivors.

With lesser tribes, Mkwawa dealt easily. His domain now stretched over fourteen thousand square miles from a line between Ifakara and Kilosa in the east to Lakes Tanganyika and Nyasa in the west; from the central caravan route in the north to the Ruhinga–Kilombero rivers in the south. He was planning to establish an even greater kingdom when an Arab from Tabora arrived with news that was to change the course of his life.

This Arab related how Tabora had fallen to the Germans. Two years ago, he said, a German merchant called Giesecke had arrived to buy ivory. There was some argument about money, an African fired a rifle and the merchant died of his wounds. For this crime, the Germans arbitrarily hanged an Arab who, so it was said, had not even been present. Siki, Paramount Chief of the Nyamwezi, whose capital was three miles from Tabora, looted Giesecke's property–ivory, arms, munitions and guns. He used the arms to attack and rob the caravans.

The Arab messenger went on to say that just a fortnight previously a German calling himself Emin Pasha had arrived with a hundred and thirty armed men and sent an ultimatum to Siki, who had restored Giesecke's property and humbled himself before the *Wadachi*. The German flag now flew over Tabora. . . .

Mkwawa was stunned by Siki's spineless submission. On the Arab's advice, he decided to fortify his capital, Kalenga. By the time the work was finished, an eight-mile-long wall, twelve feet high and in places four feet thick, surrounded it. Inside there was an armed camp, complete with peasant families in their mud huts, working their irrigated fields, grazing their cattle and carrying on their tribal existence. But pride of place went to the military barracks, where the soldiers were housed, and to the big square where they were drilled.

Any European baron of the Middle Ages would have known Kalenga at a glance. Indeed, he and Mkwawa would have understood each other perfectly.

Unfortunately the chief had no one of his own stature to consult, no one to explain to him the nature, the traditions, the military tactics of the *Wadachi*, whom one day he would have to meet in a fight to the death. Bushiri's uprising having failed, Mkwawa regarded it as his mission to halt the foreign invaders before they could conquer the interior and rob the African of his land and life.

The immediate cause of trouble was the *hongo* levied on caravans using the route on his northern frontier. Mkwawa charged reasonable sums; traders, explorers and missionaries paid without fuss, for they knew that the Hehe would wipe them out if they refused. Certain predatory clans, too far from Kalenga for Mkwawa to control, charged much more. Annoyed by this excessive *hongo*, the Germans decided to abolish the system altogether.

As they knew practically nothing about the interior, the invaders first wanted to find out to whom they were paying this money. When they learnt that it was to the Paramount Chief of the Hehe, the Governor, Hermann von Wissmann–who had put down the Bushiri uprising–decided if possible to reach a settlement by friendly means.

Von Wissman was a very different man from Carl Peters. A good soldier and a fair human being, he tried to understand the Africans and, where he saw a chance of success, to reason with them. There were many Germans of similar frame of mind; but there were also people like Peters, who believed in *Schrecklichkeit* (frightfulness) and who undermined the good work. Terrified Africans could hardly believe there were any decent Germans at all.

In the spring of 1891, von Wissmann sent two emissaries to Kalenga to open negotiations with Mkwawa. They were allowed to approach the wall and were treated to a meal, but Mkwawa would not see them. This was a mistake, but from the point of view of African tribal custom, these emissaries had offended against traditional courtesy by failing to bring presents.

Yet Mkwawa badly needed information about the military strength of the invaders. Having refused to speak to von Wissmann's representatives, from whom he could have learnt a lot, he now sent two spies to Bagamoyo, to find out how strong the *Wadachi* were, what kind of organisation they had, how efficiently it functioned.[2]

They saw warships, field-guns, troops; they watched soldiers practising on a shooting range. Their first reaction was to tell Mkwawa that these foreigners were too powerful to be taken on. But on their way back they had second thoughts. They began to fear for their own fate as the bearers of terrible news: they would be accused of cowardice They agreed to tell Mkwawa that the Germans were strong and efficient, but not to admit that they were more powerful than the Hehe. All the tribesmen were terrified of Mkwawa's brutal reactions when something displeased him.

He saw through their prevarication and came to the conclusion that, faced with such a formidable enemy, he would have to enlist allies. He approached the Ngoni, his neighbours, whom he had defeated seven years previously. But Chaburuma had never forgotten his humiliation and now saw an opportunity to get his own back by refusing to play any part in an anti-German alliance. Fourteen years later, this decision in its turn was to have fatal consequences for Chaburuma.

The Nyamwezi also held back. Chief Siki told Mkwawa he saw

[2] One of the pair has told Father Michele Musso what happened. The facts related about Mkwawa in this chapter were given to the author by Father Musso. See also Chapter 1, pp. 9 and 10.

no need for preparing a war against the Germans. Two years later he, too, was to regret his shortsightedness.

As he could get no allies, Mkwawa fell back on his second plan, to gain time by reaching a *modus vivendi* with the invaders. His next move followed the traditional ways of his tribe. He sent a magnificent gift of elephant tusks to the German garrison at Mwpapwa.

He was not to know that a local German garrison was in no position to open negotiations without orders from above. The German garrison commander furthermore failed to sit down with the Hehe emissaries for a preliminary parley and to return elaborate presents in exchange for Mkwawa's gifts. This was the second fatal mistake in Hehe–German relations.

The Mwpapwa commanding officer sent the gifts to the Governor, who invited the Hehe chief to visit him. But as he too failed to observe the formalities customary in this conservative tribe, Mkwawa interpreted von Wissmann's invitation as a ruse. Instead of accepting it, he began to make ready for battle. For his part von Wissmann interpreted Mkwawa's refusal to come as a slight on his authority, and also started preparing for the conflict that now seemed to be inevitable.

From their own point of view, the Germans behaved very correctly. To them Mkwawa seemed almost pathologically suspicious and unapproachable.

It was characteristic of the two that, at the backs of their minds, they both still hoped to put off the day of reckoning. Von Wissmann instructed Lieutenant von Zelewski, in charge of the military expedition: 'Reach agreement with Mkwawa; only fight if he won't see reason.'

When Mkwawa heard that German armed men were advancing up the Ruhaha valley, he once more tried to avert the inevitable by sending presents to the German commander. Whether Zelewski did not wish to be placated or whether he lost his head, it is impossible to tell. But the Hehe party was fired on and only one survivor returned to report to Mkwawa. He swore to repay the invaders in their own coin.

An excellent spy organisation kept him informed of every movement the Germans made. He knew when they crossed the Ruhaha river and when they marched up the Kilonga escarpment twenty-five miles from Iringa. At its brow he was waiting for them. His warriors were silently hidden in the wood a few yards from the road. It never occurred to the Germans that natives could lay a perfect ambush.

During the night they camped on the right bank of the river. Mkwawa's orders were that, as soon as the last German askaris had reached a certain point, the warrior standing opposite was to fire his muzzleloader as a signal for the general attack.

At dawn the German askaris were approaching their assigned positions. Zelewski, who had slept in his tent, stepped out and saw some guinea fowl scratching the ground. He fired at them and his shot was mistaken for the signal.[3] The Hehe flung themselves on the Germans who could only shoot once before they were massacred. But in the *mêlée*, the German officer-surgeon, helped by askaris, dragged two machine-guns, with plenty of ammunition, into a mud hut, and from there turned the tables on the Hehe. He is said to have killed about one thousand of them.

Of the German force, only two officers out of twelve (Zelewski and the surgeon), and fifteen askaris out of a hundred and fifty, escaped with their lives. A monument, a plain stone obelisk, erected by the Germans in memory of their slain comrades, still stands with the names of the fallen inscribed on a brass plate. The Hehe keep it highly polished for everyone to see and to read.

This had been a pyrrhic victory and Mkwawa knew it. The capture of three hundred rifles, three field-guns and large quantities of ammunition did not change his realistic assessment. To hide the large number of dead from his tribe, he forbade the traditional mourning, except for his son-in-law. Some of the surviving warriors fled to other tribes because they feared Mkwawa's violent temper. Others tried to endear themselves to the chief by relating old gossip. That is how he came to hear about a relation who had intrigued against him while he was a refugee. In a fit of ungovernable rage, he ordered this man to be killed.

This was not the only time he frightened his family by his brutality. When his younger brother, Mpangile,[4] did something Mkwawa interpreted as interference with his authority, he

---

[3] Another version has it that the signal was to have been the call of a bird. A German sergeant was supposed to have whistled a tune similar to this bird's call, which was mistaken for the signal.

[4] When Mkwawa had to go into exile the Germans appointed Mpangile 'viceroy' of the Hehe. Later however, they discovered that he was keeping in contact with Mkwawa; a German court martial found him guilty of treason and he was executed.

thrashed him within an inch of his life. On another occasion, he laid hands on his wife. The head-slave, who saw it, became so angry that he hit Mkwawa across the face. Everyone expected the chief to have the man hanged; if not flogged to death. He did neither, admitting that he, Mkwawa, had been in the wrong. This was unusual fair-mindedness on the part of an African chief of that period.

Until the summer of 1892, the Hehe contrived to harass the Germans with such impunity that Mkwawa felt the time ripe for a large raid against the Kilosa garrison. To draw out the invaders, he lined up some warriors along the southern bank of a near-by rivulet. The Germans took them for a handful of harmless natives, from whom they hoped to buy fruit and eggs. They hurried out, and the Hehe, emerging from their hiding places, killed them all.

One of the garrison's officers, Captain Tom von Prince,[5] was profoundly impressed by this blitz attack. In his report to Governor von Wissmann, he suggested that the Hehe and their methods should be carefully studied before further action was taken. He begged to be put in charge of the final accounting with Mkwawa.

The only hope of finding out about Hehe methods was to induce a Hehe to explain them. At this moment the brother of the man whom Mkwawa had executed for causing trouble while he was a refugee fled to German-held territory.

Personal revenge secured for Tom von Prince the knowledge he needed to defeat the Hehe. Such knowledge is always crucial when different civilisations meet in head-on collision.

In 1894 the Germans equipped a large expeditionary force. The Hehe traitor advised them to avoid the usual route to Kalenga, marching instead to Tosamaganga, where now stands the Consolata Fathers' beautiful mission. Von Prince placed his field-guns on top of this hill, bombarding Kalenga for two days. On the third day, October 30, he attacked, taking the Hehe fortress after fierce hut-to-hut fighting. A grenade fell into the powder store, causing an explosion so great that the beams of the roof were lifted over the river. Mkwawa himself escaped.

From then on, his was a losing fight. But the Germans failed to

[5] His father was a Scotsman, T. H. Prince, his mother a German, M. Ansorge. A born rebel and adventurer, he fought in the German Army and was raised by the Kaiser to the rank of 'von'. To the end of his life, Tom von Prince retained his British citizenship. He was killed in November, 1914, in the fight for Tanga.

undermine his subjects' loyalty. His guerilla activities inflicted constant losses on the invaders, who never knew where he would hit them next. The following report of a German officer shows the remarkable hold he had on his people even in his hour of defeat:

Mkwawa always moved between our patrols. He was supplied with information and food in the very localities where our troops operated. Yet the inhabitants declined to give any information and denied all knowledge of his presence. When we were on Mkwawa's trail, food and liquor would often be found in the pathless bush; his people always knew where to find him, the direction he had taken, and the points he would traverse. Altogether, Mkwawa exercised an inexplicable influence over the natives who, when the pursuing troops surprised his camp, would time after time blindly hurl themselves on the soldiers, sacrificing themselves merely to give Mkwawa the chance to escape. No scheme for his capture was possible, and no one knew even what he looked like.[6]

Any European underground leader during the last war would have been proud of such a tribute from an enemy.

In 1898, when the German Governor offered a reward of 5,000 rupees for Mkwawa's head, there was no African willing to take it. Even the traitor who had guided von Prince would not touch it, though he went out of his way to discourage Mkwawa, sending word to him: 'We've had enough of your resistance to the Germans. We won't support you any more. Go somewhere else where you're not known. . . .'

At this time—it was June, 1898—Mkwawa was hiding in the Iringa district. One day he boldly decided to return to his beloved capital, Kalenga. He wanted to see what the Germans had done to it. He knew that they had destroyed his wall. When he was half-way up the escarpment, Africans came to warn him that a company of askaris, led by a German Sergeant called Merckel, was near by.

Mkwawa realised that he could not get away. It was the end. But he was not going to be taken prisoner.

He had two 'pages' with him. He ordered one to collect firewood and light a fire. When it was burning, he sent the other to fetch more firewood. This boy, who had overheard what the Africans told the chief, realised that Mkwawa was about to kill himself but that he would first shoot his two 'pages' so that they should accompany him into the other world. This was in the Hehe chiefs' tradition.

[6] First published by Graf von Götzen, the second governor of German East Africa, in his *Deutsch-Ostafrika in Aufstand*, 1905–6.

The boy ran some way into the forest, then stood listening. When he heard the first shot he knew that it had taken the life of his companion, who had been the great chief's favourite. A few moments later, he heard the second shot and knew that Mkwawa had now taken his own life. Stealing near the place, he saw that he had been right. Mkwawa had shot himself in such a way that his body fell into the fire. This is how he hoped to prevent the invaders from capturing him even in death.

At this moment, the German patrol appeared. The boy stepped forward and told the Sergeant that Mkwawa was dead, pointing to the bodies. The Sergeant did not believe him and aimed a shot at Mkwawa's head, which penetrated the skull. Sergeant-Major Merckel then cut off Mkwawa's head and took it to the *boma* at Iringa as proof that he had earned the reward. The 5,000 rupees became his.

Mkwawa's headless body was handed over to his family for burial; his skull was sent to the Reich. The Versailles Treaty, according to which Germany lost all her colonies, stipulated that the Hehe chief's skull should be returned to his people so that he could rest, according to tradition, with elephant tusks standing at his head and his feet. This provision was only carried out thirty-five years later.

In 1920 Mkwawa's sons, whom the Germans had exiled from Hehe territory because of the popular acclaim they received wherever they went, advised the British Government not to return the skull. The tribesmen had not been told about the beheading of the legendary chief's body and there was danger of lawlessness if this was revealed. The German authorities maintained that they knew nothing of Mkwawa's skull, although von Prince himself had told the sons where he had sent it.

In 1949 the then Governor of Tanganyika, Sir Edward (now Lord) Twining, took up the matter. He sympathised with the Hehe, their traditional institutions and their conservative way of life. Feeling that the time had come to put right an unnecessary wrong, he carried out a remarkable piece of detective work. Having established that after the Second World War Mkwawa's skull had been taken to the Bremen Anthropological Museum, he asked for its official return to Tanganyika. For four years nothing happened and in 1953 he went personally to Bremen.

Sir Edward had the following data in his possession: the shape

of the skull, its cranial measurements and the place where the shot
had pierced it. The efficient forensic surgeon of the Bremen Police
helped him to examine rows and rows of African skulls laid out for
his benefit. Between them, the British Governor and the German
police doctor found what they were looking for. At that time, Sir
Edward did not know that, quite apart from the skull wound,
Mkwawa had sustained in his earlier days an injury to his forehead
which had marked the bone. His grandsons later identified this
mark.

On June 9, 1954, fifty-six years to the day of Mkwawa's death,
Sir Edward Twining handed over his skull to Adam Sapi,
Mkwawa's grandson and the present Chief of the Hehe. Lady
Chesham has described the ceremony:

During many weeks, the tribesmen walked down the narrow foot-
paths from the hills, up from the river, in from the plains and along the
European built main roads. All were making their way to one place,
Kalenga, where the Chief lives. They carried their best clothes in a
bundle, and their spears and guns on their shoulders. There was
nothing colourful about them. They were covered with dust. It was
June, the time of no-rain. The roads and paths were hard. But they
walked lightly, for they were going towards a great occasion: the day
when Mkwawa would come at last to rest.

On this day at Kalenga the sun shone, and the air was star-spangled
with gold from the yellow dust raised by the thousands of feet of a
crowd colourful and gay in their best clothes. Older men were standing
in dignified groups; young ones were laughing and dancing, while
children were running and shouting.

The Gogo and the Bennaa were there too, tribes that once paid tribute
to the Hehe. The Gogo were newly painted with ochre and coloured
mud; the Bennaa, the little hard-working agricultural people, were
smiling happily. And this being Tanganyika, the Europeans and the
Asians were there too, their women in garden party dresses and in light,
bright saris.

Then the moment came for which this crowd had gathered. Sultan
Adam Sapi walked on to the platform built for him, tall, dignified, with
an impassive face. He was dressed in the traditional long white robe,
the toga with its coloured border flung over one shoulder, his turban
tied in the Hehe way. He was followed by close members of his family.
A detachment of the King's African Rifles came to the salute, as Sir
Edward Twining, Governor and Commander-in-Chief of Tanganyika,
wearing his full uniform with white plumes flying in his hat, and sword

by his side, came on the scene surrounded by his staff. The band played
'God Save the Queen'.

Sir Edward carried a plain, well made box. In a breathless moment of
dead silence, he held it out and Chief Adam received it in his two hands,
bowing his head to the box. A shout tore the sky apart, hundreds of guns
were fired into the air, the women ululated that strange cry they make
on joyful occasions or when they urge their men to fight. The children
were silent, awe-stricken, and Chief Adam wept with joy.

At last Mkwawa, hero of the Hehe and revered by all Tanganyikans,
could be buried as a great chief should be buried, with elephant tusks at
his head and his feet.

CHAPTER 4

The Maji-Maji *Uprising*

ACT THREE opened to the sound of voices, recounting Mkwawa's heroic deeds. Events had proved what arguments had failed to prove, namely that Africans could not weather the German occupation simply by tending their fields regardless of what others were doing. Tanganyika's hundred and twenty-seven tribes suddenly felt in need of each others' support.

Long before Mkwawa's death the Nyamwezi and the Ngoni, who had refused to make an anti-German alliance, realised their mistake. Siki, the Nyamwezi Sultan, was the first to see how things stood. In April, 1892, stirred by stories of Hehe guerilla exploits, his son decided to attack a German column. In retaliation his *boma* at Ipuli was destroyed. Two months later, Siki harangued the assembled tribe. His command was to exterminate all Europeans.

In two skirmishes he was the victor. In a third, Lieutenant von Prince held his own and on January 9, 1893, attacked Siki's fort. The chief and his family fled to the powder magazine, which he blew up, destroying himself and all with him.

The Ngoni, the great fighting tribe of the south, were seething with indignation. They, who had ruled over all other tribes of this large area, were now forced to do compulsory labour on Government plantations and on private farms. Even greater indignity, they had to work side by side with their slaves, or serfs, the Sutu. The Ngoni and the Sutu were eventually to merge into one tribe, but at the time this German affront was bitterly resented.

As for their Sultan, Chaburuma the Thunderer, it is said in Songea that he had a particular personal reason for regretting his refusal to help Mkwawa in his great struggle against the German invaders. Believing that his wife had been unfaithful to him, he laid his case against her before the German D.C. at Songea. Hauptmann von Richter listened to Chaburuma's accusations and his wife's denials, then asked the Ngoni Sultan to produce his witnesses. As he had none, the German D.C. refused to condemn the wife. From that moment on, the infuriated Chaburuma hated the Germans. When the *Maji-Maji* fight began, the first Ngoni regi-

ments–the *Impi*–became known as 'The Witnesses'. Their chief
was to see them and his other *Impi* routed by the force of modern
arms.

The Germans also had trouble with lesser tribes in scattered
parts of the country, especially with the Gogo, who attacked
caravans between Tabora and the coast. Punitive expeditions
followed hard on each other. But the bush often provided an answer
to machine-guns.

At the turn of the century, two new German decrees brought
matters to a head. The hut tax of two or three rupees a year had to
be paid in cash instead of in kind as hitherto. Africans were convinced that payment in rupees meant a higher tax. The cotton they
were ordered to plant fetched such a low price that they believed
that they were being cheated. The Germans were unable to explain either the tax situation,[1] or how to grow cotton successfully.
By the winter of 1905 Africans were so incensed that they were
beyond restraint. That was the moment when Chaburuma and the
other Ngoni chiefs saw their chance. They urged their witch
doctors–under the cloak of the general dissatisfaction–to foment
a revolt which would expel all foreigners and restore the chiefs to
their old splendour.

For thousands of years, the relationship between chiefs and
witch doctors, in Swahili called *waganga*, had been a close one.
These medicine men advised the chiefs on all their problems and
assisted them in their vital function of rainmakers. To this day,
they have to foresee further developments, analyse popular
psychology and devise solutions for labyrinthine problems. Often
they do so with uncanny skill; they also have a highly developed
flair for advertising each others' prowess.

Encouraged by the Ngoni chiefs, the witch doctors started a
whispering campaign. It was that a Snake God called Koleo, living
in the Pangani Rapids of the Rufiji river, had brought a powerful
sacred water called *Maji-Maji*, which protected men against
black magic, the thing Africans fear most. From this the belief
slowly developed that a water strong enough to break black magic
must also be powerful enough to break European magic. Bullets
would be turned into water.

Africans carried *Maji-Maji* water on their persons in small con-

---

[1] The British were equally unsuccessful, and Julius Nyerere failed too. In
1962 only ten per cent of the registered taxable Africans paid their taxes.

tainers cut from millet or maize stalks.[2] If they could not receive this elixir personally from Bokero,[3] a witch doctor living near the Pangani Rapids, friends could always obtain it in exchange for presents of cloth. They were to drink a little at a time, and sprinkle it four times on head, chest and feet.

Maji-Maji followers were encouraged to pass on the secret of the magic water against a token of cash payment. This was shrewd psychology, for Africans rarely value things given away free. Everyone, including the poorest, was willing to pay. Equally shrewd was the instruction that certain things could never be mentioned. Among the forbidden words were the real names of the witch doctors. Code words were imposed for a number of things. A lion had to be called a sheep; a leopard became a cat, a snake a creeper. A European became red earth, an askari was a moth. Africans revel in the verbal mumbo-jumbo of secret societies. They paid little or no attention when the cunning witch doctors added that in war, warriors must be continent and that sleeping with a woman on the eve of battle would break the water's spell.

The chiefs and their deputies, however, knew the real purpose of the *Maji-Maji* cult. A letter, dictated by one of Chaburuma's sons and addressed to a Yao friend living in Portuguese East Africa, makes this clear:

A command has come to us from God[4] that the white men must be driven from the land. We are therefore to do battle with them. . . . I wished to send you a present now, but was unable to do so. The war ordered by God is the first consideration. Send me a hundred men with firearms! Help me to storm the *boma* of Songea! I am presenting you with a flask containing means whereby the Europeans may be vanquished. Do not doubt it, for it has great power. (*African Afterthoughts*, by Sir Philip Mitchell, p. 247.)

[2] From R. M. Bell's article, 'The Maji-Maji Rebellion In The Liwale District', in *Tanganyika Notes and Records*, January 1950.

[3] Bokero was probably a title of rank; his real name was Kinjikitira Ngwale. After his execution his younger brother continued to dispense the magic water. The Ngwales and their brother-in-law, Ngmeya, a third famous witch doctor, all belonged to the Ikemba tribe.

[4] Father Gerald Rupper, O.B., Head of Peramiho Teachers' Training College, Tanganyika, thinks that in the original 'God' may have been spelt *Hongo-Hongo*. *Hongo-Hongo*, also called *Kimulungu*, was said to be a powerful ghost, who had come either from the Luwegu or from the Mgindo country. It was connected with Koleo, the Snake God. The pagan Ngoni did not believe in God in any monotheistic sense of the term.

In setting the stage for the *Maji-Maji* uprising, the witch doctors took several factors into consideration. They knew that the old hatred of the Arab slave-traders was still very much alive. The southern slave route, running from Kilwa to Lake Nyasa and beyond, had passed through this area. In the mountains above Kibata there are enormous caves. When slave-raiders approached, an earlier generation of medicine men had hidden their protégés in them. Now, under Bokero's guidance, the caves were prepared as a last refuge in the case of war. This action, of great symbolic value among Africans, helped to merge the old hatred of Arab slavers with the new hatred of German occupiers. The witch doctors cleverly channelled this into a general hatred of all foreigners.

Moreover, although the tribes in the centre and the north of Tanganyika had been so weakened by their fights against the Germans that they could not lead a new resistance movement, those of the south, among whom the Ngoni were the most powerful, had been little affected. They had no conception of the price the Hehe, the Nyamwezi and the Sukuma had paid for their defiance of the occupiers. The southerners were chafing to hit out against the Germans, and the witch doctors played on these feelings to rouse them against all foreigners.

Finally, the southern tribes, much more primitive than those of the centre or of the north, were witchcraft riddled, as indeed they are to this day. Witch doctors wielded immense power over them, and shrewdly counted on them to accept in full the *Maji-Maji* cult, including not only the belief that the sacred water would protect them against European bullets, but the doctrine that after seven days dead warriors would rise again.

The keynote of the *Maji-Maji* uprising was hatred of all foreigners; the means to lead unarmed tribesmen against the Germans was an unscrupulous exploitation of their belief in the protective powers of the sacred water. Nevertheless, the ultimate purpose of the anti-German conspiracy was the determination of the Ngoni chiefs to restore themselves to their old position of absolute power. The witch doctors understood this perfectly. It also suited their interests, for under the old dispensation their influence was as great as that of their chiefs.

Even so, the year 1905 might have passed without a major

explosion but for German red tape. In mid-July the unpopular *akida*[5] of Kibata issued orders for cotton picking by forced labour. Instead of obeying, the Africans went to Bokero for advice. The *akida* reported to the Acting D.O. of Kilwa that Bokero the witch doctor was inciting the natives to cause trouble. But, as the Rufiji river was in the Mohoro District, the Acting D.O. sent the letter to his opposite number at Mohoro. By the time it reached there, the *akida* was besieged in his house and 100,000 square miles of Africa were in revolt.

It broke out in Kitope, in the north of southern Tanganyika. A witch doctor called Ngameya, a brother-in-law of Bokero, boasted of having rescued a young man from a lake *alive* five days after he had vanished into it. The Africans reasoned that if Ngameya could bring a man back from the dead then he could also defeat the Germans and free his followers from compulsory labour. Suddenly it was being said that Europeans were not strong enough to overcome the power of the sacred water. Then Ngameya ordered them to rise against all foreigners. They obeyed, ruthlessly killing all Europeans and Arabs and persons friendly with them— as well as Africans unwilling to join the movement. Only a few Indians (now known as Asians, because of the division of the sub-continent into India and Pakistan) were spared, because, living close to the *boma* and never venturing into the countryside, they were little known. Shops were looted and goods handed over to Ngameya.

The rising spread like bushfire, setting the pattern of the *Maji-Maji* terror.

In a village called Madaba, two Swahili overseers arrived beating the morning drum, calling people to work on the Government cotton plantation. These two men were particularly detested because, when Africans were late for work they made them chastise each other, jeering: 'You are too dirty for our hands to touch.'

Both were spreadeagled on a flagpole and horribly beaten. Then the wife of one man, on pain of death, was forced to lash her husband with a *kiboko* (a whip made of hippopotamus hide) until he died. The other Swahili had, mercifully, breathed his last by then. Other prisoners, also cruelly beaten, were thrown down a ravine.

---

[5] An *akida* was a headman, a position the Germans filled with their own protégés. In the early days, the *akidas* were Arabs or Swahilis, because these were the only people with learning and authority. Later on the Germans also appointed Africans.

Two of them survived. In the twilight they emerged. One, an Arab, crawled to a *jumbe* he knew and begged him: 'God has spared me, please save me. . . .' The African answered by calling him a dirty slave-raider and decapitated him at a sweep. His hidden Swahili friend, who had witnessed this ghoulish scene, managed to reach a woman who did save him. He was one of the few eye-witnesses to survive.

In the centre of southern Tanganyika the leader of the uprising was an elephant hunter called Abdulla Mpanda. He went to Bokero to take the sacred water mainly because the Germans had failed to make him a *jumbe*. Early in August, on his way back to Liwale, Mpanda abandoned the pursuit of elephant for human game. He visited two askaris as a friend, drugged them, and carried them to the bush. There he slit their throats. By this act he was fully committed. He set the war drum throbbing and next morning the rising broke out at a caravan halting place fourteen miles from Liwale. All former German askaris and traders were brutally murdered.

Only one Arab escaped. He fled to the German *boma* at Liwale. Faupel, the sergeant in charge, immediately posted sentries a hundred yards from its fences. One was on guard near the house of a German trader called Aimer. Aimer unwittingly played a decisive role in the *Maji-Maji* uprising; he struck the first blow for the defence by shooting two Africans dead.

This act, one of the turning points of the revolt, has been discussed by Africans ever since. It was proof that *Maji-Maji*, after all, did not turn bullets into water. Some Africans cried: 'We've been cheated. . . .' Others rushed forward, screaming even louder: 'Those killed have slept with a woman! Love-making forfeits *Maji-Maji* protection. . . .'

With their machine-guns, Faupel and his men wrought havoc among the Africans and the *boma* seemed safe. But not for long. An African tied a piece of dry bark to his arrow, set it alight and launched it into the *boma's* thatched roof. Within a minute the roof was in flames.

Several policemen and local traders, who had taken refuge in the *boma* with their families, managed to reach the hut opposite. Its roof made of caked mud could not be set on fire. But Faupel, who had fought desperately, was so weakened by poisoned arrows that he fell dead outside it.

Then occurred an episode which shows the depth of African fanaticism. Abdulla Mpanda's daughter was married to an askari stationed at the *boma*. Before the attack, her father sent word that she was to return home; she replied that her duty was at her husband's side. Forced to flee from the flames, she fell on her knees before her father, begging his forgiveness. Abdulla Mpanda spurned her, his first-born child, drew a knife and cut her throat. Of such stuff are the primitive legends of a people made.

The second way in which Aimer, the German trader, influenced the *Maji-Maji* uprising, was even more fateful. A little earlier he had persuaded an African called Msham Kinjalla to borrow money for a certain trading operation. When it failed and Msham could not repay the loan, Aimer reported him to the *boma*. Msham was promptly given twenty-five lashes and told to find the money within a few days. After borrowing from relatives, he brought half the sum, and received another lashing. Again he returned with half the amount still outstanding, and was led a third time to the flogging block.

Msham had a brother called Omari, the most influential *jumbe* in southern Tanganyika. In the early days, Omari would neither 'take the water', nor have anything to do with the uprising. For this Mpanda had him arrested and condemned to death. But when in prison Omari heard of his brother's humiliating experience, he changed his mind. Other *jumbes* pleaded his case so eloquently that Mpanda forgave him and Omari became their most effective leader.

Now there was no stopping the *Maji-Maji* madness. It engulfed innocent and guilty alike.

Particularly tragic was the case of the missionary Bishop Cassian Spiss of the Benedictine Order. Twelve days before Liwale's fall he had set out from Kilwa with two brothers, three sisters, three African servants and some Ngoni porters. Though the German D.C. had warned him of dangers on the road, the Bishop trusted in his own popularity. The day the caravan halt was sacked, the party arrived at a near-by village. The Ngoni porters deserted in a body, joining the *Maji-Maji* army. Next morning, one of the Bishop's African servants went in search of other porters. Insurgents arrested him, tracked down the missionaries and speared them to death. Eventually their remains were re-buried in St Joseph's Cathedral, Dar-es-Salaam, where they rest still.

The massacre of Bishop Spiss and his fellow Benedictines was a senseless crime. These were friends of the Africans. They did not use their arms even to defend themselves. And yet if one compares the *Maji-Maji* uprising with the Mau Mau emergency–and the two have features in common–the Tanganyikan record is far better than the Kenyan. Here a handful of European civilians were murdered; in Kenya the Mau Mau killed with ghastly brutality thirty-two Europeans, men, women and children, most of whom had shown them fairness and affection. They also murdered twenty-six Asians and close on two thousand loyal Kikuyu.[6] At their worst, the British had treated the Kikuyu infinitely better than the Germans had treated the Tanganyikans. Yet Mau Mau leaders forced personal servants to kill masters whom they loved. No such ruthlessness was recorded even at the height of the *Maji-Maji* revolt.

When Count von Götzen, since 1900 Governor of German East Africa, heard of Bishop Spiss' murder, he cabled to Berlin for reinforcements. Two cruisers and a company of marines were sent off immediately. In his memoirs von Götzen says that news of the uprising hit him like a bolt from the blue. No one, either missionary or trader, ex-askari or African, had even breathed a hint of what was to come. He believed that the rising had been planned for September, but had broken out prematurely. What amazed him was the scene on August 24, 1905, when the captured Bokero was about to be hanged. He stood under the gallows completely serene. His last words were: 'My death will make no difference, for my teaching has spread far and wide.'

Such was the effect of the dedicated fighting of the Africans, despite mounting proof that *Maji-Maji* did not turn bullets into water. According to von Götzen: 'The natives fought amazingly well, only retreating in the face of machine-gun fire, and then in good order, to reform at the earliest opportunity. Their discipline was astonishing. . . . Prisoners were totally indifferent to their personal fate.'

It was a crusade against oppression, ill-treatment by Swahili overseers, flogging for small misdeeds, but above all against all foreigners. The Ngoni chiefs, determined to regain their old power, were the leaders.

[6] Of the Security Forces, 63 Europeans, 3 Asians and 525 Africans were killed. Altogether 95 Europeans, nine Asians and 2,357 Africans, a total of 2,461 lives, were lost on the Government side in Kenya.

The uprising reached its zenith in September, 1905, when the entire territory south of the present Central Railway and east of the Great North Road (except for Heheland) was in rebel hands. In October, the German cruisers arrived, bringing not only their marine company, but also ample supplies of modern arms and ammunition. These, as could be expected, turned the tide. Systematic suppression began in November. By then the peasant population, especially the wives and mothers, had lost their enthusiasm for the fight. The sacred water clearly did not protect their warrior husbands and sons. Both sides had begun their scorched earth policy. This spelt famine for thousands of families hungry already because, believing that *Hongo-Hongo* would bring them food, they had done no planting.

Neither side took prisoners. There is hardly a single big tree in a south-west Tanganyika village that was not turned into a gallows.[7] After Dar-es-Salaam had confirmed the sentence of a summary court, the Germans hanged forty-seven Ngoni chiefs and sub-chiefs at Songea. This stern measure broke the Ngoni tribe. Its traditional regime, its military prestige and its old way of life were swept away for all time.

The worst murderers were the *rugaruga*, bands of men from tribes that had not joined in the *Maji-Maji* fighting. Armed by the Germans, they were usually commanded by Swahili sergeants and N.C.O.s. Acting as independent units, they took a vandal's pleasure in the destruction of houses and crops.

From the spring of 1906 onwards, the German plan was to round up those leaders who still had a following. Ngameya, the witch doctor, who had started the uprising at Kitope, was captured and executed in March. In April Abdulla Mpanda, Chief Chaburuma and Omari Kinjalla were driven yet further back; in June their camp was encircled – but they once more slipped out of the dragnet. A German patrol seized their possessions, which included vestments and rosaries stolen from Peramiho, the Benedictine Mission founded by Bishop Spiss in 1898. There they had murdered seven African teachers, all members of distant tribes. Now Peramiho is a Teachers' Training College.

Retreating to the south-west, a leader called Abdulla Machimaya was the first to be betrayed and hanged in Liwale. Omari Kinjalla,

---

[7] Fifty years later the elders, *wazee*, showed photographs of these trees to Julius Nyerere when he canvassed for Tanu in the south.

the most reasonable of the insurgents, was captured next, but he managed to commit suicide. Chief Chaburuma, having lost everything, fled to Portuguese territory, where he died, unhappy and deserted, regretting to the end his mistake of refusing to make a stand with Mkwawa.

Abdulla Mpanda, cruel and fanatical to the last, died fighting in January, 1907. As his right thumb had been blown off in an accident, his body was easily identified, and by then many Africans had begun to talk.

The price of *Maji-Maji* was appalling. One hundred and twenty thousand men, women and children died either fighting, by execution or from famine. After the leaders had been captured, some of the warriors formed themselves into gangs and took to the forests. From there they carried on the resistance, mixed with a good deal of brigandage. The German military commanders had crops burnt and food confiscated so that the resisters could not be helped. Of course the main sufferers were the ordinary people, who died of starvation by the thousand.

The German Governor, Count von Götzen, well understood the basic cause of the uprising. His comments were prophetic:

We have been forced to believe in a feeling of solidarity between the Negro race in face of foreign colonisers. The uprising was undoubtedly a symptom of the great movement aimed at independence which, since the beginning of the twentieth century, has made itself felt among the coloured races. This is what gives these warlike events their special significance.

Inside Tanganyika, this tremendous effort, entailing immense suffering and affecting tribes previously not involved in the anti-German resistance, should have demonstrated to the Africans that they shared a common destiny. But it was too soon for that. Intense tribal rivalries could not yet be sufficiently overcome for them to be welded into one people. None the less, the fight put up by the Hehe, the Nyamwezi, the Ngoni and their serfs and slaves gave Tanganyikans a *mystique* which was to affect succeeding generations profoundly.

Half a-century later, Julius Nyerere told the author: 'My followers were inspired by this *mystique* in their struggle for our independence.'

This then was the Tanganyikans' inheritance. They were born

on a sullen, slumbering continent still two thousand years behind the west in cultural and economic development. They belonged to a race which had been decimated by slave-raiders, a race whose strongest sons had vanished. Slaves never return to tell the tale. Although Britain had officially stopped the slave trade, the German invaders imposed their will ruthlessly, placing the African under a new kind of bondage.

Beneath the easy ripples of an African smile, there flows a strong hidden current of elemental superstition and fear. That this current has sometimes been canalised by their present leaders into a groove of principle is almost a miracle.

To ascertain how this change has come about, how elemental beliefs and the hard inheritance from the past have been turned to good account, it is necessary to relate more recent history, and to describe upbringing and home life in our time.

PART II
TANGANYIKA'S MORE RECENT HISTORY

CHAPTER 5

The German Record

THE *Maji-Maji* uprising caused a world scandal. Coming after the savage repression of the Herero and the Hottentot revolts in German West Africa, it thoroughly discredited the German colonial administration. Angry *Reichstag* Deputies and informed Liberal writers attacked German colonial officials on grounds of inefficiency as well as inhumanity. Indignation inside and outside Germany was so great that the Imperial Government had to set up a Colonial Department. Its first Secretary of State, the humane and enlightened Dr Bernhard Dernburg, was hurriedly sent to Africa to investigate the causes of the *Maji-Maji* trouble on the spot.

Dr Dernburg began his mission by visiting neighbouring Uganda. He wished to see how the British were running the country. Crossing the German territory by slow-stage *safari*, he arrived in its capital with a clear idea of what was wrong. While the *Maji-Maji* war was still in progress, he appointed a Commission of Enquiry to sit in Dar-es-Salaam – a courageous measure warmly applauded by the British.

As a result of the Commission's investigations, Dr Dernburg instituted three major changes.

He ordered officials, planters and traders to put away the lash and to rely on common sense. Until then, hardly a German was to be seen in the colony without a whip, which he used freely. The theory behind this brutality was that it was reasonable to punish natives as though they were children and the person who punished them was a surrogate parent.

The numerous 'parents' of the unfortunate Africans were absurdly stern and painfully inarticulate. They were unable either to take the Africans into their confidence, or to explain to them their intentions. They had no idea of African reactions, problems or needs. They had no knowledge of such native institutions as the *baraza*, at which the chief dispensed justice according to well understood tribal law, under the watchful eyes of the tribesmen. They had never seen a chief question a witness, nor a witch doctor, after some remarkable sleuthing, produce the real

47

criminal. The African world was a book that the Germans had never opened.

Dr Dernburg aimed not merely at making German officials and settlers study native ways. He introduced legislation to safeguard Africans against exploitation; he laid down rules for their care, their food, their housing and for their protection against rogues and usurers. His regulations regarding health and sanitation were as effective as was his fight against human and animal epidemics. In the villages he appointed Africans to apply the labour laws. On the assumption that the natives could only do four hours work a day, he fixed their tasks in fields and on plantations at a low level. What even Dr Dernburg did not realise was that Africans were quickly worn out because they were underfed.

Dr Dernburg also developed African education. In 1914 German East Africa had 99 Government schools: 89 elementary and 10 'principal' schools with 8,494 pupils. He had funds in hand for 20 more elementary schools. At the same time there were 1,852 Mission schools with 108,550 pupils.

Unlike British education, which aimed at imparting general knowledge and training 'the whole man' to become a responsible citizen, the purpose of German education was to train selected Africans to understand and carry out administrative orders. Its methods were not without success. After Britain had become the Mandatory Power for German East Africa, her officials admitted that there was more literacy in Tanganyika Territory than in neighbouring British Uganda and Kenya.

Dr Dernburg's third reform was the institution of a plan for the economic development of the colony. Under him, and his successor, considerable improvements were achieved.

Most German settlers lived in the Northern Highlands, the Pare and the Usambara Mountains. To create an outlet for their produce, the Greek contractors who had built the Baghdad Railway in the Middle East were commissioned to construct a 352 kilometre railway line from Tanga to Moshi. Owing to the completely different and unfamiliar circumstances, they ran into innumerable difficulties and muddles. Most of these, however, had been sorted out by the time they began building the 1,252 kilometre Central Railway from Dar-es-Salaam to Kigoma. Both were completed by 1914. So were roads, bridges, ports and docks, telegraph, telephone and wireless installations. For the first time, contact was established between the colony and the outside world. Public buildings, especially in Dar-es-Salaam and in Tanga, were solid and imposing.

The Imperial Government as well as private individuals devoted much money and energy to the development of plantation agriculture. They introduced sisal,[1] tea, cotton, rubber and cinchona. Coffee had been grown in Bukoba for centuries. The Germans started growing the strong but delicate Arabica coffee, which remains popular in Germany and other countries where coffee of good quality is appreciated. They spread coffee to the Kilimanjaro region where it had not been known before. Wherever coffee became established, they made each landholder grow a specified number of bushes; they also commercialised sales. They expanded the coconut plantations started by the coastal Arabs. The production of copra flourished.

The German settlers were encouraged to buy land, which became their freehold property. Most of it they had to reclaim from the bush, although some of it was, or had been, under native cultivation. The Africans, who only knew their own type of communal ownership, did not take in the white man's concept of freehold. When, years later, they came to understand it, they resented it strongly. That is why one of the first actions of the Independent Tanganyika Government in January, 1962, was to announce that all freeholds would be transformed into long term leaseholds; the area affected was less than one per cent of all arable land, but the psychological impact of the move was remarkable.

Dr Dernburg's idea was to establish large European plantations. On these Africans were to work as hired labourers. Even he did not think it desirable to teach them how to grow cash crops.[2] As the Africans had little inducement to leave their tribal lives, planters and policemen used force to procure labour. There was much less brutality than before, but constant pressure to get sufficient workers was bound to disrupt native life.

In 1911 Dr Wilhelm Solf, a Sanskrit scholar who had gained his colonial experience in Samoa, succeeded Dr Dernburg as Colonial Secretary. Another man of outstanding qualities, Dr Solf appreciated the fundamental fact that the natives were Africa's main

---

[1] In 1892 from Florida, where it had been smuggled from Mexico.

[2] Crops which the African could himself sell, as opposed to crops he used himself, or which he disposed of through the agency of the Colonial Authority.

asset. He insisted that forced labour must cease and that native production must be stimulated. Previously the authorities had actively discouraged this for fear that the European plantations might run short of labour. The colonial debates in the *Reichstag* helped Dr Solf because the many unsavoury facts revealed by the Social Democrats shattered official complacency. But by the time his schemes were authorised, it was the summer of 1914 and the days of Germany's colonial empire were numbered.

Bismarck, its architect, had never believed in his own colonial creation. He had only given in gradually to pressure from business-men and professors, who had economic and prestige reasons for canvassing the need for colonial possessions. Under Bismarck's successors, German colonial policy developed two aims: to create a new Germany on the model of the English-speaking countries in America, Australia and South Africa and to produce colonial goods in Germany's African territories, thus freeing her from de-pendence on foreign colonial powers.

Neither of these aims had been achieved by 1913. In the whole of Germany's African possessions there were only about ten thousand German settlers. In German East Africa they numbered 4,107, hardly an impressive beginning for a 'New Germany' on the Dark Continent.

All her colonies furnished Germany with less than 2 per cent of her total consumption of cotton, rubber, tobacco, copra and palm kernel. Of these, German East Africa provided 0·2 per cent. Only 0·3 per cent of Germany's total foreign commerce was with her African colonies, a figure the Imperial Government's critics did not fail to publicise.

Over the years, this general picture would have improved radically. Germany had excellent economic plans, which provided for the colony's fast and intelligent development. After December, 1961, independent Tanganyika's Government pulled the old German plans out of their dusty pigeon holes. Some of them may be realised – fifty years after their inception.

Thus the Germans had real economic achievements to their credit, and yet something was wrong with their colonial régime. For an explanation of this it is necessary to look in four directions.

The Imperial Government in Berlin was uninformed about local conditions. The German leaders would not listen to the men on the spot and sent out many orders which made no sense in East Africa.

Hermann von Wissmann, the first military governor, had the courage to stand up against what he considered 'stupid instructions'. But his successors did not dare to contradict Berlin. This situation only changed when Dr Dernburg appeared on the scene.

The officers recruited for the German colonial service were young, conceited, inexperienced and unwilling to learn. The N.C.O.s were hidebound, fit only to lick conscripts into shape. In the early days their askaris, mostly enrolled outside East Africa, brought a campaign of terror among the inhabitants. They took all they wanted, including women. When an African in righteous indignation killed a Sudanese or a Zulu, the German officer sent a punitive expedition to set fire to entire villages, or to carry away their cattle. African resentment of such flagrant injustice was intense.

As has been said before, German colonial officials did not understand native administration. Instead of letting Africans choose their chiefs and headmen, as they had always done, they nominated them. These nominees were rightly regarded as '*Wadachi* henchmen'. The Germans feared any chief who had an independent mind, because he could mobilise his tribe against them. To lessen the position of these strong chiefs, they appointed pliable men, mostly Arabs or Swahilis, called *akidas* or *liwalis*. They were really German agents and spies who undermined the foundations of the native administration. In some areas their activities were so damaging that the British, when they had become the Mandatory Power, were just not able to bring the Native Administration back to life.

Finally, and this is the most serious charge against the German colonial régime, they did not provide the Africans with any legal security. Any native could be conscripted for labour on a private farm or plantation as well as for public works. The Africans had no law and no Court of Justice to which they could appeal for protection. Without trial, almost anyone could punish them by flogging[3] and they were at the mercy of the colonial officials. They had no hope of redress, however unjust their treatment seemed to be. And they had no prospect of ever becoming anything but retainers to their German masters.

And yet, compared with the past, conditions had undoubtedly

---

[3] 1911–12: 5,944 official floggings administered; 1912–13: 8,057 floggings; 1912–13: 107 employers convicted for assaulting their labourers. But many Africans preferred to suffer their employers' beatings in silence, for any native who brought a charge without being able to prove it was severely punished.

improved. Two excellent civilian governors, Freiherr von Reichen-
berg and Dr Heinrich Schnee, saw to it that the Dernburg and the
Solf policies were carried through. When the First World War
broke out, the Africans had come to realise that the German régime
offered some advantages.

For one, they were certain that Arab rule with its slave-raids
was over and would never come back. This gave them a sense of
security they had never enjoyed before. Slavery had not been
legally abolished, but the German law of 1905 that every newly
born child was a free citizen regardless of its parents' status guaranteed its disappearance within a few decades.

The Africans also knew that, at the time the Germans imposed
their colonial rule, the Masai who had been coming down through
the Great Rift valley from the north and the Zulu who had been
fighting their way up from the south had been preparing for a
tremendous tribal war to establish which of these two great tribes
should be master of western Tanganyika. German intervention
forestalled this threat which would have inflicted immense suffering on the lesser tribes.

The Hehe and the Ngoni, the two famous fighting tribes, had
learnt to respect the Germans. They looked back on the war with
them with nostalgia, as good soldiers do when reminiscing about
former enemies. During the First World War this nostalgia was
transformed into loyal service under the German colours.

From 1906 onwards economic conditions had improved and it
became apparent that the Germans had a plan under which the
Africans also benefited. In the Northern Highlands, where the
African population was sparse and made up of non-fighting tribes
like the Chagga, several planters helped Africans to set up in trade
and to earn good money. Their descendants, well-to-do African
families in Arusha, Moshi, Tanga and Dar-es-Salaam, even now
feel very friendly towards the Germans, to whom they owe their
economic prosperity. But it would be difficult to find such families
in the *Maji-Maji* country of the south.

So there was truth in Berlin's contention that relations between
Germans and Africans had vastly improved. Nowadays many
Africans, when asked about the German colonial régime, reply:
'*Wakali lakini wenye haki,*' – 'They were strict but they were just.'
This attitude explains why they did not revolt against the Germans
in the First World War.

The only group against whom the Tanganyikans felt real resentment were the Indians, who had acquired a bad name because of their greed and usury.

The eight years between 1906 and 1914 had wrought great changes in Germany's East African colony. The Africans had learnt that Europeans had something to offer besides oppression and servitude. This was a new factor in their experience. It drained off much of the bitterness created by the anti-German wars. But it did not affect the mystique created by their heroic leaders, who had already become legendary figures. The discovery that the tribesmen must stand by each other was pushed back into the Africans' subconscious minds: there it stayed, dormant but alive.

*

CHAPTER 6

The Last Gentleman's War

TANGANYIKA was the only African country to remain a battle-field throughout the First World War, and here the German Forces were never overcome. This was due to the military skill of their commander, who is still remembered in Tanganyika and Kenya, and by both sides with warm admiration.

In 1914 all belligerents agreed to exclude their African colonies from hostilities. In private they admitted that the spectacle of Euro-peans fighting each other might undermine the white man's pres-tige. But the Commander of German East Africa's Protective Force, General Paul von Lettow-Vorbeck, held different views. He believed that it would benefit England if Germany's colonies were neutralised. He was also confident that, even with the small force at his command, he could compel the enemy to reinforce the East African front at the expense of their effort in the main European theatre of war, and that in this way he could make a really significant contribution to the German cause.

Von Lettow-Vorbeck took up his appointment in German East Africa on January 17, 1914. By August 4, he had at his disposal 216 German officers and N.C.O.s and 2,450 askaris. When war was declared, the Police Force, in which served 45 officers and 2,154 askaris, joined the Protective Force.

An excellent soldier, deeply patriotic and imaginatively re-sourceful, von Lettow-Vorbeck had received his training in the Boxer War in China, in the Herero and Hottentot rebellions in South West Africa and as Commander of the Marine Battalion in Wilhelmshafen. Now he found himself in the unexpected position of having to defer to the Governor, the quiet, peace-loving Dr Heinrich Schnee who, contrary to the usual German tradition, was Commander-in-Chief as well as Governor. And Dr Schnee was determined that, in the case of war the coastal towns should 'under no circumstances' be exposed to bombardment. Those who knew both the Governor and the General had no doubt as to which of them would have the last word.

British military authorities have stated frankly that, even if the Germans had not chosen to fight, Tanganyika would have been

54

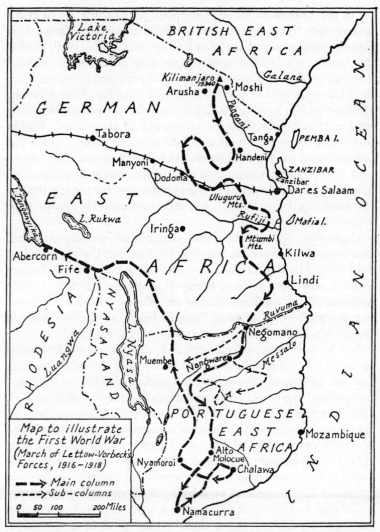

Map to illustrate
the First World War
(March of Lettow-Vorbeck's
Forces, 1916–1918)

---➤ Main column
- - -➤ Sub-columns

0   50 100   200 Miles

drawn into the war. The German Navy had to be denied the hide-
outs of the East African coast. This was borne out by the bombardment, on August 8, 1914, of the Dar-es-Salaam wireless tower,
followed by a demand for the surrender of the town. Governor
Schnee was negotiating terms with the commanders of the two
light British cruisers when von Lettow-Vorbeck took matters
into his own hands.

On the moonlit night of November 3, 1914, the Royal Navy landed eight thousand men and plentiful supplies at Tanga. Von Lettow, advised about the plan by captured Indian mail, stuffed the Governor's pacifist orders deep into his trousers pocket.[1] The stake was the strategic Tanga–Moshi railway. He was willing to risk a great deal to prevent it from falling into British hands. His men put up a tremendous fight and the inexperienced askaris rendered an astonishingly good account of themselves. Within forty-eight hours the British and Indian invading force, which had outnumbered the German defenders by eight-to-one, was thrown back into the sea. A simultaneous British attempt to advance on Moshi was also defeated. For the first, but not for the last time in the campaign, von Lettow was able to rearm his troops with captured supplies.

Contemporary accounts of the Tanga episode are very colourful. One reports in all seriousness that the German Commander had used trained bees to harass the enemy. In his memoirs von Lettow says: 'I may now perhaps betray the fact that, at the decisive moment, all the machine-guns of one of our companies were put out of action by these same "trained bees", so that we suffered from this new "training" quite as much as the English.'

Von Lettow knew perfectly well that, with his few available units he could not defend the northern border and the long coastline. Instead, he intended to stage raids against the Uganda railway, compelling 'the enemy to employ his forces for self-defence'. (*Reminiscences of East Africa*, by General von Lettow-Vorbeck, p. 4.) He could carry out this plan for more than a year because, with Turkey's entry into the war, no Allied reinforcement for East Africa was possible until 1916. This vital respite enabled the German Commander to train his troops for guerilla warfare and to muster replenishments or substitutes for dwindling supplies.

German units were established at a few points on British (Kenya) territory. From here small detachments of eight to ten men, Europeans and askaris, attacked British communications. In two months, they knocked out thirty-two trains and nine bridges.

---

[1] After the British had taken Tabora, where Schnee had transferred the capital after Dar-es-Salaam's fall, the Governor attached himself to von Lettow. He stayed with him throughout the long and cruel campaigning, adding to the General's difficulties by constantly advising him to give up the fight which he, Schnee, considered had no purpose.

One patrol observed that the British sent their riding horses to water at a certain time. Next day four Germans crept past the sentries behind the camp and covered with their rifles the English soldiers driving the horses. They ordered them to put their hands up and explain why they had only fifty-seven horses when the German scouts had counted sixty-one the previous day. Before the British had finished explaining that their officers were using the four missing horses, the Germans got the fifty-seven safely to their lines.

With the captured horses, von Lettow formed a second mounted company, which traversed the desert north of Kilimanjaro, destroying bridges, surprising guards posted on the Uganda railway and mining the permanent way. But the Germans did not have everything as they wished it. Their losses of trained officers were as serious as the shrinkage of their ammunition. A combined attack against Mombasa was beaten back. The land force was repulsed twenty-three miles from the town and the warship *Königsberg* had to seek refuge from the Royal Navy in the Rufiji delta.

In July, 1915 the *Königsberg* was destroyed by gunfire from two Royal Navy monitors, *Thames* and *Severn*. Her crew joined von Lettow's forces. Her ten 4·1 guns, mounted on heavy carriages, were of enormous help to the Germans throughout the war.

East of Kilimanjaro, German patrols had to work on foot through dense bush. Each operation lasted ten to fourteen days. Several men died from fatigue and thirst in the burning sun, for it was almost impossible to carry a sick or wounded man through the bush. Some askaris, who realised that they were lost and so a prey to the man-eating lions that infested that part of the country, offered to be left behind and to hand their rifles and ammunition to their comrades so that at least these might be saved.

In the early months of the campaign, raids were also staged in Uganda, the Belgian Congo, Rhodesia and Nyasaland. This was rendered possible by von Lettow's central position and his excellent communications along the Dar-es-Salaam–Kigoma railway. Lake Tanganyika also remained under German control until December 1915.

While waiting for a concerted Allied attack, von Lettow inspired the German colony to lead a 'Swiss family Robinson–do it yourself' existence. When cotton materials ran out in the Asian stores, he induced women and missionaries to spin and weave. The most suitable dye was obtained from the root of a tree called *mdaa* (Euclea Fruticosa), which gave a brownish-yellow colour, inconspicuous in grass and bush. From rubber vulcanised with sulphur, efficient tyres were made for motors and bicycles. A motor fuel called *trebol* was concocted from cocoa; from tallow, wax candles and soap were produced.

With constant marching, footwear was crucial. Cattle and game skins were plentiful; tanning materials were extracted from mangroves on the coast. In peace time the missions had already made boots. Now their activity was further developed and the General got his troops to establish large-scale tanneries and shoe factories.

Quinine, vital for the Europeans' health, was turned out in tablet form at Amani Biological Institute from bark obtained in the north. During the long retreat, von Lettow brewed it from different barks and it became known as Lettow *Schnapps*. Men doctored with it were unanimous that their malaria was better.

Of course, war materials were the main problem. Von Lettow set skilled artificers and armourers to manufacture apparatus for blowing up the railways. At first they had to rely on small quantities of explosives to be had from the planters; later the demolition charges captured at Tanga from the British proved much more effective.

In 1915 the German ammunition shortage was relieved in a remarkable manner. A British ship, the *Rubens*, seized in Hamburg, left that port loaded with arms and ammunition. On April 4 she appeared off Tanga. Sighted by H.M.S. *Hyacinth*, she was attacked and entered Manza Bay on fire and was abandoned by her crew. Bluejackets boarded her, finding her timbered up and battened down. On the assumption that the enemy ship would burn herself out, *Hyacinth* steamed away. However, the Germans returned and saved almost her entire cargo. Cartridges which had suffered from sea water von Lettow had broken up, their powder cleaned and damaged caps replaced by new ones.

A year later, a second store ship slipped into Saudi Bay. The Germans secured her entire cargo of 4·1 field howitzers, gun and small-arms ammunition, machine-guns, stores, provisions and clothing. She also carried the last mail the German Force was to receive in the course of the campaign.

This was a good natured war, in which the two sides sent each other messages. Askaris carrying letters between the commanders were given a great reception by friends and relatives 'on the other side'. On one occasion, General W. Malleson wrote to von Lettow complaining that a woman was taking part in German patrols, which had 'perpetrated inhuman cruelties'. He accepted the German assurance that this was sheer fantasy. Later several British diaries were picked up by the Germans which contained notes to the effect that no prisoners were to be taken. It was von Lettow's turn to enquire whether this was true. No such order had been given.

During this period British and German officers treated each other with great chivalry and so did their askaris. On March 10, 1915, a badly wounded young Englishman, captured by German askaris who had no European with them, thought his last moment had come. When they tied him up as best they could and carried him to a doctor, he exclaimed: 'You askaris are gentlemen. . . .'

Wounded prisoners, on giving their word of honour not to fight again in that war, were sent back to their respective sides. Everyone of them kept his word. Information about missing men was promptly provided. Symbolic of the spirit of this campaign was the manner in which von Lettow learnt of his *Pour le Mérite* order. Lt.-Gen. Smuts sent it on to him with a covering letter, expressing the hope that his cordial congratulations 'will not be unacceptable to you'.

When the conquest of German South West Africa had been completed in July, 1915, the campaign entered a new phase; in the second half of the year, thorough preparations were made. In February, 1916, the following Allied units arrived in Mombasa: from South Africa, six brigades with auxiliary units and large supplies; from Britain, six batteries, and from India, ten Indian regiments. All these joined the seasoned King's African Rifles (K.A.R.) who since August, 1914, had carried the burden of withstanding the German attacks. The commander of this considerable force was Lt.-Gen. (later Field-Marshal) Jan Christian Smuts, who had become famous as a guerilla leader against the British in the Boer war.

His first two-pronged attack, one force moving along the coast and another inland, with a reserve detailed to cut off the enemy's retreat, pushed the Germans back. But von Lettow managed to retreat with his force intact. During the rainy season both sides reorganised. Meanwhile the Belgians in the north-west and a force from Nyasaland in the south-west were also advancing. The aim was to concentrate all forces on Morogoro and there compel von Lettow to fight.

In one month, Smuts had advanced two hundred and fifty miles, although malaria had reduced the strength of all his units, some to thirty per cent of their original numbers. Practically every animal succumbed to tse-tse fly. With the aid of the Navy, Tanga, Pangani, Bagamoyo and Dar-es-Salaam had been occupied. The Belgians captured Kigoma and Tabora. But once more von Lettow foiled the attempt to intercept him, directing the remainder of his forces to safety through the Uluguru Mountains. Eventually he retired to the Mgeta river, where he encamped. During the last three months of 1916, the two sides faced each other in trenches: the only trench warfare in East Africa.

In the spring of 1917, having forced the Germans to retire on Mahenge, General Smuts joined the War Cabinet in London. To his colleagues he reported: 'Everything is over in East Africa, von Lettow-Vorbeck is hiding in the jungle. . . .' He could not have been more wrong, as his successor, General J. L. Van Deventer, soon found out. Far from hiding (the German Commander never went near a jungle area) von Lettow fought every inch of the way, kept the initiative and constantly re-equipped his men with captured arms and ammunition.

By then the large force commanded by Smuts had been withdrawn and the task of driving von Lettow from German territory had been entrusted to the K.A.R. Surprise attack was impossible as the defender waited concealed and was forewarned by the laborious approach of an adversary who had to cut roads and to bridge rivers. Supply and transport were exceedingly difficult through the bush, while the defending force fell back slowly upon supply points posted in the rear.

If General Smuts was wrong in his estimate of the situation, General von Lettow was even further off the mark. In his memoirs he states:

At the end of 1916 I regarded the military situation as remarkably favourable, for I knew that the South African troops were, for the most part, worn out with battle casualties and sickness, while a large proportion of the remainder were returning to South Africa at the end of their engagements . . .

Cut off from the outside world, the German commander had no idea of the immense forces and supplies at the disposal of the Allies. It is a tribute to him that he kept up the morale of his men, who had had no news from home for years and who were retreating into the unknown from March, 1916, until November, 1918. They were short of everything. For a long time, von Lettow and his officers had to provide meat and fat by shooting big game. A hippopotamus, killed with one shot, would reappear ten to fifteen minutes later, with its legs upwards. Experts would tow it to the river shore with ropes made of bark, and extract about forty kilograms of appetizing white fat. Elephants were stalked not for their tusks, but for the amount of fat and meat they would yield. Yet the rations shrunk constantly, and on one occasion the women, who were following their men in the forces, staged a 'lie down strike' for better food.

And still the men marched on. Von Lettow used every advantage of terrain with cunning skill and bravado. The hardest fighting of the whole campaign took place while the Germans were slowly retiring south. On October 17, 1917, at Mahiwa, the K.A.R. forced them to fight a pitched battle lasting three days. Of the outcome, von Lettow said: 'At Mahiwa we inflicted a real defeat . . . the greatest since Tanga.' But Lt.-Col. N. Moyse Bartlett, official historian of the K.A.R., put his finger on the crux of the situation when he said: 'This battle virtually destroyed von Lettow-Vorbeck's offensive power.'

Because of this, the German commander had to make a hard decision. A grass shed was set up in a clearing. German doctors weeded out the hopelessly disabled; they were to stay behind and be captured. When the British warily closed in on the silent camp, all they found were rows of litters with sick and wounded askaris.

On the night of November 18, 1917, von Lettow had crossed into Portuguese East Africa at the head of 2,000 fighting men, determined to find food for them, for they too were hungry and exhausted. His luck still held. Opposite the place at which he forded the Rovuma he came upon a Portuguese camp, Ngomano, full to bursting point with arms, food and medical supplies. The Portuguese did not even try to defend it. Their askaris joined the Germans in the looting. Only with great difficulty did the German officers put a stop to such 'criminal waste'.

During the rainy season in January, 1918, von Lettow's forces were able to rest and to feed really well. From then on, operations on both sides were carried on almost entirely by Africans. Commanders on both sides fell back on guerilla tactics. Columns sent against von Lettow from the east and the south shores of Lake Nyasa and from Porto Amelia missed him. In July he captured a Portuguese supply base large enough to enable him to carry on the war for another two years, had it lasted that long. Once more, in August, 1918, he eluded envelopment by converging columns.

The anger of the K.A.R. over Portuguese non-resistance can be imagined. There is an apocryphal story that the Army Order allegedly issued when Portugal entered the war – 'From now on the Portuguese are no longer to be referred to as "pork and beans", but as our gallant allies' – had to be rescinded!

The pursuit of von Lettow's army was a harrowing experience. In September, 1918, he doubled back from Portuguese East Africa into Tanganyika, from there to march into Northern Rhodesia. The K.A.R. have never received proper recognition for their endurance, especially for the engagements they forced the Germans to fight on August 31 and on September 6, 1918. The enemy not only chose the terrain, but employed scorched earth tactics. The climate also told on the Europeans. Lt.-Gen. Sir George Gifford, who was with one of the pursuit columns, says that the regiment never suffered anything like it before or since.

On November 13, 1918, in Northern Rhodesia, a dispatch rider carrying a white flag caught up with von Lettow, who was about to cross a river under enemy fire. He gave him a personal letter from General van Deventer, saying the war was over and Germany had surrendered. It was part of the surrender terms that he should hand over his war material to the British Commander, but 'in consideration of the gallant fight you have made' he and his officers might keep their personal weapons. On November 25, 1918, at Abercorn, before a special guard of honour, General Paul von Lettow-Vorbeck drew up his band of ragged veterans and proudly surrendered.[2]

There was no doubt in East Africa who the hero of that war had been: it was the German commander who, with at most 14,500 men, held down over the war years 134 Allied general officers and 160,000 men. Characteristically, British officers were most anxious

[2] Von Lettow's maximum number of men, at the end of 1915, was 3,007 Europeans and 11,900 askaris.

to see and to shake by the hand an enemy whose achievements they were loud in appreciating. Dr 'Battling Bill' Williams, M.O. with the K.A.R., and now eighty-eight years old, still gets excited when describing the meal von Lettow had at his unit's mess. Everyone present toasted the little man with the beaked nose and twinkling eyes. He carried himself with calm and courtesy at a moment when his country's defeat five thousand miles away had torn from his hands the fruit of four years' brilliant generalship.

Despite the consideration shown to him personally, the German commander felt aggrieved that his men had to be interned. Before being repatriated, they had to wait in Dar-es-Salaam for over a month under the same conditions as prisoners of war. Nor would the British advance funds to enable von Lettow to settle the back-pay of his faithful askaris.[3] On January 17, 1919, exactly five years after his arrival, he set sail with 114 of his men for Amsterdam. There an enthusiastic reception showed him that his exploits had not passed unnoticed.[4]

In 1920, von Lettow became one of the leading figures in the Kapp putsch and, egged on by Field-Marshal von Hindenburg, led the revolt against the German Social Democrats. For this he was court martialled, imprisoned and temporarily deprived of his rank. Later he was elected a member of the *Reichstag*, but soon grew disillusioned with the cynicism and corruption of German politics. Hitler offered him the post of Ambassador to Britain, provided he joined the National Socialist Party, but this he would not do as he abhorred the Nazis.

Sad to tell, Adenauer's Germany has paid little attention to her distinguished son. In 1951 Field-Marshal Smuts discovered him in Hamburg, living in poverty from the proceeds of his wood-carvings. He arranged for the South African Government to give von Lettow a small pension and invited him to visit the Union. The respect shown him there in 1953 was as nothing compared to his welcome in Tanganyika, where he paid a visit on his way back to Germany. The K.A.R. paraded before him and officers flocked from far and near to the dinner in his honour.

[3] In 1927 von Lettow at last managed to pay them. They received seven million Marks, roughly £600,000.

[4] In 1913 he had become engaged to Margarethe Walbrath, but had received no communication from her since 1916. From Dar-es-Salaam he cabled her to ask whether she still considered herself engaged to him. She did and they were married on March 12, 1919.

As the applause died away in the African night, it probably did not occur to either the English officers or to the German general that they belonged to a passing age. To an age in which men were proud to have waged a gentleman's war.

*   *   *

What the Africans felt about it all is illuminating. Two prisoners of war gave their views to von Lettow; one, in Belgian uniform, said: 'You know quite well that we always side with the stronger man.' Another, a Masai in British uniform, said: 'We don't care whether it's the Germans or the British who rule us.' And yet devoted askaris fought bravely under the German colours to the bitter end and their descendants take pride in their achievements. How this came about despite the suffering endured by Tanganyikans during the anti-German wars of resistance is to be explained on several grounds.

In the first place, certain African tribes, such as the Hehe and the Ngoni, like soldiering. They are the Irish of Africa, who seem to enjoy any scrap. In the past they would have served under anyone who led them well and paid them handsomely. That von Lettow certainly did; moreover his black *effendis* (officers) and his askaris had great authority. Provided they did their duty, German officers backed them unquestioningly against the civil population. The troops were the *élite* of society, a position they loved. This is the story their children and grandchildren have been told.

With the British advance into Tanganyika, some of von Lettow's askaris were captured. They refused to sit out the war in the tedium of a P.O.W. camp, and unhesitatingly enrolled themselves with the British, as did their friends and relations. In the unit thus formed, K.A.R. battalion orders had to be given for a time in German.

The same factor had also worked to von Lettow's advantage. In 1911 there was a big economy drive in British East Africa. The K.A.R. were cut down from six battalions to three. This meant that many askaris had their service terminated. Most of them walked across the frontier to enlist with the Germans.

Native porters, pressed into service by both sides, had a tough time. Spirited Africans preferred to volunteer for fighting, which meant a reasonable load and a certain amount of service from camp followers.

A very important point in von Lettow's favour was that he allowed the *bibis* (women) to follow their men. They waited for them in the evening, cooked for them, moved with the force and formed part of the German camps. During the long retreat, they kept their men cheerful (many babies were born on the way) and helped by carrying supplies. Every time the Germans captured fresh supplies, the *bibis* shared the rations. Von Lettow says in his memoirs that when his force marched single file through the bush the women in their bright *kangas* as often as not carrying babies on their backs and a load on their heads, looked like a carnival procession.

The loyalty of von Lettow's askaris reflects a traditional African concept. Africans are loyal to a person, usually to their tribal chief or headman. In the First World War the Tanganyikans also served a person–a German or a British officer–not a regiment, least of all a country. With a man of such strong personality, courage and resourcefulness as von Lettow, the Africans had a trebled incentive to loyalty. Those who served directly under him were loyal to the end. (Without captured supplies and good pay, it might have been different. It should be remembered, too, that altogether less than 20,000 men out of a population of seven and a half millions were involved.)

From their experiences in the war the final conclusion the Africans drew was that the Europeans were not gods. Even the most powerful among them had been defeated. If the British could beat the Germans, without ever visibly defeating the famous general, perhaps one day the Tanganyikans could defeat the British? This thought, present in the subconscious, was slow in maturing.

In 1954, when Nyerere started on his campaign to build up Tanu, one of his strongest arguments in persuading people to join the battle for Tanganyika's independence was: 'What the British did to the mighty Germans, we must do to the mighty British, especially as we have friends in America to help us!'

CHAPTER 7

The Mandate and After

In 1919 a new name appeared on the world map: Tanganyika Territory. Sir Cosmo Parkinson, a distinguished British civil servant, had invented it, and in the Versailles Peace Treaty it replaced 'German East Africa'. At the end of the Second World War, 'Territory' was dropped and the country became just Tanganyika.

The Germans have complained bitterly that in 1919 it took the victorious powers ten minutes to rob them of their colonial empire, despite President Wilson's pledge of a peace without annexations. But a lot of thought and hard bargaining had gone into the preparation of those ten minutes.

Great Britain entered upon the First World War with no desire to add to her vast underdeveloped areas. Not so the Dominions. Already during the war they had declared that, if they conquered areas contiguous to their boundaries, they would hold on to them, as they feared German submarine bases, air stations or black armies near their respective countries. They meant to annexe conquered territories.

A clash between President Wilson and the British Dominions seemed inevitable. To reach a compromise, General Smuts suggested that the German colonies should not become the possession of the conquerors, but be administered under mandates associated with the League of Nations. From the ensuing discussions emerged Article XXII of the Covenant of the League, which divided the territories 'inhabited by people not yet able to stand by themselves under the strenuous conditions of the modern world' into three classes: A Mandates, B Mandates and C Mandates.

B Mandates, the category which applied to Tanganyika Territory, were to be administered so as to

guarantee freedom of conscience and religion . . . prohibit abuses such as the slave trade, the arms and the liquor traffics . . . prevent the establishment of fortifications or naval bases and the military training of the natives for other than police purposes . . . secure equal opportunities for the trade and commerce of other Members of the League.

66

Article XXII also laid down that Mandated Territories had a distinct status, which could not be unilaterally altered either by the League of Nations or by the Mandatory Power.

The peoples of the Mandated Territories were to be trained or tutored until they could stand by themselves 'socially, economically and politically'.

The Mandatory Power had to accept international supervision by the League of Nations, and report to it annually through the Permanent Mandate Commission sitting in Geneva. This system of administration by a Great Power under international supervision was a historic innovation.

General Smuts put in a powerful plea that the Mandate over German East Africa should be entrusted to Britain, the greatest African Power, linking her possessions 'from the Cape to Cairo'. When this was agreed to, the Belgians protested and the question was reopened. In recognition of their military aid against von Lettow-Vorbeck, they received a Mandate over Ruanda-Urundi, the highland area of 20,000 square miles and three million inhabitants in the north-west of the Territory. This left Tanganyika with 365,000 square miles and four million people.

Had the Tanganyika Africans been consulted, the Belgians would not have received this Mandate. The barbaric conduct of the Congo troops, especially during the occupation of Tabora Province, is still vividly remembered. Many Congolese askaris were cannibals, who ate their Tanganyikan (mostly Nyamwezi) prisoners, not to mention what they did to the women. When the Congo trouble flared up in 1960, Nyamwezi tribesmen were ready to fight against the Congolese on anybody's side as long as they could avenge the past.

At the end of 1916 General Smuts vested all administrative power north of the Central Railway in H. A. Byatt, a civil servant who had gained his experience in Malta and in Somaliland. By January 31, 1919, when a knighthood was conferred on him, Sir Horace Byatt was administering the whole of Tanganyika Territory. On July 22, 1920, he became the first Governor and Commander-in-Chief.

It has to be emphasised that Byatt was faced with an almost superhuman task. The entire country was devastated; both sides had practised a scorched earth policy, and when food crops were at last sown the rains failed two years running. Famine came on top of the influenza epidemic, which in Tanganyika Territory had claimed about 70,000 victims – almost two per cent of the population. As Government House in Dar-es-Salaam had been bombarded by British men-of-war, Byatt set up headquarters in the German Museum attached to the Botanical Garden. To build the new Government House, he used green (living) coral reef brought in from the sea in dhows.

Byatt had to start from scratch, relying exclusively on Tanganyikan resources. No help came from England. The great majority of Englishmen, even of educated people, was as yet indifferent to the newly emerging problems of the empire. Besides, England was engrossed in her own problems, in the aftermath of war.

With only 108 administrative officers, Byatt had to re-create a complete departmental system, including police, posts and telegraphs, communications, health and education, down to the last details of office administration and filing. Matters were further complicated by the need to repatriate all Germans, a step which Britain was entitled to take under the terms of the Versailles Treaty. The care of their estates and plantations was placed in the hands of the Custodian of Enemy Property. In the early 1920s these were put to auction. As there was no scheme to help British settlers, who had no money to buy, Indian and Greek settlers snapped up the German properties for about five per cent of their real value.

There was a special reason for Indian interest. Although India could not be a member of the League of Nations,[1] the India Lobby made its influence felt through those provisions in the Tanganyika Mandate which prohibited overt and hidden segregation. This was the reason why the Aga Khan advised his followers to open up 'the furthest recesses' of the Territory. The Ismaeli Community obeyed and made a home there, although it is more influential and wealthier in Kenya. Four decades later, its schools and hospitals were among the best in Tanganyika.

Under Article V of the Mandate, Britain was pledged to abolish slavery where it still existed. The Germans had prohibited the slave trade, but shrank from overnight emancipation because of the expense of compensating owners and for fear of political disturbances. On June 16, 1922, Byatt published the Involuntary Servitude (Abolition) Ordinance, and slavery disappeared from Tanganyika Territory once and for all.

---

[1] Because India was still not an independent country.

He also banned forced labour, with the result that both de-mobilised askaris and former plantation labourers returned to their tribes. They now spent their days idling and drinking *pombe*, the cheap liquor brewed from fermented maize. Lack of workers, however, spelt disaster for the white settlers and British D.C.s and D.O.s were soon forced to bring pressure to bear on Africans to return to work. If their methods were not as harsh as those of the Germans, they were not soft either.

Byatt was driven by his enormous difficulties to make do with the remnants of the German system. He maintained the twenty-two German provinces, although their boundaries ignored tribal divisions. The only exception to this was the creation of the Masai reserve, a continuation of the Masai Territory in Kenya. To this day the Masai have remained nomads, and with their herds of cattle roam the reserve Byatt gave them.

He also appointed Provincial Commissioners, District Com-missioners and District Officers, but his staff shortage was acute and despite much talk about the reform of the German *akidas*, it was the former German *akidas* who remained in control of every-day affairs. Yet in 1908 the German Count von Götzen had written: 'They resort to oppression and fraud, which makes our Adminis-tration detested by the people.' In 1919, Captain G. St. J. Orde-Brown, O.B.E., said:

I am convinced that many of the evils which brought about the per-petual punitive expeditions of German days arose solely because the white official was shut off from direct dealings with the natives. To put it bluntly, *akidas* save trouble. A lazy district officer will appreciate an efficient *akida* and therefore tend to be biased in his favour. If an *akida* is efficient, he is dangerous, if he is inefficient, he is redundant.

The British D.C.s and D.O.s remained almost as shut off from direct dealings with the Africans as their German predecessors had been. It was unfortunate that Sir Horace Byatt appears not to have thought out, and certainly did not put into writing, the principles on which he expected them to operate. The result was that they had to use their own judgment, often disregarding what their predecessors had done and what their colleagues were doing. The African, with his sixth sense for noticing discord among the white *bwanas*, was well aware of any rows going on. Stories began to circulate about D.O.s writing each other intemperate letters, or descending to professional intrigue against each other. The performance of the D.O.s varied according to their personalities.

Among the Gogo in the Central Province, for instance, the war was followed by a devastating famine. Even in 1924 many human skulls lay in the countryside between Kondoa-Irangi and Dodoma, the remains of those who tried to walk to the Central Line to buy food. Survivors sold their cattle for one rupee a piece in the Dodoma market. When in 1921 the harvest failed for a third time, many Gogo tribesmen fled to other parts of Tanganyika. Some pawned their children for food; husbands left their wives, mothers deserted their babies, family life had nearly ceased to exist and over thirty thousand people died of hunger.

The English D.O. in the Gogo country did what he could, but there was no possibility of bringing in relief food from outside the Territory. At last, in 1922, there was a good harvest; corn bins were filled, ribs became covered and at their *barazas* the Gogo began to sort out family tangles. The D.O. ordered all children to be returned and himself paid off the loans against which they were being held. He worked day and night to get the children back and is still gratefully remembered. Yet his opposite number among the Nyaturu, who suffered nearly as much from the famine as the Gogo, failed to measure up to his task, pleading that he had neither funds nor time enough for unravelling the infinite complications which confronted him.

It was in part because of the debts assumed by Africans during the famine that Byatt passed in 1923 the Credit to Natives (Restriction) Ordinance, as a result of which traders could not sue Africans for the recovery of debts incurred by way of credit if those debts were in excess of a certain amount.

Byatt increased the hut and poll tax, but issued no clear instructions as to how it was to be collected. The chiefs were to be compensated for the tribal tribute by direct payment from the Treasury, but there were no directives as to how the new tax was to be distributed. And if an old-fashioned chief ordered a tribesman to be beaten because he refused to pay tribute (or indeed for some other misdeamour), the British interfered, saying that he had no right to do physical violence to another man. The Germans had supported such tough measures; now the chiefs were resentful of a British humanity which they did not understand.

And little was done to increase their understanding of British intentions. The key to this problem lay in a rapid expansion of education; but to say this with the advantage of hindsight is to underestimate the immense difficulty of meeting, with insufficient staff and hopelessly inadequate funds, even the pressing practical needs on which the day-to-day life of the community depended. In the early days of reconstruction Byatt certainly gave a low priority to education: this department was run by one officer, Stanley Rivers-Smith, and two clerks, and their budget was less than one per cent of the total, less than the sum earmarked for the maintenance of Government House. By 1920 only twenty schools for Africans had been re-opened, with two European teachers. By 1924 this situation began to improve and young, dedicated men were being enrolled in England for Tanganyikan service (see Chapter 9). This meant the beginning of a new era.

The famous Amani Institute, which the Germans had established in 1902 as a centre of tropical research and which under their rule had been admirably equipped with buildings and staff, was now, to quote Major Sir Ralph Furse, 'so to speak in mothballs. A Kew gardener was acting as caretaker and the mules were eating the experimental maize.' (*Aucuparius: Recollections of a Recruiting Officer*, p. 143.)

Byatt's small health staff did a remarkable job. They were on the look-out for plague, smallpox, cerebro-spinal meningitis, influenza, sleeping sickness and yaws. Smallpox was difficult to control because of the deterioration of imported vaccine; eventually the Territory produced its own. In 1922 a significant number of sleeping sickness cases was detected. The population was concentrated into close settlements, where regular medical examination and treatment was possible. In 1924 a nation-wide campaign against yaws was organised, based on treatment with bismuth sodium tartrate, a medical innovation infinitely cheaper than anything used before.

Of economic matters Byatt had an admirable grasp. Under the terms of the Mandate, he was required to honour the land titles (freeholds) granted by the Germans, but he would only allow new land to be obtained on a leasehold basis. Under his encouragement the former German sisal estates were first of all put in order. The cotton plantations in the north and in Tanga Province came next. In the Kilimanjaro and Bukoba Districts Africans participated effectively; in 1924, in the Bukoba District alone, their income exceeded £100,000. Cotton farms were revived and Africans did well on their own land around Lake Victoria and in the eastern districts. Tea, copra, groundnuts, grain, hides, skins and oil seeds followed suit. Only the derelict German rubber plantations could not be saved.

By 1924 the economic position was so well restored that the war interruption could be discounted and all domestic exports (except rubber, the third largest export under the Germans) were significantly greater than in 1913. The first budget surplus showed in 1923-4; this was exclusive of the railway deficit, a constant headache for Tanganyika. On account of the latter, a £300,000 Treasury Loan had to be granted by London, the repayment of which was to become a heavy burden.

In all this there was little reference to the Mandate and officers outside Government House probably had scant idea that they were administering anything but a British colony. In this they could hardly be blamed, for it was the Colonial Secretary, Leopold Amery, who in June, 1925, said:

We have got rid of that intrusive block of German territory which, under the name of Tanganyika, has now been permanently incorporated in the British Empire. I stress—permanently. It is an entire delusion that it is any less British than any other colony. Though we have laid ourselves under an obligation of the League of Nations, it is not one whit less British nor does it make our tenure there one whit less permanent.

The Governor, naturally, was aware that Tanganyika Territory had a status of its own. After all, he had to write yearly reports to the Permanent Mandate Commission. And when in 1924 the Ormsby-Gore Commission came to East Africa to effect a 'Closer Union' between Kenya, Uganda and Tanganyika, Sir Horace acidly reported to the League: 'There appears to be an impression abroad that the population of the Territory includes large numbers of unemployed labourers who form a useful reservoir from which to draw for the development of adjoining territories. The contrary is the case.'

(Much more was to be heard about 'Closer Union' with neighbouring British colonies in the future.)

If British officials knew little about the Mandate, Africans knew nothing. No one had told them that their position in a Mandated Territory was different from what it had been in a colony. As far as their experience went, German masters had been replaced by British masters. True, the British began by pulling down the high walls surrounding the *bomas* and widening their machine-gun slits into proper windows. In historic perspective, the symbolism of this British measure, the first to be carried out all over Tanganyika, is now being appreciated. At the time, it was not understood.

British officials told Africans that from now on they need no longer bow from the waist and could come up to the *boma* to look through the windows. But they, no more than the Germans, thought of shaking hands with the average African. Chiefs, especially paramount chiefs, had, however, always been shown special consideration.

As the British régime settled down and the old *akidas* (with a few exceptions) retained their position, everything seemed to go on as before. Comparisons between the old masters and the new were inevitable. Conclusions went, more often than not, in favour of the Germans. The main reason was: 'The Germans beat us, but they paid more than the British for the agricultural products we sold them.' And this was true.

The second reason was usually stated this way: 'With the Germans we knew where we stood, with the British who can tell?' By this, Africans meant that the German rules, however harsh, were clear. For instance, the methodical Germans had placed white kilometre stones on all roads. In the Lushoto (Wilhelmstal) area they kept on disappearing. So the Germans published an order that the next person caught stealing a kilometre stone would have his hand chopped off, as used to happen to thieves under tribal rule.[2] This was done twice and from that day to this no kilometre (or mile) stone has been touched.

British laws, much more humane than German laws, were full of 'ifs and buts'. Instead of swift retribution, the person caught in the act was arrested and kept in prison. Meanwhile, there was no one to look after the family. Long proceedings in a British court were unintelligible to Africans, who were deeply shocked when someone got off on legal technicalities. Nor could they grasp

[2] In 1962 a Member of the Tanganyika Parliament wanted to reintroduce this tribal punishment for theft, but his motion was not carried. However, in April, 1963, it was announced that theft would be punished by a minimum sentence of two years imprisonment, during which the convicted person would receive twenty-four strokes of the cane each year. Six strokes every three months.

why a man, sentenced to a term in prison, could not bring his entire family with him. Death sentences on men who had killed someone, on grounds which were perfectly reasonable from any African point of view, filled them with horror. (They had felt no happier under the Germans when a murderer was hanged.)

On the whole at this time the Africans regarded the British, compared to the Germans, as soft, undecided people, who had to look up rules, who argued with each other and wasted a lot of time. The Germans had never boggled over brutality, which suited the strong, that is to say the chiefs. Several of these were sorry that the Germans had gone, for the British would not tolerate their harsh practices.

A final factor in the preference for the Germans arose from the approval of discipline by older men, especially if they belonged to the great fighting tribes. They admired, particularly in retrospect, the bravery and military skill of the Germans. Among the Arusha, the Chagga and the Sukuma there was a strong Lutheran element and Lutheran missionaries were either Germans or pro-German. Broadly speaking, Roman Catholic missionaries and Moslems were anti-German.

In the early 1920s the impact of the British régime on the Tanganyikans was not startling. Yet one has to bear in mind that Byatt had to deal with a devastated country, and he was given no money—on the old principle that colonial possessions had to maintain themselves on their own resources. Therefore he had to devote all his resources to building up the economy. Because of this, the Africans saw little that was different from German days and such things as were different did not impress them. Had anyone suggested that Tanganyika Territory was no longer a colony, but had a special status as a Mandate, they would have thought this a white man's joke.

CHAPTER 8

The First Great Governor: Sir Donald Cameron

In April, 1925, Sir Donald Cameron succeeded Sir Horace Byatt as Governor of Tanganyika Territory. He arrived from Nigeria, where he had served under Lord Lugard.

Officials at Government House had heard that Cameron was an enthusiastic exponent of Indirect Rule, the method of governing Africans through their own institutions. They were somewhat apprehensive about the innovations he might introduce.

The new Governor was a controversial figure who had climbed the ladder without connections or diplomas. Born in Demarara, in the West Indies, he was the son of poor Irish parents. At the age of twelve he took an unpaid job as mail sorter at Christmas time, hoping this would lead to more worth-while employment. Having fallen out with his neighbour, a Negro, he kicked him—and was sacked on the spot.

'In South Africa they would have kicked out the Negro,' he confided to a friend. 'It was my first lesson in race relations and I learnt it.'

He joined the colonial service as a fifth grade clerk. Fortunately in Nigeria Lord Lugard recognised his talents and promoted him. Sheer ability did the rest. The few friends he made were willing to fight his battles all the time. But his caustic tongue swelled the number of his enemies, about whom he told outrageous stories. Cameron's passionate sympathy was reserved for the underdog and nothing gave him greater pleasure than to make sure such a one had his chance.

A small incident on the day of his arrival showed what kind of a man the new Governor was. When told that it was seven o'clock, he looked at his watch and remarked that it was five minutes past six. From this discrepancy it emerged that the Post Master General and the Director of Public Works could advance (or retard) the clock of the Lutheran Church, from which Tanganyika Territory derived its time. Next morning the Governor introduced zonal time. Private tampering with the hour of day was over.

He then amazed his Chief Secretary by analysing the Mandate, with this conclusion: 'We're here on behalf of the League of

75

Nations to teach the Africans to stand by themselves. When they can do that, we must get out. It will take a long time, yet everything we do must be based on this principle.'

The Chief Secretary objected that it would not be fair to the Europeans, Indians, Arabs and other foreigners working and trading in the Territory to ignore all they had done.

'If we're dissatisfied because the Mandate ignored European participation, or because of something else, we should have said so *before* accepting its administration,' was the dry and precise retort. 'If enough people feel as you do, we can still return it. As long as I'm here, we'll live up to our obligations.'

The Chief Secretary sought to press the point by mentioning the current imaginative conception of a Great European Dominion in Africa, reaching from Kenya and Uganda. . . .

'Nonsense,' said Cameron. 'The trouble with your Great European Dominion is that the gods saw fit to place a large and predominating proportion of Africans in these territories. We've no right to squeeze them out of here.'

A few days later, white settlers from Kenya applied for land in the Southern Highlands. Knowing that they were the dreamers of the Great European Dominion, Cameron informed them: 'I've passed on your applications to the District Commissioner in Iringa, who will pass them on to the Native Authorities, who in this Territory decide who may or may not obtain land, taking into consideration the present and future interests of the Africans.'

Lord Delamere came down from Kenya personally to discuss with Cameron the terms on which white settlers could stay in Tanganyika. He drove by Ford from Arusha to Mbeya. This road, the beginning of the Great North Road, had been built by District Commissioners with native labour, linking up individual stretches.

Cameron explained to Delamere at Iringa that settlers had to have capital, otherwise in the cruel climate they were bound to fail as planters. They had to accept leases to be revised every five years. Finally they had to recognise that Tanganyika was a British Mandate, not a British possession.

Few new settlers accepted these terms.[1] The old ones in the Northern Highlands, closest to Kenya, petitioned the Colonial Secretary in London to recall the Governor because he did not see

[1] Among them were Lord Francis Scott, Arthur Fawcus and Rodney Kenyon-Slaney.

eye to eye with them. Whatever answer they received Cameron was not required to change his ways.

But long before he went on the Iringa *safari*, Sir Donald had found out that the methods of the German régime had been continued; that the Governor ruled unassisted by Legislative Council or public opinion; that he had never visited the area south of the Central Railway; that flogging and whipping were normal punishment in the K.A.R.; that there were hardly any schools and that his predecessor had ignored the missions, as the Germans had done.

Convinced that the Africans had not had a fair deal under the rudimentary organisation he had inherited, Cameron started to create an administration they could understand. He was determined that they should participate in it and eventually become African citizens proud to be members of the African community.

To attain his objective he needed men who shared his ideals. Cameron could not stand yes-men. He wanted courageous partners who in an argument gave as good as they got and helped to find solutions. He was lucky in the members of his staff at Government House, most of whom supported him enthusiastically. His real problem was with the men in the field, the D.C.s and D.O.s who hardly ever came to Dar-es-Salaam. As there was not a single road from the coast to the south-west region of the Territory, some went to their stations travelling via Nyasaland or Southern Rhodesia.

To visit his D.C.s and D.O.s Cameron spent a great deal of his time in tiring and uncomfortable *safaris*. He discussed all new measures with them, giving each one an opportunity to object and to criticise. In this way he inspired and engaged their loyalty, and the old discords were no more. Cameron in effect applied to civilian problems the military doctrine, applied so effectively by Field-Marshal Montgomery, that the good general must know and be known by his troops.

He had great faith in Lord Lugard's system of Indirect Rule, which he preferred to call Native Administration, because its essence was to administer the Africans through their indigenous institutions instead of communicating orders to them directly. This system had moreover two practical administrative advantages. On the one hand, it was financially impossible to employ a sufficient number of administrative officers to get in touch with the whole of a primitive people. Working through indigenous institutions, a

D

limited number of officers could achieve this and see to it that Government orders were carried out. From this point of view, Native Administration was extremely practical. On the other hand, indigenous institutions, purged of their abuses, were democratic in the sense that all members of the tribe understood their purpose and participated in them. On to these institutions in due course British forms could be grafted, eventually bringing modern democracy to Africa as a practical and workable form of Government.

Cameron did not believe that this could be done either quickly or by means of the ballot box. He knew that it was part of the Africans' need to argue out their beliefs, even if it took three days to reach agreement. That was the meaning of the *baraza*, the meeting under the big tree, at which every member of the tribe had a right to speak up.

In order to build up the Native Administration, Cameron's first move was to find out which chiefs carried out their duties and were accepted by their people. He sent out his most trusted officers and also went himself to investigate. He much regretted that under his predecessor no such research had been done. He believed that if Byatt's *akidas* had gone on much longer, the Native Administration would have been completely destroyed.

He backed genuine chiefs to the full. The hut and poll tax, the native court and market fees, and the ferry tolls were now collected according to clearly defined rules; from these he provided the chiefs with a publicly known income. He was proud that, by not paying unrecognised or inactive chiefs, he had saved the Tanganyika Treasury thousands of pounds.

On his endless travels through the Territory, Cameron held *barazas* and addressed African crowds, explaining how his administration worked and what he expected from the Tanganyikans. He spoke eloquently about the chief's duty to ensure security of life and property, about the peasant's duty to work and to produce, about his own duty to help and to support the people. He wanted to buy a loudspeaker van and send it to every village of the Territory, so that all should get to know his voice as well as his views. But the Colonial Office vetoed this as an unnecessary expense.

A classic incident took place at Mwanza. After three years in office, he reported that he had built the railway as promised, that he had constructed feeder roads as promised and that he had sent good agricultural officers as promised. Now it was up to the Tanganyikans to grow more cotton, more groundnuts, more *sim-sim*....

A man put up his hand. Cameron immediately ceded him the right to speak.

'You've done all you said,' the African began. 'What we now want is that you should provide regular rain. Then we'll grow much more food....'

History does not record what Cameron replied, but this scene was something completely new in African experience.

Most chiefs had never even set eyes on a Governor. In Tukuyu, in the south-west, the local chiefs asked Cameron point blank to prove that he was the Governor.

'Only he has the right to wear this blue uniform, this golden braid, this hat with white plumes,' he told them pointing at each in turn. 'Now let's all be photographed together, so you don't forget what a Governor looks like.'

With his profound faith in the democratic ideal, Cameron was unhappy to enact legislation and to prepare the annual Budget without debate in a Legislative Council. He insisted that the Colonial Secretary should create an elective body; it seemed to him that the Permanent Mandates' Commission could not accept the excuse that the Africans were too young a community even to elect a dozen wise men. In Geneva Britain was unopposed, but all he got from London was authority for a Legislative Council he had to appoint himself.

At first, he was reluctant to accept a mere talking shop, yet it was better than nothing. He inaugurated it on December 7, 1926, with twenty members. Thirteen were senior officials of the Government, seven nominated members. The latter consisted of five Europeans and two Asians, but no African. In Cameron's words: 'No African could be found with a sufficient command of the English language to take part in the debates of the Council.'

He had the text of all intended legislation published, and encouraged criticism. Thanks to his strong personality, the Legislative Council meetings became worth-while exchanges of argument.

He intended to make education the keystone of his state edifice. In his view Indirect Rule, preparation for self-rule and eventual independence were all conditioned by education. Funds for three Superintendents of Education started the process by expanding existing schools and by founding new ones. These three men worked themselves to the bone; between 1925 and 1931 education estimates increased by more than eight times, pupils by more than ten times. The main difficulty was the dearth of competent European and African teachers and of suitable premises.

Cameron's inspired act was to call in the missions and to ask for their help on a grant-in-aid basis. Both Roman Catholics and Protestants responded enthusiastically. The number of schools soared, at little cost to the Tanganyika Treasury, as these dedicated teachers were not paid, just maintained. Mission schools cost half the amount of Government schools (see Chapter 9).

He was frequently attacked for wanting to train Africans to replace Europeans and Asians in higher positions. That this was his ultimate aim he never denied. It formed part and parcel of the Lugard policy which aimed at self-rule for Africans at the earliest opportunity. Cameron could not have put it more plainly: 'We must determine from the start the place of the African in the political structure and how he is to achieve it. We must not allow the European to become so entrenched that there will be no place for the African, except at the white man's pleasure. . . .'

Of course white settlers, who drew their inspiration from the Kenyan dreamers of the Great European Dominion, were shocked. Realising that outright opposition only made the Governor more determined, they tried paying compliments to his idealism, while begging him not to stir up beliefs among Africans that they had a right to any position.

'That's a policy of sheer negation, which would allow our obligations under the Covenant to go by default,' Cameron retorted. 'No British Government would dare declare that policy to the world.'

This unanswerable argument silenced his critics.

Cameron's interest reached into every field. Early on, he replaced the twenty-two German districts by eleven Provinces. He had no time to eliminate all arbitrary boundaries, but the worst mistakes were made good.

He recast Tanganyika's labour laws; he revitalised her industry; he gave a new lease of life to her agriculture. His officers went out to teach African peasants how to grow new cash crops and how to improve the old ones. The result was that the national income rose from £1,324,670 in 1925 to £1,992,675 in 1930, despite the considerable drop in agricultural prices on the world market from 1926 onwards.

When he arrived the Territory depended on Treasury loans. He induced London to cancel one-third of this debt, the remainder to be repaid over a long period. Even this was so onerous a burden that it continued to stultify social and economic developments.

As Tanganyika was not a colony, he could only borrow in the London market if Parliament guaranteed the interest on a loan, even if that loan was to be used for development purposes specifically authorised by the Mandate. These included the building of roads and railways, but not schools and hospitals. By first reconditioning German roads, then building new ones, he enabled Africans hitherto cut off from any market to dispose of their cash crops.

Considerable funds were needed for extending the Tanga railway line from Moshi to Arusha and the western line from Tabora to Mwanza. It so happened that Cameron had obtained these funds just before a conference with the Governors of Kenya and Uganda about bringing the salaries of all East African rail and port workers into line. Tanganyika being the poorest of the three, he had to raise wages. The two new railway lines were included in his plans for increasing revenue. He outlined his prospects to the other two Governors, who did not comment. But the next thing Cameron knew was that they had appealed to the Colonial Secretary to restrain Tanganyika from further work on the Mwanza line, as this would create unfair competition to the Kenya–Uganda line!

London refused to interfere, but this was not the end of the matter. Two months later there was a meeting in Nairobi, attended also by the Governors of Nyasaland and Northern Rhodesia and the Resident of Zanzibar. The subject on the agenda was Closer Union between Kenya, Uganda and Tanganyika. It was put to Cameron that he should drop the Tabora–Mwanza railway as it meant duplication inside an economic unit. To Cameron's amazement, a vote was taken and Nyasaland, Northern Rhodesia and Zanzibar voted with Kenya and Uganda–against *his* railway! With deep indignation he told his colleagues that their votes were of no interest to him, as all decisions rested with the Colonial Office. Then he betook himself to London.

There he wove a complicated web of stratagems to defend

Tanganyikan interests. He asked for his resignation[2] to be accepted if Closer Union went through. It did not; instead, several commissions travelled to East Africa, to report on Closer Union, Federation, Economic Unity or any other name thought up for the same problem. Thanks to Cameron, one postponement followed another. By the time he left Tanganyika in 1931, he was confident that Closer Union was a dead issue.

Actually it was still very much alive; but thirty years later an independent Tanganyika, dealing with an independent Kenya and an independent Uganda, all three led by African politicians, presents a different problem from a Mandated Territory dealing with a colony and a protectorate. Even now, it remains to be seen on what terms, if at all, Tanganyika will join an East African Federation or Confederation.

Two more achievements gave Cameron great pleasure. The first time he left on a *safari*, driving out of Government House he saw a little bugler boy being officially and formally whipped for having polished a stone against a mango tree in Government House park. K.A.R. officers assured him that they could not maintain discipline without flogging and whipping. He had to accept their advice, but demanded to be informed every time such punishment was inflicted. Papers outlining the offence, the circumstances, the presiding officer's opinion and the man's defence had to be sent to him. In view of the Governor's intervention, suddenly no more flogging or whipping sentences were imposed. In 1928 both were quietly abolished, without any detriment to regimental discipline.

At about the same time he judged that supplies could reach their destination by mechanised transport, and banned head porterage. Despite dreadful predictions the change-over worked smoothly.

The second achievement on which he prided himself was the foundation of the Tanganyika African Association. This was a platform for Africans in urban areas where Native Administration had never existed and in districts where the Germans had destroyed it so thoroughly that it could not be revived. The T.A.A.'s purpose was to provide the Africans with one more means of developing self-reliance and responsibility. At its meetings they could discuss

---

[2] The first of Tanganyika's three great governors placed his resignation in the hands of the Colonial Secretary rather than accept a measure he regarded as inimical to Tanganyikan interests. Another great governor, Sir Richard Turnbull, was to apply different tactics under even more dramatic circumstances.

any subject of their choice. Its premises were the only places where they could meet Europeans on equal terms. Branches were opened in all towns and large communities.

The original African founders of T.A.A. were Mwalimu Mdachi Shariff, a teacher; Martin Kayemba, the first African private secretary to a Governor, and Kleist Sykes, the first African to be employed in the railway service as an accountant. Subsequently he became a member of the Dar-es-Salaam town council.

Twenty-five years later young Tanganyika nationalists, among them Kleist Sykes' three sons, staged the opening moves of their independence campaign at T.A.A. meetings, gaining experience for later party political activities.

Summing up his six years in Tanganyika, Cameron said: 'We have not created a new heaven and a new earth. But we have improved conditions and we have sorted out some of the native situations.'

When asked whether this was mainly due to the Mandate, his answer was: 'I would not say so. The object of modern British colonial policy is the development of free institutions in the dependent countries leading to ultimate autonomy. The principles embodied in the Mandate are in complete accord with the views to which I had grown used in Nigeria.'

His example of working on a principle, and of doing so even if subjected to public criticism, had a tremendous effect on Africa, particularly on Tanganyika. In his view the Tanganyikan chiefs were anything but primitive illiterate men, and the tribesmen showed a high degree of intelligence and adaptability. He never stopped warning the British Administration that any organisation with which Africans came in contact had to be genuine.

'Nothing harms so much as sham,' he used to say, 'and no one spots sham as quickly as the African. He may not react at once, but the bill will come in due course.'

When he left in 1931, chieftains from every part of the land trekked to Dar-es-Salaam. They wished to attend his departure. He promptly sent word that they were to return to their homes as their costumes were unsuited to the coast's tropical climate. The answer came equally promptly:

If the Governor had sent for us, and now told us to go back, we should have no hesitation in obeying his wishes. But we came here of our own accord, because we believe that such is the course that our people desire. If they heard that we had left Dar-es-Salaam before the Governor sailed, they would be ashamed of us.

Letters poured in, expressing friendship, appreciation, gratitude. When boarding ship to sail for England, he had in his pocket one from a distant tribe, which ran: 'Tell him we do not wish him to go. We hope he will not forget us. We shall not forget him. He has done much for us. Our children will not forget him; nor yet their children.'

On this day Cameron gave up the pretence of being a hard, fierce man. The contrast between his arrival, unknown to all, and his departure, surrounded by tokens of affection from thousands of Africans, left him greatly moved. Had his next appointment not been as Governor of Nigeria, in succession to his own great teacher, Lord Lugard, his heart would have been much heavier.

In the lean years to come Cameron watched with distress how the foundations laid by him in Tanganyika were knocked about. But his theory that the bill always comes in worked in this case in reverse. With the trend of the age and the force of African nationalism, nothing could have stopped Julius Nyerere and his supporters from succeeding in their struggle. Without Sir Donald Cameron it would have been a violent struggle. His six years bore fruit when Tanganyikan independence was obtained without bloodshed.

CHAPTER 9

'A Due Supply of Persons Well Qualified to Serve . . .'

LORD LUGARD'S Indirect Rule could only work if chiefs and headmen carried out their duties effectively. To make them efficient, Sir Donald Cameron saw that they had to be trained. For future chiefs, a school modelled on a British Public School was founded at Tabora; for talented commoners Native Administration Schools were devised which set a pattern for the whole country.

In a traditional bidding prayer often used in public schools and university colleges, especially of old foundation, comes the petition:

'And that there may never be lacking a due supply of persons well qualified to serve Thee in Church and State; pour down, O Lord, Thy blessing on all schools and seminaries of sound and religious learning.'

These words, whatever else may be said, truly reflect the ideas for which, at their best, the English Public Schools have stood: sound learning closely harnessed to the concepts of public service and religious duty. These also have been the ideas that have been the inspiration of Tabora. Because, moreover, 'What Tabora does today, all other schools do tomorrow', they have suffused the whole educational system that was possibly Cameron's greatest achievement. But to measure the full greatness of this achievement it is necessary to examine what went before.

*   *   *

During the First World War, once German East Africa had become a battlefield, all education stopped within the Territory. The German Principal Government Schools had catered for 2,500 pupils and the elementary schools for 3,700, employing 16 European and 159 native teachers. The Europeans joined up or returned to Germany; the Africans dispersed to their homes or entered other employment. This meant that the education of promising boys, from whom normally the new recruits to teaching would have come, suddenly ceased.

The main purpose of the German educational system had been
the practical one of training Africans who might become either
clerks or N.C.O.s, who would understand and transmit orders in
writing. Yet the results were far from negligible, for, as stated
earlier, in 1919 British observers reported that the literacy level
in German East Africa was higher than in neighbouring British
colonies.

Possibly the most notable share in this achievement was made by
mission schools, of which in 1914 there were 1,800, with 110,000
pupils on their registers. Mission activities went back to Livingstone's appeal to Oxford and Cambridge in 1857 'to join in making
Africa free, civilised and Christian'. This led to the creation of the
Universities Mission to Central Africa (U.M.C.A.), which in 1864
set up its headquarters in Zanzibar. Eleven years later a station
was established at Magila in what is now the Tanga District; then
two others at Masasi and at Newala, and finally one in 1888 on
the shores of Lake Nyasa.

The Church Missionary Society, founded in 1897, became firmly
established in the Kilosa and Dodoma District of the Central
Region. With the awakening of German interests in East Africa
came the Lutheran missionaries of the Berlin mission, which in
1892 began work in the southern area near Lake Nyasa, and in
1903 took over the work of the Bethel mission on the coast, with
stations in Dar-es-Salaam and its district.

More numerous, although somewhat later in the field, were three
great Roman Catholic Orders. In 1867 the Fathers of the Holy
Ghost landed in Bagamoyo, where eventually they erected a
hospital and an industrial school, and introduced such plants as
coffee, which later was to flourish in mission stations in the more
suitable climate of the Highlands. In 1877 they founded a station
in the Turiani hills of the Morogoro District, the first of a long
chain stretching as far as Lake Tanganyika.

In 1878 members of the *Societé des Missionaires de Notre Dame
d'Algérie*, known from the colour of their habits as the White
Fathers, reached Tabora and began their evangelical and educational work. From here one group set off for Uganda in the north
and another for Ujiji on Lake Tanganyika.

In 1887 the Benedictine Order of St Ottilien of Bavaria started
work in the south. Their main centre became the Teachers'
Training College at Paramiho near Songea. In 1900, when the

German Government offered them a central site in Dar-es-Salaam, they built a handsome church known today as St Joseph's Cathedral.

By 1914 there were few areas in German East Africa which were not served by missionaries of one denomination or another, who brought to thousands both spiritual light and the humanising influence of medical attention and education. They also trained artisans and were the first to enable Africans to earn a cash income by handicraft in industry. Their primary purpose was to make converts, but they also wanted to raise the spiritual and cultural level of the Africans.

The war, however, wrought havoc among the mission stations. British and German missionaries were interned in succession, the former on the outbreak of war by the German authorities, and the latter by the advancing British forces. In accordance with the Treaty of Versailles, the ex-enemy missions were handed over to missions of the same denomination but of allied or neutral origin. Even before the Armistice, the German Benedictine missionaries had been replaced by French and Swiss workers, while some of the German Lutheran missions were taken over temporarily by the Church of Scotland and the Wesleyans. Soon the British Administration agreed to return the ex-enemy missions to their former owners, but legislative sanction for the transfer was only completed in 1925.

Thus it was that in 1918 there were no foundations on which Sir Horace Byatt's Administration could build. A new educational system, of which in 1928 Tabora Government School was to become the centrepiece, had to be started from scratch.

In 1920 the Department of Education came into being, with instructions to trace natives with previous teaching experience, and to reassemble the more promising pre-war scholars whose tuition had been interrupted by the war. Thus was to be formed a nucleus of a teaching staff who, after a refresher course, could carry on until a new generation of teachers had gone through the schools.

Shortage of money rendered this difficult task almost impossible; moreover, as late as 1922, Government schools in Tanganyika could boast only two European teachers. Fortunately Stanley Rivers-Smith was Director of Education. A graduate of Cambridge, he was determined that a proper educational system should be

developed in Tanganyika so that a sense of service could be inculcated into the young Africans. He put his philosophy succinctly
when he interviewed a prospective teacher, John Blumer, also
just down from Cambridge. Rivers-Smith recognised that here
was the type of man he needed, saying: 'You have the right ideals.
Always keep them before you and always remember that we are
training these people for self-government.'

'And then what happens to us?' asked twenty-two year old Mr
Blumer.

'We shall go, but our job will have been done.'

A. A. Isherwood,[1] Rivers-Smith's deputy and in 1931 his successor, was a man of the same way of thinking. Educated at St
John's, Leatherhead, and Oxford, he was indignant over the
pittance allocated to education in the Byatt era. Rivers-Smith and
Isherwood were scouring the highways and by-ways for the right
men, to create the right schools in Tanganyika. A friend of both
of them, by name A. Travers Lacey, a Bedford and Cambridge
man, tall, with a slight stoop due to bad gassing during the war,
agreed to come. They appointed him the first Superintendent of
Education of Tabora Province.

Previously the few village schools in the Province had been
dependent on the D.C. In 1922 the Provincial Commissioner,
Major Herbert C. Stiebel, a South African, turned the elementary
school in Tabora town into the European Hospital and built a
new school two miles away. Although it seemed a long shot, Lacey
was inspired to see this as the chance to create a school which would
teach the future leaders of Tanganyika the spirit of service, and
eventually train them to assume full social, economic and political
responsibility.

*   *   *

To Dar-es-Salaam, Lacey put up the sober and eminently
respectable suggestion that at the new school in Tabora the sons
and heirs of chiefs should be educated on English Public School
lines. By then Sir Donald Cameron had replaced Sir Horace Byatt.
He understood what Lacey wanted to do and heartily approved.
He also saw that the premises, consisting of mud huts surrounding
a flagstaff, were not good enough for a school of the type Lacey
had in mind. He provided £20,000 for a double-storied building,

[1] He died in August, 1957, in Tanganyika.

designed to hold 180 boarders, with cloisters running round a court. Preliminary work having been completed in 1928, the laying of the foundation stone was carried out by the Governor himself. The north block, the dormitories on the upper floor, and the large refectory in the main floor were finished in 1929, the rest of the compound in 1930.

The first thirty pupils had already been enrolled in 1925, and on February 26, 1925, there was a formal opening ceremony by the Acting Governor, John Scott. Founder's Day is still kept on the Saturday nearest February 26, and is marked by a traditional game of *Karamojo* football, a cross between Rugby and Association football, which has no boundaries and no rules, except that biting and punching are not allowed.

Lacey's original idea was to blend British Public School ideals and rules with African tradition and administration. The tutorial system and training for responsibility were to be linked with the African system of obedience to elders, of *baraza* justice and of absolute respect for the chief. Along with these ideals, Lacey saw clearly that the first practical aims of Tanganyikan education had to be to combat illiteracy and to produce Africans qualified to do jobs as farmers, clerks, administrators. Due weight therefore had to be given to vocational education.

In the first four forms the boys were taught the three Rs in Swahili,[2] plus a little native administration and history. It was Rivers-Smith's idea to institute Swahili as a *lingua-franca* throughout the Territory, a policy from which Tanganyika is now reaping dividends. In the higher forms the boys had to learn English, grammar and literature, mathematics, history and geography. Lacey realised that practical vocational training and advanced learning were both necessary, although at that stage it was more important that future chiefs should understand modern agriculture than that they acquire a purely academic education.

In those early days Tabora schoolboys were older than they are now: many were eighteen, some even twenty years old, married, living with their wives and children. Some were rulers, whose duties were carried out in their absence by a regent or a board of elders. Today the average boy goes to Tabora at the age of

[2] Swahili is Bantu in origin, enriched by words of Arabic, Persian, Hindustani, Portuguese and English. It grew out of the long contact between Bantu and Arab in Zanzibar.

fourteen, though some are still sixteen years old. There are three hundred pupils, who stay for eight years, and about a quarter obtain the Overseas Cambridge Higher School Certificate, which qualifies them to go to the East African or to any British university.[3]

From 1928 onwards Lacey felt able to promote a school curriculum that would strike a balance between classroom work, agricultural training and organised sport. Africans being traditionally community minded, the boys adopted the team spirit with a zeal which would have rejoiced Dr Arnold: singing, music and chess competitions have taken their place along with football, netball and hockey.

With the realisation of how much English educational practice has changed in the last thirty years, it may seem that the system introduced at Tabora was typical of the so-called 'Public-School spirit' at its most primitive and slightly ridiculous level. But it should be judged according to the principles generally accepted at that time; even if more progressive attitudes have since developed, the old methods had many constructive results to their credit. Thus it would be wrong to dismiss as useless spit and polish the weekly inspection of dormitories carried out like a military parade. The boys took great pride in having their House declared the best. That they had a terrible battle at home during the holidays proved that school had taught them principles of discipline and service they could not have learnt from their parents.

John Blumer, the young master whom Rivers-Smith interviewed in 1928, took a special interest in the school band. It had been started in 1925 with a drum and six bugles; in 1926 six flageolets were added, in 1927 it greeted a Belgian cabinet minister with his national anthem, which earned the boys an ox for a feast. From 1936 onwards the entire European community attended its excellent concerts.

Discipline at Tabora, adapted for African conditions, was maintained by a tribal system. Travers Lacey organised the boys into tribes, corresponding roughly to the districts from which they came. Each tribe elected a chief and one or more subchiefs who,

[3] In 1962, 693 Tanganyikan students studied in Britain. Of these, 150 were studying at universities, 228 were enrolled in technical colleges and 57 at Inns of Court. Teacher training occupied 38, while 74 nurses were at work in British hospitals. Practical training occupied 64 Tanganyikans and 82 were studying at private and other colleges.

subject to the headmaster's veto, were responsible for the discipline and general behaviour of their tribe.

Lacey also set up a school court, on the lines of a native court, the purpose of which was to train the boys in Native Administration procedures. It consisted of the chiefs and subchiefs, with the headmaster (or his representative) acting as president. Later on a European only attended when serious offences were being tried. Meetings provided an opportunity for boys and European staff to discuss school problems. The accused was questioned by the chiefs; his own witnesses had also to be heard. After all the evidence had been presented, the court took its decision. If the accused was found guilty, his punishment was either extra work in the fields or caning. The latter was carried out by Maliakini, an ex-K.A.R. sergeant-major, who fulfilled the functions of head-porter. The boys were devoted to Maliakini, and wept bitterly when he left for his native Nyasaland. There was a free fight over who should carry his kit to the station.

Unfortunately the tribe system was not a complete success. African boys showed little respect for any but their own tribe. Most of them would not obey the orders of another chief. Gradually tribal rivalries began to upset school discipline. To this were added two specifically African difficulties. One was that an African, unless he is a chief, dislikes giving unpleasant orders and will hide behind any excuse rather than say disagreeable things to a person's face. The second was *fitina*, which means jealousy leading to rivalry or vendetta, and remains one of independent Tanganyika's greatest problems.

In 1934 the tribes were replaced by Houses, in which the boys from all districts were mixed up. The Houses were originally named after well-known wild animals; after the war they were re-named after distinguished personalities, such as Sir Donald Cameron, A. Travers Lacey, Patrick Williams, and John Blumer, but retained the wild animals as their emblems. Painted on wooden shields, they adorn the dormitory doors.

With the introduction of Houses, discipline improved and tribal rivalries died down.

African parents believe that learning is the key to all success, and do not object to discipline, however stern. If a boy plays truant and the headmaster sends word to his father, he will be brought back in no time. A headmaster had to do this on one occasion. It happened to be a chief who returned the culprit. Before leaving, he asked: 'What will happen when I have gone?'

'Your son will get six.'

'Make it twelve and give him another twelve next week,' said the irate father.

Another boy, who had had a very bad school report, returned the following term with a note from his father saying: 'Please keep him. Give him thirty-six and I do not mind if you give him all the thirty-six right now, as long as you go on teaching him. . . .'

Like every other school, Tabora was faced with difficulties in maintaining discipline, but by and large the system worked, and within the context of African life the boys of Tabora had as good a record of behaviour as their contemporaries in English schools.

Until the middle 1930s admission to Tabora and expulsion from it was a complicated affair. In the early days, Travers Lacey consulted the teachers of village schools about talented pupils. Having made a list of suitable boys, he showed it to the D.C., who had a say where the son of an influential family was concerned. If the headmaster wanted to get rid of a lazy boy, or one obviously unsuited to book learning, he had to discuss it with the D.C. of the district. Often the D.C. would appeal to him not to expel the boy as it would make great difficulties for the whole family. In the case of a boy who would one day hold an important position, the headmaster would be urged to try and make something of him. Except for extreme cases, the headmaster invariably co-operated.

The academic content of the curriculum required a long period of adjustment, both in regard to Tabora School and the whole educational system that Sir Donald Cameron had inspired. As early as 1930 it seemed that the attempt to merge two traditions, the British and the African, had not worked out, and a decision had to be made as to whether it was more important that future chiefs and headmen should become expert farmers and cattle breeders, or that they should prepare themselves for higher education. It was clear that ultimately the demands of higher education had to prevail. Gradually agriculture and cattle husbandry were cut out. By 1935 the Tabora curriculum differed little from that of an average English school. The lower forms had been dropped, which meant no more teaching in Swahili; at the other end of the scale, boys who reached the top of the school and secured a School Certificate, could go on to Makerere College in Uganda.

Another change, effected in 1935, brought Tabora completely into line with British schools; the entrance examination was made competitive. No longer had candidates to be chiefs' or headmen's sons; gifted commoners could also sit for it. This meant that the most promising young Africans from all parts of Tanganyika went to Tabora.

Tabora Government School rose to what was probably the height of its reputation between 1932 and 1939. And with this progressive rise two outstanding Africans should be remembered: Mwalimu Stephano Mgalawe, the head African teacher, and Abraham Pitso, the agricultural instructor. These two senior members of the African staff set an example both in school and out which was quite unsurpassable. The subsequent reputation of Tabora School was partly due to their sound and cheerful influence.

During the war few changes took place, although the old saying, 'What Tabora does today, all other schools do tomorrow,' still prevailed. By 1949, when Makerere College was upgraded to a university college status, a special course was provided to prepare boys for the intermediary examination. Already in 1946 they could enter Makerere direct from Tabora; in 1948 for the first time they took the Cambridge School Certificate examination, and the Makerere intermediary was dropped. By this time two excellent mission secondary schools, the Roman Catholic Pugu and U.M.C.A.'s Minaki, were also in existence, training their pupils for the Cambridge School Certificate, thus practically trebling the number of young Tanganyikans who could go on to a university.

In 1947 John Blumer returned as headmaster, with the special task of concentrating School Certificate teaching at Tabora. He inaugurated a class of twenty-five pupils, drawing gifted boys also from other provincial secondary schools. By 1950 there were fifty boys in Tabora preparing themselves for higher education.

Blumer thoroughly revitalised the spirit of Tabora School by aiming at restoring the high standard of discipline, work, games and music which had been achieved during the 1932–9 period, under the headmastership of Patrick Williams. Unfortunately, he left in 1950. After an interregnum, he was succeeded by John Crabbe, whose immediate task was to consolidate Blumer's work and to add more pupils to the School Certificate stream. In 1950 no Tanganyikan boy got a first class certificate; in 1953 forty-five passed, with twenty in the first class. Since then the number going from Tabora to Makerere, or other parts of the East African University,[4] has been a steady twenty a year.

In 1959 John Crabbe set up the sixth form. In 1960 twenty-seven boys obtained their Cambridge Higher School Certificate and went on to university training. Tabora's sixth form is now open to boys from all Tanganyikan secondary schools. In 1961 and again in 1962, 1963 and 1964, eighty boys attended the sixth form. In this respect Tabora can compare with public and grammar schools in Britain, and its pupils can compete with British boys. The rapid attainment of such a level was the contribution of John Crabbe, who resigned and left Tabora on January 1, 1963.

At the moment of writing, in addition to Tabora there are twenty-two secondary schools in Tanganyika. Ten of these have sixth forms, also preparing their pupils for the Overseas Cambridge Higher School Certificate.

Considering the economic stringencies that plagued the development of education in Tanganyika, it is much to the credit of those responsible for administering Tabora that such notable educational standards were achieved at a minimal cost to the pupils. Tabora fees in any event have only been intended to cover maintenance; education as such was free. Boys who enrolled before 1928 paid £4 per annum; those after 1928 £5 per annum. Fees could be remitted if parents proved unable to pay. All school children were given free vouchers on the railways. In 1962 the annual fee at Tabora was £48, but this was only paid by twenty-five out of the three hundred boys. Eighteen per cent paid nothing, the rest varying fees in accordance with the father's income, some as little as £7 10s. 0d. a year.

*   *   *

The educational vision of Sir Donald Cameron's period, which produced Tabora Government School for the *élite* among young Africans, likewise inspired an entirely new approach to the task of providing schools for the mass of African children. That is when a remarkable D.O. at Shinyanga in the neighbouring Lake Province, Cecil McMahon, entered the picture. Charles Whybrow, one of the

---

[4] Makerere achieved university status in 1962, forming the University of East Africa with the Royal College of Nairobi and the Law School of Dar-es-Salaam.

three Superintendents of Education who went to Tanganyika in 1924 and subsequently became headmaster of Tabora, has recalled:

He was a crazy South African, known to everyone as Mac. It was Mac who moved the *boma* from Old to New Shinyanga, and it was he who started the first Chiefs' Federation, consisting of all the Sukuma Chiefdoms in Shinyanga District, with headquarters at Ibadakuli.[5] He was a great character and kept a gang of looters to steal building materials from the Railways and P.W.D.[6] for his Native Authority schemes. His unusual method came to light when Sir Donald Cameron congratulated him on a magnificent bridge which he had built between Shinyanga and Ibadakuli, and asked him where he had got the materials, which were mainly railway sleepers. Mac confessed and was let off with a caution, but he had to disband his looters. He and Travers Lacey were great friends.

McMahon picked up an idea thrown out by Travers Lacey that something had to be done for the children of African commoners. He suggested that for them boarding schools should be built on Tabora lines, but financed by the Native Authorities (except for teachers' salaries) and therefore called Native Authority Schools. As McMahon had hoped, the Sukuma chiefs liked Lacey's idea and Sir Donald Cameron approved it. Building began at four places; one was at Ibadakuli, where Travers Lacey, Charles Whybrow and Cecil McMahon together pegged out the foundations of the N.A. School. McMahon saw to it that this news reached the furthest corner of Tanganyika.

There was considerable rivalry as to which of the four N.A. Schools would be finished first. Kizigo, near Tabora, won by a short head and a hundred boys were admitted on December 1, 1928. Ibadakuli, near Shinyanga, was completed a few weeks later and the pupils of two village schools were transferred to it *en bloc*.

Overnight, N.A. Schools became an important factor in Tanganyikan education. The boys lived in symmetrically arranged 'villages', in accordance with the district they came from. Each village consisted of six to eight dormitory huts, a refectory, a kitchen and a teacher's hut. The dormitory huts were round grass huts, with windows and large doors, higher than the native pattern. They originated from South Africa, where they are called

[5] Ibadakuli, more correctly Kipatakuli, means the place of the Augur buzzard.
[6] Public Works Department.

rondavels. It was hoped that the boys, when they left, would build their own huts in this improved manner.

Each hut elected a father, each village a headman, the whole school a chief. The chief and his headmen formed a school court, for which a court house of African type was provided. All offences against discipline were tried in it. Tribal autonomy was thus brought into the school and boys learnt the meaning of authority and discipline. As all pupils were local boys, there was none of the strain caused by different tribes at Tabora and the system proved most successful.

A council or a committee composed of chiefs and headmen was responsible for the maintenance of the buildings, the proper feeding of pupils and for the teachers' activities. All teachers were Africans, who taught in Swahili. Relations with Administrative and Education Officers were friendly throughout.

Some Native Administration Schools took girls as well as boys, while others were reserved for headmen's sons. After four and a half hours classroom work a day, the children did agricultural work, carpentry and tailoring, drill and games. On leaving, many boys went on either to a Teachers' Training College, or to an industrial school, or to the Railway-Telegraph School at Dar-es-Salaam. The K.A.R. were also anxious to recruit them as signallers or members of the band.

In the early days it was difficult to find pupils for the N.A. Schools. At the request of the British authorities, the chiefs duly filled them, but until the Second World War many children could not be induced to stay. After 1945 this changed completely. Then fathers applied for all their children, so that suddenly there were more pupils than places. This has by now been made good, though today they are called lower primary schools.

Until 1961, N.A. Schools were, in fact, financed by the Government. The procedure was for Government to meet all costs, including equipment and teachers' salaries. The Native Treasury was then required to make a direct annual contribution of a small proportion of these costs to Government. In years of crop failure and financial strain in a district, the contribution was remitted in part or *in toto*. In this way basic requirements were provided. Gifts from chiefs, occasionally very generous gifts, donations from England and the sale of books and school materials provided the extras.

Since 1962, the procedure has been reversed. Government makes a direct grant for primary education to the Native Treasury, or to the District Council, which is then responsible for finding the balance.

Fees in the early days varied between 7s. and 10s. for nine months. Even these small sums had to be remitted sometimes, especially if there were several clever children in one family. Such remissions are still being granted.

* * *

By 1929 government schools had been provided for the sons of Tanganyika's aristocrats and commoners, but nothing had been done for their daughters. In the Annual Report of 1925, the Director of Education had called the absence of any provision for girls' schools a serious defect in an otherwise comprehensive scheme. Before initiating female education, however, it was thought wise to give assistance to the missions to improve their existing facilities for girls' training and to investigate how far these would meet the needs of specific districts.

Provision has been made in the draft Grant-in-Aid Code[7] to assist wherever possible any attempt to train women teachers and health workers under mission auspices [the Director reported]. I am of the opinion that it will be impossible to evade the necessity to make provisions for girls' schools in the estimates for 1927–28.

Admittedly it was a complex and contentious problem, especially on account of co-education. In the words of the report:

In a scheme of education based on the ideal of training for community life, there must be a basis for co-education which, while overcoming prejudices which may exist among the natives, will provide a type of education which will give the woman a higher conception of her duty in the community than might be possible in a wholly separate institution.

The Director added that if the Advisory Committee in London saw its way to throw open the service to women teachers, a channel to admit the necessary confidence would at once be opened.

The report recognised that wives of future chiefs needed a different type of education from girls who would marry into the

---

[7] In 1925 a Grant-in-Aid Code was framed under which grants could be made to Mission Societies in respect of certain recognised types of schools, based on the number of qualified European instructors, the salaries of the native teachers employed, the efficiency of the school and the cost of maintenance.

commercial community of Moshi. This could be planned for. It was suggested that in Moshi girls' villages should be created, similar to the boys' villages which the Moshi school had adopted, under close European supervision. The girls were to run the Moshi school kitchen, also learning invalid cooking and nursing in the school hospital. (In 1946 a girls' school in fact, opened in Machame, in rural surroundings twenty miles from Moshi.)

A year later, in the Annual Report for 1926, the Director said that the Government had made a very small experimental beginning with two day schools for girls and that a few girls were continuing here and there to attend village schools. The scheme for girls' boarding schools under mission auspices, provided for by the Grant-in-Aid Code, had been launched and proved a great success. The Church Missionary Society, the Holy Ghost Fathers and the Consolata Fathers (who had arrived in the early 1920s from Kenya, where they had been active since 1903) had led the way. But, the Director concluded, female education would not be fully met by the missions and the Government would have to accept the obligation of establishing a girls' school.

At last in 1929 Stanley Rivers-Smith founded a girls' boarding school in Tabora. Inside a ten-foot-high, enormously thick wall, three classrooms and four dormitories were erected, housing thirty girls and four teachers. At night, two watchmen locked the outside gate, all the doors, and patrolled the grounds. Miss Hake, a woman with a first class honours Cambridge degree, was invited to become headmistress. She saw the school through its initial teething troubles. A year later she was replaced by Miss M. H. S. Hanna, who had firm ideas both about education and the proprieties of life in any climate. She decided to have a formal opening for Tabora Girls' School, for which great occasion she ordered uniforms for the girls, which included–knickers. Her charges had never seen such a garment, let alone worn one. Comment about this innovation turned into hilarious gossip when, despite the two watchmen, the wall and the doubly locked doors, on the eve of the opening ceremony all the knickers were stolen! Miss Hanna was so put out that she cancelled the celebrations until a new consignment of knickers had been imported to Tabora. In 1931 she was succeeded by Miss Mary Hancock, who was not only devoted to the girls, but befriended their parents. Africans of all stations were welcome at her house.

In the beginning it took a lot of persuasion for parents to let their daughters come, especially as Moslems and pagans were stubbornly opposed to female education. Appeals were made to chiefs, but they were inclined to send the daughters of their junior wives or concubines. It was a great day when Chief Makwaia of Usiha, one of the most powerful men in Shinyanga and a strict Moslem, sent both his eldest daughter and his favourite young wife to Tabora Girls' School. His example turned the tide. Later on Christian converts became the school's staunchest supporters.

At first Tabora Girls' School was the equivalent of an elementary school; it laid great stress on housecraft–cookery, domestic science, mothercraft–though at an early stage girls were trained as teachers. A real change came after the war, in 1946, when Miss Violet Charman was headmistress. Classes were remodeled to teach to a higher standard and the teacher training course was developed. This trend was further stepped up from 1949 to 1953, when Miss Maureen Cowan was headmistress. By 1950 Tabora Girls' School virtually came up to matriculation standard and in 1953, for the first time, girls sat for the Cambridge School Certificate examination. Under Miss E. Webber and from 1960 onwards under Miss G. P. M. Hurley not only has the school become a first class secondary school, but the first one in Tanganyika to train girls for the Overseas Cambridge Higher School Certificate. In 1960, three out of four candidates succeeded in their exams, but all four got to a university. One was a Moslem girl, who went to Trinity College, Dublin. In 1961 five, in 1962 five and 1963 six girls obtained the Overseas Cambridge Higher School Certificate. In 1964 Miss Barbro Johansson, Member of Parliament and Lutheran missionary, became headmistress.

Miss Cowan, Miss Webber and not least Miss Hurley have watched with pride the erection of new buildings. In 1961 there were 185 pupils, with a staff of eleven European and two African teachers; in 1963 the figures rose to 276 pupils, with twelve European, three African and one Goan teacher. The reason for the low number of African teachers is that there are very few African women qualified to be secondary school teachers.

The new buildings are outside the wall, and the staff long for the day when the compound wall will no longer divide the school into an old and a new part. So far finances have not permitted the tearing down of the wall and its replacement by new modern fencing.

At the moment of writing there are eight secondary girls' schools in Tanganyika, but only two, Tabora and the Janwani Girls' School in Dar-es-Salaam, prepare pupils for the Overseas Cambridge Higher School Certificate. The Morogoro Secondary School, run by the American Maryknoll Sisters, may soon be the third.

*   *   *

In the Cameron era many new village schools were also opened. In these teaching was entirely by Africans in Swahili. Built either of mud brick or of wattle and daub with thatched roofs, they contained a classroom for each teacher and usually a small store. As a rule, there were two classes to each room. The system was known as the double session. Two of the four classes attended in the morning, the other two in the afternoon. So only two teachers and two classrooms were needed for four classes. Though unsatisfactory, this was unavoidable as long as the dearth of teachers continued.

The village schools were crowded. To enable children living at a distance to attend, huts were built where they could spend the nights from Monday to Friday and cook their own food. The chiefs made themselves responsible for these hostels. They also decided what punishment a young offender was to receive, as teachers were not allowed to punish pupils.

By now all village schools have been transformed into lower primary schools. Outside townships, the district councils are responsible for the maintenance of the primary schools, and approve any expansion (on which Tanu secretaries are very keen) provided the local authorities bear the total cost and do not ask the central government for any help. Until the end of 1965, all finance from the central government is to be used for the expansion of secondary level education.

Nowadays parents must contribute modest fees, according to their ability to pay, to the maintenance and the classroom expenses. The long term aim is to expand all lower primary schools into eight classes, that is into lower and upper primaries, so that every Tanganyikan child may receive eight years of schooling.[8]

*   *   *

[8] In 1963 out of 480,000 children of school age 267,118 (56 per cent) attended Standard I–II; out of 460,000, 196,713 (43 per cent) attended Standard III–IV; out of 440,000, 30,638 (9 per cent) attended Standard V–VI; out of 420,000, 27,849 (5 per cent) attended Standard VII-VIII. Approximately one fifth of the latter went on to Secondary School, that is 1 per cent.

The great innovations made during the Cameron era laid the foundations of future educational developments in Tanganyika. And yet the central,[9] the N.A., the village and the girls' schools between them only catered for ten per cent of African children who received education. The remaining ninety per cent[10] were taught at mission schools, which until Cameron's arrival had received neither financial assistance, nor even encouragement from the administration. In 1921 C.M.S. missionaries importuned Sir Horace Byatt to introduce a system of grants-in-aid to mission schools, in exchange for which they promised to augment the number of their schools, to raise their educational standard and to introduce a large measure of industrial training, with qualified instructors from England. Byatt, however, for lack of resources, could not take up this offer.

Yet the Protestant missions had rendered services of a type which changed the Colonial Office attitude to them. This was due to their stand over the severe Labour Ordinance issued by the first post-war Governor of Kenya, General Northey. Northey, who had encouraged his ex-officers from the campaign against von Lettow-Vorbeck to settle in the colony, in 1918 instructed Government officials and chiefs to exercise every possible lawful influence to induce able-bodied male natives to go into the labour field, in other words to impress them for work on white settler farms. In view of the dependence of chiefs on D.C.'s, and of their ignorance of the difference between lawful and unlawful influence, this was equivalent to compulsory labour for private individuals. Local mission protests achieved nothing, but fortunately in London there had been set up the Conference of Missionary Societies of Great Britain and Northern Ireland, and the eminently able, energetic and tactful secretary of this body, Dr J. H. Oldham, succeeded in drawing the attention of the Colonial Office to the pernicious implications of the Labour Ordinance. Leading into a

---

[9] The original name for what were to become upper primary schools.

[10] Altogether only about 10 per cent of African children went to any kind of school. Their own education, *Jando*, took place in the bush, where the boys were sent when they reached puberty. They were instructed in tribal history and custom, put through physical endurance tests, taught how to take a beating, and initiated into the mysteries of sex and marriage. The Masai were par excellence *Jando* conscious. When back from *Jando*, a boy had achieved a higher stage of social life. The missions attacked *Jando* and eventually smashed it because of the sex teaching.

much wider field, Dr Oldham propagated the need for a policy which would realise the Double Mandate of training Africans for self-government while administering the colony.

With his expert knowledge of East Africa, reinforced by frequent local reports, Dr Oldham suggested to the Colonial Office that the most effective means of carrying out the Double Mandate would be to establish an educational policy for Africans; and that such a policy could not be operated unless the missions were enabled to teach a sufficient number of pupils. His arguments were borne out by the Report of the American Phelps-Stokes Commission, based on West and South African experience. In 1923, the then Under-Secretary for Colonial Affairs, William Ormsby-Gore (later Lord Harlech) accepted Dr Oldham's advice. He introduced a new deal in education for East African natives and invited the missions on a grant-in-aid basis to help carry it out. Due to Dr Oldham, the Grant-in-Aid Code was so worked out that, in order to qualify, the missions had to modernise their teaching methods and personnel.

Although in the early days the Protestant missions alone advocated a forward native policy which would keep open the road to racial equality in the future, once the policy had been established, the Roman Catholic missions took their full share in making it work. This was brought home by the appointment, in 1927, of Mgr Arthur Hinsley (later Cardinal Hinsley) as Apostolic Vicar to The Catholic Missions in the British Colonies in Africa. In August 1928, at Dar-es-Salaam, he summed up the Catholic point of view, naturally backed by the Vatican, in his address to a conference of bishops and leading missionaries in Africa: 'Collaborate with all your power, and where it is impossible for you to carry on both the immediate task of evangelisation and educational work, neglect your churches in order to perfect your schools.'

Three years before this remarkable order, in fact soon after his arrival, Sir Donald Cameron sent for the representatives of all the missions and offered them co-operation on the basis of the Grants-in-Aid Code his Education Department had worked out for Tanganyika. (See Chapter 8, p. 80.) The missions responded enthusiastically. They put their house in modern order and then literally hundreds of Roman Catholic and dozens of Protestant schools were opened in all parts of the Territory. The missions also taught industrial crafts, forerunners of the later Trade Schools.

The White Fathers had, moreover, set up a seminary for training priests.

Grants to the missions increased steadily over the years, from nothing in 1923 to £285,000 in 1949 and £824,000 in 1963-4. Their popularity was due, in part, to the fact that they Africanised themselves long before any other institution by training African monks, nuns and lay teachers, all of whom have worked with singular dedication.

* * *

When the whole field of Tanganyikan education has been surveyed, the most outstanding single monument to Sir Donald Cameron's activities is still Tabora Government School. The achievements of this great institution both speak for themselves and symbolise the devoted work which was done in the many schools of Tanganyika during the governorship of Cameron and thereafter. All former pupils of Tabora are proud of having been there and feel that they have a special link with each other.

Sir Donald thought in terms of training chiefs and headmen. Today, under changed conditions, it is no longer chiefs and headmen, but political leaders, economic experts and trained administrators who shape the destiny of the new Tanganyika. Men educated at Tabora have the equipment of mind and character to acquire political and economic qualifications.

Had Cameron lived, he would have approved of this adjustment to the needs of the times. And he would have been proud indeed had he seen the 'old boys' who foregathered at Founder's Day in 1961. Julius Nyerere, then Chief Minister, was there; so were Abdulla Fundikira, Minister for Legal Affairs, Rashidi Kawawa, Minister of State, Cardinal-Archbishop Laurian Rugambwa, the Apostolic Delegate from Mombasa, two Archbishops, one Archbishop-Designate, a number of Bishops and a galaxy of lesser notabilities.

Julius Nyerere was the speaker of the day, and he made one of the best speeches of his life.

You are the real privileged people of Tanganyika [he told the assembled school]. Not the Europeans, not the Asians but you pupils of Tabora School fall into this category. You are among the lucky boys who went to primary school. Remember, at least fifty per cent of your contemporaries cannot go to school at all. Of those who have had any schooling at all you are among the doubly lucky few to come here, to the finest school in Tanganyika, if not in the whole of Africa. It is your responsibility to take full advantage of your chances and to study diligently, so as to get to a college or a university. Then it will be your responsibility to act as teachers to the vast majority of under-privileged children in our country. You are the future leaders of Tanganyika, for remember Tabora has a unique record in turning out leaders for our country.

In 1963, Tabora Government School started on yet another phase of its history, under the headmastership of Peter Partner. In the wider field of education the future will likewise bring changes. Changes and fresh ideas are good, yet it will be a sad day for Tabora and for all education in Tanganyika if there is any falling away from the ideals of its English founders to produce 'a due supply of persons well qualified to serve. . . .'[11]

[11] To enable every talented child in Tanganyika to obtain secondary education, on January 1, 1965, all fees in secondary schools were abolished. This applies only to Tanzania citizens; non-Tanzania citizens pay the following fees: those already in a secondary school on January 1, 1965, pay £24 a year for tuition and £24 a year for boarding; those who entered them after January 1, 1965, pay £48 for tuition and £24 for boarding. Now pupils must provide their own uniforms and their own bedding which previously they received free. Now as before books and copybooks are a Government responsibility, as is transport beyond a certain radius from school.

In all primary schools a nominal fee is being charged.

Since January 1, 1965, pupils are no longer enrolled by the schools directly, except in lower primaries. In all other schools they are enrolled by Selection Boards. Each one of Tanganyika's seventeen zones has a Selection Board, consisting of the regional education officer, headmasters and headmistresses, and one or several representatives of the voluntary agencies within the zone. (The voluntary agencies are: the Tanzania Episcopal Conference (Roman Catholics), the Tanganyika Christian Council of Churches (Protestants), the Moslem Welfare Society and the Tanganyika Parents' Association.) The regional education officer or his representative is chairman of the Selection Board.

The present system of enrolment means two things. Denominational schools must accept children of any religious denomination, provided they live within the zone; priority is being given to pupils having Tanzania citizenship.

After the completion of the Five Year Plan, which aims at raising the average standard of living by fifty per cent, this generous education policy may be revised.

CHAPTER 10

Tanganyika in the Doldrums

EVERYBODY knew that the Governor who would succeed Sir Donald Cameron would have a difficult time living up to his standards. But it is unfortunate that Tanganyikans do not even remember the names of the three men who held this office between 1931 and the outbreak of the Second World War. These eight years showed up the weariness of the British colonial system.

The theory behind it was admirable. Based on the highest principles, it was flexible and adaptable to most varied local conditions. But the Colonial Office was permitted to frame policy without consulting its vastly differing territories.

To understand this part of the Tanganyika story, it is necessary to visualise the structure of British colonial administration in the 1930s. It was built like a pyramid. At its apex stood the Governor: on the level below, the Executive Council and the Legislative Council; on three subsidiary levels were spread the Provincial Commissioners, the District Commissioners and the District Officers, assisted by the police and if occasion should arise, by the armed forces. On the lowest level but one stood a few thousand Europeans and Asians; at the very bottom were the millions of Africans, with no political rights at all.

The Governor, who was also Commander-in-Chief of the armed forces, was under the firm control of the imperial government, which laid down policy. He had immense statutory and discretionary power. The Colonial Secretary appointed the judges on behalf of His Majesty, in consultation with the Governor and the Chief Justice. The Governor had no power over the High Court, but the Crown's prerogative of mercy was vested in him.

It takes a man of strong character like Cameron to use so much power for the creation of a new nation and to stand up to the Colonial Office when he judges certain instructions from it to be harmful. That is why the London civil servants regarded Cameron with suspicion and disapproval. Great men must suffer the disadvantages of their greatness, one of which is that they arouse the obstructionism of a harassed and possibly somewhat obtuse higher authority. A man has to be lucky as well as great to overcome obstinacy in high places.

The first Tanganyika Executive Council was created in 1920. It had four members: the Chief Secretary, the Attorney-General, the Treasurer and the Director of Medical and Sanitary Services.

The Chief Secretary played the part of all Permanent Secretaries rolled into one. He was the head of the Civil Service. His duty was to keep the Governor informed of the work, the policy, the aspirations, etc., of various departments and to make sure that the Departments operated efficiently. Generally speaking all communications to the Governor went through him.

The Attorney General was the Governor's legal adviser. He and his office drafted all new legislation. Legislation concerning fiscal measures and measures which might adversely affect Africans had to be reported to the Secretary of State. The Royal Assent could be withheld on his advice.

The Treasurer was in charge of Government finance. The Director of Medical and Sanitary Services dealt with all matters of health. In 1926, Sir Donald Cameron appointed a fifth member to the Executive Council, the Secretary of African Native Affairs, responsible for Native Administration. He supervised the system of indirect rule.

These five officials held their places at the pleasure of the Crown as represented by the Governor. If they disagreed with the Governor or with the policy he enforced, they would, quite properly, have to resign from the Council. The Governor was required to report to the Secretary of State if this happened.

In 1926, as related earlier, a Legislative Council (commonly referred to as Legco) was set up. Although according to the strict letter of the constitution, its function was to advise the Governor, it was to all intents and purposes the law-making machinery of the country. Some of its legislation had to be approved by the Secretary of State.[1] The Governor was chairman; its membership com-

---

[1] An Order in Council, dated March 19, 1926, laid down: 'It shall be lawful for the Governor, with the advice and consent of the Legislative Council to make laws for the administration of justice, the raising of revenue and generally for the peace, order and good governancy of the Territory. Such laws shall be styled "Ordinances" and the enacting words shall be "Enacted by the Governor of Tanganyika" with the advice and consent of the Legislative Council thereof.' (Section XIV.) According to Section XV, it was within the discretion of the

prised the members of the Executive Council *ex officio*, plus 'unofficials' appointed by the Governor. These 'unofficials' held their places at the Governor's pleasure; he could not compel them to support legislation of which they disapproved. (In fact the position never arose.) No African belonged to Legco until 1945.

Under the Governor served the Provincial Commissioners (known as P.C.s), the District Commissioners (D.C.s) and the District Officers (D.O.s). Within their respective geographical areas they had great power over the day-to-day affairs of the Africans, although this power was bounded by policy and by finance and, of course, by the relevant legislation. They supervised the Native Authorities, who could do nothing without the sanction of the P.C., the D.C. or the D.O. They made local regulations or, rather, they instructed the Native Authorities to make them. They acted as magistrates to the natives; they controlled the Native courts; they supervised the collection of native house and poll taxes. They were justifiably called 'fathers of the people' and certainly no father could have had more complete mastery over his children. The justification of the system lay in the manner in which this power was exercised.

This is the side of British colonial rule which has called forth much resentment among Tanganyikans. With so much power over day-to-day life, the character and attitude of these civil servants was tremendously important. Some were outstanding men who are still remembered with love. Some were of a calibre which would not have been acceptable in India, where Britain sent the best of her talent and where the heads of departments refused to tolerate second class men. Some were rough and ready, but they had a rough and ready country to cope with, and their charges had, through the years of tribal wars, become accustomed to a climate of violence. Some were remote, but in a country split by feud and counter feud, by quarrels, intrigues and rival factions, and by bitter animosities between chief and chief, and witch doctor and witch doctor, remoteness was no bad thing.

The large majority of these men loved their work and the people whose affairs they were administering. Darrell Bates, who went to Tanganyika as a cadet in 1935, gives this description of his work:

Governor 'but subject to any instructions addressed to him under His Majesty's signed manual and signet or through a Secretary of State' which laws he assented to and which ones he referred to the Secretary of State.

In backwater Districts where there was only a District Commissioner and, with luck, an Assistant, there were no magistrates (Inner Temple and all that), no police officers, no agricultural or forestry or veterinary experts, no proper builders or roadmenders. So we did the lot. One spent a lot of time in court and, although in practice we mostly just used our common sense to find a fair answer, we often had to thumb through Archbold or somebody on torts afterwards to see if it also agreed with the law. People in England, particularly judges, often looked surprised when they heard that as well as being a magistrate I ran the police detachment, and the prison as well. In between times we read books on soil erosion and dipping of cattle and ring-barking and so were able to pass on the benefits of western civilization to our flock. We also mended and, if need be, built roads and hospitals and houses and schools, and one or two other things as well. . . . Our job was not to rule but to help and, if need be, make them rule themselves. We wanted something that would last, so that when we left it would run by itself. (*A Fly-Switch From The Sultan*, p. 19.)

Bates also relates that until the end of the 1920s, members of the Colonial Administrative Service were recruited mainly from individualists bored with the routine and slow promotion in the Army or the Navy, from those who had acquired some experience of Africa in other fields, like the British South African Police, and from men who had useful relations and liked outdoor life. But from 1930 onwards, due to the stimulus and imagination of Ralph (now Sir Ralph) Furse at the Colonial Office, recruits began to be drawn from the universities. 'There were no exams and plenty of interviews, and the system and the nature of the job gradually attracted some of the best people Britain and the Dominions had to offer.' (Ibid. p. 56.)

Of course there were failures, men who ruled with an alien and unsympathetic hand. Speaking Swahili does not necessarily mean understanding Africans. Some D.C.s and D.O.s had no idea what their charges were feeling and thinking, especially not the small number of educated Africans who had begun to question the whole system of being ruled by men with a different colour skin. Some European women did further harm by their deliberate apartness. To give just one illustration. At this time, in the 1930s, the wife of a civil servant would not have dreamt of inviting an African woman to her house, except as a servant.

Another aspect of the British colonial pattern was the impossibility of complaining about the shortcomings of the D.C.s or

2 (b) Sir Donald Cameron

2 (a) General von Lettow-Vorbeck

3 (*a*) Karamojo Football at Tabora

3 (*b*) Tabora School, 1926

the D.O.s. The Africans had no one to turn to. They could, in theory, have written to the Colonial Office, but at this time ninety-eight per cent of them were illiterate. And without higher backing, they were afraid, justifiably, of the retribution of the D.C. or D.O. in question. Although most of them would have done nothing, the African was not to know that. Even a European, who observed treatment which would not have been tolerated by the British public had it known about it, got no hearing at Government House. The line was that any criticism of officials was subversive and could not be countenanced.

Yet this was the period of early African awakening. It was in the 1930s that Jomo Kenyatta studied at the London School of Economics and wrote his book *Facing Mount Kenya*. It was at this time, too, that a fundamental change took place in the principle underlying British colonial rule.

From the eighteenth century until the 1920s, this principle had been the paramountcy of native interests. From Edmund Burke, to David Lloyd George, all great English politicians used this ponderous term when referring to their responsibility as custodians for the well-being and advancement of colonial peoples. Its primary aim was to safeguard native interests and to train Africans so that, eventually, they should stand on their own feet.

This classic policy was first questioned by the white settlers who went out to Africa. In the wake of Cecil Rhodes, Englishmen and Dutchmen settled in what are today Zambia and Rhodesia and Malawi; under the leadership of Lord Delamere many hundreds of Englishmen, with their families, went to Kenya. Having sunk their capital and invested exceedingly hard labour in the land they had purchased with Colonial Office blessing, they wanted not only to be sure in its possession, but on the basis of their superior knowledge and experience, to be in a position to rule the areas in which they lived. From this followed the dream of the Great White Dominion, challenged by Cameron, and today's acute political problems in Kenya and Rhodesia. As Cameron rightly said, the bill always comes in.

It was the Conservative Party that replaced the old principle of paramountcy of native interests by a new concept, 'co-ordination of interests', meaning co-ordination of African and European interests. Anyone familiar with conditions in the colonies understood that this was bound to mean subordination of African to

E

European interests. Otherwise the Great White Dominion made no sense.

And this was not all. Shift in principle was to be accompanied by change in practice. The white settlers persuaded the Conservative politicians that they should, logically, be associated with the great task of administering Britain's trust for her African territories. The trust was still to be exercised for the benefit of the African; but the policy had become an ambivalent one.

In a series of White Papers and in instructions to Commissions sent out to East Africa, L. S. Amery, Colonial Secretary in successive Conservative administrations, made it plain that he wished the immigrant communities domiciled in the country to be more closely associated in the responsibilities and trusteeship of Government. The trend was for the white settlers to become more and more powerful; in Kenya the situation moved in this direction, while in Southern Rhodesia they were firmly in control. It was Uganda's fear of domination by Kenya settlers that put a stop to further progress towards the Great White Dominion. As for Tanganyika, she was protected by the Mandate.

When the Labour Government came to power in 1929, Lord Passfield (Sidney Webb), brushed aside L. S. Amery's plans. He issued two White Papers which stunned the Kenya settlers by restating Tanganyika's special position under the Mandate; and he scotched any notion of 'Closer Union' on the ground that, politically, Tanganyika could not be brought into federation with territories in which the Africans had no political rights and, as long as the white settlers had a decisive say in the matter, never would have any. Under the Mandate, Tanganyika had to be trained for independence. But this political security did not help from an economic point of view; indeed, the reverse was true.

In the summer of 1931 the world economic crisis hit Britain with full force. The Labour Government was faced with what seemed bankruptcy. No saving loan came from Washington. The Labour cabinet refused to agree to the full measure of economies urged by Ramsay MacDonald and Philip Snowden, including cuts in welfare payments; MacDonald therefore resigned –but promptly undertook the leadership of a new 'National' coalition with Conservatives and Liberals in which few Labour members served and which the party as a whole opposed. In spite of initial assurances that the coalition was to be a purely temporary measure, to meet the crisis, its leaders soon asked the country for a mandate for its continuation. They secured a considerable majority. It was a time when patriotic Englishmen queued at the office of the Inspector of Taxes for the privilege of paying what was due from them.

Cameron's successors carried out the Colonial Office instructions to retrench and economise. They did not like to close down promising development or to sack experienced staff, but Britain did not have the means to keep them; not even the Labour Government were prepared to make concessions on this score. They felt that they were helping their country by saving every possible penny; that they were damaging the foundations of a young country seemed in the context of a world slump a remote issue.

In this contemporary context it was doubtless inevitable that expenditure in the colonies should be slashed. In Tanganyika Cameron's road and railway building programme had to go. Not only were no new roads built, but some existing ones were no longer maintained. A number of villages lost their market exits. The atmosphere of confidence created by Cameron wilted and living standards slipped back almost to the 1925 level.[2]

Even in 1960, when a great road building programme had been carried out, there were only 3,774 miles of territorial main roads, 5,176 miles of local main roads, 10,883 miles of district roads and 495 miles of roads running through municipalities and townships. (In addition there were 8,000 miles of dirt tracks, euphemistically called village roads.) This adds up to a total of 18,278 miles of roads within an area of four times the size of Great Britain. In 1931, the total mileage was 3,587. At that time, the United Kingdom refused to provide money for road building, both on the principle that colonies had to maintain themselves and on the practical consideration that there was no money. Tanganyika was desperately poor and could not help herself.

Three extensions of the railway line had been planned under Cameron: one from Kilosa to Ifakara; a second from Kilosa to Korogwe connecting the Northern and the Central Railway; and

---

[2] Retrenchment was the order of the day the world over. A comparison between the British colonies in Africa and the mid-Western States of the U.S.A. might well show that the latter's losses and sufferings were relatively greater than those of Tanganyika.

finally one from Dodoma to Iringa. All three were cancelled. Twenty-five years later the Kilosa–Ifakara line got as far as Mikumi and in 1960 Sir Richard Turnbull, the Governor, drove the first train on it. In 1963 Kilosa and Korogwe were connected by train; only at Iringa are the railway station and depot sad reminders of Tanganyika's doldrums in the 1930s. With an airport at Iringa, and the excellent new road as far as Dar-es-Salaam, it seems unlikely that the Dodoma–Iringa railway line will be built.

Retrenchment in the field of education is revealing both of hard economic realities and of lack of foresight on the part of H.M.G. What happened between 1931 and 1939 can best be understood by looking at the following figures. Here is the first:

Year	Total Expenditure on Education £	Total Revenue £	Per cent of Total Revenue Spent on Education
1923–24	13,156	1,257,540	1·05
1924–25	15,754	1,324,670	1·18
1925–26	24,491	1,975,400	1.44
1926–27	45,923	2,202,908	2·08
1927–28	59,692	2,486,278	3·21
1928–29	75,947	1,972,858	3·85
1929–30	89,829	1,992,675	4·50
1930–31	111,302	1,749,478	6·36
1931–32	122,666	1,522,368	8·06
1932[3]	100,393	1,624,918	6·18
1933	89,355	1,564,538	5·71
1934	86,704	1,720,285	5·03
1935	81,104	1,973,863	4·10
1936	84,619	2,206,417	3·83
1937	92,313	2,345,004	3·94
1938	99,717	2,100,414	4·75

[3] From here on, calendar and financial year coincide. 1932 = ten months.

These figures show that Sir Donald Cameron had steadily raised the education appropriation, in absolute figures from £13,156 in 1924 to £122,666 in 1931, in proportion to total income from 1·05 per cent in 1924 to 8·06 per cent in 1931. Under his successors it was reduced from £122,666 in 1931 to £81,104 in 1935, and from 8·06 of the total revenue in 1931 to

4·10 per cent in 1935. In 1936 it fell to 3·83 per cent of the total revenue. After that it crept up slowly to £99,717 in 1938, by which year Tanganyika's economic life had long thrown off the effects of the depression. But education still formed only 4·75 per cent of the total revenue.

The full import of these figures only emerges on reading the annual reports to the Permanent Mandate Commission of the League of Nations. Reviewing 1932, the report states that there had been a further advance towards economic stability; with increasing imports and exports, the economic overdraft had been reduced by £780,000; but the education appropriation was cut by £5,324. In 1933 there had been a steady improvement in tax collection, economic prosperity was returning and the financial position was better than expected. That year the education appropriation was cut by £11,342. In 1934, trade returns had further improved, sisal, coffee, cotton and tobacco exports had reached record figures and trade exceeded that of 1933 by £527,000. But the money spent on education was reduced by another £6,328. The 1935 Report was enthusiastic about economic improvements, stating that exports had reached £3,500,000, a figure only exceeded in the 1928 and 1929 boom years. But the education appropriation was once more reduced by £4,604. In 1938, when the national revenue was over £2 million, the education appropriation was still under £100,000 and £23,000 less than in 1931.

Only in 1933 was the percentage of children, European, Asian and African, who went to school published: 51 per cent of the Europeans, 49 per cent of the Asians and 1·84 per cent of the Africans.

There is one redeeming aspect in this barren period: the record of the missions, Protestant and Roman Catholic. Although in 1933 their educational grants-in-aid were reduced by ten per cent, their maintenance grants halved and their examination and capitation grants abolished, they increased their educational activities. That year, the Government closed two central and four industrial schools. In 1934, the report to the Permanent Mandate Commission had this to say:

An outstanding feature of missionary work has been the marked increase in the activities of the Roman Catholic missions, who applied to register over two hundred new schools in the Kigoma District, and over one hundred in the Iringa Province, apart from several hundred applications spread over other provinces. (p. 88.)

Yet in this same year, the grants to the missions were cut by another ten per cent.

Despite economic improvement, these cuts remained in force until 1936, when grants to the missions were increased from £19,171 to £20,698.

In 1936, the report to the Mandate Commission stated: 'The European staff of all foreign missionary societies continue to increase and their building activities are noticeable everywhere.' In 1938, the grants-in-aid to the missions were increased to £24,110. But by then the economic blizzard had blown itself out and Tanganyika had repaid all the loans the Home Treasury had given her.

With this education policy, Tanganyikans could not replace Europeans and other foreigners in the Civil Service and in commercial positions. In 1937 fourteen of the Secretariat's eighteen clerks were foreigners; thirty-seven out of thirty-nine Treasury clerks were foreigners; one hundred out of one hundred and fourteen customs officials were Asians.

In the 1930s salary cuts were imposed throughout the Civil Service and the number of officials reduced. Africans were affected in the first place. Cameron had set up a Labour Department to investigate all questions connected with labour economy, waste of labour, methods of rewarding labour, feeding, medical treatment, housing, inspection of labour conditions on public undertakings such as railways and road construction, and on private plantations, and supervision of the erection and control of labour camps. Cameron was convinced that the German system, which fixed the daily task of labour so low that an ambitious man could carry out separate tasks for three different employers, had its roots in underfeeding, wrong treatment and poor organisation. The purpose of his Labour Department was to remedy these conditions. After his departure, on grounds of economy his Labour Department was abolished; it was restored in the late 1930s.

*   *   *

In addition to shortsightedness and lack of comprehension of local conditions, there was one more powerful reason why Tanganyika suffered economically. The Mandate put it in a special position in more senses than one. Hitler was claiming that the Mandate system had been specially devised to despoil the Germans of their colonial possessions, and demanded the return to the German Reich of Tanganyika, the erstwhile German East Africa. In the face of these provocative statements, the British governments of the day, the National Government, the Baldwin Government and the Chamberlain Government, remained silent. By the time of the Munich crisis, British policy was openly one of appeasement, with the result that investors kept their money back. Tanganyika went on floundering in economic frustration.

British officials and settlers in Kenya as well as in Tanganyika were deeply concerned over rumours that the Territory might be handed back to the Germans. The settlers, headed by Ferdinand (now Sir Ferdinand) Cavendish-Bentinck (who later became one of the leaders of the Kenya white settlers), formed the Tanganyika League. In 1939 its president, General Boyd Moss, threatened: 'to fight to the last cartridge before we allow London to give our country away'. In October, 1938, the Governor invited the members of the Legislative Council to make a protest on behalf of the five million Africans. They were delighted to do so.

Fortunately, at this time, the question of Tanganyika's future was raised in the House of Commons. The then Colonial Secretary, Malcolm MacDonald, made the following statement:

I do not believe there is today any section of opinion in this country that is disposed to hand over to any other country the care of any of the territories or the people for whose government we are responsible either as a Colonial or a Mandatory Power. That view has been expressed this afternoon in every part of the House and it is a view which is shared by H.M. Government. We are not discussing this matter; we are not considering it; it is not now an issue of practical politics.

This was not exactly a fiery reassurance, but after years of painful uncertainty, it did bring some relief. Sir William Lead, owner of Tanganyika's largest sisal plantation and leader of the Nominated Members of the Legislative Council, promptly requested the Governor to set up machinery for a large-scale development programme. This was not only to further the interest of all; it was to be an earnest of confidence in Tanganyika's future. For once, quick action followed. Within a few days a Central Development Committee was inaugurated, which did excellent work.

The space of eight months before the outbreak of war was not enough fully to explore Tanganyika's economic potentialities. Meanwhile German business men, well provided with capital, were standing in the wings, poised to swoop into a restored German colony. Their economic plans were worked out to the last detail.

For Hitler Tanganyika may have been a sideline. But he despised nothing. In the great conflict that was coming, everything could be of value.

CHAPTER 11

To Whom Hitler Meant Nothing

To millions of Tanganyikans the name Hitler meant nothing. They did not know that the German Führer claimed the return of what used to be German East Africa. Even less did they know that this was part of his aim to achieve world domination.

Tanganyikans were also unaware that Neville Chamberlain, then Prime Minister of Britain, was considering the cession of their country to Germany if, by doing so, he could avert the horrors of a second world war. They did not know that British business men were hesitant to invest money in the Territory because of the political risks attending its future.

And they never noticed the events shaping before their eyes. More and more Germans arrived, some of whom took over an organisation called the Usagara Company. This had been started in 1926, quite legitimately, as an organisation backed by the German Government. Its purpose was to help settlers with loans and advice during their first crucial twelve months.

When Hitler came to power, his henchmen grabbed the company. Analysed and tabulated by Gestapo-trained minds, its files revealed the secret weaknesses of every single member. Under the threat of this hidden blackmail, all Tanganyikan Germans were pressed into the Führer's service.

By then the Usagara Company was the third largest trading concern in Tanganyika. It bought coffee, tea and sisal from German settlers, paying them in *Aski* Marks, the cover name for a typical Nazi business arrangement. The settlers received payment in the form of credit at local German stores and in the form of 400s. (£20) cash a month. The rest of their sales' proceeds remained in Germany to benefit the Fatherland.

A subsidiary of the Usagara Company, the Uhehe Company, had its ramifications in the Southern Highlands. In exchange for credit, this Nazi organisation forced German planters to hand over the title deeds of their farms. Once the so-called loans had been paid off, these were to be returned. In no case was this promise fulfilled. Shortly before the war the settlers sent a spokesman to Berlin to find out what was happening. The Nazi

Government then made such a slave-driving offer that even these enthusiastic Nazis turned it down.

For that is what most of the German settlers in Tanganyika were. The exceptions, those who voiced their dissatisfaction too boldly, were summoned before secret party tribunals. It is believed that, as a result of sentences passed on them, some stubborn individuals met with fatal accidents. In other words, under the nose of the British colonial administration, a miniature underground Nazi state was in full working order.

In the old Berlin Mission Building in Dar-es-Salaam, for example, a German baker painted a large mural of the Führer, taking up most of one wall of this Lutheran chapel. During the day it was covered by a picture of Our Lord. But when the Aryans met in secret, Our Lord's picture was shoved into a corner and services were held under the likeness of Adolf Hitler.

The British administration was not quite as naïve as the Germans imagined, but reports of the security authorities on Tanganyika were merely pigeonholed in the pious hope that a peaceful solution with the Nazi Government might even now be arrived at.

After Munich, these hopes were dashed for ever. After the rape of Czechoslovakia, coded instructions were issued from London whereby all German men and some German women, should be interned in case of hostilities. In the event these arrangements were carried out so quietly and efficiently that, by noon on Sunday, September 3, 1939, all the 1,470 Germans on the list were under lock and key.

Herr Troost, the Führer of all the Germans in Tanganyika, was bald and bespectacled and well into his fifties. He was motoring peaceably in the countryside when a constable waving a warrant for his arrest, stopped his car. Baron Oenhausen, as fair and as tall as Herr Troost was dark and small, wore a monocle. This Nazi peacemaker of the Southern Highlands was politely handed a towel while in his bath. Neither put up any resistance, believing that 'the British farce' would soon be over.

During the first six months of 1940, 572 German men and 780 women and children were repatriated. The astonishing thing was that some of these Germans begged to be allowed to stay in British captivity. They have since returned to Tanganyika and become steady, loyal citizens.

After the fall of France and Italy's entry into the war, 500 Germans and Italians were transferred to South Africa for internment. This left 1,700 internees in Tanganyika, of whom 656 were missionaries. While on parole, the Italian Consolata Fathers built a boarding school, a hospital and a cathedral at Tosamaganga, that hill in the Southern Highlands from which half-a-century earlier German field-guns had bombarded Mkwawa's fort.

Camps of a very different nature welcomed thousands of refugees, among them many Poles. A million of these unfortunates had been deported from the eastern half of their country to the frozen north or to the burning deserts of Soviet Russia. When, as a result of the 1941 Stalin–Sikorski agreement, they were 'released', some succeeded in trekking to India. From there, 6,500 were sent via Persia to Tanganyika, slowly to recover from the indescribable hardships they had endured and to start a new life.

Still they longed for Europe. At the end of the war, few Poles made their homes in Tanganyika, but 396 missionaries and 369 German and Italian internees wanted to stay and were allowed to do so. The mistake of repatriating wholesale *all* Germans, committed at the end of the First World War was not repeated. This time the sheep and the goats were divided.

To young Tanganyikans all this seems ancient history, with no bearing on themselves. They have not heard about Hitler and to them von Lettow-Vorbeck still seems the only German who ever mattered.

CHAPTER 12

From a Different War
Emerges the Trust Territory

MOST settlers in Tanganyika joined up in 1939. One of the first
to go home and to join R.A.F. Fighter Command was Lord
Chesham, who in 1936 had been granted by the Colonial Office a
110,000 acre concession for his Southern Highland Scheme. He
had land cleared and surveyed, roads made and a clubhouse built,
complete with golf and tennis courts. It was a well conceived
colonial settlement scheme, designed to fulfil local demands on a
co-operative basis. Lord Chesham's American wife, Marion,
took up war work in London. Twenty years later she was to play
a part in Tanganyika politics through her friendship with two men,
an African called Julius Nyerere, and a European called Derek
Bryceson. Both were seventeen years old when war broke out, and
one day they were to become close friends.

The white settlers who stayed behind grew commodities needed
in Britain and other allied countries. One of these was pyrethrum,
the plant which looks like a daisy and is a superb insecticide.
Another was sisal, which became a top priority product when Japan
seized Phillippine and Javanese supplies. A third was rubber, produced at great expense on old, derelict German plantations. After
Japan had overrun Malaya, it was such an essential war material
that price no longer mattered. The great difficulty Tanganyikan
farmers had to overcome was the weather. During four of the
six war years, there was a disastrous lack of rain. Because
of the drought, maize had to be imported, rice and groundnuts had to be rationed, and wheat, badly needed all over East
Africa, yielded poor average crops. Despite all this, Tanganyika
helped to save shipping space. Prices rose steadily during the
war and income tax was introduced. The overall result was that
revenue increased from £2,308,108 in 1940 to £4,768,465 in
1945.

Of Tanganyika's African population, ninety-two thousand
joined the ranks of the King's African Rifles, the highest ratio of
volunteers in Britain's territories. They served under General

120

Wavell in Somaliland and Abyssinia, and took part in the victorious entry into Addis Ababa on April 6, 1941.

When Italy declared war, it had looked as though Tanganyika might once again become a battlefield. After Italy's collapse Tanganyika was safe until Japan's entry into the war on December 7, 1941, and the danger of Japan dominating the Indian Ocean soon faded as American mobilisation grew apace.

In the spring of 1942, owing to the doubtful attitude of the Vichy French Government, Madagascar had to be occupied. The K.A.R. had a share in garrisoning Diego Suarez and later in occupying the rest of the island. With the extension of the war to South East Asia, the K.A.R. were for the first time sent on duty outside the African Continent and its adjacent islands. In the Burma campaign they were in the vanguard of the advance down the Kabaw Valley, the notorious Valley of Death. Japanese rear-guard actions, appalling weather and disease made it a nightmare test of endurance and casualties were high. When the campaign was over, it was realised how bravely and well the K.A.R. had carried out this very difficult operation. From Burma they only returned to Tanganyika in 1946.

While awaiting repatriation in Kalieni Camp, outside Bombay, a small band of Tanganyikans were drinking rum and talking politics. One of those present was Ally Kleist Sykes, son of one African founder of the Tanganyika African Union. He has described how the all-absorbing topic was what were they to do when they got home. They were unanimous that conditions could not remain as they were, and that they would not put up with discrimination such as being banned from travelling first class, from entering hotels, from being served with drinks, even with a pint of beer. But how were they to change all this? Abdul Sykes, Ally's brother, said that they had to awaken the political conscious-ness of the people and form a political organisation.

All agreed on this. While discussing what kind of an organisa-tion it was to be and how to set about creating it, various names were suggested. Some said that the Tanganyika African Associa-tion should be changed to Tanganyika African Union. Then someone said that the word national should be added. Thus it came about that in 1946, at Kalieni Camp outside Bombay, the four words Tanganyika, African, national and union were linked together.

No minutes were kept, for this was not a meeting. Yet all the men who sat there, that day, trying to look into the future, remember it. Some made notes in their diaries. One actually put down the four initials – T.A.N.U. – which were to become famous eight years later.

The idea shot up in the air like a flame, momentarily throwing light on a wide area. But nothing further happened. There was no leader to formulate a practical plan, and time was not ripe.

The askaris who returned home were so much improved physically as to be almost unrecognisable; yet they lacked the qualifications and skills they needed to set themselves up in any life but the old tribal subsistence economy. The British Administration did much to re-establish them. At a cost of nearly a quarter of a million pounds men were trained in trade schools as motor mechanics, masons, bricklayers, carpenters, joiners, shoemakers, blacksmiths, tinsmiths, painters, signwriters and cycle repairers. Courses lasted between six and twelve months.

There was plenty of work waiting for them in post-war East Africa, the greatest demand being for trainees in carpentry, plumbing, building and house painting. By 1950, over two thousand ex-servicemen had taken advantage of the scheme. This had the effect of upgrading human resources, the key to all economic growth. The more politically minded of the Africans levelled one criticism against this useful and costly programme: it was carried out in too much of the old paternalistic spirit.

What the young school teacher and the young clerical worker wanted was not a skill in handicraft, which although useful in a way might have the effect of chaining the African to the workshop bench; but the chance to have a responsible say in the central direction of the affairs of the country; they welcomed trade training up to a point, but they nourished an uneasy suspicion that the Europeans had the intention of continuing to run Tanganyika in just the same way as before the war.

Attempts by the authorities to arouse the interest of returning askaris in the duties and responsibilities of local government met with a somewhat similar response; the majority of the soldiers were resolved only on getting back to their wives and families; and the interested minorities felt themselves worthy of something better than the local District Council. To the British, brought up on the principle that experience in local government is the best possible training for a career in Parliament, it was a surprise and a disappointment; they did not realise the depth of the ambition that was stirring within this group of forward looking young men.

They had been educated in good secondary schools and in many cases at Makerere College, and they now questioned everything around them with the critical mind all the young turn on their elders. They had a premonition that they might be called upon to achieve independence for their country, although they had no idea how to set about this tremendous task, or how to make the best of the new possibilities opening up before them.

The most important of these was the change in Tanganyika's status from a mandate to a trusteeship, resulting from the setting up of the United Nations Organisation in 1945. In the Preparatory Commission Arthur Creech Jones, Under-Secretary at the Colonial Office under G. H. (later Lord) Hall, represented Britain at San Francisco.

The Trusteeship Agreement with the United Nations grew out of the Mandate arrangement: the alternative after the Second World War could have been annexation, though this would have constituted a blatant betrayal by the British Government of its pledges and loyalties. All the same many Europeans in East Africa, including Tanganyika, urged Mr Creech Jones to recommend to the Government the transformation of Tanganyika into a British Colony.

This plea I resisted [Mr Creech Jones has told the author]. One of the first tasks of the Labour Government was to implement the San Francisco agreement concerning the U.N. Charter and to attend the Preparatory Meeting of the United Nations. There I moved that the Trusteeship arrangements be formally established and agreements made with the U.N. respecting the three main territories in Africa which the U.K. was administering.[1]

The basic principles of the Mandate and the Trusteeship were the same. Both conferred a distinct status that could not be uni-

---

[1] On April 18, 1946, in Geneva, at the last meeting of the Assembly of the League of Nations, a resolution was passed that the mandates would cease with the termination of the League itself. The Mandatory Powers expressed their willingness to administer the mandated territories until other arrangements had been agreed between The United Nations and themselves. This means that the Trusteeship system did not apply automatically.

laterally abolished; both involved tutelage by advanced nations to enable backward peoples 'to stand by themselves'.

The U.N. Charter laid down much more specifically than the League of Nations Covenant that the Administering Authority had to provide educational, social, economic and political advancement; that it had 'to encourage respect for human rights, and for fundamental freedoms for all without distinction as to race, sex, language or religion'.

Unlike in Mandate days, the people in all Trust Territories had to be consulted whenever their interests came into play, and their economic requirements had always to take priority over those of outsiders.

Under the League, the Mandatory Power was forbidden to exploit the military potential of Mandated Territories, but under the U.N. the Administering Authority was under an obligation to 'make use of volunteer forces, facilities and assistance from the Trust Territory' to further international peace and security.

The greatest difference, however, was in international supervision. While the members of the Permanent Mandate Commission were non-political experts sitting in their own right, those of the Trusteeship Council were representatives of the great powers and approached all problems from a political angle. Moreover, while under the Mandate members of the indigenous population could only launch complaints through the Mandatory Power, under the Trusteeship they could appear before the Council and complain in person.

In the Trusteeship Council, the Soviet delegate, assisted by his satellites, has taunted, abused and humiliated the representatives of the old colonial powers who, during the war, had already suffered from American censures. President Roosevelt and his advisers had often, in their anti-colonial attitude, deliberately sided with Stalin against Churchill (and the Dutch and the Belgians). But for this American policy, the Soviet conduct would not have been so violently provocative in the post-war period.

African and Asian representatives from Trust Territories at the Trusteeship Council have often made fiery and vituperative attacks on former and present 'colonialists'. It was also before the Trusteeship Council that, in 1955, Julius Nyerere was to expound his moderate demands and for the first time to influence the course of events in his country. In Tanganyika, strange as it may sound, not a word had been breathed about Trusteeship until January 19, 1946, when in the House of Commons the Foreign Secretary, Ernest Bevin, said:

We welcome the Trusteeship Council to which we made our contribution in the Preparatory Commission, and we are ready to accept the obligations which will rest upon us as administering authority under the new system. The peoples of the territories themselves and the world at large should be left in no doubt that the continuity of administration will be maintained, until the ultimate object of the Trusteeship system, selfgovernment or independence, is attained.

Soon after, Mr Creech Jones toured Tanganyika and discussed the change with representative Europeans and Africans in several parts of the Territory.

I met the criticisms of Europeans and the apprehensions of Africans at a number of groups and felt in respect of the Africans that the U.K. had their endorsement [he has told the author]. But at the time Africans were outside territorial political institutions and the Governor could only proceed by the recognised government bodies.

Mr Creech Jones had seen a limited number of persons, and the majority of Europeans and Asians, who listened to the radio or received British newspapers, were amazed. Why had they not been told about Mr Bevin's announcement before? What was the British contribution? How could it affect Tanganyika?

For an answer, they had to wait until March 7, 1946, when the Governor, Sir William Battershill, in his opening speech to the Legislative Council, announced that Trusteeship would apply to Tanganyika. No member raised the subject, or asked for further information until the next session four months later.

On July 23, 1946, two things happened. The administration published Command Paper 6840, entitled: 'Trusteeship Territories in Africa under United Kingdom Mandate', and E. C. (later Sir Charles) Phillips, C.B.E., introduced a motion: 'Be it resolved that this Council approves the draft terms of Trusteeship for Tanganyika as set out in Annex VI of Command Paper 6840.'

The members had not even had time to look at Command Paper 6840. Some of them were more than a little annoyed. F. J. Anderson asked pointedly whether Government considered that Trusteeship would be in the best interests of the inhabitants, and if so why? Why had the inhabitants not been given an opportunity to express their approval or otherwise? Were not between five and six million Tanganyikans being handed over to a foreign organisation 'as yet untried and untested'?

The Chief Secretary replied that the first point would be discussed when E. C. Phillips' motion came up; as to the second point, 'the terms of Trusteeship have been widely circulated in the Territory to obtain peoples' reactions'; as to the third point, the British administration would be maintained.

At this, Brigadier W. E. H. Scupham intervened abruptly. He quoted the Secretary of State's promise that before an international agreement would be entered into 'the wishes of the inhabitants of the Territory concerned would be ascertained. This, Sir, in the case of Tanganyika has most definitely not been done. To pretend that any attempt has been made to sound the views of the inarticulate masses of the African population would be nothing short of disingenuous.' He demanded more time to study the implications of the draft agreement.

Thereupon E. C. Phillips withdrew his motion and until the young nationalists became Members nothing further was heard about Trusteeship in the Legislative Council.[2]

From the point of view of international law, Britain had no obligation to consult the inhabitants of a Mandated Territory to discover what they felt about becoming subjects of a Trust Territory. Yet morally and in view of the Secretary of State's promise, British subjects expected to be informed and given a chance to comment (if not to consent or to refuse) on their new status. Mr Creech Jones did his best to inform the Tanganyikans, but with a ninety-two per cent illiterate population, this was no easy matter. As he has said:

The complaints of the Europeans, as embodied in Scupham's speech, veiled their real purpose, which was to create a colony. It must be added that it was I who had to create the interest of the Africans in the matter. Their apprehensions, where they existed, were slight and they preferred the Secretary of State to the local Europeans.

In August, 1946, at the Dar-es-Salaam Chamber of Commerce, Mr Creech Jones answered questions regarding the trusteeship of Tanganyika. He explained that, in accordance with

[2] Based on *Tanganyika Hansard* of the period and private conversations.

Article 77 of the United Nations Charter, trusteeship applied to territories held under a mandate; and in accordance with Article 79 the terms of trusteeship for each territory had to be agreed upon by the States directly concerned. This included the Mandatory Power in the case of a territory held under mandate by a member of the United Nations. A draft agreement of Tanganyika's trusteeship would be submitted to the United Nations in September.

We made it clear [Mr Creech Jones said] that we would not accept the transfer from mandate to trusteeship except on our terms, which included an agreement satisfactory to Great Britain and the continuance of British administration. In this respect there can be no ambiguity, because the charter provides that the administering Power must give its consent to the terms. (*The Times*, August 12, 1946.)

Negotiations about the terms took three months and Tanganyikans were never formally told that their country had become a Trust Territory. Diplomatically informed people inferred that this had come about from the fact that on August 27, 1947, diplomatic privileges were conferred on the United Nations and their representatives within the area, which would not have been done under any other circumstances. Europeans and Asians of Tanganyika regarded this as high-handed treatment, especially on the part of a Labour Government.

The status of a Trust Territory, the last landmark of the old Tanganyika, came about in a way typical of the whole history of African development. The force of world opinion and the atmosphere within Tanganyika combined to make the change inevitable, but there had been hitches and backslidings. Though these defects seem in the light of hindsight to have had little justifiable excuse, it would be surprising if, in the handling of an age-old continent which was still in many respects so primitive, undue caution and timidity by the authorities concerned had not played a part in the outcome. Be that as it may, the final landmark of Trust Territory status was reached on December 13, 1946, when it was passed in the General Assembly of the United Nations. From then on there was little holding the pace of events which were to lead to Tanganyika's Independence Day on December 9, 1961.

PART III
AFRICAN AWAKENING

CHAPTER 13

Post-War Reconstruction and Constitutional Change

In 1945 the Labour Government came to power in Britain. In its attitude to the colonies, the new Government almost immediately introduced a new and revolutionary policy. Before the Second World War, Government policy had been to leave colonies and other dependencies to their own resources. Governors of these territories had to do the best they could without much material help from London. The turning point came with the Colonial Development and Welfare Act of 1945. This Act brought to its conclusion a trend begun by the Acts of 1929 and 1940, but it went so much further than previous legislation that the result was a radical change in British colonial policy from negative patronage to sustained and positive action.

It meant, in practice, vast expenditure on under-developed areas, a new concept in colonialism. By implication, it also meant the more rapid approach of independence, for an impoverished and war-weary Britain could not carry this heavy colonial burden indefinitely. Here lies the real source of the Winds of Change, about which so much was to be heard ten years later. Under post-war conditions the dissolution of the British Empire may in any case have been inevitable, but the idealistic Labour attitude to colonial territories hurried up this process.

Few people realised this in 1945. In Tanganyika, the immediate pattern of events was settled by the recommendations of the Central Development Committee. Set up on December 21, 1938, 'to examine and report on methods whereby the development of the Territory by non-native and native enterprise may be encouraged', the Chairman, G. R. (later Sir George) Sandford, expressed its real aim: 'To make Tanganyika a country.'

As the Sandford Committee was unable to complete its work within the eight remaining months of peace, the Colonial Secretary, Malcolm MacDonald, asked it to carry on during the war. Its report, published on May 1, 1940, reflected the spirit in which it worked. Not only had it tried to discover Tanganyika's actual and potential resources, but it had assessed the chances of each one: pyrethrum, sisal, cotton, tea, rice, beeswax, gold, diamonds, cattle ranching and all. Its main conclusion was that development could not be effected unless communications were much improved.

The Territory, four times the size of Great Britain–Tanganyika being 365,000 square miles against Britain's 94,210–had 19,000 miles of 'passable roads', but only the Great North Road, part of the longed-for Cape to Cairo Highway, could carry traffic during the rainy season. There were many regions that could not be reached by motor vehicle for three consecutive months each year.

The Sandford Committee's road plan allocated £1 million[1] for arterial and feeder roads. Calculations were based on an estimate of £1,150 for transforming one mile of earth road into a carpet construction road with macadamised surface. After the war, with the adoption of metalled surfaces, costs soared. Eventually the British government spent over £4 million[2] on Tanganyika's road system.

Towards the end of the war the Governor, Sir William Battershill, had appointed a new committee to bring the Sandford Report up to date. The result was *An Outline on Post-War Development*, published in 1944.

Two years later, in 1946, it was followed by *A Ten Year Plan for Tanganyika*, with a £19 million budget. Of this, in accordance with Labour's new colonial policy, the British Government provided the major part, £13 million, in grants or loans. Territorial revenue and Native Treasuries contributed the rest. This Plan remained Tanganyika's blueprint until she achieved independence in 1961, when it was superseded by the Vasey Plan (see Chapter 37).

Its most interesting section was that which dealt with education. The Sandford Report had first commented that only 7·5 per cent of Tanganyika's African children could go to school, and suggested that this figure should be doubled. The Ten Year Plan allocated £2 million to achieve this by 1956. In fact, over ten years £5,550,000 were spent on education. Tanganyikan sources provided £2·2 million and Britain £3,350,000. In 1959, 40 per cent of the African children went to school.

Of the three reports, only the Ten Year Plan made reference to the African attitude: 'There is also the insistent demand of the

[1] Pre-war pounds.   [2] Post-war pounds.

Africans themselves for a more rapid expansion of educational services. This demand is a growing one and cannot be ignored' (p. 55).

The young African nationalists were deeply shocked by the reports. Not a single African had been consulted by the Sandford Committee, or any other committee. Non-natives, that is Europeans, invariably figured in the first place and they were to maintain their ruling positions. In their resentment over this attempt to perpetuate the pre-war situation, the nationalists failed to appreciate the good will, hard work and ability of the British civil servants who were carrying out the Ten Year Plan. This is one instance where the sometimes derided methods of modern public relations might have been usefully applied.

The Ten Year Plan met with difficulties, but shortage of money was not one of them. In the late 1940s, as the prices of Tanganyika's main products went on rising, there was a large budget surplus. The annual income from sisal increased from £4 million in 1946 to over £11 million in 1949; the annual income from diamonds (which paid a 15 per cent royalty to the Treasury) increased from £638,000 in 1945 to £1 million in 1949; the annual income from coffee increased from £675,580 in 1946 to £1,460,768 in 1949. The cotton crop increased three times in bulk and five times in value. The total value of trade was £17 million in 1945 and £52 million in 1949. Some £15 million had been accumulated and over £7 million was in hand.

The real difficulty was the world shortage of machinery, raw materials and technical experts. The supplementary Development Reports are studded with sentences like: 'Shortage of trained supervisory staff and of essential materials imposed a definite limit to a number of schemes.'–'The Central Breeding Station of Mwpawpa could make no headway because of lack of materials and supervisory staff.'–'The girls' school in Mbeya could not be started owing to lack of supervisory staff and materials.'

In 1949, thanks to world economic recovery, staff and materials became available. This coincided with the appointment of the new Governor, Sir Edward Twining, and with the collapse of the Groundnut Scheme, to be discussed in the next chapter. A new era of economic development was about to begin.

*   *   *

Already, before the war, the Colonial Office had realised that the constitutions of the East African Territories needed modernising. In Tanganyika, tribal unions were developing among the Chagga, the Haya, the Sukuma and the Zaramo. Old Tanganyika African Association groups were being revived and new ones founded. Inter-connections soon developed through men who belonged both to a tribal union and to the African Association of the nearest town. T.A.A. branches now began to grow because they had a useful function: to provide information and articulate support for newly appointed members of the Legislative Council, commonly referred to as Legco.

In 1939, the first Unofficials had been appointed to the Executive Council–Exco; in 1945, on Arthur Creech Jones' insistence, the first two Africans, Chiefs David Makwaia and Abdiel Shangali, were appointed to Legco.[3] Four years later, in 1949, the Tanganyika Constitution was to be overhauled.

Inevitably the British administration chose for official appointment Africans who were friendly to them. David was the son of Chief Makwaia, the proud and powerful Sukuma, who sent him to Tabora Government School, and from there to Makerere. He had to interrupt his studies when his father died and he succeeded to the chiefdom. Later on he got a scholarship to Oxford. At Makerere he was a leading member of the group of aristocrats. To his friends he was known as the Hamlet of Tanganyika, for he could always see both sides of a problem and was always torn by doubts and uncertainties.

Makwaia had become a Roman Catholic and in baptism received the name of David, which he uses in preference to his tribal name, Kidaha. Being a deeply conscientious man, he felt it was wrong for a Roman Catholic to be the chief of a predominantly Moslem tribe. He therefore resigned his position and was succeeded by his brother Hussein, who tried to carry out his intentions, for he was not only devoted to David, but greatly admired him.

Abdiel Shangali was a different type. A divisional chief of the Machame Chagga, he owned lucrative coffee plantations. He was not sent to Tabora, and had little academic education. But he had a good mind and taught himself English. A friend of his has told the author: 'Abdiel, being a chief, had the chance to meet

[3] In June 1947, Adam Sapi and in April, 1948, Juma Mwindadi were also appointed to Legco.

people, to travel to many parts of the world and to pick up quite a bit of general knowledge.' Shangali, although the most astute of the Chagga, relied greatly on his friend David Makwaia.

Makwaia and Shangali had no easy time in Legco. On the one hand European members were courteous but did not accept them as social equals. They were invited to official functions, but not to private parties. On the other hand, the African nationalists regarded them with a certain suspicion as possible British puppets, who might not stand up for African interests and dare not voice views unpopular with the British. Makwaia and Shangali were bound to find themselves in an awkward position as soon as there was any real test of opinion between the administration and the nationalist leaders. The test came, in fact, when the possibility of union between Kenya, Uganda and Tanganyika became a topic for serious debate.

In December, 1945, the nationalists' suspicions were aroused by a proposal put forward in London, and embodied in Non-Parliamentary Colonial Paper No 191, for creating an East African High Commission and a Central Legislative Assembly, both with headquarters in Nairobi. Knowing how much Africans in Tanganyika and Uganda feared Kenya influence, the Colonial Office proposed in Paper 191 that the East African Central Assembly should be composed of twelve official and twenty-four unofficial members. Six of the unofficial members would be Europeans and six Indians; these would represent primarily the interests of their communities. Six were to represent African interests and as many of these as possible were to be Africans. The High Commission was to nominate two members to represent Arab interests and four members for general interests. The principle on which this representation was based, was stated in Para. 22 of Paper 191:

Equality in numbers the only practicable basis for unofficial representation of the three main races.

The suggestion that the unofficial members of the Assembly chosen by the territorial legislatures should represent the three major communities in equal numbers arises from the impossibility of devising any generally acceptable formula by which to decide the relative importance or the respective claims of the communities concerned. The racial composition of the Legislative Councils differs from territory to territory and none offers a satisfactory pattern for a joint assembly. It was this question of representation which proved to be the most controversial part of the report on a scheme for closer union made by Sir Samuel Wilson in 1929 and it was found impossible to secure agreement at that time. It does not appear to His Majesty's Government or to the East African Governors that, in the case of a joint legislature of this type now proposed, there is any logical alternative to equal representation.

On this principle, the chances were that the Central Legislative Assembly would have seven European, seven Indian, seven African and three Arab members; the twelve official members being necessarily Europeans, there would have been a total membership of nineteen Europeans, seven Indians, seven Africans and three Arabs.

What followed is best told in Julius Nyerere's own words,[4] which vividly reflect the African reaction:

What did our White Neighbours, who form the smallest of the three major races, say to these proposals which . . . made sure of their predominance in the Central Assembly? . . . They denounced it. They denounced the whole idea of closer union and declared that they would boycott it unless the Colonial Office recanted the principle of racial equality. They would not sit on any Assembly which was based on such a principle; they would only agree to the formation of the Central Assembly provided that the principle was denounced and they were given an unofficial majority. It sounds hard, but it is a historical, and indeed a historic, fact. The Colonial Office and the East African Governors had confessed that they saw no logical alternative to the principle of equal racial representation; these indomitable Europeans were now asking them to recant that confession; and terrible Indian and African admirers of the Labour Government and in particular of the Colonial Secretary, Mr Creech Jones, these terrible Africans and Indians were quoting that principle of equal racial representation and that confession that there was no logical alternative to it, these terrible Africans and Indians were quoting those things and these indefatigable Europeans were demanding their recantation.

We did not believe that the British Government, and a Labour Government at that, could yield to such hysterical demands as our White Neighbours were making. We firmly believed that H.M. Government would put its mighty foot down and uphold a principle to which it confessed there was no logical alternative. Indians and Africans submitted memoranda to the Colonial Office expressing that belief. But we were to be disillusioned. Our indefatigable White Neighbours went on

[4] From Nyerere's unpublished essay, *The Race Problem in East Africa*.

denouncing Paper 191 and asking the Colonial Office to recant the principle of racial representation.

In February, 1947, the Colonial Office issued in White Paper 210 its revised proposals to meet the Europeans' demand. To our horror and dismay H.M. Government had indeed dropped the principle of equal racial representation! The Europeans had triumphed and they rejoiced everywhere. The British Socialists can hardly realize how much that event lowered the prestige of the Labour Government in the eyes of the Africans and Indians of East Africa. The great faith which they had in the Socialist Government was shattered to pieces by that single event and will never be the same again. My own faith was shaken even more when I discovered later that the principles embodied in Paper 191 were those of a Conservative Colonial Secretary, and that the real Labour Government principles were those embodied in Paper 210.

The eventual establishment of the East African High Commission (later the East African Common Services Organization) in 1947, was the work of Arthur Creech Jones, who had been Colonial Secretary since October 7, 1946. He believed that to unite would not only benefit Kenya, Uganda and Tanganyika economically, but that it would build up racial co-operation between them. There had been formal conferences between the three governors since 1926. These had later been supplemented by technical conferences to co-ordinate scientific research. During the war, many inter-territorial commissions had been set up. Not one had either a constitutional or a juridical basis. This had to be remedied, especially as a long-term customs agreement was under negotiation, the hope being that it would lead to a customs union.

At that time Tanganyikans as well as Ugandans resisted these constructive moves because they feared Kenya domination. Even under a Socialist Government, the Kenya white settlers seemed to get their way in the highest London circles. Tanganyikans, especially Africans and Asians, wanted no truck with the Kenyans. Now, with all three countries independent, the African leaders themselves approve of the same kind of union that Arthur Creech Jones had in mind, and have even taken tentative steps, on the initiative of President Nyerere, to establish an East African Federation. Unhappily, the jealousies and suspicions which in 1947 were racial jealousies and suspicions, have re-emerged as national rivalries, to hamper the present leaders in their search for unity.

In actual fact, the Central Assembly, about which Nyerere felt so bitter in 1947, had only limited powers to control strictly defined subjects. Of its thirty-three members ten were to take their seats by virtue of the offices they held in the High Commission and the High Commission's services, and thirteen were to be unofficials (twelve of them chosen by the Territories) thus providing for a permanent majority on the 'non-Government' side. The first nine of the unofficial members were to be a European, an Asian and an African from each of the three Territories, but owing to the differing racial composition of the three Legislative Councils, the method proposed for their selection was not entirely uniform; in Uganda and Tanganyika each of them would be appointed by the Governor of the Territory; but in Kenya the Governor would appoint the African only, the European and the Asian being chosen by the respective vote of the European and Asian elected members of the Legislative Council. The next three members would be elected, on a basis of one for each Territory, by the vote of all the unofficial members of each of the Councils. The tenth member was to be an Arab, appointed by the High Commission.

As Nyerere saw it, the ten *ex officio* members were certain to be Europeans; and since there was a great preponderance of Europeans in each of the three territorial Councils, it seemed to him inevitable that the three members elected by the unofficial members of the Council would be Europeans. The overall racial composition of the Assembly would therefore be one Arab, three Africans, three Asians and sixteen Europeans. Until 1958, Nyerere's gloomy prediction proved correct, but after that, within four years, the Africans obtained an overwhelming majority in the Central Legislative Assembly.

Unlike the Trusteeship question, Colonial Paper 210 did come up for debate in the Tanganyika Legislative Council. On April 15, 1947, the Chief Secretary moved the following motion: 'Be it resolved that this Council accepts the proposals for Inter-Territorial organisation in East Africa as set out in Non-Parliamentary Colonial Paper No. 210.'

All the European speakers, led by E. C. Phillips, echoed the Colonial Office point of view. It was left to two Asians, I. C. Chopra and V. M. Nazerali, to oppose it and to voice the views held by the overwhelming majority of Tanganyikans. The country, if not Legco, applauded them. Said Mr Chopra: 'The ego or the superiority of the Kenya settlers would upset anyone with a particle of self respect and would breed innumerable prejudices.'

Mr Nazerali said that the Kenya settlers had managed to have the non-racial representation proposed by Colonial Paper No. 191 changed to racial representation, as put forward by Colonial Paper No. 210.

The behaviour of the two African Members was astonishing. Chief Abdiel Shangali said:

> Your Excellency, I am not opposing this paper nor supporting it, but I understand that this Colonial Paper No. 210 has been translated into Swahili in order to enable Africans to understand and to study it so that they may give their views. I was given a copy of this translation yesterday here in the Secretariat. Meanwhile I tried to see the Tanganyika African Association in Dar-es-Salaam that I may get their views and they told me that they have not held any meeting to study the Paper because they have seen it just recently. In my opinion, I suggest that since the majority of Africans have not studied the Paper, therefore they should be given sufficient time to study it and they will then be able to express their view before the final discussion in this Council. (*Tanganyika Hansard*, April 15, 1947.)

David Makwaia supported Shangali's demand for delay until the next Legco meeting. 'It would give an opportunity for the Africans to study the proposals and it may be in the Chiefs' Council and so on that valuable information may be obtained.' (Ibid.)

In his reply the Chief Secretary brushed aside the Asian objections with pointed references to the financial gains the Asian community had made from trading with Kenya. He apologised for the delayed publication of Colonial Paper No. 210 on the grounds that it was very difficult to translate this complicated text into Swahili. However, he refused to postpone the vote. In fact, it was taken the same day: all Europeans voted for it; the two Asians voted against it, and the two Africans abstained. In Kenya and Uganda also the official majorities voted for the proposal and the East African High Commission and the Central Legislative Assembly came into being on January 1, 1948.

The abstention of David Makwaia and Abdiel Shangali was to bedevil relations among Tanganyika Africans of their generation until the present day (see also chapter 19).

*　　　*　　　*

For reasons very different from those that agitated the Tanganyikans, the U.N. Trusteeship Council was also suspicious of the two new East African bodies. To allay its fears and to disprove the malicious insinuation of its Soviet member, the British Administering Authority imposed two important restrictions.

The new organisation was not to diminish the final responsibility of the British Parliament for administering the three African territories.

It was not to involve closer political ties among the territories, nor fusion of their Governments. This was tantamount to guaranteeing Tanganyika's special status as a Trust Territory.

Finally, to reassure everyone, a typically British compromise was worked out. The East African High Commission and the Central Legislative Assembly were to be set up for a four-year trial period. During this time only such additional Common Services as were unanimously approved by all three territorial legislatures were to be transferred to it. In 1951 and again in 1955 the life of the Assembly was extended for further periods of four years; in 1959, when the economic situation had undermined Tanganyika's desire for co-operation, its Legislature only voted for a two year extension, although Kenya and Uganda voted for four years. Once more the Secretary of State recommended a compromise, this time of three years, during which period the functions of the Central Legislative Assembly were to be subjected to review.

One of the greatest benefits the Assembly conferred on Tanganyika was the amalgamation of the East African Railways on May 1, 1948, four months to the day after it had come into being. This relieved the Treasury of the annual railway deficit, a perennial headache. The railway loans, needed for post-war development, were guaranteed by all three East African countries.

Advance was also made in local government, where the British aim was to democratise the Native Authorities. The first step, to break the dictatorial powers of the chief as both ruler and judge, was the most difficult. It was tackled in two ways. On the one hand, attempts were made to abolish the autocratic authority of the chief in favour of the far more democratic concept of the Chief-in-Council. This move was helped by the Nyamwezi chiefs who, in the early 1940s, in the Tabora District, formed a Chiefs' Council, which decided on policy and on specific subjects of joint interest. The D.C. gave them guidance.

The Nyamwezi example was followed in other parts of the country; but much depended on the personality of the D.C.; a popular, constructive man could achieve much; with an unimaginative or unapproachable man the useful results were limited.

The second way in which the Native Authorities were democratised was the transformation of two Provincial Conferences into Provincial Councils by appointing to them unofficial Europeans, Asians, and, for the first time, Africans. In the Lake Province, the Provincial Council tended to become an offshoot of the Central Government. In the Southern Highlands it took an independent attitude, akin to British local government bodies. Both experiments were to prove useful later.

All these changes were good as far as they went, but they did not go far or fast enough. The complete apartness of Europeans and Africans had remained unchanged. Rulers and ruled, regardless of the Trust Status, were hardly speaking to each other. The Asians, in theory standing between the two, were of no help.

Unorganised and un-unified, the masses of African peasants were plodding along as their ancestors had done for thousands of years. The young nationalists were earning their living in humble positions, far from the political arena.

F

CHAPTER 14

Groundnut Interlude

THE Groundnut Scheme was a sudden, fantastic incursion of Europe into Africa, ending in an equally sudden, inglorious withdrawal. A thousand men, with excellent war records and a war-ingrained indifference to costs, rushed in with the enthusiasm of crusaders to grow groundnuts, from which oils and fats were to be made for a world threatened with hunger.

There was grandeur about the conception of this scheme. To grow 600,000 tons of groundnuts a year, five thousand square miles of territory, an area the size of Yorkshire, were to be cleared with fleets of bulldozers advancing on the African bush. Heavy earth-moving machinery left over from the war was to be put to good purpose. The project was to be run not for private profit, but by a Government-sponsored Public Corporation, eventually to hand over one hundred units of 30,000 acre farms–three million acres–to the African peoples. This was to pave the way for co-operative farming. Everything was to be on a gigantic scale, planned and run as a military operation, a method unprecedented in the history of colonial development.

Yet the inception of the scheme was quite ordinary. At the end of 1945, Frank Samuel, Managing Director of the United Africa Co., met R. W. R. Millar, Director of Agriculture in Tanganyika. Mr Samuel said that his company was anxious to expand in East Africa and to take an interest in agriculture in addition to trading and asked Millar whether he had any ideas. As oil products were then in short supply, Millar suggested that United Africa might make a useful start by putting in 2,000 acres of groundnuts. Land could be made available in some promising area so that groundnuts would be produced and the possibility of growing them on a plantation scale tried out. Greatly interested, Samuel asked a few more questions, promising to follow the matter up. In the period of gestation in his mind and, no doubt, in consultation with his colleagues, the idea got expanded into the very large-scale production of groundnuts under high pressure methods. Proposals were submitted to the Labour Government at the end of March, 1946.

To understand what followed, it is helpful to look at the chronicle of relevant events.

March 28, 1946. Frank Samuel submits to the Labour Government his scheme for the mechanised production of groundnuts in Tanganyika.

June 20, 1946. Sir Ben Smith, Minister of Food, sends out a three-man official mission to find suitable areas in Kenya, Tanganyika and Rhodesia for growing groundnuts.

September 20, 1946. The Wakefield Report is published, recommending three areas in Tanganyika and outlining the structure of a Government corporation to run the scheme.

September 27, 1946. John Strachey, successor to Sir Ben Smith, reads and is enthralled by the Wakefield Report.

October 31, 1946. The Government accepts the Report and decides that the Ministry of Food should carry it out.

December, 1946. John Strachey reports to the House of Commons that the Report has been checked and that 'no unjustified financial risk is involved'. Necessary legislation is passed and the United Africa Co. is to act as H.M.G.'s Agent until the Overseas Food Corporation is set up.

January 30, 1947. The first Groundnut Party leaves for Tanganyika, where the U.A.C. makes Kongwa the headquarters of the scheme.

April 1, 1948. The Overseas Food Corporation takes over from the U.A.C. with Leslie Plummer as Chairman.

January, 1949. Second disappointing harvest after protracted drought.

Spring of 1949. Serious doubts assail Administrative Executives about prospects of the scheme. Plummer is distrusted.

November 21, 1949. House of Commons vote of confidence in Strachey and in Plummer.

December 11, 1949. Strachey flies to Nairobi secretly and quells local critics.

February 25, 1950. John Strachey becomes Secretary of State for War, succeeded by Maurice Webb as Minister of Food.

May 24, 1950. Sir Leslie Plummer resigns.

August, 1950. Instructions are given to wind up the Groundnut Scheme.

The three-man mission Sir Ben Smith dispatched to East Africa to investigate Frank Samuel's proposals for the mechanised production of groundnuts, consisted of John Wakefield, former Director of Agriculture in Tanganyika, David Martin, Plantation Manager of the United Africa Co., and John Rosa, a banker by profession who during the war had served with distinction in the Treasury and the Colonial Office. At first they chose areas in southern and western Tanganyika, in Northern Rhodesia and in Kenya, on the grounds that a variety of scattered places would prove a safeguard against simultaneous drought.

Then they received a letter from a farmer called Tom Bain, who for years had farmed successfully near Mpwapwa. He lived twenty miles from a tiny village called Kongwa, where good groundnuts were being grown and are still growing well. Because of its position under a line of hills, running east to west, Kongwa itself enjoyed a modest rainfall. Bain recommended that the Groundnut Scheme should develop the area to the north.

When the Mission accepted Bain's invitation to view Kongwa, he prepared some facilities for soil inspection, including traces cut into the bush. The party stayed the night with him and he was at his most convincing. Yet John Wakefield and his friends were impressed not by Bain's talk, but by the fact that he had farmed successfully in the area. All his ground was, however, in the hills or fed by water furrows, which he had laid out with remarkable skill, even if the water did not always belong to him. Here was one piece of concrete evidence, which went a long way in compensating for the absence of rainfall statistics. Still, in their final recommendations, the Wakefield Mission chose three areas in Tanganyika: Nachingwea in the Southern, Kongwa in the Central and Urambo in the Western Province, in this order. It was the United Africa Co. that made Kongwa its centre and headquarters because communications to it were better than to the southern or the western areas, although clearing had commenced in both before the end of 1947.

Bain certainly had an interest in encouraging a development like the Goundnut Scheme because it would allow him a ready market for the vegetables, pigs and other foodstuffs which he hoped to supply – and did supply – to a large concentration of European and African population. He is the only person who can be accused of having made money out of the scheme.

Even more interesting is what his guests failed to find out from their visit to the farm. It is not to be supposed that Bain had heard of Dr E. J. Baxter of the Church Missionary Society, who in 1878-9 had failed to develop the agricultural possibilities of this area 'because of the uncertainty and shortness of the rainy season' (J. H. Briggs: *In The East African War Zone*, Church Missionary Society). He may not have seen the official rainfall map published in 1932, which showed the projected groundnut area well inside a yellow band which marked the lowest rainfall in Tanganyika. And even if he had, there was, after all, no reason why he should have told his visitors of them; for his purpose was to encourage the establishment of the scheme near his farm, and he was entitled to assume that the visiting Mission had access to all the relevant climatic records and that it had informed itself as thoroughly as possible. He had demonstrated that the wide, monotonous bush-covered and largely uninhabited plain had much the same soil as Kongwa; it was up to the Mission to satisfy itself about the rainfall.

One member of the Tanganyika administration at the time has commented to the author:

It must be remembered as an important fact that Wakefield himself had served for some twenty years in Tanganyika, starting as a junior Agricultural Officer and ending up as Director of Agriculture. He had a close knowledge of the Territory as a whole and would certainly not need to be given detailed information as to the aridity of our central plateau. Furthermore, the Wakefield Mission received all the information from official sources that it asked for and was offered a great deal more. One cannot, however, force information into a body that is not desirous of receiving it.

The Wakefield Report said that in three years 600,000 tons of groundnut could be grown in Tanganyika. The cost per ton was estimated at £14 4s. 5d., against the world price of £23 per ton, representing a saving of over £500,000 per annum. The total capital to be expended over six years was estimated at £24 million. £5,750,000 would be spent on agricultural machinery, to be amortised in five years; the balance, spent on clearing, in twenty-five years. The cost of clearing was estimated at £3 17s. 4d. per acre.

As will be seen, all these figures were to prove hopelessly off the mark. But before going on with the story, four points must be clarified.

Why was there no pilot scheme? Why was no study made of rainfall records? Why was the soil not subjected to full analysis? Why were the local people not consulted?

There was no pilot scheme because to have undertaken one would have meant the loss of a year, possibly eighteen months. And speed was vital, especially as embittered British housewives were threatening to vote against the Labour Government unless their fat rations were increased.

Detailed rainfall measurements were not made for the same reason. Instead, the classic device of measuring all neighbouring rain gauges and taking an average, was resorted to. In this case the calculated average bore no relation to the real rainfall, or rather the lack of it.

The soil was not tested because, in the planners' view, as no African could be dispossessed, it had to be taken where it was available. All the same, some hundred families had to be moved from the Kongwa area.

(On this point a Member of the Tanganyika Administration has commented:

Of course ground tests could easily have been taken without disturbing any African occupants for the very good reason that hundreds of square miles of the country had no occupants at all. It was just because of this lack of occupants that these areas came to be singled out as suitable for large-scale agriculture of the kind intended.)

The local people were not consulted because, owing to the shortage of time, no methodical enquiry could be conducted among them. The Mission had to rely on Directors of Agriculture, and Provincial and District Agricultural Officers. Most of them did possess local knowledge, but some apparently did not.

Yet the local inhabitants of the Kongwa area could have provided interesting information. The Gogo are a charming, rather backward people, who copy the Masai by painting their bodies with red ochre and rancid butter. They could have told the Wakefield Mission that, when they wished to provide an almost impervious and cement-like covering to their flat-topped huts, all they had to do was to dig down six inches into the Kongwa soil, where such material was usually to be found. In other words, the soil had a high clay content, which would make it difficult to harvest such groundnuts as managed to grow despite the usual drought.

The Gogo might also have told them that in Ki-Gogo, the native tongue, Kongwa means 'to be deceived'. . . .

By the end of 1946, after intensive examination by experts of the Ministry of Food, the Government and the House of Commons had accepted the Wakefield Report. The necessary legislation was passed for starting the Groundnut Scheme and in January, 1947, the advance party left England for Tanganyika. It was expected that there would be wide support among the public for such a scheme, and that many men and women would be keen to apply for posts. In the event, over 100,000 applied for 1,200 posts.

To join the scheme there came a host of men of all calibres and professions—administrators, doctors, agriculturalists, mechanics, electricians, accountants. Many of these came with the highest sense of purpose, and subsequently worked in a way that has never been suitably acknowledged. Some came to develop social services for the Africans, and to them the growing of groundnuts was much less important than the building of schools and hospitals, and the improvement of public health. David Martin, of the United Africa Company, at the time in charge of operations, deplored the fact that almost every aeroplane and ship brought out a number of self-appointed social welfare officers, to be dumped on him at Kongwa, together with public health planners, educationists, and so on. He was having great difficulty in housing his staff and was crying out for a few practical men who would actually carry on with the work of knocking down the bush and reclaiming the soil. For every practical man he got, he had to put up with some twelve airy-fairy individuals for whom he was hard-put to find employment.

Barclay Leechman, Member for Social Services in the Tanganyika Administration during this period, has told the author:

Many of the Groundnut people were first class in every way, but there was a large swarm who were definitely fifth class. Up till 1946, except for a few of the old African prospectors and digger types, chiefly in the Lupa area, there had been no Europeans in Tanganyika who were not of the educated classes; there were, of course, a small number of high quality artisans (engine drivers and the like) employed on the Railways and in the Public Works Department; all highly respectable people. The Groundnut Scheme, however, brought out other types in large numbers over a short period. Most of these were flown direct from the U.K. to Kongwa without touching at any other point, so that there was not even the short initiatory stage given by a sea-voyage. Results were often quite disastrous. I remember once seeing a chartered 'plane returning some twenty-five Europeans from Kongwa. They were, I think, in general appearance and in the manner they were behaving, even at the airport, the lowest types of European that I have ever seen in my life. David Martin told me that these people had been recruited in Liverpool–they had arrived shortly before–and had been quite useless; they had refused to work and behaved like a set of hooligans. He had been compelled to arrange for a charter 'plane to fly them out to get rid of them.

Fortunately for Tanganyika, when the scheme failed, many of the best men decided to stay.

The initial development was entrusted to the United Africa Co. as managing agents. On April 1, 1948, the Government-sponsored Overseas Food Corporation, set up by the Overseas Resources Development Act, took over the management of the Groundnut Scheme. The Overseas Food Corporation had a capital of £50 million and authority to borrow another £5 million, but by March 31, 1948, £7,730,000 had been spent, and expenditure was running at the rate of £1 million a month.

The Overseas Food Corporation had a Board of Governors with adequate Government representation, sitting in London. There were nine Directors (called Members) of whom three were part-time, six full time, the latter including the Chairman, the Deputy-Chairman and the Members who acted as senior executives, but there was no local board in Africa.

To head the Overseas Food Corporation, Strachey[1] made the remarkable choice of a business executive from the *Daily Express* newspaper. His name was Leslie Plummer.[2] When the scheme was already experiencing serious difficulties, he became Sir Leslie Plummer. This was the first of several moves to pretend that success was attending the effort.

When the Overseas Food Corporation took over from the United Africa Co., the higher grade executives seemed almost

[1] John Strachey died in June, 1963.
[2] Sir Leslie Plummer died in May, 1963.

deliberately unheedful of advice both from the retiring company and from experienced public and private sources in Africa. Yet these were useful sources of knowledge of bush clearing and estate development. They were made to feel that their advice was too old-fashioned and too slow to appeal in the prevailing, over-confident mood of speed.

The machines had begun to arrive. The heavy caterpillar tractors had been bought as surplus war material in the Pacific and some of them appeared to have spent quite a period of time under water. The majority were in poor condition and required a considerable amount of repair and re-fitting. The original estimates had not envisaged such a huge workshop requirement.

Lord Twining, who became Governor of Tanganyika in 1949, has told the author:

Owing to the impossibility of obtaining new machinery due to post-war shortage, the Groundnut men had to buy and adapt war material. For instance, on one occasion they had heard that there were safari lamps in Mombasa. They found them, but were told they could only have them provided they bought everything else besides the lamps in the lot.

Everything else in this case meant machinery for the scraping of the plates of battleships. . . . It was purchased and taken to Kongwa. There it eventually sank into the earth, never to be retrieved. Should archeologists in A.D. 3000 come upon the keel scrapers, they may deduce from them that the British had a naval base as far inland as Kongwa!

The Rover factory sent a few of its first prototype Land-Rovers for trial, which proved very successful. They were followed by new inventions of other firms, unfortunately much less suited to East Africa. New equipment in the nature of agricultural tractors, implements and vehicles, on the whole gave good service. There was an endless stream through the port of Dar-es-Salaam of lorries, combines, water-carriers, fire engines, ambulances and all manner of equipment. Contractors were collected to do some of the preliminary clearing, build houses and supply furniture. Minor roads, tennis courts, clubs and hospitals (the best equipped in Tanganyika at the time) were constructed.

The job of clearing the bush was dramatic. Over a period of time, by trial and error, the staff evolved a technique which in many places proved very effective. The surface cover, trees and bush, was felled and uprooted by two heavy, specially armoured bulldozers dragging between them a third bulldozer which, rather like a scrum half, followed behind the two to add its own strength against any tree which resisted the efforts of the two alone. The trash was bulldozed into rows and burned. Then huge rippers prepared the soil for subsequent ploughing, harrowing and planting.

However, the Kongwa soil was abrasive in the extreme. Plough shares, hoes and anything else which had to be pushed into the soil were quickly torn away, a feature well known to the Public Works Department, which had always had to make an extra issue of standard road-making tools in this area. Moreover, when it came to harvesting, it was found that the Kongwa soil had a facility for compaction which made the lifting of the groundnut plant out of the soil by the use of slowly revolving finger tines very difficult. The high clay content nobody knew of now came into play. To the delight of the Gogo, so much was left behind the combines on the ground that during harvesting unauthorised gleaning became a full-scale operation.

Urambo and Nachingwea also had their problems, although abrasion, compaction and clay content were not at the head of their list.

The difficulties of the soil, the vagaries of rainfall, the problems of maintenance and repair and the age-old puzzle of trying to hurry Africa, together began to put the whole planting programme seriously behind schedule. It was clear that this was the time for complete re-appraisal and the institution of a more careful approach. The heads of the Administration and Servicing Departments pressed strongly for it, but their first attempt did not get past the Resident Member, General Harrison. When the situation became desperate, they wrote a memorandum and sent it direct to the Chairman, Plummer. Much of the blame for what followed must rest on him.

Plummer was a man who had a theatrical approach to life, possibly springing from his newspaper background. He shared some of the qualities and some of the faults of his former employer, Lord Beaverbrook, with his vision and his blindness for facts he did not wish to see. Plummer was fond, for instance, of saying: 'Do you realise I shall have more tractors here than Montgomery had heavy tanks at Alamein?' He seemed either unaware of, or disinclined to examine, the reason why out of a hundred big crawlers available, frequently only five were in operation. Instead of recognising the warning signs that were becoming apparent to a great many people in the middle ranks of authority in the scheme, the Corporation Board drove the programme on faster and faster. Estimates and progress reports were produced which, if not deliberately falsified, were prepared in such a way that a totally unreal picture could easily be gained by the authorities in England. Many people feel, in retrospect, that these estimates bordered on deliberate deceit.

On one occasion at Kongwa 15,000 acres of sunflower were hastily planted so late in the season as to make success almost out of the question. However, as soon as the planting was over, the House of Commons was informed that a further large acreage of planting had been completed. Members there, with their minds on groundnuts, assumed that the planting had been of groundnuts. The sunflowers perished; the guile employed to mislead the authorities in England was not missed by members of the Corporation in the field.

Disillusionment was added to the strain of the staff still working hard in fairly tough circumstances. Families could not join the breadwinner sometimes for eight to ten months; when at last they arrived, his job was, as often as not, about to be abolished. Discontent slowly spread until the senior executives in Kongwa began to feel that the Chairman, Plummer, was unsuited in personality, knowledge and approach to lead the scheme. He was not popular, he was not trusted and, in many quarters, he was actively disliked. Senior members of the Tanganyika Government, not renowned at this time for their flexibility or tact to newcomers or new ideas, found him overbearing, and the gap between them and the Overseas Food Corporation widened.

Misgivings were enhanced by the dismissal in November, 1949, of two London Board Members, John Wakefield and John Rosa. Both were non-political appointees. Obviously, their views must have been in conflict with those of their colleagues and of the Minister. Had the reason for their dismissal been, as John Strachey stated in the House of Commons debate on November 21, the failure of the Overseas Food Corporation to carry out its mandate (that is to grow groundnuts) he should either have dismissed the whole Board, since Board responsibility was joint, and not several; or he should have dismissed the man who, as Chairman, presided over the Board.

In the Commons debate, the late Oliver Stanley put his finger on the crux of the matter:

The Minister wanted scapegoats and he chose the two most convenient. He made use of the analogy of the military operation, in which the penalty of failure is dismissal. That is not a bad principle. Though sometimes not very just, it is sometimes very effective. However, if that principle is to be applied, it must be one of general application. In this case it was one of particular application. When this military operation fails, we sack the battalion commanders, but we do not touch the general who planned the attack, still less the commander-in-chief who ordered it. (*Hansard* November 21, 1949.)

The published views of the two sacked directors indicate on what points they had disagreed with Overseas Food Corporation policy. On December 12, 1949, the day the House of Lords was to debate groundnuts, John Rosa set out his views on the future of the scheme in a letter to *The Times*. He rejected both immediate liquidation and continuation of large-scale operations. Instead, he recommended a middle course, consisting of a combination of experiments, pilot projects and a minimum of large-scale operations. He estimated the costs at another £10 million to £12 million, for which he only promised 'conclusive answers to the question of whether, and if so at what level, development of this kind in Africa can be made self-supporting'. This answer is still not available.

Earlier in 1949, Rosa had spent three months in Tanganyika. The men on the spot had endorsed his middle course; he seemed also to have convinced Mr Strachey of its soundness. Sir Leslie Plummer thought otherwise and induced Mr Strachey to change his mind. Hence the dismissal of John Rosa and of John Wakefield, who strongly backed Rosa.

In that same House of Commons debate of November 21, 1949, a backbencher asked Strachey whether it was true that senior executives of the scheme had no confidence in their Chairman, Plummer. Without a pause, Strachey replied that there was no foundation for such a belief, adding that when last he had been at Kongwa 'separately, privately and alone' he had consulted them on this point. He had demanded and had received a vote of confidence in himself and Plummer.

When reports of the debate reached Kongwa, the senior executives were outraged. In their opinion no such conversations with Strachey had ever taken place. They protested and had, of course, to send their protestations through Plummer.

On December 11, 1949, Strachey flew out from England secretly, with his name kept off the passenger list. Ironically he was hotly pursued by a *Daily Express* reporter. He summoned the two managing directors, Professor John Phillips and George Raby, to Government House in Nairobi, and overwhelmed them by alleging considerable Cabinet concern over the protest that had emerged from Kongwa. He hinted that it was the opinion of many in England that there was Communist influence behind this action. This, coming from Strachey, was unexpected, yet he succeeded in cowing the managing directors. After their retraction, the remaining so-called Kongwa rebels collapsed.

In February, 1950, there was a general election; in the following government reshuffle John Strachey was moved to the War Office and Maurice Webb became the new Minister of Food. At last in May, 1950, Sir Leslie Plummer resigned and many improvements were made. In three years over £30 million had been spent, but the Scheme had failed in its prime objective: to grow groundnuts. By 1950 vast quantities of groundnuts were becoming available from West Africa and the world was no longer threatened by any serious shortage of fats and oils.

John Strachey has stated to the author:

John Wakefield could not have been more wrong in choosing the area he did. Kongwa was utterly unsuited for it. Everything else, expensive machinery, erroneous accounting, numerous mistakes, etc., would have eventually righted themselves had groundnuts grown in reasonable quantities.

This could serve as an obituary of the whole operation–provided it is remembered that groundnuts did not grow in Urambo or Nachingwea either.

During the summer of 1950, an attempt was made to put the Scheme on a self-supporting basis, with farm managers participating in a bonus scheme. Overnight enormous economies were effected, but at this stage the Government would not face further expenditure. It was a strange twist of fate that the order to close down arrived when John Dugdale,[3] Under-Secretary of State for the Colonies, was visiting Tanganyika.[4] Later on, it will

---

[3] John Dugdale died in 1963.　　　　[4] See Chapter 18.

be seen that there was another significant side of his visit. He went to Kongwa with instructions not to inform the staff of the winding-up and had the eery experience of going over the fields, listening to reports and being shown plans for the future, knowing full well that within hours the groundnut machine would be brought to a standstill. This was precisely what John Rosa's middle course had tried to avoid.

Sir Eric Coates, India's last British Finance Minister, was Plummer's successor. His first task was to make a realistic re-appraisal of the scheme. It was now admitted that instead of 600,000 acres 150,000 had been cleared; that the clearing per acre had cost over £50 instead of £3 17s. 4d.; that one ton of Tanganyika groundnuts had cost more than the highest world market price. Total expenditure had been about £35 million instead of £24 million.

Coates submitted a plan to the Government which limited land clearing at Urambo and Nachingwea to approximately sixty-five thousand acres. There was to be large scale experimental development to establish the economics of clearing and mechanised or partially mechanised agriculture under tropical conditions. Funds were made available for the continuation of the plan on this basis.

At this time, responsibility for the Overseas Food Corporation passed from the Ministry of Food to the Colonial Office. Sir Stuart Gillett succeeded Sir Eric Coates as Chairman and two years later, in 1953, was instrumental in bringing about the forma-tion of the Tanganyika Agricultural Corporation, which was to succeed the Overseas Food Corporation and be run from Tanganyika. The Governor, Sir Edward Twining, agreed, provided the T.A.C. took over the assets, but not the liabilities of the Over-seas Food Corporation, and was run on an economic basis. This was done and the T.A.C. has not disgraced itself. Its Chairman until January 1964, Chief Harun Msabile Lugusha[5] had this to say about the assets the Corporation took over:

£36,000,000 were spent on the Groundnut Scheme. John Strachey has told you that £25,000,000 were lost, so what you really want to know is, what happened to the £11,000,000?

The most important gain Tanganyika achieved out of this was the building of Mtwara port south of Lindi for the export of groundnuts from Nachingwea. This port may prove to be a great asset in the future.

[5] See also Chapter 19.

Kongwa had houses, land and equipment, which we took over. This is excellent cattle ranching country, and African settlers are doing well on it.

Urambo had houses, land and equipment; here mainly Virginia tobacco is being successfully grown.

Nachingwea, with houses, equipment and land has been settled by peasants, who are developing into successful farmers.

Under the Groundnut Scheme a number of Africans were trained, who are now employed by us and are very useful indeed. They are earning good salaries.

In the above mentioned places, agriculture has been transformed from hand hoeing to mechanised farming. Individual tenants, not collective farms, are being put on their feet. These tenants have access to machinery and experienced staff.

But in view of Tanganyika conditions, all this could have been achieved for a fraction of the £11 million which were profitably invested, if—and I repeat if—Mr Strachey is right that only £25 million were lost. Frankly, I would find it impossible to account for more than about £7 million worth of assets, including the training of Africans, at 1950 prices. In my view the loss was nearer to £30 million than to £25 million.

Chief Lugusha added sadly: 'Under Tanganyika conditions, with our desperate need for capital, what a waste. . . .'

African views, at their most restrained, can be summarised thus. The scheme struck them as incredibly wasteful of money and of the people working on it. These men came either from the Army, or from the lower ranks of society, and did not behave in the exemplary fashion Africans had grown accustomed to expect from the British. Some reeled about drunk in the daytime, others went to prison for stealing. Africans were deeply shocked by all this. They add bitterly that if on Independence they had received £20 million they could have done immense good with that money, adding that Kenya got £19 million on her Independence, while Tanganyika had only £6 million.

CHAPTER 15

The Penultimate Phase – Sir Edward Twining Becomes Governor

ARTHUR CREECH JONES, Colonial Secretary since 1946, was determined to inaugurate a new era in Tanganyika. He had established the principle that Britain was responsible financially as well as administratively for her underdeveloped territories; he had set up the Colonial Development Corporation and the Colonial Food Corporation; he had pushed through legislation for the development of overseas resources. Yet by 1949 none of these measures had helped Tanganyika, because there was no firm leadership on the spot.

The Governor, Sir William Battershill, had been a sick man for three years. Most of 1948 he spent in Britain, trying to find relief from excruciating arthritic pain. Without leadership, the Territory's officials felt frustrated and became cynical. The excellent Ten Year Plan became a dead letter and the much heralded Groundnut Scheme was a resounding failure. As Labour's bold new colonial policy showed no sign of fulfilment, the Administration and the technical services were running down and thoughtful Tanganyikans were haunted by the spectre of the pre-war doldrums.

The Colonial Secretary was forced to undertake the disagreeable duty of inducing Sir William Battershill to resign. This was the more difficult as both the Governor and his wife believed that he could be cured. (Actually, his condition never improved.) Creech Jones chose Sir Edward Twining, then Governor of North Borneo, as Battershill's successor; it was he who was to initiate the new era.

The Colonial Secretary visualised the new era as one of gradual, systematic preparation for independence before the end of the century. He did not yet grasp that nationalist aspirations were stirring in Tanganyika as in all other parts of Africa, although far-sighted observers had predicted that after the war Africa would never be the same again. For instance, at the end of the Abyssinian campaign, General Sir Alan Cunningham had warned the

156

Kenya Government that, judging by the mood of the askaris, Africans would not be content to remain junior partners in their own country. Yet when hostilities were over, demobilised askaris seemed only interested in getting home to their wives and families, and even the more astute political analysts failed to realise the strong hold nationalism had established on their minds. No one in authority had heard of the young nationalists who were to play leading parts a few years later.

When Sir Edward Twining was sworn in as Governor of Tanganyika in 1949, he received no hint that the nationalist struggle was about to begin in earnest. Nor, indeed, did he observe anything untoward until July, 1954, when a young teacher, by name Julius Nyerere, founded a nationalist movement which promptly passed a resolution declaring that the Queen's authority did not apply to Tanganyika. There was no reason in the world why the Governor should foresee that this inexperienced young schoolmaster would become the architect of modern Tanganyika and that he, Twining, would be so deeply involved in the anti-nationalist campaign as to wage a personal struggle against Nyerere. Nonetheless, despite the notable achievements of Twining's first two terms of office, it was this unforeseen issue which was to dominate–and to sour–his third term.

*   *   *

The Governor in whom Arthur Creech Jones put such great trust was born on June 29, 1899, son of the Vicar of St Stephen's, Rochester Row, a parish church with a notable pastoral reputation on the borders of Pimlico and Westminster. He belonged to the well known family of tea merchants in the Strand. A plaque once on the shop front indicated that the original Twining had a jolly sense of humour, for it bore the jingle:

> 'Tis seldom kind Nature hath planned
> That names with their calling agree
> But Twining the tea-man who lived in the Strand
> Would be wining deprived of his Tea.

Young Twining had a conventional upbringing; from prep. school he went to Lancing College, a Public School in the High Anglican tradition, where he did well. Yet his subsequent career in the early days can hardly be said to have foreshadowed the eminence he was to reach twenty-one years later.

Wanting to become a soldier, Twining just scraped into the Royal Military College at Sandhurst. On his own admission, he was 315th in the competition for a theoretical quota of 300 vacancies. But this was in 1916, when great numbers of young men were needed for the fighting units, so he obtained a place. Two years later, he passed out bottom of the Sandhurst list, was commissioned in the Worcestershire Regiment and spent three years in Ireland during the Trouble. As he had no money, and as Army pay was considerably better in the colonies than at home, he transferred to the K.A.R., and from 1923 to 1928 he served in Uganda. As an impoverished subaltern he had already married the future Lady Twining, a young woman of character who was also a first-class doctor. In Uganda he failed three times to pass his captain's examination, and was glad of a chance to transfer to the Colonial Service. In 1939, after ten years of routine work in the Kampala Secretariat, Twining failed his language examination and once more transferred, this time to Mauritius, as Deputy-Director of Labour.

Then suddenly his career earned real advancement. Promoted Director of Labour after the outbreak of the Second World War, he participated with zest in work which even now, twenty-five years later, has to remain a secret. His contribution must have been considerable, for in 1943 he was made a C.M.G. and appointed Acting Governor of St Lucia in the Windward Islands. From 1946 to 1949 he was Governor and C.-in-C. in North Borneo.

In Tanganyika, Twining's instructions from the Colonial Office and from the Trusteeship Council were to prepare the Territory for self-government and independence, but in the meantime to develop the administration and to strengthen the economy. In his own words: 'Two main things had to be done: an infrastructure had to be provided, and the people had to be associated more closely with Government on a local and on a national level.'

The first task was relatively easy. Because of the war, much money had been spent on stepping up Tanganyika's economy. Considerable sums had come from Allied treasuries; an excellent development plan had been drawn up and some £15 million had accumulated, with an additional £7–£8 million in hand. In addition, the Governor had obtained power to raise loans.

Civil servants and technicians, who had hated the enforced idleness while Sir William Battershill would take no decisions, went to work with enthusiasm when Twining gave the word. Among their number were many who might be described as keen amateurs, yet they built good roads, serviceable aerodromes, waterworks, railways, docks, hospitals, schools and agricultural stations, and they opened up the Territory's economic resources. Twining himself did his utmost to put Tanganyika on the map by interesting business men and industrialists in its possibilities. When in London, he entertained potential customers and acted as a high-power publicity agent. During the Korean War, when certain Tanganyika products like sisal, tea and coffee, were in urgent demand, his efforts were genuinely successful. In view of rising prices, he imposed an export tax which brought in good revenue. The export tax on sisal paid for the fifty-nine mile Tanga–Korogwe road, and for the Colito Barracks outside Dar-es-Salaam, a set of buildings that was to figure prominently in the news in January, 1964, at the time of the Army mutiny.

The second thing which had to be done was much more difficult: the Constitution had to be modernised and constitutional life placed on a new basis. Before taking action, Twining interviewed, individually and alone, the fourteen unofficial members of the Legislative Council: seven Europeans, four Africans (appointed since 1945) and three Asians. He asked for their views and suggestions. Each member professed to be content with colonial rule and wished for no alterations.

The Labour Secretary of State was very disappointed by these passive reactions. Under pressure from America and the Trusteeship Council, Creech Jones decided that in any event the Constitution must be modernised. This problem Twining tackled along two main lines.

First we streamlined the Native Administration and introduced democratic methods [he has told the author]. Every tribe was to have its own tribal council, tribal court and other tribal institutions, schools, dispensaries, and so on, based on the elective principle. Actually, the Sukuma Chiefs had shown us the way, as they had started doing all these things in the early 1940s. Now we were determined that in all tribes decisions were to be taken by the Chief-in-Council, not by the Chief alone.

Twining entrusted Robert Hall, an able administrative officer (later, as Sir Robert Hall, Governor of Sierra Leone) with the task of modernising the Native Administration, above all, the Native Courts. In these the village elders, who used to pass judgment sitting under a tree, were replaced by stipendiary magistrates. He also recast the tribal, district and provincial councils, although only the district councils had the right to raise and spend money, the essential characteristic of such councils in a democracy. Working with the material that was available, and within the limits prescribed by prevailing British policy, Hall accomplished a great deal.

On December 2, 1949, Twining appointed the Attorney-General, Sir Charles Mathew, as chairman of a committee consisting of all the unofficial members to thrash out the new constitution. The Commission's terms of reference were: 'To review the present constitutional structure in the Territory, both local and territorial, and to make recommendations for future constitutional development in the Territory.'

The Constitutional Committee took eighteen months to produce a report. For the first time, African nationalists succeeded in giving evidence before it, although they made no great impression on Sir Charles, who cannot recall the occasion.[1] The members of the Constitutional Committee travelled widely, argued a lot, but ended up by working well together. The four African members became liked and respected by the rest. Mathew wrote the Report himself and, after treating his Committee to an excellent dinner, induced the members to sign it unanimously. The main recommendation was the notorious one–one–one formula. Legco was to have twenty-one unofficial members: seven Europeans, seven Asians and seven Africans. Parity in political representation, as this principle was dubbed, was based not on population statistics, but on the respective contribution of the three communities to Tanganyika's development.

The twenty-one unofficial members were to be appointed by the Governor for three years, on a territorial basis, from lists submitted by representative groups. Eventually, but at some indefinite time in the future, the members were to be elected, each voter having three votes: to be cast for one representative of each of the three races. This formula was intended to canalise racialism

[1] See also Chapter 18.

in parallel channels. It did nothing of the kind, and seven years later one–one–one became a central issue of the nationalist struggle. Yet at that time it was a great step forward, although it may not seem so now. Besides, Twining nominated as members farmers, women and Africans who, although they had never been in public life, accurately reflected the mood of the country.

In 1951 Twining set up a new Committee under the chairmanship of W. J. M. Mackenzie, Professor of Government at Manchester University. Known as the Election Committee, it was to gather material on how, and under what circumstances, elections could be held. Its report, published in 1952, proposed that there should be thirty instead of twenty-one unofficial members, and that on the Government side there should be thirty-one official members, who should constitute a permanent Government majority. The members were to represent constituencies based upon the existing administrative provinces, together with the municipality of Dar-es-Salaam. If the elective principle were introduced, the Committee considered that it should be based on a common roll.

Professor Mackenzie's report coincided with the return from Britain of Julius Nyerere, the first Tanganyika African to obtain a degree at a British university. He provided a rallying point for the young nationalists, who hitherto had scarcely known each other. Now they began to build a movement, using the Dar-es-Salaam African Association as their platform. Security officers paid little heed to this; the Governor never heard about it. Indeed, Twining had far more important problems on hand than parleys among what then seemed starry-eyed Africans. An outstanding achievement of his second term, for which the future rulers of the Territory could be deeply indebted to him, was the manner in which he killed Mau Mau in Tanganyika.

In 1950, some sixteen thousand Kikuyu were living in Tanganyika. The first Mau Mau oaths were administered in Moshi. When this was discovered, action was taken against the two Kikuyu in question. Unfortunately, they got off on appeal and then wreaked vengeance on the two witnesses who had given evidence against them. One was murdered, the other disappeared from his police sanctuary. His body was never found.

When there was further Mau Mau trouble, Twining went to Nairobi, where Sir Evelyn Baring (later Lord Howick) had by then succeeded Sir Philip Mitchell as Governor. Baring agreed that certain categories of the Kikuyu in Tanganyika should be repatriated and sent a police detachment to help sort them out. By this time, an emergency had been declared in Kenya, where Mau Mau terror was nearing its full horror.

At Christmas, 1953, Sir Edward and Lady Twining were at Lushoto, the Governor's summer residence. There he read an intelligence report which contained information to the effect that a Mau Mau organisation in the Northern Province planned to massacre all Europeans on Christmas Eve. It was also to burn all garages, tear down all telephone wires and isolate the area.

Twining summoned the leaders of his administration from Chief Secretary down, to Lushoto. Then he ordered the entire Security Organisation to be brought north; the police force and K.A.R. units were to stand ready at Moshi. When Kenya had returned the Tanganyika Police detachment he had sent up on loan, Twining also declared an emergency.

Altogether eight hundred policemen and one thousand soldiers were concentrated in the North. As the clock struck midnight on December 24, 1953, 640 Kikuyu were arrested. To this the other Kikuyu reacted by murdering the families of two informers. When Twining heard of this, he ordered fifteen thousand Kikuyu to be taken into custody.

Five hundred loyal Kikuyu, who had given information, were speedily repatriated to Kenya. The others were rounded up. The really dangerous suspects, some nine hundred actual Mau Mau men (Category I), were held in Miombo, in the Urambo District of the Western Province, until Kenya agreed to take them back. Those charged and convicted by Tanganyika Courts (Category II) were to be deported to Kenya after having served their sentences. Their families, with those of Category I, were sent back to Kenya forthwith. Kikuyu 'undesirables near the Kenya border' (Category III) were interned near Tamota in the Handeni District of Tanga Province. They were given some rough bush land, which they turned into a well organised settlement, with village shops, a hospital, a school and a church. They had their families with them. Many of Category I and III were rehabilitated.

In March, 1954, an armed band of Mau Mau from Kenya came as far south as Mount Meru. Twining enlisted the support of the loyal citizens of the Province. The tribes polished up their spears and went for the Kikuyu. The hard core were driven into a grove where a brave policeman arrested them; of the remainder some escaped, the rest were captured by the tribes.

By the summer of 1954, Twining had cause to be pleased with the progress which had been made in Tanganyika both in the constitutional and in the economic field. His efforts to attract capital for the development of the Territory's resources were beginning to meet with success. It was then that he received a report on Nyerere and his followers–the young nationalists who wanted to run their country and to decide its future. Twining was horrified by the very thought of an African demanding rights instead of being grateful for the efforts the British Administration generally, and he personally, were making on Tanganyika's behalf. A sight of the document the founders of the Tanganyika African National Union had signed on July 7, 1954, made him even more indignant.

When Julius Nyerere, with his Zulu, Nyasa and Kikuyu friends set up Tanu, I read his original Manifesto very carefully [Lord Twining, as he now is, has told the author]. It demanded that Africa should be for the Africans, Tanganyika for the black Tanganyikans. We Europeans were not even allowed to join. This policy of black racialism was contrary to the principles of the Trusteeship Agreement and to the policy of the British Government.

It did not occur to Twining that, since ninety-eight per cent of Tanganyika's population were black Tanganyikans, Nyerere's demand would hardly qualify as rabid racialism. Nor did he appreciate Nyerere's reasoning that his political party could not admit Europeans because the African had to win the nationalist struggle by himself, in order to prove that he could run his country.

The arrival, a month after the foundation of Tanu, of the third U.N. Visiting Mission, which under the opinionated leadership of the American Mason Sears countenanced even Tanu's wildest demands, further infuriated Twining. He made the sweeping statement that the Africans had neither a national organisation, nor an articulate spokesman. This roused Nyerere's anger, and persuaded him not only to put his complaints against the British Administration into writing, but to petition for an invitation to appear before the Trusteeship Council and to speak for the

Tanganyika Africans in person. When Nyerere not only obtained the invitation, but scored a great personal success in New York, the chasm between the Governor and the nationalist leader became unbridgeable. It cannot be denied that it was Twining who allowed the struggle to assume an intensely personal character. In an attempt to destroy the young African who would not accept the advantages the British Administration had to offer, but who proposed to go his chosen way, Twining descended into the arena of active politics.

Not that Twining and Nyerere would ever have seen eye to eye. They were opposites in every possible way. Twining was a big, heavily built man; Nyerere was small and very thin. Both had excellent minds, but while Twining was dictatorial, and would brook no criticism, Nyerere listened to friends, however critical, and liked to delegate authority. Twining was set in his views, anchored in Kiplingesque traditions; while Nyerere had the ability to step back and take a look at Africa, and then to draw conclusions for Tanganyika and himself. Twining was a child of the successful British middle class; Nyerere an African aristocrat, with the pride and poverty this entailed.

Their political philosophies were poles apart. Twining represented the imperial past, Nyerere the African national future. Twining was fighting for his belief in England's civilising mission; Nyerere for the demands of young Africans to share in the political and economic life of their country, and to have at least a date set for its independence. To Twining, Nyerere was a rebel, an upstart and a rabble-rouser. To Nyerere, it was incredible and hurtful that his efforts to achieve his political aims by constitutional means, even at great risk to his own political future, were not realised, let alone appreciated, by the Governor.

Against this background of personal clash and political animosity, the constitutional advance recommended by Professor Mackenzie's committee seemed to the nationalists to be far too insubstantial. With developments in Ghana to demonstrate that Africans could rule themselves, they wanted elections, which they were convinced they would win and responsible positions they knew they could hold. They were particularly determined to achieve ministerial positions, because in Kenya from 1954 onwards not only Europeans and Asians but an African as well were styled ministers, although no African had risen sufficiently high in the ranks of the Civil Service to be the head of a Government Department. Finally they wanted London to fix a date for self-rule.

Nyerere and his friends were determined to fight until they reached their goal. Their activities were aimed primarily and, it must be said, most unfairly, against civil servants on the spot, D.O.s, D.C.s and P.C.s, agricultural officers and policemen. In the past, most of these men had been their friends, and had sympathised with their nationalist aspirations. Some had actually advised Africans how to prepare for their political future. Now everything seemed to have changed, and they were being provoked and harried by people whose interests they had served and to whom they were genuinely devoted.

The Africans knew that, whatever they did, Britain would not resort to force. They believed that Twining, fundamentally a kindly man, would rather ask for a Royal Commission to be appointed than for the military to be called out. A Royal Commission would have suited the nationalists too, for judging by West African precedents, it would have accorded them seventy-five–if not 100 per cent–of their demands.

Sir Edward Twining has admitted that he committed three mistakes during his nine years of office. (His first term was twice extended.)

His first mistake was to turn official Legco members into ministers.

Ministers must be able to defend their policies in public [he has commented], but my men were still civil servants who did not know how to do that. They could and did reduce my powers as a Governor, because they feared interference by me, but they had not been trained to do the sort of thing which wins over people.

Twining's second mistake was the formation of a government party.

Under the Trusteeship Agreement, it was the Governor's duty to foster political activities, in order to teach Africans democratic methods in preparation for self-rule [he has explained]. Until 1956, we had been pursuing a policy of non-racialism. I changed this to one of multi-racialism, and it was in the name of multi-racialism that we carried out elections to district and provincial councils. But this was not enough, something on a national level had to be done. That is when I called in the Europeans, the Asians and a number of friendly Africans, and asked each one in turn what he proposed to do in view of the black nationalist challenge.

They confessed they did not know what to do and asked the Governor to advise them. Twining suggested that they form a multi-racial party, with African backing. He told them candidly that they could not win, because they could never compete with Tanu's emotional appeal, but that if they mustered a large enough following they might make a deal with Julius Nyerere. According to Twining's information, Nyerere was at this time worried about his future, as he was still not certain how he and Tanu would fare in the elections. That is why this seemed the psychological moment for the United Tanganyika Party (as this party founded by Europeans and Asians was called) to reach agreement with the Tanu leader. But in Twining's view, the Europeans in Tanganyika had no political gifts and missed their chance.

Twining's third mistake was that he could not prevent the Attorney-General, John S. R. Cole, from bringing a case against Julius Nyerere. 'I advised against it, I brought the matter before the Executive Council, I did all I could to stop Cole,' he has told the author. 'Cole was a stubborn Irishman and there was no holding him. He had the right to overrule me and he did so.'[2]

Nyerere, for his part, took full advantage of the situation, and played his cards with great skill. His ace of trumps was that he understood the Governor and his methods very well indeed.

We owe a great deal to Twining [he told the author on November 30, 1961, in Dar-es-Salaam]. Without his peculiar characteristics, we could not have built up Tanu and we could not have welded our backers into accepting our non-racial ideas.

Had Twining been the type of man Andrew Cohen is, things would

[2] One of Twining's former Ministers has told the author: 'Cole was stubborn and unperceptive, but it is nonsense to say that he had a "right to overrule the Governor". In an ordinary criminal prosecution no sane Governor would dream of interfering with the Attorney-General carrying out his duty; and no such matter would ever be brought to the Executive Council.

'But the question as to whether or not to prosecute Julius was *political*; it *was* brought to the Executive Council because it was a political, and not an ordinary criminal matter. The Governor had both the *responsibility* and the *power* to decide the issue. If the Attorney-General did not like the decision he could resign; but he could not override the Governor, and even Cole would never have attempted to do so.'

have been very awkward for us. Cohen in Uganda killed the nationalist movement by falling in with it, by agreeing with it to such an extent that there was nothing left to fight for. Every nationalist movement must have something, or somebody, to fight *against*. Twining provided this foil for us. Had he stopped me going round the country when I still had to convince my people of the possibility of obtaining *uhuru* without creating a violent movement, things would have worked out very differently. Had he given me complete freedom to go ahead without opposition, it would also have been different, for we would have had no cause. But he did the perfect thing: he opposed us, thus giving us a foil; yet he only once barred me for three months from speaking all around the country!

Twining proved a godsend on the racial issue too. When the Kenya white settlers were looking for backers in Tanganyika, he threw them out. When David Stirling arrived with his Capricorn idea, he was shown the door. Twining was not going to tolerate anyone having any influence in Tanganyika except himself. By his conduct he enabled me to say in London that all races in Tanganyika were agreed on *uhuru*.

It was also lucky for us that Twining turned down any possibility of an East African Federation at a time when this would have involved us in an unholy fight. Naturally, Federation will come, but at a time when we will be ready for it, and when our partners will have disposed of their own difficult problems. As I said before, we owe much to Twining, for with another man at Government House, Tanu's story would have been a much less happy one.

Nyerere's political and philosophical ideas represented a force as powerful and as uncontainable as the nationalism that had swept Europe in the nineteenth century. He was bound to win. Yet for four years, from 1954 to 1958, under Twining's dominating influence, no one at Government House realised that Julius Nyerere, with his gentle nature and Christian principles, was, as nationalist leaders went, an unusual and welcome phenomenon. Instead, the colonial administration did their utmost to put him behind bars in the mistaken conviction that, deprived of Nyerere's leadership, the nationalist movement would fall to pieces, and the old tempo could be maintained. Tanganyika would achieve independence perhaps by the end of the century.

Fortunately, Twining's third term ended in the spring of 1958, and his successor, Sir Richard Turnbull, knew the realities of modern Africa.

Had Twining left Tanganyika at the end of his second term,

in 1955, he would have gone down in history as one of the three great governors of Tanganyika. As he misjudged both the personality of Julius Nyerere and the character of his movement, after the beginning of the nationalist struggle his actions were out of touch with reality. It must have been a bitter experience for him to see how the moving sands of time, stirred up by the Winds of Change, covered up the achievements of the first six years.

*   *   *

The ensuing chapters relate the story of Julius Nyerere, and the way he obtained Tanganyika's independence in seven years. Why he could do this, regardless of Twining's mistakes, can be stated in almost statistical terms.

1. Tanganyika's population was ninety-eight per cent African. There were only three thousand European owned estates, no white highlands, no native reserves, and consequently much less racial prejudice than in neighbouring Kenya or the Rhodesias.

2. Tanganyika has 127 tribes, not one of which dominates the country as the Kikuyu dominate Kenya. Nyerere did not have to fight on two fronts, against rival tribes as well as against the British, as many African nationalist leaders have had to do.

3. The tribes can understand each other, for Swahili–thanks to the early history of the Territory and to the educational system devised by Stanley Rivers Smith and Travers Lacey in the early 1920s–is the country's *lingua franca*. Any broadcast in Swahili is understood by the overwhelming majority of Tanganyika's Africans.

4. Julius Nyerere is a Zanaki, and the Zanaki are one of the smallest tribes in Tanganyika. His rise to great prominence did not arouse tribal jealousies; his modest, almost humble, attitude has gained him veneration among Tanganyika Africans.

5. Nyerere was a Christian not only in name but in faith and ethics. During the whole time he fought against the British, he regarded the democratic system as the application of Christian principles to politics. In Britain, he had learnt the rules of the democratic game, and played it with brilliant skill against the British, who observed the same rules. Later, when faced by his own less highly principled fellow Africans, he discovered that democracy was not enough, and that violence (from which he shrank with intellectual as well as physical aversion) could not

be held at bay by parliamentary tactics which his opponents neither understood nor observed. But that was after the British had departed from Tanganyika.

When Sir Edward Twining arrived in 1949, Tanganyika was asleep. When he left in 1958, not only was it awake, but in political turmoil, and the people were on the march, following the lead of Julius Nyerere.

CHAPTER 16

Julius Nyerere, Youth and Early Manhood

JULIUS NYERERE was born in March, 1922. His mother Mugaya is not certain of the day, although she remembers that the rains were exceptionally heavy. That is why she called her newly born Kamberage, which is the name of an ancestral spirit living in the rain. The boy's father was one of the eight chiefs of the Zanaki, a very small tribe, even now numbering less than fifty thousand. He was called Nyerere, which in Ki-Zanaki is the name of a caterpillar, the army worm, because in the year of his birth, 1860, the country was riddled with army worms.

The story of Julius Nyerere is the story of all Black Africa, of a continent struggling to emerge from the tribal past. For many centuries the Zanaki had lived close to the eastern shores of Lake Victoria. In the plural, Bazanaki means poor people, literally translated: 'Those who came with what?' They are still a poor people, although the dam they built by self-help in 1962 has improved their farming prospects.

Racially they are a mixture of several tribes whose members fled east of Lake Victoria because of famine, or for personal reasons. They also have Bahima blood;[1] the Bahima are the kingly tribe whose members moved about a thousand years ago from the north into Buganda, Buhaya, Ruanda-Urundi and Zanakiland. The Zanaki divided a very long time ago into two nations, the Biru and the Baturi; Nyerere belonged to the Biru.

Zanaki tribal laws and customs were similar to those of other East African tribes, and had detailed rules about marriage, divorce, theft, murder and inheritance. Until recently, a Zanaki tribesman paid bride-price for a wife, usually so many head of cattle. He could divorce her if she was 'barren, ugly and unfit' (unfit to do field work), if she had committed adultery or was found guilty of theft or arson. A woman could not divorce her husband either for adultery or for committing a murder, but she had this right if he inflicted grievous bodily harm on her, or disgraced her by stealing or setting on fire a fellow-tribesman's

[1] Bahima blood means Hamitic blood. Julius Nyerere's Hamitic blood shows in his features.

property. In all divorce cases the wife's father or brother had to repay the bride-price, or part of it, according to the period she had been married, provided the husband had been blameless. The amount of the bride-price to be restored was a frequent cause of litigation. Nowadays a wronged Zanaki wife can claim alimony–to the great disgust of the tribesmen.

The Zanaki being polygamous, the rules were clear on what each wife was entitled to: the husband had to provide her with a grass hut and a *shamba*, farm. The first wife had a special position, in that the husband had to consult her about each new wife he brought home. If she withheld approval for good reason, he was supposed to accept her objection. Younger wives waited on the first wife hand and foot, and treated her like a mother.

Theft and arson were the most shaming crimes of all, as being those which most endangered tribal welfare and were most severely punished. While the murder of a fellow tribesman could be atoned for by a fine, the death penalty was imposed for theft, especially theft of cattle. If a man caught a thief and recognised his animals, he had the right to kill him then and there.

The payment of workers and the treatment of old people was clearly laid down. Among the Zanaki, as among other tribes, the elders, in Ki-Zanaki called *bakaruka*, have a special position and take decisions on social and political problems. Age symbolises the welfare of the clan, far more important than any individual member. This is the basis on which blind obedience to old people and elders is demanded and obtained. The *bakaruka* are kept by their sons and looked after by their daughters-in-law.

Justice used to be dispensed by the ruler, the *mwami*, at a *baraza*, a meeting held under a big tree which could be attended by any member of the tribe. The Zanaki were democratic in the sense that every tribesman and woman understood the law and knew if and when it had been broken. In 1962, when the Tanganyikan chiefs abdicated their powers, a District Magistrate took over the judicial functions of Chief Edward Wanzagi, Julius Nyerere's eldest half-brother, although he maintained his honorary title. The chief is occasionally still asked for advice on the settlement of disputes.

Although Zanaki tribal laws and customs in general were like those of other tribes they differed in several particulars.

The ruler or *mwami*, who was also rainmaker and witch doctor, could only exercise his immense powers in co-operation with the *bakaruka*. They could control a *mwami* who proved too cruel or too grasping by withholding tribal dues and refusing to hold tribal sacrifices. These sanctions were always effective.

Each of the two Zanaki nations consisted of several clans; each clan had an elected leader called *Murwazi*, who was its spokesman and who advised whether or not the clan should go to war. The clans fought independently of each other; only in times of famine did they unite, except on one celebrated occasion. This is how the story is told:

Like every tribe in our part of East Africa, we suffered from the Masai, who raided our cattle and kidnapped our women. Sometimes our women did not want to return from their Masai captors, which was most humiliating for us.

When the bush drums next spread the news that the Masai were on the move, the *mwami*, the *Bakaruka* and the *Barwazi* (*Barwazi* is the plural of *Murwazi*) got together and hatched a plan. It was a good plan.

All our warriors were drawn up to wait for the Masai. When they appeared, the first round of arrows was aimed at the attackers' heads. Instinctively the Masai raised their shields. Then the second and much stronger round of arrows was aimed at a lower part of their bodies. Their aim was true. Howling with pain, the Masai fled, and from that day to this they have never troubled us again.

A Zanaki tribesman will add: 'Julius applies similar tactics in his verbal battles: while an opponent is thinking about one argument, he slips in another one. That is why he usually gets his way.'

Warriors and workers ruled the Zanaki clans. Attendance at meetings was compulsory; a man who did not turn up had to pay a fine. Their specific duties were to build the house of the *mwami*, to protect the land against attack and to collect fines from people who refused to do communal work. This is interesting in view of the Tanganyikan law, passed in October, 1962, that people who fail to participate in self-help schemes must pay a fine.

*   *   *

The Germans were the first to modernise ancient tribal life with the intent of weakening influential chiefs. They broke up the Zanaki into ten tiny chiefdoms, headed by the most important clan, which lived at Butiama and appointed its *mwami*, Buhoro, as chief. In 1912 he was succeeded by his cousin, Nyerere. When the British took over Tanganyika, the Zanaki had reunited into one tribe, but under Sir Donald Cameron they broke up again into seven chiefdoms, which in 1932 formed a federation presided over by Chief Ihunyo of Busegwe.

Chief Nyerere was on good terms with the elders and had no trouble in obtaining tribal dues, consisting of so many head of cattle, sheep, goats and fowls, as well as hoes, spears and shields. The Zanaki were not supposed to taste any of their harvest without giving him a share for the sacrifices. As most Zanaki are still pagans, tribal sacrifices are held to this day. Chief Edward Wanzagi has nine wives and twenty-six children. Once Julius Nyerere teased him: 'Why don't you get rid of that lot and buy a tractor?'

Chief Nyerere must have had considerable diplomatic skill, for he got on both with the Germans, who wanted a weak chief, and with the British, who wanted a strong one, although under the latter Zanakiland was for six years administered by an *akida*. From 1923 onwards, Chief Nyerere ruled undisturbed.

Two years earlier, aged sixty-one, he took his eighteenth wife, a young girl of fifteen called Mugaya. She was pretty and gay, and bore him six children who say that she was the beloved wife with whom their father spent more time than with any of his other wives. In 1942, when Chief Nyerere died, her grass hut was destroyed and she moved away from Muhunda, the tiny village where he is buried. His grave is the size of an average plot in a cemetery, surrounded by a low wall on which is written in Ki-Swahili: 'Here lies Chief Nyerere, son of Burito, who ruled from 1912 to 1942.'

Mugaya's children, like other Zanaki children, did not belong to her but to the clan. Her sole privilege was to kiss them on the face, anyone else being only allowed to kiss their little hands. Later in life kissing on the face or the mouth is for lovers or spouses only; that is why Zanaki women kiss each others' hands.

Zanaki children are educated by all their female relations; their aunts and grandmothers and cousins are all called 'elder sisters'. They are taught courtesy from the cradle; they cannot speak to an elder person unless spoken to first. Younger boys carry out the orders, even the wishes, of older boys unquestioningly. Before strangers children must be silent; they must not reach for food, especially meat. To eat without washing hands is rude. Ill-mannered boys and girls are a disgrace to their parents and will have difficulties in later life in finding spouses.

Even by African standards Kamberage Nyerere had a hard childhood. The few acres of Mugaya's shamba were poor quality land. However hard she worked, and her children helped her from a tender age, the harvest would not provide sufficient food for the family. Maize and millet porridge were the mainstay of their diet, although Chief Nyerere often brought meat and fish. During the rainy season vegetables and fruit were plentiful, and children could pick paw-paws and groundnuts. But when it rained, it was also cold; Mugaya could only put some old sacking over Kamberage's shivering shoulders. She placed earthenware pots under major leaks in the roof; the rhythmic plop-plop of the raindrops is one of his earliest memories.

At the age of eight, he started taking out Mugaya's goats and watching over them all day without food until evening, when the family ate its one meal of the day. About this time he saw his first white man and his first motor car. He was not frightened of either; he would have liked to know more about both.

Neighbouring chiefs often joined Nyerere at Mugaya's grass hut. Although poor and unimportant, they were proud men who stood on their chiefly dignity. Chief Ihunyo of Busegwa and Chief Marwa of Butuguri were the most frequent visitors. Their sons, like the sons of other chiefs of this part of Tanganyika, were Kamberage's friends.

Another welcome guest in Muhanda was Chief Makongoro of Ikuzu. The Makongoro and Nyerere families were good friends and inherited property from each other. Twenty-three years later Chief Makongoro was to play an important role in Kamberage's life. (See also Chapter 31.)

There was no indication at this time that the boy might lead a life different from his forebears or his contemporaries. Although he was quick and bright, and asked a great many questions, no one paid much attention to them until he began to beg his mother to let him go to school because his friend, Mwanagwa Marwa, son of Chief Ihunyo, had been sent to Musoma. The British Government had made repeated appeals to the chiefs to have their children educated, and some had responded.

Marwa told Kamberage about what he learnt, what school was

like, what games they played. He also spoke about a priest who came over from Nyegina mission, and talked about Jesus and the saints and the Roman Catholic feasts. Kamberage's imagination was touched by all this, and he also wanted to learn to read and write. His mother could not understand why her fourth child should not be satisfied with the traditional life of the Zanaki. Like her people, she felt no desire to change it, or raise it to the level of the Arabs or the Asians. It never crossed her mind to want to have a house or clothes like the white people.

The old chief was very fond of Kamberage and wanted to provide for his future. When he was a small boy, he bought him a bride on the principle that a girl was less likely to die or to deteriorate in value than the cattle one gave for her, which could catch all sorts of diseases.

His 'child bride' is still a good friend of Julius Nyerere's, although he retrieved the cattle by passing her on to another husband when he had to pay bride-price for Maria Gabriel, the girl he eventually married.

Kamberage was indubitably clever; he played *Soro*, a complicated African game, with Chief Ihunyo, constantly beating the older man. Much impressed, Chief Ihunyo told his friend Chief Nyerere to let the boy go to school. Nyerere accepted the advice and Kamberage went off to a Native Authority boarding school in Musoma.

A boarding school in an African town is rudimentary indeed compared with its counterpart in Britain. In Musoma it meant a large grass hut, where little African boys slept and cooked for themselves their single daily meal.

Kamberage soon headed his class. He learnt in three years what took other boys four years, and became very interested in the catechism classes. It is a strange sequel that Marwa, the boy who first told him about Christianity, has remained a pagan. He is at present a headman in Zanakiland.

It was the Musoma N.A. school teacher who insisted that Kamberage should sit for the Tabora Government School entrance examination. As admission to this splendid school meant paying a tuition fee, his father's agreement had to be obtained.

Kamberage was lucky in easily overcoming family resistance to his wish of going to school. Other boys had far greater difficulties; some had to put up with beatings and privations before they could achieve their aim. Andrew Tibandebage, who later became a close friend of Kamberage's, had to wait until his fierce grandmother died to insist openly on being educated in the European way. His parents would never have agreed had he not fallen ill. When their witch doctor had proved powerless and the boy appeared to be dying, a white priest was allowed to baptise him. Because Andrew improved, his parents regarded the white medicine man as more powerful than their own witch doctor and when the priest advised school, Andrew got his wish.

In 1937 Kamberage entered Tabora Government School. He was an excellent student, but showed no special aptitude for leadership. He was, however, twice made prefect of his House, then called *Kifaru* (rhinoceros), now Blumer House. The future Julius Nyerere showed his mettle when he discovered how great were the privileges of the prefects. They received almost twice as much food as the other boys and had excessive power over them. Kamberage decided that these privileges were unjust and should be abolished. His agitation against them was so effective that the headmaster quietly cancelled them.

This was a great success, and Kamberage became known to everyone in the school. Thanks to his quick wit and ready answer, he soon figured in school debates. Tabora Government School was one of the few places in Tanganyika where political discussion flourished. In their lively debates the boys continually talked over things which affected themselves, their country and the whole of the African continent.

Looking much younger than his age and wearing the shortest shorts ever seen, Kamberage had the rare gift of helping his friends to clarify their thoughts.

'Could an African make a good headmaster?'

'Could an African run his country?'

'Could Tanganyika, at however distant a point in the future, shake off colonial rule?'

'We can try—we must try. . . .'

Kamberage's answers pointed towards an unknown path. Though the entrance to this path was blocked by Britain's power, he convinced his friends that the path was indeed there.

During the war years, such embryonic nationalist ideas were in the air all over Africa. Nyerere readily admits that Tabora Government School was the British devised platform on which the future

Tanganyika nationalists met and befriended each other while still in their teens. Had it not been for Tabora, it would have taken them much longer to set out on their common road towards Tanganyika's independence.

While at school, Kamberage continued attending catechism classes, held by White Fathers from the Tabora Mission. He was not baptised there, as it was normal practice to leave this decision to the Superior of the mission where the boy's instruction had begun. In Kamberage's case this was Nyegina mission on the outskirts of Musoma.

Having obtained his School Leaving Certificate, Kamberage went back to Musoma. On December 23, 1943, he was baptised by Father Mathias Koenen together with a group of young Africans in the Nyegina mission chapel. His godfather was Petero Masive, a Nguruimi, who is now head catechist at Iramba mission.

Father Koenen was unaware of Kamberage Nyerere's identity until years later, when he saw his picture in the *Tanganyika Standard*. That is when he realised that he had baptised and given the name of Julius to the famous Tanu leader. As he put it to the author: 'I'm afraid I can't claim to have consciously met Julius Nyerere. . . .'

*   *   *

Two questions arise from the story of Julius Kamberage Nyerere's early years. Why did all these African boys suddenly want to go to the white man's schools? True, the young always want something different and more advanced than the old, yet these lads were setting foot on the bridge between a stone age existence and the modern world. With the chasm between the two being so vast, they could scarcely have realised what they were doing.

If we are forced to accept that they did this instinctively, in response to the spirit of the age, we are faced with the even more puzzling question: What effect did this fantastically quick transition from their pagan world into a western way of life have on these young Africans? Only ten years elapsed between Kamberage watching tribal sacrifices at Muhanda and Julius Nyerere going to communion at Nyegina mission. The pressure on his mind during these ten years must have been tremendous.

His nationalist friends passed through similar experiences while joining either a Christian Church or the Moslem discipline. All of them seem to have adjusted themselves amazingly well. It is a truism to say that many average Africans have reacted differently. An imposed development, with tremendous demands on simple minds, this, in a nutshell, is the core of the African drama. It is also one of the basic problems with which President Nyerere of Tanganyika has to deal.

CHAPTER 17

The Makerere Intellectuals

THERE can be no disputing that the birth of national consciousness was the product of education: at the same time, the growth
of national consciousness itself inspired an ever more urgent demand for more education. The Africans' awakening promoted an
entirely novel attitude to it. In particular, Makerere College at
Kampala, Uganda, played a unique role as the cradle of Tanganyika's future leaders.

Makerere was founded in 1922 as a college for training clerks.
Thanks to its first-class staff, it developed steadily, and by 1945
was pressing forward towards university college status, which it
attained in 1949. The Governments of Kenya, Uganda and
Tanganyika had agreed to share the costs of maintenance of
Makerere College, the University College of East Africa, as it was
called until 1961, when it became Makerere University College.
They did this in two ways. Each paid a contribution, fixed for a
period of years, towards recurrent costs, such as staff salaries. In
1960–1, the Tanganyika Government contributed £137,677, in
1961–2 £154,155, in 1962–3 £165,575 and in 1963–4 £221,000.
In addition to this basic contribution, each government paid a
capitation fee, which varied from year to year, according to the
number of students at the college. In 1954, each of 113 students
at Makerere cost the Tanganyika Treasury £740. Bursaries of
about £220 a year each were awarded, varying slightly according
to the faculty and the number of examinations taken.

In the early days, college students studied free of charge, but
when Makerere became a university college costs rose so much
that parents had to contribute according to their ability. The
balance between the cost and the parental payment was borne by
the Central Government. This system still prevails under the
government of independent Tanganyika.

Every year a quota of students was allocated to each of the three
East African Territories. It is a bitter complaint of Tanganyikans
that they were unable to fill their quota of places at Makerere
because Britain had not set up enough good secondary schools to
turn out a sufficient number of qualified candidates. There is,

undoubtedly, some truth in this criticism, for in some years there were genuinely not enough candidates. Yet from the figures below it becomes clear that, until 1958, the number of students steadily increased. In this, the peak year of Tanganyika students at Makerere, their upkeep cost was £47,520, of which the Administration paid £47,000. This indicates that finance was an additional reason why an unlimited number of students could not go there.

STUDENTS AT MAKERERE

Year	Total Number	Tanganyikans Men	Tanganyikans Women	Total	Tanganyikan Degrees
1949	222	32	–	32	
1950	237	41	–	41	
1951	245	48	–	48	
1952	273	59	1	60	
1953	367	88	1	89	
1954	449	110	3	113	2
1955	560	146	4	150	7
1956/7	625	163	5	168	8
1957/8	696	179	4	183	11
1958/9	823	212	4	216	12
1959/60	881	192	8	200	10
1960/1	912	159	9	168	25
1961/2	951	145	11	156	–
1962/3	782	124	24	148	–
1963/4	–	–	–	170	

The largest contributor to Makerere was the British Government, the stipulation being made that money coming from Colonial Development and Welfare Fund, was to be used for capital development, e.g. for building and equipment. From 1949 until Uganda's independence in November, 1962, the British contribution amounted in round figures to £3,350,000.

In 1960 another step forward was made. It was decided to set up the University of East Africa, consisting of Makerere University College in Kampala, the Royal College in Nairobi and the University College in Dar-es-Salaam. In October, 1961, a Law Faculty was inaugurated in Dar-es-Salaam, in a spacious building originally intended as the new headquarters of Tanu. For Julius Nyerere this meant the realisation of a dream; it was even more rewarding that the Law Faculty soon became the nucleus around which the University College was formed. On June 29, 1963, the University of East Africa came into being, with President Julius Nyerere as its first Chancellor.

In October, 1961, another Nyerere dream also became reality: Kivukoni College, founded with funds raised entirely in Tanganyika, was opened in Dar-es-Salaam.[1] Its purpose was to train students for responsibility, regardless of what school standard they may have reached. They were to receive no certificate, for the aim was not to produce good examinees, but Tanganyikans with enough knowledge to appreciate what is impracticable and what should be undertaken. In May, 1963, in London, the Principal of Ruskin College, Bill Hughes, and the former Commissioner of Community Development in Tanganyika, Horace Mason, formed a group calling itself 'The Friends of Kivukoni College'. The response to their appeal for a fund to ease Kivukoni's financial problems has been gratifying.

Without having gone to Tabora Government School and from there to Makerere College, Julius Nyerere could not have conceived Kivukoni. E. S. Williams, headmaster of Tabora when Kamberage Nyerere secured his School Leaving Certificate, was determined that this clever boy should have a university training. He did not anticipate trouble with the Nyerere family, for the African attitude to education had begun to change. Even the N.A. Schools, to which earlier on it had been difficult to attract students, were well attended. It was at this time that Africans started to talk about the Golden Book the Europeans kept locked and hidden because it contained all their secrets.

'If our children learn to read and write, they will find out what the Europeans know,' they were saying. 'Then the white men won't be able to order us about any more. Then we'll become our own masters.'

The young Africans who were to play a decisive role in the future would have put their faith in education in less naïve terms. Had anyone asked what they wanted most, they would have replied–schools.

Kamberage, who now wished to be called Julius Nyerere, was very anxious to go to college. His father, who had died at the great age of eighty-two, was succeeded by his eldest son as chief of

[1] See also Chapter 29.

the Zanaki. Chief Wanzagi was pleased at the prospect of his third brother becoming a teacher. With Mr Williams' backing, Julius Kamberage obtained a bursary and arrived at Makerere in January, 1943.

If Tabora had been a meeting place of future nationalists, Makerere was doubly so. Not only Tabora boys came to it, but the *élite* of the pupils from all Tanganyika secondary schools. For instance the White Fathers' St Mary's College, Tabora, had an enviable record of turning out boys who obtained scholarships to Makerere.

There young Nyerere renewed acquaintance with Abdulla Fundikira, son of the great Nyamwezi chief; Ibrahim Sapi, grandson of Sultan Mkwawa, the famous Hehe chief; Kidaha Makwaia,[2] son of the first Sukuma chief to send a wife and a daughter to Tabora Girls' School. He also met many other young aristocrats, all of whom had been brought up to believe that they were the natural leaders of their country.

Among the commoners, Vedast Kyaruzi, Andrew Tibandebage, Luciano Tsere and Hamza Mwapachu were leading figures. They were playing an important role in student activities, and were canvassing political ideas. Anti-Nazi or anti-Communist propaganda made no impression on them. They resented Hitler because of his racialism, but neither Nazi nor Communist dictatorial ways shocked them. As both Germany and Russia were geographically remote, they did not think that either could interfere with Tanganyikan affairs. Their interests centred nearer home.

In one of his essays written at Makerere, Andrew Tibandebage, then studying for a teaching diploma (he is now in the Tanganyika diplomatic service), compared Tanganyika with Buganda, saying that Buganda was more advanced because Bugandans were headmasters of secondary schools, while not a single African was headmaster in Tanganyika. His last sentence read: 'Buganda proved that Africans can get ahead on their own.'

'What exactly do you mean by that?' his tutor asked.

'I mean that we in Tanganyika can and must do the same. We must play an important part in the affairs of our country,' he replied, closing the argument.

Between the two groups, Julius Nyerere was something of a lone wolf. By birth an aristocrat, by inclination a reformer, he

[2] See also Chapter 13.

shared the nationalist views of the commoners. Soon he became the star debater of Makerere College, and introduced international affairs into discussions. He looked for statements about brotherhood, equality and equal opportunities, whether emanating from Washington or Moscow, trying to figure out how these would apply to his own people. Soon his friends also grew excited by anti-colonial declarations.

This is how Luciano Tsere remembers this period:

Before Julius' arrival, the students had been playing with political ideas in an unthinking way. Perhaps it would be more accurate to say that political ideas had been creeping in, but we had hardly any interest in the war and none in National Socialism or Communism. Julius' brilliant performances in the students' debates clarified our minds and made us think.

Yet his intellectual arguments did not appeal to all students. Most of the young aristocrats kept away from him because he did not share their pastimes. As one of them said:

Julius was not active in our Students Union, he did not play games and he did not go to dances. I would have been exceedingly surprised had anyone told me that he had been up until midnight. The usual pursuits of young people held no attractions for him. Nor did he display signs of his talent for leadership, that was to come much later. I for one did not anticipate that he would develop into a great leader.

The Tanganyikan commoners regarded young Nyerere from a different angle. This is how Vedast Kyaruzi, who, with Luciano Tsere, studied medicine and who from Independence until March 1963 was Permanent Secretary of the Foreign Ministry, has described him:

Julius was a reserved, courteous young man. He was in no hurry to get up and speak; he would answer questions but he would make no statements. He was also deeply religious. He had an outstanding mind and his academic achievement was a remarkable one. He won first prize in the regional literary competition with an essay on the application of John Stuart Mills' arguments for feminism to the tribal societies of Tanganyika.

Tibandebage also has memories of those college days.

Julius and I were members of the Makerere Debating Society [he has said]. We also belonged to Catholic Action, in fact between us we had founded it. Hamza Mwapachu used to call it 'mass action' because we organised such religious activities as annual retreats and pilgrimages to Namugongo, the place where Charles Wanga, Mathias Mohumba and other Christians had been murdered. We also got a choir going, which had its ups and downs both vocally and organisationally.

In his second year, young Nyerere began to grope for a political organisation, something that could, eventually, be transformed into a political party and help the Tanganyikans to work for self-government. He and Hamza Mwapachu, his closest friend, founded the Tanganyika African Welfare Association, known as T.A.W.A.

I drafted T.A.W.A.'s constitution [Julius Nyerere has told the author]. It was frankly political. Then I sent it to a number of friends and to people who I thought might sympathise and join. One of them wrote back saying that there existed an organisation in Tanganyika which would be excellent for my purposes, the Tanganyika African Association. It had quite a past, Sir Donald Cameron having founded it to provide Africans in towns with a sounding board and a place where they could discuss their views. It had the further advantage, he said, of having branches in all sizeable towns. Cameron had not intended it as a political organisation, although he had not forbidden political discussion. Unfortunately T.A.A. had sunken to a tea-party organisation, and my friend suggested that we bring it to life again.

Tibandebage visualised T.A.W.A. very differently from Nyerere.

T.A.W.A.'s prime aim was to improve the peoples' physique [he has said]. We knew that the actual bodily well-being of the Tanganyika Africans had to be bettered. We as students of Makerere were to prepare ourselves for carrying out this task. We also wanted to extend the rights and privileges accorded to Africans, especially to civil servants. Most of us were training to become teachers, and if we found employment in Government schools, we would automatically become civil servants. Only if we happened to be employed by a private agency, such as a mission school, could we avoid Government service.

In my last year, in 1944, I became chairman of T.A.W.A. and Julius secretary. This was the third organisation in which we alternated in this fashion. I was one year ahead of Julius in my studies, but he was ahead of all of us in his brilliant debating. Yet as a leader he came forward only very gradually,

he ended, agreeing with other observers.

While Julius Nyerere and Hamza Mwapachu were discussing the chances of creating a political platform, Vedast Kyaruzi also suggested that they should use T.A.A.

I told them [he has said], that in Bukoba, where I come from, we had a branch, but people were dissatisfied with it because of its uneven activities. When there was a public issue, say criticism of an agricultural policy or some other Government measure, then it was active. It was up to us, I argued, to keep T.A.A. always active.

This was sound, and it bore out the argument of the letter Nyerere had received. He and Mwapachu regretfully dropped their own creation and transferred their activities to T.A.A.

I became secretary of our T.A.A. group [Dr Kyaruzi has explained]. We wrote letters, some very pungent ones, to T.A.A. headquarters in Dar-es-Salaam, but for a long time received no answer. Then we heard from an official who had unearthed our letters and promised to deal with the problem we had raised. This was the last communication we had from him. Later friends in Dar-es-Salaam told us that he had been 'too active'. They believed that 'too active people', meaning naturally Africans, were apt to be transferred. This was particularly so if they were officers of T.A.A. Of course some transfers had genuine reasons, but many were due to fear on the part of the colonial authorities that there would be too much probing. The T.A.A. secretary in question was definitely transferred for political reasons.

Andrew Tibandebage left Makerere in 1944, Julius Nyerere and Hamza Mwapachu a year later. By then Dr Vedast Kyaruzi and Dr Luciano Tsere had been admitted as house physicians to the Sewa Haji Hospital in Dar-es-Salaam.

Before scattering for their first jobs, the intellectuals of Makerere pledged themselves to continue their nationalist activities through T.A.A. Little did they realise how intertwined their lives would become, and how useful their first uncertain steps on the political platform provided by Makerere would prove in the future. They wondered who among them would have an opportunity to strike the first blow for their great purpose.

The young men who went to Dar-es-Salaam were to have that distinction.

CHAPTER 18

First Into Action

EVEN in the late 1940s, Dar-es-Salaam was still a small town. As in other small towns, everyone knew everyone else's business. Makerere graduates, of whom there was only a handful, found each other within hours of arrival there. And it did not take them much longer to become acquainted with Africans who during the war had served with the K.A.R. and whose minds had been broadened by their experiences overseas.

So it came about that, soon after their arrival at the Sewa Haji Hospital, Dr Vedast Kyaruzi and Dr Luciano Tsere befriended nationalists among the ex-servicemen. No one regarded this as an event. Yet it was more than an event, it was a landmark. They met the brothers Abdul and Ally Sykes, James Mkande, Dossa Aziz and others, who had discussed Tanganyika's future over mugs of rum while waiting for repatriation at Kalieni Camp outside Bombay. It was a thrilling experience for them to find each other in fundamental agreement on the burning need to rid Tanganyika of colonial discrimination, to enable Africans to hold responsible positions, to create a political organisation for Africans and, eventually, to secure the supreme aim – independence for Tanganyika.

The opportunity they awaited presented itself in 1950. The Governor, Sir Edward Twining, had announced on December 3, 1949, that a Constitutional Committee would hear evidence about political changes to be made in Tanganyika. The young nationalists unanimously resolved to place their views before the Committee.

This was a revolutionary decision. Never before had Africans had any say *in public* about the future of their country. Four Makerere graduates and six ex-servicemen formed themselves into an Action Group. Their purpose was to draft a meticulously worded memorandum and to submit it to the Constitutional Committee. They were happy to sacrifice their Saturday afternoons and their Sundays to discuss the demands this memorandum was to incorporate.

Not one of them had a house or a flat where they could meet.

They shared narrow, cramped quarters with wives and children or with parents and a large family. Hospitality being a virtue as well as a compulsion among Africans, it can never be refused. Its duration cannot be limited and privacy is unknown. To be able to thrash out undisturbed their difficult problems, the Action Group met at the Ilala Community Centre. This was a whitewashed house with a verandah running along two sides, built outside the city in Sir Donald Cameron's day. It consisted of two large rooms. A child clinic was held in one; a modest teashop occupied the other. When Dr Kyaruzi and his friends were in funds, they walked in proudly through the main entrance, sat down at a corner table and ordered tea. When funds were low (more likely non-existent) they came in through the side-door, and were allowed to sit on the verandah without ordering anything. Secret meetings, held behind closed doors in the room used as a child clinic, were restricted to the hard core of the Action Group.

There were no police spies, and no one tried to listen in to their conversations. Whether this was because the authorities respected their right to think, or because they were unaware of the kind of thinking they were doing, must remain an open question. As related earlier on, before the Constitutional Committee began its work, the Governor had private talks with a number of Africans, all of whom said that they were satisfied with the administration and had no suggestions to make. It is puzzling how they could have been so uninformed about the nationalist desires of their contemporaries.

The memorandum drafted by the Action Group contained three main proposals: To organise Tanganyika's local government on the basis of rural, district and provincial councils, elected from a common roll of Africans and Europeans. On these councils, the Europeans were to be assured of forty-five per cent of the seats. For thirteen years, the provincial councils were to be electoral colleges for the Legislative Council. 'In the thirteenth year of this programme, the whole electorate in the Territory shall elect common representatives by a common electoral roll and the elected representatives shall acquire majority power in the council.'

It is unlikely that these young men really expected events to move as fast as, in fact, they did. The District Councils were introduced in 1958 and 1959, and, after a difficult start, are now working well and have largely replaced the chiefs' functions; they

have not, however, a minimum European representation upon
them. The first 'one man, one vote' election, the presidential
election of 1962, was held in the thirteenth year after the presentation of the memorandum. By then, of course, fifty out of seventy
members of the Assembly–the successor to the Legislative
Council–were Africans.

Two men were mainly responsible for shaping the memorandum: Hamza Mwapachu and Luciano Tsere. Mwapachu had
just returned from Britain, where he had trained as a social worker
and therefore was familiar with British local government. Steeped
in Moslem discipline, he provided the solid facts on which
Tanganyika's constitution was to be based.

Luciano Tsere acted the part of the devil's advocate. Born into
the Iraqw tribe in Mbulu, he obtained his first education in a
mission bush school and became a Roman Catholic. At one point
he wished to embrace the priesthood and went to the Kipalapala
Seminary. Realising that he had no vocation, he switched over to a
medical career. But at Kipalapala he had studied logic. This now
enabled him to bring up the kind of arguments an Englishman
might be expected to use to rip the memorandum to pieces. For
three months he forced his friends to redraft their work again and
again. At the end of it, the memorandum was so solid that no holes
could be bored in its reasoning.

Brilliance was provided by another Makerere graduate, Steven
Mhando, later for a short time Tanu's organising secretary.
Abdul and Ally Sykes, James Mkande and other ex-servicemen
provided the practical element, asking the simple questions which
must be answered to everyone's satisfaction if there was to be
popular support.

By early 1950, the memorandum seemed very good to its
authors. They knew that nobodies like themselves could not
appear before the Committee. They had to find an umbrella of
respectability under which to range themselves. There were two
alternatives: Either to become members of the Tanganyika
African Association, T.A.A., which had branches in many parts
of the country, or of the Tanganyika African Government Servants Association, T.A.G.S.A., of more recent origin and function-
ing mainly in Dar-es-Salaam.

Obviously, T.A.A. was much more important than T.A.G.S.A.
The question was whether it would admit them as members, and

whether it would allow itself to be used for nationalist purposes. Like all young men, they felt that they were embarking on an important struggle.

While at Makerere, they had vainly tried to join T.A.A., and the office bearers were still anxious to keep Kyaruzi, Tsere and Mwapachu out. So they applied for T.A.G.S.A. membership, hoping that it could be put on a proper footing. To find out in what shape it was, they asked to see its books. Heavy with dust, they were produced for them.

'When I established that T.A.G.S.A. had Shs/- 27,000 in the bank,' Dr. Kyaruzi has recalled, 'I was asked to take office. I refused with thanks, as by then things had begun to move ahead with T.A.A.'

They had again written to the Secretary saying that they wished to join T.A.A. although their previous approach had been turned down for reasons which were by no means clear. This time there was a prompt answer: apply for membership. They did. Then: subscribe for a full year. They did. Then all of them were again turned down.

Dr Kyaruzi has told the rest of the story:

The leaders who wanted to keep me and my friends out–they called us trouble makers–advertised in March, 1950, in the *Tanganyika Standard* that new elections had been held in T.A.A. They did not know that one of their secretaries, James Mkande, was secretly an important member of the Action Group. Hamza Mwapachu, then a welfare officer in Dar-es-Salaam, had asked his boss's permission to explain the meaning of the Constitution to Africans. This man did not relish the idea of an African addressing the people, so he suggested that his father-in-law, Mr Russell, a European lawyer practising in Dar-es-Salaam, should speak about it. Hamza agreed and called a meeting, although he did not advertise it in the *Tanganyika Standard*.

Then Mr Russell had a talk with the Governor. No one knows for certain what passed between them, but at the meeting Mr Russell did not even mention the Constitution. Instead, he compared British rule to German rule and to chiefly rule. . . .

Gloom and disappointment settled on the hall. As the audience was moving out, a member of the Action Group called Schneider, a South African Moslem, suddenly shouted: 'Stop–stop–don't go out . . .'

Everyone stopped as in a pantomime.

Schneider was no intellectual, he was not even very intelligent, but

being brave and bold, he went on shouting: 'Just a moment. Think. We
are members of T.A.A. We have a Constitutional Committee moving
about the country. What have we to say? How will we express our views
before the Committee?'

The effect was electric. Everyone talked at once. Then a voice
was heard above the rest: 'Let's meet on Sunday and decide what to
do!'

T.A.A.'s President could but agree. Dr Kyaruzi and his friends
then instructed James Mkande, who was naturally present,
promptly to insert a notice in the *Tanganyika Standard*, calling a
meeting for the following Sunday at the T.A.A. headquarters in
New Street. Should the President subsequently remonstrate for
not having been consulted on the proposed advertisement,
Mkande was to reply: 'You agreed to the meeting being held,
how could this have been done without advertising it?'

Now the Action Group had to decide on crucial strategy. The
stakes were high. If they could not achieve office in T.A.A.,
they could not present their memorandum on the Constitution.
If the memorandum was accepted, but if its authors could not
discuss its contents with the members of the Committee, half of
their purpose would have been nullified. In other words, they *had*
to take over T.A.A.

In planning the next moves, again Luciano Tsere proved the
master mind. He regarded this as a case in which the end justified
the means; consequently his aim was to take advantage of the constitutional forms, or rather the lack of them. The tactics he suggested and which his friends enthusiastically accepted, were
plainly opportunist. They agreed that if the President and other
T.A.A. officials failed to turn up, they should be ousted. Not one
of them came. Having waited nearly an hour, Dr Kyaruzi put the
decisive question: 'Have the members confidence in officials who
do not attend a properly called and advertised meeting?'

There were tumultuous shouts: 'No–no–no . . .'

Dr Tsere cautiously advised: 'Whatever you do, it must be
strictly constitutional.' Turning to James Mkande, he asked the
pre-arranged question: 'Mr Secretary, when you were elected
this year, was it at a General Meeting?'

'There was no meeting, certainly none called or advertised,'
Mkande said, shaking his head in mock distress. 'I was just told
to take on the job.'

'Then you were not constitutionally elected,' Dr Tsere stated gravely with his tongue firmly in his cheek. 'What's more, without a General Meeting, this year's President, Chairman and other officers were not properly elected either. In fact, there are no Officers at all!'

Wild cheers greeted this statement. Then it was agreed that the 'non officers' should be informed in writing. That is when the Action Group realised that it had no money, not even a few shillings to buy stationery and stamps. . . .

Again Dr. Tsere had a bright idea. 'Before you elect your officers, you must become members,' he said. 'Pay your subscriptions against receipts, then you can vote.'

This done, the new members wanted him to become President, but as his transfer to Tanga Province was pending, he would not stand. Dr Vedast Kyaruzi was unanimously elected in his place.

Now the memorandum's fate was secure. But even T.A.A. aegis was not enough. The nationalists had to have age on their side too, partly because the backing of elders mattered so much to Africans, partly because some British listeners might have ignored the memorandum as the work merely of some young African demagogues. So the Action Group invited four very old Moslem Africans to become their sponsors and coached them on what to say. The sheiks learnt their parts with alacrity.

Roping in four old figureheads to lend an air of respectability to the proceedings was, perhaps, disingenuous. It is remarkable how instinctively the young nationalists picked up the ways of certain politicians in the Western world.

At last the great day dawned. On June 8, 1950, they filed into the hall where the Committee was sitting. The sheiks led the way, resplendent in ceremonially tied turbans, flowing beards and loose robes. Behind them walked Dr. Kyaruzi, his round face smiling. Hamza Mwapachu and Steven Mhando brought up the rear. Dr Tsere, whose help had been so vital in drafting the memorandum, was not there, as he had already been transferred to Tanga Province.

When they were all seated, the sheiks bowed with immense dignity to the Chairman, Sir Charles Mathew, Attorney-General of Tanganyika, and said in Swahili: 'Sir, we would like our boys to tell you in your language what we want. We agree with everything they are going to say.'

Dr. Kyaruzi was the chief spokesman, who explained to Sir Charles in English that they wanted no more discrimination and intended to practise none. 'We want Europeans also to be elected and to sit on the Councils with us.'

Sir Charles turned to the elders: 'Are you prepared to sit down with Europeans?'

'Why not?' the sheiks cried, raising their eyebrows. 'Why not?'

Sir Charles looked at them as though wanting to say something, but never articulated his thought, whatever it may have been. He accepted the African memorandum as it stood. This triumph was further enhanced by the fact that the Tanganyika European Council and the Asian Council were told to re-write their memoranda.

One amusing moment of the hearing was when Steven Mhando told Sir Charles: 'Sir, you have heard that we want elections. You haven't asked how we propose to carry them out with a largely illiterate population?'

'Well, how will you do it?'

'We will have different colours for different candidates, or different trees; in that way everyone can identify his candidate.'

In the 1962 presidential election on the voting slips Nyerere was represented by a round black disk; his opponent, Zuberi Mtemwu, by a lion. Despite careful instructions, some Nyerere supporters put their crosses against the lion, as they could not believe that the emblem of the ruler of the animal kingdom was not Nyerere's emblem!

On the morning of their appearance before the Committee, the Action Group held its last war council. It was then that Dr Kyaruzi told his friends: 'You know, our main trouble is that we have done nothing to excite the popular mind. People regard us as plain dull. We must give them and Government something to think about!'

Hamza Mwapachu had a prompt remedy: they were to spread a rumour that, unless T.A.A.'s demand for fifty-one per cent of the Legco seats was conceded, a general strike would be called. They quickly wrote a leaflet to this effect and pressed a copy into the hands of a Special Branch man who had kept uncomfortably close to them. He believed what he read; the colourful report he submitted to his superiors caused quite a flutter in government circles.

*　　*　　*

While the Constitutional Committee was collecting evidence an extraordinary episode took place in Arusha, in the Northern Province.

The then Minister of State for Colonial Affairs in the Labour Government, John Dugdale, visited East Africa. Before leaving London, he had already made it plain that he would go to no place where Africans were unwelcome. Staying at Government House, Nairobi, he refused an invitation to lunch at the New Stanley Hotel because it did not admit Africans. When assured that the luncheon would be held in a private room with Africans present, he made public the reason why he had changed his mind.

From Nairobi, Mr and Mrs John Dugdale drove by car to Arusha, where a Greek settler was giving a party for them. Unfortunately, they were involved in a motor car accident, which made them two hours late. The other guests had been there a long while when they finally arrived. While the Greek hostess introduced them, Mr Dugdale had the impression that no one in the room desired to talk to him, that people actually turned away when he was shaking hands. Finally, one white settler did speak.

'What is all this nonsense about you not going to places without Africans?' he asked bluntly. 'I for my part would rather sit down with my pigs than to eat with an African.'

John Dugdale turned on his heels and stumped out of the house, followed by his greatly embarrassed wife, the Provincial Commissioner and his wife, and the Greek lady who begged him, on the verge of tears, to stay. But he was adamant, although, to make matters worse, the P.C.'s chauffeur had gone off to have his meal and the Dugdales had to hang around the drive until the car turned up.

The Action Group had by then been dissolved, but its old members were jubilant when they heard about John Dugdale's stand. Here was a man, a Socialist, who understood their feelings, their pride, their ambitions. They could not wait for his arrival in Dar-es-Salaam.

As soon as news reached them that he was at Government House, Dr Kyaruzi asked for an appointment on behalf of the T.A.A. spokesmen. The time and place were communicated to them by letter, which they found in the T.A.A. box–three hours before the appointed time. In Dr Kyaruzi's words;

We arranged a hurried meeting of the Executive Committee; we collected three parts of the memorandum we had prepared for Mr Dugdale and which had been written by different people. We managed to put these parts together just before Mr Dugdale arrived and presented our memorandum to him. But there were so many errors in the hurriedly typed text that we had to send a corrected copy by air the following week. Mr Dugdale was very sympathetic towards our aspirations.

*　　*　　*

The Makerere nationalists, led by Dr Vedast Kyaruzi, had taken two important steps forward. Linking up with the nationalists among the ex-servicemen, they had bridged the gap between intellectuals and ordinary, unsophisticated Africans. Together they had, for the first time, publicly voiced African demands. Among thinking Tanganyikans this had created a deep impression. Now they dared to believe that events were on the march. In view of this wonderful result, small blemishes like the opportunist tactics they had employed either seemed justified or were forgotten. A few men were proud of such cunning.

CHAPTER 19

Nyerere Prepares for the Future

WHILE the young nationalists in Dar-es-Salaam were involved in their first political venture, their compatriots in other parts of the country were working at their jobs and founding families. Julius Nyerere, following in the footsteps of his friend Andrew Tibandebage, was about to become a schoolmaster at St Mary's College, Tabora.

Father Richard Walsh, Director of St Mary's, has an important place in the great record of the White Fathers in East Africa. Not only did he love and understand his pupils, but he had the supreme gift of evaluating their characters and abilities, and of inspiring them to prepare for their future roles as leaders of Tanganyika.

One day, Tibandebage remembers, Father Walsh was talking to the boys about developments in Egypt since 1936 and they were not particularly interested.

'Boys,' he concluded on a crescendo note, 'bear in mind what I've told you. You'll have to head the independence struggle in Tanganyika. Then you'll have to hold important positions. You'll have to become the leaders of the Tanganyikan people.'

The class sat up. This was different from other lectures. No one else had said such things to them. It is understandable, that, at times, the British administration had misgivings about the teachings of this particular missionary.

In 1945, when Julius Nyerere had obtained his Diploma in Education at Makerere, Tibandebage asked Father Walsh to invite his friend to teach at St Mary's. At first the Director was unenthusiastic, as he had reservations about Tabora Government School boys. But Tibandebage insisted and, as he was still busy turning St Mary's into the first Catholic secondary school, Father Walsh gave in.

To be correct, he asked the headmaster of the Government School for his approval to approach young Nyerere. The reply was a polite agreement, in the belief that Nyerere would turn down the poor pay of a mere £6. 5s. a month, when an African teacher at a Government school earned more than twice this amount. (A European teacher earned £36 a month.)

The Headmaster and the education authorities were much put out when Nyerere accepted Father Walsh's offer. They told him that his years of work at St Mary's would count neither in his promotion, nor in his pension, and that he was spoiling a promising teaching career. Nyerere's reply was: 'If that is so, if there is such a discrepancy between salaries and promotions of Government teachers and mission teachers, I shall have to fight for the rights of the mission teachers.'

He taught history and biology in the top forms, and his pupils gave a good account of themselves. He was one of the first Africans to read science. Also interested in botany, he put little plates on trees in the mission grounds bearing their Latin and African names. His original ideas impressed everyone, yet he was modest and exercised rigorous self-discipline.

Father Stanley, who eight years later was to succeed Father Walsh as Director, was a fervent exponent of physical training and one day asked for volunteers. Nyerere volunteered and after Mass, but before breakfast, did Father Stanley's exercises for all to see. As this was during the rainy season, he took off his shoes and socks, and performed barefoot. He wanted to prove to the boys that one need not lose face even if one did a comic-looking thing in public. The purpose mattered, not the appearance.

Within a week of his arrival, Father Walsh had become his friend. Their relationship deepened over the years and the President of Tanganyika still appreciates an occasional piece of advice from the Second Assistant to the Superior General of the White Fathers, as Father Walsh now is, at the headquarters of the order in Rome.

Julius was an excellent teacher [Father Walsh has recalled]. He had a real gift for funnelling knowledge into the heads of his pupils. He first showed his metal by his prompt defence of a fellow teacher, Joseph Kasella, who had been given a raw deal. Here was a potential leader, who would act with force whenever he believed a principle was at stake. Kasella was reinstated and Julius scored his first success against the Colonial Administration.

Although he worked conscientiously as a teacher, Nyerere's mind was more than ever concentrated on political problems. Soon after his arrival he joined the Tabora T.A.A., and at its next general meeting was elected Treasurer.

'It was my determination to restore T.A.A. to life,' he has told the author, 'and to use it as a means to further the awakening of the Tanganyika Africans to fight for independence.'

He also made a great impression on the boys at Tabora Government School, where he was frequently invited to participate in debates, usually having Mr Blumer as his opponent.

From among the boys at Tabora, a special tribute to Nyerere's skill in debate has come from Michael Lukumbuzya, the youthful chief of the Ukerewe, who had inherited his position, as a small boy, and gone to primary school with two bodyguards. These not only protected him against possible assassination, but did his chores and, in good feudal fashion, suffered his punishments for him. At Tabora, Mr Blumer guaranteed Lukumbuzya's safety, sent the bodyguards packing and made him rough it like other boys. To this day, Michael Lukumbuzya, now Permanent Head of the Foreign Ministry in Dar-es-Salaam is resentful of the corporal punishment he had to endure because of the democratic Mr Blumer.

As a good nationalist, Lukumbuzya approved the political views expressed by Nyerere. As a young aristocrat, he was at pains to point out that Nyerere too was the son of a chief. And he also welcomed Nyerere's bettering Mr Blumer in debate, probably as vicarious revenge for his own unwelcome chastisement.

We all knew about Julius, we all admired him, we all hoped to meet him [he has told the author]. He was reserved and modest, and it was not easy to get at him. We used to look forward to any meeting of the School Debating Society when he had been invited to participate. My first impression of him is indelible: he was tiny, terribly thin, he wore shorts and a short-sleeved shirt. He seemed no older than his pupils, but when he began to speak, something happened. It was thrilling to hear him develop his arguments.

While Nyerere was still teaching at St Mary's College, his political activities provoked one incident which was significant because it was the first occasion when young Africans of the same generation clashed on the nationalist issue almost in hatred.

In 1947, when the East African High Commission was set up, the nationalists were indignant. They feared domination by Kenya white settlers and the introduction of methods which, thanks to Sir Donald Cameron, had never been practiced in Tanganyika. When Colonial Paper 191, which proposed equal representation for the three communities in the Central Assembly of the three

Territories was replaced by Colonial Paper 210, setting out much less favourable terms for Africans and Asians,[1] Nyerere, with the help of Tibandebage, at once organised several T.A.A. meetings in Tabora in protest. The T.A.A.'s first large meeting in Dar-es-Salaam had the same purpose. (By then the T.A.A. had many branches in the Lake, Northern, Eastern and Tanga Provinces, members paying an annual subscription of 6s. In 1947 and in 1948, these branches held provincial conferences in Mwanza.)

Nyerere and Tibandebage then heard that Chief David Makwaia, one of the two African Legco Members, was passing through Tabora on his way to the Legco debate on Colonial Paper 210. Nyerere, accompanied by Chief Harun Lugusha, went to the railway station to impress on Makwaia their grave misgivings about the vital paper. They recalled the general opposition of Africans in East Africa to any form of Closer Union and reminded him, in particular, of the resentment felt by Tanganyikans at the injustice of the proposals contained in Paper 210. They left Makwaia in no doubt as to the views of the Tabora branch of the African Association and assured him that these were shared at headquarters. Nyerere declared that this issue above all offered the ideal opportunity for Makwaia to make a rousing speech in the forthcoming debate.

When the train steamed out, Nyerere and Lugusha were confident that Makwaia would voice their views. They were equally confident that Chief Abdiel Shangali, the other African Legco Member, would no less speak on their behalf, since in April, 1946, at the annual conference of T.A.A. held in Dar-es-Salaam, as chairman, he had roundly denounced the whole idea of Closer Union as embodied in the earlier Paper 191. They assumed, therefore, that it could be taken for granted that Shangali would be bitterly opposed to the even less justifiable politics of Paper 210.

When Nyerere and his associates learnt from the *Tanganyika Standard* that in the crucial debate the two African Legco Members had remained neutral and abstained from voting, their fury knew no bounds. As though to rub salt into their wounds, summing up for the Government J. E. S. Lamb said that the silence and abstention of the two African Members could be interpreted as indicating their tacit acceptance of Paper 210.

No one cared that the two African votes could, in any event,

[1] See above, Chapter 13, pp. 135–9.

have made no difference to the outcome. Makwaia and Shangali had betrayed the African side and with Julius Nyerere this counted more than anything else.

In his own defence Makwaia put forward the arguments that the Tanganyika delegation to the Central Legislative Assembly included an African member and that the first meeting of the Assembly saw the introduction of income tax in all three Territories as a Common Service. For Nyerere this was nothing but a piece of face saving.

*   *   *

As early as 1946 Nyerere told Father Walsh: 'I'm dissatisfied with my education, I must improve myself by continuing my studies.'

'In that case we will send you to the U.K. to study,' the Director replied.

'I'm not ready,' Nyerere shook his head, 'there is a lot more reading I must do. . . .' He wanted to pass the London matriculation examination before going to Britain. This he eventually did, biology being his best subject, but not until 1948.

When Father Walsh offered him a scholarship for a second time, he again refused saying: 'I don't want it because I don't know how I'll come back. . . .' He was afraid that such a long stay in Britain might damage his African roots, and he would not accept anything that might make him less African. It was only when Father Walsh pointed out that this danger was removed by the very fact that he already sensed it that Nyerere was able to resolve his moral doubts.

One practical obstacle remained to the fulfilment of young Nyerere's educational aspirations: how was he, while in Britain, to support his family and in particular the girl he wanted to marry, Maria Gabriel?

Maria was the daughter of Gabriel Magige, a venerable African elder, whose son Joseph has become a land surveyor. Gabriel and his wife, Anna, were of the Msimbiti tribe, both from Kinesi, in the North Mara District. He was among the first five Msimbiti to be baptised at Butuli mission, now called Kowak mission. Gabriel and Anna then moved to Komuge mission, to work among the Msimbiti people. He is buried within the mission precincts; Anna still lives and lends a hand with mission work.

Her parents sent Maria to the White Sisters' Girls' School at Sumve, near Mwanza, where after eight years tuition she obtained a teacher's certificate, becoming the first woman teacher of her tribe. She was well known and much admired in her part of the country. Although an educated woman and a teacher, she helped her family, working in the fields like any African peasant woman. She had many suitors, but she only thought of the young teacher called Julius Nyerere. He wrote often from Tabora and she knew that he did not take out other girls.

Once again, Father Walsh came to the rescue. The scholarship he obtained for Nyerere included a grant for his widowed mother, Mugaya, for his brother, Chief Wanzagi, and for his fiancée, Maria.

When his scholarship was approved, Nyerere came to Musoma and proposed to Maria. During the Christmas holidays of 1948, they became formally engaged. He found the customary dowry, six head of cattle, by arranging the marriage of the girl his father had bought for him. Her prospective husband paid six head of cattle for her and these Nyerere passed on to Maria's parents. Father W. Collins of the Maryknoll mission drew up the documents; it was also arranged that he would receive the scholarship grant through St Mary's College, Tabora, and divide it between Julius' mother, eldest brother and Maria.

In April, 1949, Julius Nyerere at length arrived in Britain. Under the terms of his scholarship, he was to study biology and at the Colonial Office he was told to go to Durham University. He had a long argument with well meaning officials to whom he tried to explain that he had done as much science as he needed to. He wanted to take an arts degree. The officials objected that he was not qualified for that course. Then one suggested that he should study Arabic. Nyerere could see no point to that. At this moment David D. Carmichael, Welfare Officer for Edinburgh, walked into the room and wanted to know what all the talk was about.

Nyerere outlined his problem and Carmichael said: 'Why don't you come to Gordon College, Aberdeen? If your English is not good enough, we'll have you tutored. Later you can go over to Edinburgh.'

This plan worked. In October, 1949, Nyerere enrolled himself at Edinburgh University for the Ordinary Degree of Master of Arts. In a letter to George Shepperson, then a lecturer in history and now Professor of Commonwealth and American History at Edinburgh University, he has since explained why he did not attempt an honours degree.

A reasonable application made certain that I would collect my pass certificates. I had never intended to pursue a strenuous course of studies and the subjects I chose enabled me to get a fairly broad one without bothering too much about the details of a specialist. Had I the inclination to take an honours degree, I should have liked to take one in philosophy. (*Gazette of Edinburgh University*, October, 1960, pp. 22–6.)

He chose as his subjects British History, English, Moral Philosophy, Political Economy, Social Anthropology, Constitutional Law and Economic History. From his marks and from comments by those who taught him, it is evident that he was an able student. His tutor in British History often commented that his English style was the best in the group, having a polish unusual not only in a foreigner, but also in a British student.

As a result of my choice of subjects, I found that I had ample time to read many other things outside my degree course, and I did [Nyerere has written to Professor Shepperson]. I also spent much time arguing with fellow students about everything under the sun, except Marxism which is above the sun. I did a great deal of thinking about politics in Africa. . . . I evolved the whole of my political philosophy while I was there. I wrote an MS on race and politics in East Africa . . . in which I expressed for myself what I have since been trying to put into practice.

This MS is written in long hand, in a small, taut script, closely filling forty-four pages of an old University of Edinburgh copybook. Its title is: *The Race Problem in East Africa*, and it is divided into five parts.

In Part I, *The Problem Stated*, Nyerere said: 'Our problem is of living together in harmony and mutual respect.' Yet there were grave signs that racial hatred was beginning to reign in East Africa, including Tanganyika, although it was fashionable to say that racialism was exclusively a Kenya disease. 'Hatred exists on both sides and it cannot be cured by hypocrisy.'

The interpretation of the racial problem was completely different on the European and on the African side.

Africans did not question the whites' right to stay. 'I have yet to meet an African who really believes that to achieve our common goal in East Africa the non-African races must be liquidated, or relegated to a place of secondary importance. . . . What we claim is the right to be masters of our own fate.'

Against this the whites were saying that they would either dominate Africa, or they would leave. This was the basis of Dr Malan's *Apartheid* theory.

In Part II, *The Root of the Problem*, Nyerere asserted:

The real cause of racial hatred is racial discrimination in order to protect the vested interests of one race and to exploit the other race. These are political and economic causes, not as many say, cultural ones. . . . We resent the idea that the power to shape the destiny of our country should be exclusively vested in the hands of an alien and minority group which is sworn to use such power to maintain its own privileged position and to keep us for ever in a state of inferiority in our own country.

To prove his point, he quoted not only Dr Malan, but Sir Godfrey Huggins, who had said: 'Every step in the industrial and social pyramid must be open to the African except only–and always–the very top.'

Nyerere's retort was: 'Africa is our own and only inheritance. . . . It is our main duty to recover its control from those who have grabbed it from us.'

In Part III, *Segregation and European Domination*, he summed up his views in one paragraph: 'It is my firm belief that the solution to our problem ultimately depends upon the distribution of political control . . . upon the acceptance by all communities concerned of the principle of social, economic and, above all, political equality.'

All the schemes so far submitted for a solution of the racial problem had assumed that the white man had the right to rule Africa. Nyerere quoted at length the latest resolution passed by the Tanganyika European Council, which demanded: 'The European community must have elected representation on the Legislative Council, and the number of seats allocated to them shall not be less than half of those held by non-official members.'

As Europeans alone formed the official majority in Legco, this ensured their domination of Tanganyika. By claiming on top of that at least fifty per cent of the unofficial seats, they in fact claimed a preponderant majority for 17,000 Europeans, against seven million Africans and 80,000 Asians.

In Part IV, *Racial Equality*, Nyerere argued that, except for Africa, where Europeans found themselves in a minority, numbers always counted in representation. 'We reject the principle of equal representation on the same ground on which we condemn European domination,' for it amounted, in a different form, to the same principle of racial superiority. 'It assumes that in East Africa 50,000 Europeans, because they happen to be Europeans, are equal to 17,000,000 Africans; that their inferiority in numbers is made up for by their superiority in wealth, intelligence, moral virtue and colour.'

In Part V, *The Will of the People*, Nyerere came to the point bluntly:

Our quarrel boils down to the simple question: 'Who are the people of East Africa?' . . . The Europeans and the Africans are the people of East Africa. For a small white minority to come to our country and to tell us that they are the people of the country and that we are not, is one of those many insults which I think we have swallowed for too long. The sooner we tell the Europeans that we will no longer tolerate such monstrous impudence the better for us all. . . . The Africans' capacity for bearing insult is not limitless. The day may come when someone may want to incite them. How easy it is to inflame an insulted people! I shudder when I think of the terrible possibility, but it will not be a mere possibility if our White Neighbours insist on this vulgar doctrine of the Divine Right of Europeans and refuse to live like 'ordinary sort of fellows'. Such a doctrine may have to be uprooted with all the vulgarity of a bloody revolution. I say this in perfect honesty. . . . A day may come when the people will prefer death to insult and woe to the people who will see that day! Woe to them who will make that day inevitable!

Nyerere however did not end on this sombre note. Throughout his essay he hinted at an alternative, possible in Tanganyika, which he now spelt out:

We must build up a society in which we shall belong to East Africa and not to our racial groups. And I appeal to my fellow Africans to take the initiative in this building up of a harmonious society. The Europeans have had the initiative and all the opportunities for over two hundred years and everywhere they have succeeded in producing interracial chaos. We have a great chance in East Africa. Let us use it well.

Implied in this dignified appeal was the conviction that, with the type of Europeans living in Tanganyika, this peaceful solution could succeed.

It is a pity that because of its length, the Fabian Society could not see its way to publish Nyerere's essay in its colonial series. It could have been cut without interfering with its logical sequence. In that case Twining's Administration would have known not only the main principles of Nyerere's future platform, but also his reaction to racial parity, which he called just another disguise for racial superiority. One passage, in particular, should have given the Governor food for thought:

Africa is for the Africans, and the other races cannot be more than respected minorities. . . . Should it come to a bitter choice between being perpetually dominated by a white or an Indian minority and between driving that minority out of East Africa, no thinking African would hesitate to make the latter choice. (Pp. 7 and 8 of MS.)

It is revealing of Nyerere's character that he did not talk about his ideas at Edinburgh. His contemporaries do not remember him as a student politician. Those who were in touch with him describe him with such phrases as 'quiet and unassuming'. He kept his political ideas to himself, although when in 1950 the proposal to federate the Rhodesias and Nyasaland was made public, he addressed Scottish groups on the problems of Central Africa. No record of these speeches seems to be in existence, but the general impression was that he was critical of the proposal, unless democratic institutions were first established in the territories concerned. The prediction that the Federation would fall apart unless based on African support has since come to pass.

Of the many friends Nyerere made in Edinburgh, Professor George Shepperson has told the author: 'I have made it my business to check with all the people who knew him at the University. In my mind there is no doubt that three things stand out about this period of his life: his remarkable good humour, his linguistic fluency and his definite interest in every academic subject he tackled.'

During the first week of his stay in Edinburgh, he was taken to visit Mrs Jean Wilson, who had spent seven years of her life in Angola, where her husband had been a missionary doctor. Throughout his career at the university, Nyerere came to look upon Mrs Wilson's house as a home and for her part Mrs Wilson welcomed him as one of the family.

When Nyerere invited Mrs Wilson to the Tanganyika Independence celebrations, the Press erroneously reported that she had been his landlady. When she tried to correct this mis-statement, telling reporters that he had never at any time lived at her house, they replied: 'It doesn't make such a good story now.'

He lived at the British Council Residence, although Mrs Wilson and her son took him to spend Christmas with their relatives. He stood up well to the rigours of the Scottish climate and never complained about the cold. 'But then he never did complain,' was Mrs Wilson's conclusion.

During his three years in Scotland, Nyerere wrote regularly to Father Walsh. Unfortunately these letters, revealing the mental struggle this young African endured, have been lost. This is a great pity, for they portrayed the effect a British university, British surroundings and British friends had on a sensitive, receptive African mind. Still, Father Walsh remembers the main problems which occupied Nyerere's mind.

He was torn by a personal dilemma of how to serve his country without becoming egotistically prominent. He thought for a while that he should become a priest. When he had become a bishop—for he never doubted that he would reach an eminent position—he would have a chance to give spiritual leadership. After months of struggle with himself, he realised he had no vocation for the priesthood; besides, there had to be a popular movement. He felt it had to be a non-racial movement, although in Africa it had to be led by Africans. In other words, his non-racial movement had yet to be a racial movement. Here was another dilemma. . . .

Nyerere was also deeply preoccupied with the consideration that the money which the Tanganyika Government was spending on his education was so much money taken away from the impoverished educational system in Tanganyika. He once calculated that with the money spent on him, two or three schools could have been built and staffed.

How conscious he was of the importance of the money spent on him is borne out by a letter he wrote prior to going to Edinburgh, to the Editors of *Makerere*, the publication of Uganda's University College. They published it in their first issue, in November, 1946:

Sirs,
The Dean of the College was kind enough to forward to the old students of the College a copy of the speech made by the Under-

H

Secretary of State for the Colonies, Mr Creech Jones, when he visited Makerere on the 30th July.

The Secretary of State told the students that they are enjoying a precious gift which masses of the people outside would like to share. I feel that this is a true statement of a plain fact. But I must confess that although while I was at Makerere I had some idea that I was somehow more fortunate than the great masses of my people, yet that statement would have meant nothing or very little to me while I was still at the College; far less, in fact, than it does today.

While I was at Makerere I understood that my Government was spending annually something in the neighbourhood of £80 on my behalf. But that did not mean very much to me: after all, £80 is only a minute fraction of the total amount which is collected every year from the African tax-payers. But today that £80 has grown to mean a very great deal to me. It is not only a precious gift but a debt that I can never repay.

I wonder whether it has ever occurred to many of us that while that £80 was being spent on me (or for that matter on any other of the past or present students of Makerere) some village dispensary was not being built in my village or some other village. People may actually have died through lack of medicine merely because eighty pounds which could have been spent on a fine village dispensary were spent on me, a mere individual, instead. Because of my presence at the College (and I never did anything to deserve Makerere) many Aggreys and Booker Washingtons remained illiterate for lack of a school to which they could go because the money which could have gone towards building schools was spent on Nyerere, a rather foolish and irresponsible student at Makerere. My presence at the College, therefore, deprived the community of the services of all those who might have been trained at those schools, and who might have become Aggreys or Booker Washingtons. How can I ever repay this debt to the community?

But why did the community spend all that money, run all those risks and miss all those chances of schooling? Was it for the sake of building a magnificent but useless apex of a stagnant pyramid? Surely not. The community spends all that money upon us because it wants us as lifting levers, and as such we must remain below and bear the whole weight of the masses to be lifted, and we must facilitate that task of lifting.

'And if this gift has come to you, when you go out from College devote yourself to the service of your people and do not regard education as something which is for your own individual advancement only,' said Mr Creech Jones. And that reminds me of a short but remarkable speech which was given to the boys and staff of the Government School, Tabora, by Dr Lamont. He likened education to a pair of spectacles: it enables those who have it to see things more clearly than they would have done without it. And he likened the educated person to the eyes: the eyes are not important in themselves, but merely in what they can do for the body. The educated man is not important in himself; his importance lies in what he can do for the community of which he is a member. That analogy will always be with me, and will always make me realise my unworthiness to the community.

We old students envy the present generation at Makerere both for having heard Mr Creech Jones and also for having Dr Lamont as their Principal. May I end by quoting the former once again?

'I hope that this message has gone home to you – do share in the work of your people and don't regard toil as a thing to be done for you. You cannot go forward unless prepared for hard work yourselves . . . '

Yours etc.,
Julius K. Nyerere

St Mary's School,
Tabora, Tanganyika.

Another problem which deeply concerned Nyerere in Edinburgh was his discovery of Communist sympathies among African students. They were rife in colleges and universities all over Britain, especially around Edinburgh. He attended several meetings and was shocked to discover that Catholics were among the most vociferous African antagonists of mission work. He was equally shocked that the British authorities had no understanding of this problem and its implications.

In July, 1952, Julius Nyerere obtained a good pass degree, thus becoming the first Tanganyikan M.A. and the first African of political importance at Edinburgh to study any subject other than medicine. Then he got a six weeks' travelling scholarship from the British Council. In September he met Father Walsh in London and they discussed the advantages or otherwise of Nyerere continuing his studies to get another degree, this time in law. He told Father Walsh spontaneously that he would interrupt his scholarship journey and repay the British Council the money he had received. Eventually he decided to return to Tanganyika and to teach in the new college of St Francis, Pugu, since the top classes of St Mary's, Tabora, had been transferred there.

As to what his years in Britain did for Julius Nyerere, Father Walsh summed up in this way:

Julius had the advantage of receiving all his basic political education from one school of thought. Unlike many Africans, he was not bothered by a cacophony of directives and siren cooings from friends of Tanganyika and Africa, whose existence he had scarcely been aware of a year or two ago. He was big enough to be able not only to assimilate what his teachers said and did, but as he went along, to adapt it so that it could also be assimilated by an ordinary African. He was politically minded from birth because of the colonial regime. He wanted answers to such questions as to why his country was not free, why there was a colonial administration, why his people—and in a wider sense the African people—were centuries behind the Europeans. The answers he found in the Catholic faith and in the teaching at Edinburgh did not clash, and did not confuse him.

Nyerere practically continued Father Walsh's trend of thought when he told the author:

One wanted, from the earliest days of one's life, to get rid of the foreigners, that is why, for thinking Africans, there was no alternative but to be politically minded, and at one point or another, to become politically active. On my return in 1952 from Scotland, I was determined to go into politics, in fact to make politics my career.

Nyerere took none of his European fellow students at Edinburgh into his confidence. Nor even did he trust himself to an African. Seemingly mild and just interested in his career, he yet during his years in Britain laid the foundations for his political credo. His unpublished essay on the racial problem, written as a young student in Edinburgh, remains as his political testament for all to read.

CHAPTER 20

The Meru Case

IN Tanganyikan memory 1951 will always stand out as the year of the Meru evictions. Yet there were other events of importance. That same year the first African was appointed to the Executive Council; also in that year the Constitutional Committee published its report, based on the one–one–one principle, the cause of so much controversy.

The Meru affair served as a catalyst in the early 1950s, providing a rallying point for forces which were in existence, but had hitherto lacked cohesion and purpose. Also, for the first time, it enabled a Tanganyikan, as inhabitant of a Trust Territory, to speak up before the United Nations.

To understand this episode in perspective, it is necessary to go back seventy years. At the end of the last century, when German settlers occupied the fertile slopes of Mounts Meru and Kilimanjaro, they also occupied the saddle linking the two, known as the Sanya Corridor, which was a Masai grazing area. The German Government granted them freehold rights, thus creating 'an iron ring of alienated land clamped round the native lands on the mountain'. (Report of the Arusha–Moshi Lands Commission, commonly known as the Wilson Report, p. 17).

The German settlers acquired their land from the Meru, Arusha and Chagga chiefs by signed agreements, and, probably, personal gifts not mentioned in writing. It is likely that the chiefs were glad to put Europeans into the Sanya Corridor, unhealthily close to the Masai roaming the plains below. In theory these were perfectly legal arrangements, except that 'neither the chiefs nor the people understood fully that they were giving away the land for the permanent or exclusive use of Europeans'. (Ibid., p. 15.) Africans had always lived under communal tenure and knew none other. Their first misgivings arose at the end of the First World War, when they observed that the German farms were sold to Greek and British settlers. And by then, thanks to European protection, they were no longer afraid of the Masai.

About the same time, owing to increasing wealth, disease control and freedom from war and slavery, the Chagga, Meru and

Arusha tribes began increasing in numbers. With an influx of Africans from other parts of the country and even from across the border, the tribal homelands proved nothing like enough to satisfy the tribesmen's land hunger.

The British authorities were aware of all this in broad outline. That is why, in 1920, they retained twenty ex-enemy farms for African use. However, to quote the Wilson Report again:

> There would appear even then to have been no proper appreciation of the future land needs of the Arusha and Meru tribes and the re-alienation of the majority of the farms so thoughtlessly demarcated by the Germans proceeded without protest. An unparalleled opportunity for readjustment was lost. This was very soon realised but it was then too late. The farms had been sold and the ring was once more in place. (P. 17.)

In the 1930s, the British authorities bought a few pieces of land to make gaps in the ring, through which the Arusha could expand to lower lands outside it, 'but without any effort to organise such expansion or preparing the ground for it'. (Ibid.) They did nothing for the Meru, who bought Farm 31, near Engare Nanyuki in the Sanya Corridor, by public subscription organised by their chief. He himself put up most of the money for the purchase.

After the Second World War, the Government appointed Mr Justice Mark Wilson, Puisne Judge, as a one-man committee to make recommendations for the re-distribution of alienated and tribal land 'with a view of improving the homogeneity of both, and of affording relief to the congestion of the native population in tribal lands with particular reference to the question of providing them with adequate means of access to other areas'.

Wilson did a remarkable job. His very readable report is the only British recommendation which had far-reaching African support, especially among the Chagga.

Mr Justice Wilson recommended that both the European and the tribal lands should be consolidated. Meru who held land in the Sanya Corridor were to be moved; Chagga on Mount Kilimanjaro were to receive twenty-one thousand acres of formerly German lands and selected white settler leases were to revert to the tribesmen. Only the Masai were to receive nothing at all. . . .

In view of the population growth, the Wilson recommendations were mere palliatives, and of this the Judge was fully aware. He put the number of Chagga at 175,000, of Meru and Arusha at 50,000, but two years later the 1948 census showed that there were 230,655 Chagga and 78,810 Meru and Arusha. The only hope for a solution on both mountains lay in opening the way, physically and by improvements, to the large tracts below the European holdings. This was the crux of the Wilson Report. People abroad can be forgiven for overlooking this because of the unexpected uproar caused by Meru tribesmen in the Sanya Corridor.

Some ten miles from Farm 31, in the Kingori area, alternative farms had been staked out for the Meru, supplied with water for domestic and cattle use and with two cattle dips. The veterinary station and the Lutheran mission's dispensary from Engare Nanyuki had also been transferred to Kingori. Moreover, the Meru were offered about £14,000 cash compensation.

Neither Mr Justice Wilson, nor anyone else in authority, had foreseen the violent indignation of the tribesmen over moving, although the Lutheran pastor of Engare Nanyuki, E. R. Danielson, had written to the Provincial Commissioner on January 11, 1951, drawing his attention to the smouldering resentment among Africans who believed that European farmers were forcing the Goverment to remove them from their land. 'This resentment might cause trouble in years to come,' he added.

Danielson's letter was quietly pigeonholed. On this one important issue, the Wilson Report was out of touch with African feeling.

Three more factors helped to bedevil the situation. Between 1948 and 1951, the Government decided its policy on land alienation. It came to regard estate farming as an essential prop of the economy. As a result all ex-enemy lands, as well as some fresh ones, were allocated to Europeans, while only a few hundred acres of wheatland reverted to tribal use.

A logical outcome of this policy was the extension of leaseholds from thirty-three to ninety-nine years as essential for healthy, long term farm planning. Thirty-three years, little more than three planting cycles for sisal, was inimical to fertility conservation and the full capitalisation of farms. Leases marked down for reversion on expiry were now extended to ninety-nine years.

At this time, the political ferment, reflecting events described in the previous chapter, was affecting not only Africans in Dar-es-Salaam, but also in the Northern Highlands. The Arusha branch of T.A.A. took a radical stand on the Meru case. Its secretary, an African farmer called Kirillo Japhet, with a gift for articulating Meru feeling, formed the Meru Citizens' Union, which soon claimed eight thousand paid-up members. Its first objective was 'to stop the evictions' and eventually 'to remove all European settlers'. Japhet was goaded into a more and more radical course by Earle Seaton, a Jamaican lawyer who practised at Moshi. The newly elected Meru tribal council strongly censured the chief, who, while sole Native Authority, had agreed to surrender Farm 31 in the Sanya Corridor.

The British authorities took none of this very seriously. According to well established practice they held *barazas* to explain the reasons why the Meru had to move and the generous arrangements made for them at Kingori. The tribesmen seemed unwilling to appreciate the argument that the move was in the public interest and the new land they were being given was better than their old farm. They sent appeals to the Governor, to the Secretary of State for the Colonies and finally even to the United Nations.

As luck would have it, the 1951 U.N. Visiting Mission arrived just then in the Northern Highlands. Kirillo Japhet, with Earle Seaton as his interpreter, lobbied its members about the raw deal the Meru tribesmen had been given all along, and the new sufferings in store for them. The U.N. representatives advised him to petition the Trusteeship Council and also promised to include the case in their report. Before it was published, however, the Meru had been evicted.

The evictions took place between November 17 and December 12, 1951. According to the Government, 330 Meru taxpayers and their families, 1,000 men, women and children, were moved; 492 huts and store-houses burnt or destroyed; 400 cattle and 1,200 sheep impounded and removed to Kingori. In the first twelve days, twenty-five arrests were made and the Africans sentenced, from two weeks to six months imprisonment. According to the Meru all the figures were much higher.

Now the Meru agitation began in earnest. Japhet, with the aid of Seaton, petitioned the U.N. for permission to appear in person before the Trusteeship Council to plead the case. As he spoke little English, Seaton had to go with him as his interpreter, which meant two return tickets and funds for two peoples' stay in New York. Seaton, as a Jamaican, had a passport; Japhet, as a

Tanganyikan, had to obtain one from the British Authorities. On both counts, they went to T.A.A. for help.

At this time, T.A.A. had its own troubles. It had grown considerably, there were branches in every town of importance and it claimed five thousand members. But tribal associations had not disappeared and T.A.A. had little influence among rural Africans. It was loosely organised and lacked a precise programme. In March, 1951, Dr Kyaruzi had been transferred from the Sewa Haji Hospital in Dar-es-Salaam to the Morogoro Prison Hospital. Whatever the British official version, every African in the capital regarded this as retribution for his political activities. They were so indignant that the Government appealed to Dr Kyaruzi himself to reassure them that there was nothing unfair about his new appointment.

After Dr Kyaruzi's departure, things went badly for T.A.A. While he had been president, every letter and every minute had to be approved by him. This applied even to Steven Mhando, one of his cleverest supporters at the time of the T.A.A. take-over, and to Tom Marealle, a sophisticated, intelligent and witty young African.

The Marealles had been for two hundred years a ruling family of the Chagga, the most progressive and the wealthiest tribe in Tanganyika. Tom, the young head of the family, had obtained a social science diploma at the University College of Aberystwith in Wales, where he also learnt to speak perfect English. On his return, when working in the Social Welfare Department in Dar-es-Salaam, he joined T.A.A., becoming one of its secretaries.

A year later, in 1952, on the Governor's initiative, the Chagga were induced to revive the old institution of a single Paramount Chief. For a time, they had had three group chiefs, who quarrelled constantly, and administration had suffered. The older generation of Chagga tribesmen formed the Kilimanjaro Chagga Citizens' Union and put Tom Marealle up as their candidate for Paramount Chief. The Moshi T.A.A. branch, made up of younger and more radical elements, opposed their choice and took the name of the Chagga Congress. But the Citizens' Union overwhelmed and eventually absorbed the Congress. In 1952, Tom Marealle received over eighty per cent of the votes; in the course of an elaborate installation ceremony, the Governor, Sir Edward Twining, anointed him as Paramount Chief.

*

From then on, Twining relied on Tom Marealle's support, as he did on that of other important chiefs, like Adam Sapi and David Makwaia, who were friendly to the British. In 1953, when in London for Queen Elizabeth's coronation, Marealle had great success both in high society and on television. This may have gone to his head, for from then on he revealed his autocratic nature and alienated in particular the younger, educated Chagga. In October, 1959, when Tanu had already made great headway, another plebiscite was held, and Marealle was swept from office by an overwhelming majority. In 1963 he successfully sued the Chagga Council for compensation for losses suffered as a result of the cancellation of his life-election. But as Parliament passed, by means of a Certificate of Urgency, retroactive legislation that no chief could obtain compensation for losses suffered in connection with his de-stooling, Marealle was not paid any of the £43,000 awarded him by the Tanganyika High Court.

But in 1950–1, when all this was still in the distant future, Marealle was loyal to Dr Kyaruzi. Only when Kyaruzi had been transferred to Morogoro, did he try to establish a hold over T.A.A. Some people were impressed by Marealle, while others instinctively rallied around the nationalists. T.A.A. was split right down the middle.

Japhet, who was the energetic secretary of the Arusha branch, wrote to Dar-es-Salaam headquarters on behalf of his proposed journey to the United Nations with Seaton. Not much came of this officially, as Tom Marealle did not want to take sides. The Africans said, probably rightly, that he did not want to offend the British. But the nationalist section of T.A.A. decided to do something. They could not help financially, as T.A.A. only had £4. 7s. 6d. in its account at Barclays's Bank. A fund raising safari was the only answer.

It was arranged that Kirillo Japhet should meet Abbas Sykes at Dodoma and set out in the direction of Mwanza and Arusha. Their success was wholly unexpected. Even in tiny villages their meetings were well attended. Land, and the ownership of land, struck a sympathetic chord in African peasants. Many of these simple people did not have one penny, but promised to sell a calf or a goat and contribute its price to the fund enabling the Meru to go to far-away America 'for justice'. They were as good as their word and the money raised, supported by the contribution of the Meru

Citizens' Union, amounted to £350, a small fortune for Africans in those days.

The British Government maintained that the Meru case was a local issue, blown up out of all proportion to its realities. This was technically true. What the Administration failed to realise was the extent to which the land problem, as symbolised by Farm 31, had acted as a detonator, and the reason why it caused such a loud bang: the Meru had been evicted from land they had purchased with their own funds. Yet when Abbas Sykes, John Rupia and Dossa Aziz, the core of the T.A.A. nationalists in Dar-es-Salaam went to see the Chief Secretary and showed him the £350 they had raised, he waived any objection he may have had to Japhet's obtaining a passport. In typical bureaucratic fashion, having ensured that there was enough money for a return ticket and hence no danger of Japhet having to be repatriated at the public expense, his attitude became detached.

The Meru case was heard by the Trusteeship Council in July, 1952. In New York, Kirillo Japhet and his interpreter, Earle Seaton, were faced by Sir Edward Twining, who had come to defend the Government's action. The tall, imposing Governor and the young nationalist went for each other full tilt. Some wild, unsubstantiated accusations were flung at Twining, but he was equal to the occasion. Contrary to the general belief in Tanganyika, Seaton was not deported because of what he said in New York. He left of his own accord and is now living in the U.S.A.

In the autumn of 1952 the Meru case was taken to the General Assembly, where it failed to obtain a two-thirds majority. Even if it had, the British Administration would not have been bound by a resolution to restore Farm 31 to the evicted tribesmen. Later on, the Government tried to make amends by allowing some Meru to graze their cattle in the Sanya Corridor, provided they used the cattle dips and there was no danger of infection. But as the bulk of the white settlers with their ninety-nine year leases could not be dislodged, the Meru could not reoccupy their farms. Nothing less than that would have satisfied them and their bitterness remained a festering sore until Independence.

There were two strange aspects of this unfortunate affair. The white farmers at Engare Nanyuki had extraordinary bad luck. Their cattle died, their crops failed, their families fell ill. Of their own free will, they all decided that the time had come for them to leave, and bitterly regretted ever having settled there. Some suspected the Meru witch doctors of having extended their activities into fields in which they had not hitherto practiced.

The Lutherans complain to this day that the military, who assisted at the evictions, had turned one of their churches into a cookhouse and the story is generally accepted in Tanganyika. Yet there is no truth to it at all.

The evictions were effected by the police; the military, the keepers of the peace, were nowhere near the scene. The church had been abandoned by the Lutherans long before. It had no roof or doors, but was otherwise soundly built. The police were encamped four miles away. Even though the Lutheran leader, Dr Reusch, assured the D.C. and the Police Commander that, according to Lutheran tenets, these buildings were not hallowed things, these two experienced British civil servants would never have made such a gross error of tact as to use the abandoned church building. Many months later the military held manoeuvres near by and may have used it; or even the police, when in 1954 they were hunting Mau Mau on Mount Meru. If they did put a cookhouse into the ruin, this had no connection whatsoever with the Meru case.

Yet it would be difficult to convince either the Lutherans, or the Meru, or the Arusha or the Chagga, or any African, that the church at Engare Nanyuki had not been desecrated during the Meru evictions. This is an interesting illustration of how legends are created, especially when it suits people to have martyrdom, for without it there would have been no crusade.

The Masai also cursed the newcomers, and with some justification. They were left out in the cold without even a suggestion of compensation, although originally the Sanya Corridor had been their grazing land.

As the Meru case marked a new milestone in African nationalist awakening, it also opened the eyes of the British to the forces at work against them. Although the Governor underestimated their strength, he realised that some measures had to be taken to shore up the dykes against the beating waves of the rising political storm. Therefore he did two things.

He ordered the tightening up of a long standing departmental regulation, forbidding civil servants to become members of any political organisation, which in the case of Africans mainly affected

T.A.A. Two years later he followed this up by the Societies Bill (April 14, 1954), which made it compulsory for all organisations to be registered, listing not only their aims and rules, but their organisers and officers, complete with their names, occupations and addresses.[1]

It was as though Twining had sensed, instinctively, that an organisation was about to be born which would spell danger to the British administration.

* * *

At last with the coming of independence, the Meru case has had a satisfactory ending. The Meru have settled densely in the lands opened up for them: there is not an unoccupied acre available in the Kingori area, proving, as was foreseen, that this fertile and prosperous country is ideal for Meru expansion. With no 'iron ring', expansion is continuing into the surrounding plains.

With the compensation money they had received from the British, the Meru have re-purchased Farm 31. There is already a complaint that, by present standards, it is insufficiently fertile to support the evicted families who have now returned to it. Several units in the homogeneous block of alienated country which Wilson sought to establish have become available to the Meru for settlement. In some cases the European settlers have surrendered their leases to the Government, and the Government have decided against re-alienation. In others the Meru have acted on their own initiative and clubbed together to buy land from freeholders and leaseholders.

Now, as before, only the Masai have gone empty handed.

[1] The present Tanganyika Government has not revoked this bill.

CHAPTER 21

T.A.N.U. is Born

AT the time the Meru case reached the General Assembly, Julius Nyerere returned from Edinburgh. Archbishop Edgar Marantha, going to meet him at the airport, offered a seat in his car to Maria Gabriel, Nyerere's fiancée. She was studying at the Dar-es-Salaam St Joseph's Convent to perfect her English and general education. Not having seen Julius for three years, she was worried lest he had changed and she turned down the Archbishop's offer saying: 'My Lord, I am not sure he is the same man I'm in love with. Anyhow, it is not a girl's place to run after a man, not even in a bishop's car. . . .'

Nyerere soon reassured her and after his salary had been settled, together they went to Musoma. There, on January 24, 1953, they were married by Father William Collins, a Maryknoll Father, at the Parish Church. The long wait for twenty-four year old Maria was over. Six years is a long engagement in any country. . . .

A representative of Barclay Leechman, the Member for Social Services in Twining's Administration, had also greeted Nyerere at the airport. Leechman was interested in the young African who had studied in his native Scotland. When he learnt of Nyerere's M.A., he suggested that he should be given a European teacher's salary. The Governor and the Colonial Office agreed, but they had reckoned without Kenya's officialdom, who feared local repercussions if an African or an Asian were to be paid a European salary. Barclay Leechman could show Nyerere all the good-will in the world, but he could not give him the practical acknowledgment he deserved.

Leechman never told Nyerere about this. Nine years later, when Nyerere was already Prime Minister of Tanganyika, he authorised the author to tell the story.

Nyerere's appointment as history master of St Francis' College, Pugu, near Dar-es-Salaam, was officially made on October 9, 1952. The decision had actually been taken when Father Walsh told him in England that the three top classes of St Mary's College, Tabora, were being transferred to Pugu, where the Catholic Hierarchy was setting up its first territorial secondary school in

218

Tanganyika. Nyerere was now offered a salary of £300; after a lot of argument between Father Walsh and the Government, this was raised to £450, plus a thirty-five per cent living allowance.

Naturally Nyerere made haste to see his nationalist friends in Dar-es-Salaam. He had read, while in Edinburgh, accounts of their performance before the Constitutional Committee; now he heard details, which lost nothing in the telling. Yet these excited tales invariably ended in sadness, with an account of the Meru case.

After the wedding, when taking his bride from Musoma to the capital, Nyerere stopped in Mwanza for a discussion with Hamza Mwapachu and Abdulla Fundikira, old friends from Makerere days. They agreed to write essays on various subjects: Fundikira on agriculture, Mwapachu on social development, and Nyerere on political theory. All of them were quietly preparing for the day when they would embark on political action.

In February, 1953, Julius and Maria started life in Pugu in a new house built for them, with a reasonable salary and the prospect of three peaceful, studious years. Soon Nyerere began to meet new people, some as intelligent and stimulating as those he had left behind in Edinburgh.

One of them was Amir Jamal, a young Asian business man with a first class brain. Born in Tanganyika in 1920, he went to school there and then to India to train as a doctor. Despite his high marks, he could not get into the overcrowded Medical Faculty of Bombay University and therefore studied politics and economics. Back in Dar-es-Salaam in 1942, he entered the family business. Financial success, however, did not satisfy him. He was looking for something more important, more creative than lucrative transactions.

In the autumn of 1953, at a British Council sundowner, he met Julius Nyerere. They only exchanged a few words, but Jamal had the feeling that this was a man well worth knowing. He wrote to him, but received no reply. Later on Marjorie Nicholson, Secretary of the Fabian Colonial Bureau (now the Fabian Commonwealth Bureau), told him to get in touch with Nyerere. To his second letter, mentioning her name, he had an apologetic answer and a meeting followed. This was the beginning of a relationship which was to develop into a close friendship.

Another man Nyerere met at this time was Fraser Murray, a barrister and an idealist who, during the war, had served with the

K.A.R. and lost an arm in Burma. His wife, Moira, became secretary of the Tanganyika Council of Women, founded by Lady Twining in 1953. The purpose of the T.C.W. was to bring about co-operation between European, Asian and African women. European and Asian women got on well, but the gap between the European and African women was enormous.

Mrs Murray's office was at the Arnautoglu Community Centre, run by Denis Phombeah, a Nyasa, at that time in the thick of African affairs. His closest friends were Oscar Kambona and Zuberi Mtemwu, who in 1962 was to oppose Nyerere in the presidential election. All of them were much influenced by Jimmy McGairl, a remarkable Scot who did more for Africans in urban areas than any other European. A Community Development Officer, he started his activities in the Arnautoglu Community Centre in Dar-es-Salaam, on a brother-to-brother basis. News of this got around quickly and young Africans flocked to him. One of them was Rashidi Kawawa, who obtained his first social service job on McGairl's recommendation.

Murray was much concerned about these young men, and the thoughts awakening in them. To give them an opportunity to clarify their minds, he invited them to his house. Julius Nyerere, whom he had met through his wife, was among his guests.

We had a little group which we called *The Oracle* [Murray has told the author]. Our idea was to run it on the lines of an Oxford discussion group. A nucleus of eight people formed *The Oracle*, its mainstay being two Asians, Amir Jamal and Eddy Cooper, my two oldest friends in Tanganyika. Cooper, a builder, was also *The Oracle*'s secretary. It was a non-racial group, including a few broadminded Europeans, such as Basil Thompson, who had a genuine approach to people, regardless of their colour. Every Friday we used to meet in each others' houses without refreshments, as these might have embarrassed the Africans who could not have afforded to return the courtesy. The host's duty was to get someone to lead off the discussion.

One Friday the meeting was held at Amir Jamal's house, and he introduced Julius, saying that he would talk on conscription. This was at the time of the Mau Mau emergency in Kenya, when security and military preparations were in everyone's mind. I cannot remember all Julius said, but I remember that all of it was sensible.

Fraser Murray told his friends about Nyerere, predicting that he would become Prime Minister of Tanganyika one day. Randal

Sadleir, then Assistant Secretary for Legal Affairs, asked to meet him. This was arranged to take place at the Cosy Cafe in Dar-es-Salaam, where the three argued until two a.m. over brandy for which Murray paid. Sadleir was greatly impressed by Nyerere.

It was a common myth that I was the power behind Julius and Tanu [Murray has said]. I never gave advice. Julius knew that I supported him politically, but it was much more important for me that I was his friend. Later I did legal work for Tanu. The first big case was that of Ali Migeya, in Bukoba. He was an early 'agin the Government' chap, basically bolshy, but not a political figure. At that time Tanu was just a dirty word; it was almost seditious to talk about Tanu.

I brought Migeya before a D.C. who was a friend of mine. This was the first time that Tanu defended one of its own members. Julius attached such importance to this that he met me at the airport when I returned from Bukoba. Later I tried many big Tanu cases, and defended Julius himself in 1958.

But this still lay in the future.

In the early months of 1953 an increasing number of leading Africans came to Pugu to discuss affairs with Nyerere, bringing him more and more into politics. Yet he did not neglect his classes or students, although clearly the latter were bound to suffer. Some of the visitors were indignant, others sad, yet others frustrated. Nyerere, they said, had to do this, that, or the other. The most urgent thing was to recapture T.A.A.

They insisted that the good work done by Vedast Kyaruzi and Luciano Tsere must not be wasted. For the first, but by no means the last time, Julius gave way to pressure and in April, 1953, ran for office in T.A.A. Opposed by Abdul Sykes, the outgoing President, who at that time was much better known in Dar-es-Salaam than Nyerere, his chances were less than even. Fortunately, Denis Phombeah, the returning officer, considered him the better man of the two. As manager of Amautoglu Hall, he knew many people and canvassed for Nyerere. To save both Sykes and Nyerere embarrassment, he asked them to withdraw while the voting by show of hands took place. Nyerere was elected by a small margin, thus stepping on to the first rung of the political ladder.

His friends now urged that he must turn T.A.A. into a political organisation, and pointed to Harry Nkumbula,[1] who in neighbour-

[1] Harry Nkumbula was succeeded by Kenneth Kaunda, now President of Zambia, as the nationalist leader of Northern Rhodesia.

ing Northern Rhodesia had organised the National Congress Party.

Nyerere began to study T.A.A.'s constitution and the rules originally laid down by Sir Donald Cameron. In Britain, he had talked to many Ghanaians and analysed Kwame Nkrumah's constitution. Every day he realised more clearly that the Government would pay no attention to nationalist demands, however reasonable, unless they had the organised power of the people behind them. Only a political party would enable him to fight it out with the British. When on August 1, 1953, Twining banned civil servants from T.A.A., Nyerere wrote to protest against this:

In this Territory, the majority of educated Africans are in the civil service. Banning them from membership of political organisations is equivalent to banning T.A.A., the only political organisation in the Territory. This, Your Excellency, is a serious blow to our political development. (August 10, 1953.)

In conclusion, he asked for a compromise which would enable civil servants to play some part in political organisations.

His letter was ignored. This high-handed treatment rankled.

It partly explains why Nyerere lifted the ban on civil servants joining Tanu after he had become Tanganyika's first President. His new, young country, he believes, cannot afford to exclude a large segment of its educated population from participation in public life.

On October 10, 1953, there was a T.A.A. meeting in the little house with the beautifully carved Arab door which Sir Donald Cameron had built in New Street. Because T.A.A. was very low in funds, one of its rooms had been rented to an Asian, who was running a laundry. The other was the T.A.A. office.

In the small airless room Julius Nyerere sat on one chair at a decrepit desk, John Rupia on another chair, the Sykes brothers and Dossa Aziz perched on packing cases. Nyerere opened the meeting by saying that he had given much thought to T.A.A., but he could not transform it into a political organisation. His friends were thrilled, as this meant that T.A.A. was finished and that they would now form a real political party.

There were many suggestions as to what to call it. Abdul Sykes remembered that while waiting for repatriation at Kalieni camp outside Bombay, they had discussed political organisation and tried all sorts of names, of which he liked Tanganyika African Union best.

To Nyerere this sounded too much like Kenya African Union, and he thought that something, for instance 'national', should be added, calling it Tanganyika National African Union.

Ally Sykes remarked that the initials of Tanganyika National African Union, T.N.A.U., were a tongue-twister; but if the name were rearranged to Tanganyika African National Union, T.A.N.U. would be easy to say.

'T.A.N.U.'—they all repeated the four initials which were to become famous in African history. 'T.A.N.U.' Thus was the Tanganyika African National Union born.

Nyerere modelled its constitution on that of Nkrumah's Convention Peoples' Party; the basic structure and much of the actual phrasing was taken over. Tanu was 'to fight relentlessly until Tanganyika is self-governing and independent', 'to build up a united nationalism'; it was to fight for 'elections for all bodies of local and central government . . . to have African majorities'; for small industries, training schools for artizans, fair prices for consumers and producers, a minimum wage and compulsory primary education. Tanu was to fight against 'tribalism and all isolationist tendencies amongst Africans . . . against racialism and racial discrimination'; against land alienation and foreign immigration and federation until the demand 'comes from the African inhabitants of these territories.'

Membership was to be open to Africans only, from the age of eighteen; trade unions and tribal associations could affiliate provided they charged their members a political levy which would be paid to Tanu.

If Tanu was to become a political party, it had to have mass support. Already in 1948 T.A.A. had thirty-nine branches, with 1,780 members. The chances were that all would join Tanu. But without money, without a publication, without means to advertise, it seemed hopeless to attempt to build these few hundred educated Africans into a popular following.

Then came an incident which convinced the nationalists more than ever that they had to organise themselves. In Lusaka, Harry Nkumubla's National Congress Party sponsored a Pan-African Congress, to which for the first time British, American and Far Eastern friends were also invited. It was a matter of prestige that, when the slogan was: 'Yours is the national struggle for free-dom . . .' T.A.A. should be represented.

Money was once more the main difficulty. The Secretary of the Mwanza branch of T.A.A., Bokhe Munanka, collected a sum sufficient for his own expenses. As the British authorities would not grant Munanka a passport, in the end Ally Sykes and Denis Phombeah became the Tanganyikan delegates. Ally was one of the three Sykes brothers, who had served during the war in the K.A.R.; he had then found employment in a dance band in Nairobi. In 1948 he returned to Dar-es-Salaam to become a civil servant; by 1952 he was running the Dar-es-Salaam employment agency, a Government concern; he was also Secretary-General of T.A.G.S.A., the Tanganyika African Government Servants Association. Denis Phombeah was in the happy position of owning a motor bicycle, the only means of transport the young nationalists had.

Ally Sykes induced T.A.G.S.A. to pay for the two air tickets to Lusaka; from the funds left over from Kirillo Japhet's trip to New York, they paid in advance for hotel accommodation in Salisbury, where they had to change aircraft and spend the night, and for their stay in Lusaka. Nothing was left to chance–or so they thought. . . .

Sykes' and Phombeah's troubles began in Salisbury. They were given a form to sign which would have declared them prohibited immigrants. Both refused to put their names to this document as they were merely in transit to Lusaka. Then they were placed under arrest at the airport, and their luggage was confiscated. Sykes' suitcase contained, so he says, a cine-camera which had cost £90, the result of years of economy. He never saw it again.

Next morning, without being allowed to touch down in Lusaka, they were flown to Blantyre in Nyasaland. They had neither money, nor accommodation. An African friend, Charles Mwin-geri, wanted to put them up, but he could not do so without per-mission from the Superintendent of Locations. This official turned out to be a decent fellow, but he could not grant permission, as it was against the law for Africans in a white area to receive visitors in their rooms. The Superintendent put his garage at the two Tan-ganyikans' disposal; they could not wash, nor did they have a change of shirts. In Zomba they approached a European lawyer, but he told them that he never took on African cases.

Even a man much less sensitive than Julius Nyerere would have been shaken by Sykes' and Phombeah's experiences. Granted, such things could not happen in Tanganyika, a Trust Territory, but even there in a public place no African would be served a drink without a drink permit, and no African would be served a meal in a European restaurant. There was nothing Nyerere could do to get redress for his friends, except go ahead and organise Tanu. And that is what he proceeded to do, with furious determination.

Nyerere had a few small cards up his sleeve. Sent to a teachers' conference in Tabora, he talked to friends and colleagues about the aims of the rejuvenated T.A.A., of which he had been elected president. He explained his political concepts and asked that they should be discussed at T.A.A. branch meetings. He also went to conferences in Dodoma and Iringa, where he sounded T.A.A. members on his proposals for a new constitution. These were conversations among individuals, and some of those who took part developed into staunch helpers. At Dodoma, Nyerere re-met Oscar Kambona and Kanyame Chiume, another Nyasa, both dedicated nationalists who taught at the Australian Church Missionary Society's secondary school.

Next he went to a conference in the Lake Province, when the headmistress of the Kashasha Girls' School in Bukoba, a Swedish Lutheran missionary called Barbro Johansson, first heard about him. Then he paid a visit to Bukoba, where Africans gave him a warm reception. Realising how much depended on his personal appearances, Nyerere came to see one important fact: the headquarters of T.A.A. in Dar-es-Salaam had no authority. On his return he told his friends that to achieve a national position, they must concentrate on developing their organisation in the capital.

Thanks to the devoted spadework which followed, Tanu, when it came officially into existence, had a solid base in Dar-es-Salaam. And yet there was no short cut to national publicity. Nyerere and his band of helpers wrote pamphlets, planned membership drives, dreamt about advertising. As they had no funds, not even money for postage, the best they could do was to ask the railwayworkers to take their duplicated leaflets to the places they went to in the course of their duty, and to entrust their distribution to local sympathisers. The railway workers and their contacts proved surprisingly efficient. After some months, subscriptions began to come in, and the nationalists saw their following grow. They decided to proceed with the registration of Tanu.

This proved a tricky matter. The Registrar General found fault both with Tanu's aims, some of which he regarded as bordering on sedition, and with the list of its office-bearers, which did not contain the correct name, occupation, address and tribe of each man. Although they had done their best to comply with the Registration Ordinance, Tanu's application was turned down.

Sitting at home, Ally Sykes was thinking about Tanu's difficulties. He looked through his books and came across his British Legion card. This gave him an idea. He designed a card, with two flags, one green symbolising peace, the other black, symbolising Africans. To this day, the Tanu cards bear Ally Sykes' design. In 1954 Nyerere and his friends gladly accepted it.

As Ally Sykes was Tanu's first treasurer, he went next day to the *Tanganyika Standard* to ask the printers how much they would charge for printing 5,000 cards. They demanded 50 cents (6d.) per card. Sykes beat them down to 35 cents. At this time, for Africans even that tiny sum was a great deal of money.

In addition to holding the Tanu treasurership, Ally Sykes was General Secretary of T.A.G.S.A.; he turned therefore to the Executive of this organisation, which donated £25; from his own pocket Sykes contributed £30. The rest of the money for the party cards was guaranteed by Francis Kaskaiga and Dr Michael Luguzia.

When the cards were printed, the first seven made out were: No 1–Julius Nyerere; No 2–Ally Kleist Sykes; No 3–Abdul Sykes; No 4–Dossa Aziz; No 5–Denis Phombeah; No 6–Domie Ockochi; No 7–John Rupia.

Tanu could not expand, however, unless its leaders secured registration. Nyerere used every possible opportunity to visit the provinces, where the old T.A.A. branches received him with growing excitement. Local people proved enthusiastic supporters and white settlers for the first time heard about Tanu men going from mud hut to mud hut telling people to educate themselves and to prepare for the day when they would be running their own country.

On July 7, 1954, T.A.A. had its Annual General Meeting in Dar-es-Salaam. On this occasion Julius Nyerere and his friends took a historic decision. Regardless of registration difficulties, they announced the transformation of T.A.A. into the Tanganyika African National Union, the first African political organisation in their country's history.

Nyerere was unanimously elected President, though he laid it down that both he and the members of the National Executive should be subject to re-election by the Annual Delegates Conference. The National Executive was to meet quarterly, but in view of communications difficulties, there was to be an Executive Central Committiee, consisting of the President and nine members, all residing in Dar-es-Salaam. Denis Phombeah was elected its first Secretary; it was to meet weekly and have full responsibility 'in the event of an emergency'.

Thus was Tanu officially born and thus did Julius Nyerere become leader of his own political party. He was thirty-two years old.

Since Independence, 'the seventh day of the seventh month', is a national holiday in Tanganyika.

CHAPTER 22

T.A.N.U. Begins to Grow

TANU'S National Executive held its first meeting in August, 1954. There was only one item on the agenda: to draft a memorandum for submission to members of the U.N. Visiting Mission, due to arrive in Dar-es-Salaam in September. Chairmen of all provincial Tanu–formerly T.A.A.–branches were present, each accompanied by two of their local representatives. Julius Nyerere presided and members of the Dar-es-Salaam Executive acted as hosts.

This gathering of young nationalists framed what amounted to the first Tanu programme. It embodied an eloquent plea for the eradication of ignorance and poverty. It declared the financial assistance received from Britain inadequate, and asked for U.N. educational and economic aid. It insisted on immediate democratic elections at least in Dar-es-Salaam; it would only accept the Government's multi-racial policy of parity representation for the three races on Legco as a necessary expedient for three years, and proclaimed the goal of a democratic African country. Finally, it was resolved that all wages and salaries should be frozen and all funds be used to raise the tragically low living standard of the African masses.

The *Tanganyika Standard*, so often at this time a reflection of Government opinion, characterised the resolutions as 'not a nice document', being 'completely anti-Government and biased in the extreme' (September 13, 1954).

At least one member of the National Executive was worried by the proposal for the freezing of all salaries and wages. It was Andrew Tibandebage, Nyerere's old friend from Makerere and Tabora, by then teaching at Karagwe and Provincial Chairman of Tanu in the Western Province.

He knew that educated Tanganyikans, who hoped to get on in life, would resent a resolution which prevented them from improving their standard of living. Because of it, they might ignore all the other constructive demands. As for the British, Tibandebage had no doubt that they would exploit it to do maximum damage to Tanu. Deeply concerned, he decided to take a hand in flat contradiction to the policy of Nyerere, who had approved the idealistic resolution about wages and salaries.

Andrew Tibandebage managed to get himself sent with Patrick Kunambi, Sultan of the Luguru, and Kirillo Japhet, the by then famous Meru spokesman, to inform the editor of the *Tanganyika Standard* about the decisions taken by the first Tanu National Executive. They described the various resolutions, but before his colleagues had a chance to explain about the planned freezing of wages and salaries, Tibandebage got up and said that they had to be on their way. Ignoring both Kunambi's signals and Japhet's stage whispers, he rushed out of the room.

He and Japhet were staying with Nyerere at Pugu. Andrew Tibandebage brooded uneasily on how he should tell Nyerere that the salary and wage freezing decision would not be reported in the *Tanganyika Standard*, and therefore could not figure in the Legco debate. . . .

'We forgot to mention it,' he said lamely over dinner, hardly daring to look at Nyerere, who stopped eating, stared at him for some time, then without saying one word, left the room.

Neither man slept that night. Nyerere never asked Tibandebage how it was possible for such an important resolution to have been 'forgotten'; for his part, Tibandebage never raised the matter either, hoping that Nyerere would understand his motive and forgive his insubordinate action. It is typical of both men that they did not face up to the event, which they must have known would affect their friendship. They just quietly drifted apart.

As Tibandebage was teaching in a mission school, the Ordinance banning civil servants from political activities did not affect him. Yet owing to the change in his relations with Nyerere he decided to turn his back on politics and to devote his entire time to earning a living for his large family. At the moment of writing he is educating eight children and is Tanganyika's Ambassador in Leopoldville.

It was encouraging to have held a National Executive meeting one month after the official foundation of Tanu. But with Nyerere's time taken up with teaching and no funds available, nothing had been done about enrolling a massive membership and preparing the documents required for Tanu's registration. That is when Oscar Kambona appeared on the scene.

The son of a Nyanja Anglican priest of Nyasaland, he was a strange mixture of intelligence, enterprise and diffidence. After his father had settled in Tanganyika, he went to primary school under the proverbial mango tree at Kwambe, near Songea; then on to U.M.C.A.'s Liuli Mission School for a teacher's training course in Swahili. As he also wanted to learn English and to obtain a good education, and as all local secondary schools were overcrowded, he enrolled himself at the new secondary school the Australian Church Missionary Society had just opened in Dodoma. Young Kambona relied on a light-hearted promise of the Bishop of Nyasaland, the Rt Rev Frank O. Thorne, to pay his tuition fee. Somewhat annoyed to have his hand forced, Bishop Thorne did nonetheless enable Kambona to go on with his studies, paying £15 a year, for three years running. In 1945 Kambona passed the entrance examination to Tabora Government School and obtained a complete remission of fees.

There he arrived with his hair so long that it stood out around his head like the crinkly mane of a black Struvel Peter. It achieved what must have been young Kambona's intention—to be noticed. The headmaster sent for him, and ordered him to return next morning at ten, having had his hair cut.

Job Lusinde, a fellow pupil from Dodoma, dealt with his hirsute mop. Mr Blumer passed the result and advised Oscar to have his hair cut every fortnight. This he has done ever since. About Blumer he has told the author: 'He was a tough man, but very fair. I owe him a great deal, for he gave me self-confidence. In some ways, he has made me what I am.'

In 1948, Kambona left Tabora for St Paul's Teachers' Training College; two years later he went from there to teach at his old school in Dodoma. By then his main interest lay in politics, which Kanyame Chiume,[1] a friend and Nyasa fellow teacher, shared with him. Their pupils heard a good deal about the misdeeds of the Colonial Administration—real or imaginary: too few schools, too few educated Africans, too few teachers and not the right teachers, who would teach their pupils patriotism and pride in the country. Kambone and Chiume enlarged upon the lack of proper health institutions with thousands of people suffering from eye trouble, many of them going blind and the British doing nothing about it. Much was said of malnutrition all over the country, a rich agri-

---

[1] In 1963 Kanyame Chiume became a Minister in Dr Hastings Banda's Government. In September, 1964, he was one of the five Ministers who resigned.

cultural land, where there should be enough for all, yet as long as the colonial government was in power, there never would be.

One afternoon, in August, 1954, a small boy put up his hand and asked: 'Sir, you've told us what's wrong with our country. Why don't you do something about it?'

Oscar Kambona felt as though someone had hit him. The child had voiced the thought which had been pricking his conscience for quite a while. He was talking instead of acting. Since his recent meeting with Julius Nyerere at the Dodoma teachers' conference, he had been on the point of resigning more than once. The rejuvenated T.A.A., now transformed into Tanu, needed help. Of course it meant throwing away his career. The little boy's question made up his mind.

Oscar Kambona reached Dar-es-Salaam by goods train, for he could not afford to buy a ticket on a passenger train. From the railway station he went to a friend's house, and was promised hospitality for three months. Then he was off to Pugu, where Julius Nyerere invited him to his home and where they had a long talk. Oscar Kambona offered his services to Tanu.

Nyerere told him sadly that he could not possibly employ him, as Tanu had no money. To this Kambona retorted that Tanu had no money because it had no organiser. Let him be Tanu organiser, and there would be funds.

Nyerere was sceptical; nevertheless he agreed to appoint Oscar Kambona as Tanu's Organising Secretary.[2] The Lidbury Commission had awarded civil servants salary increases retroactively from 1948 onwards; and although he had resigned his post as a teacher, a lump sum was due to Kambona for the intervening six years. On this he proposed to live until Tanu had sufficient funds to pay him a salary.

At Tanu headquarters in New Street, Kambona worked out his plan of campaign. He was going to visit chiefs and elders, the men with real influence in the country, and tell them of Tanu's aims

---

[2] He was the third man to hold this difficult position. The first had been Domie Ockoshi, a Kenyan deported because of his Mau Mau friends; the second, Ally K. Sykes, who did his best to grapple with this sisyphean problem. When in 1955 Kambona went to study in Britain, he was succeeded by Steven Mhando; after Mhando's dismissal (see Chapter 25) Kambona regained the title which he still holds. But ever since the work has been carried out by his deputy, Elias Kisenge, who is now also a Junior Minister dealing with economic affairs.

and hopes. If they showed an inclination to help he would request them to advise friends and tribesmen to join and pay their membership dues. This, in his view, was the quickest way to induce the conservative African peasants to accept a new organisation. Julius Nyerere backed his judgment to the full. At the end of six months, over ten thousand members had enrolled themselves. A year later, Tanu had over a hundred thousand members. But that was after Nyerere had appeared before the Trusteeship Council in New York. (See Chapter 23.)

Another friend of Julius Nyerere's who gave particular help at this time was Paul Bomani. Born in 1925 in Musoma, he was the son of a Protestant minister. The Seventh Day Adventist Teachers' Training College, where he was educated, wanted him to take up teaching. But Bomani longed to go to Tabora, then to Makerere, possibly to a foreign university. Annoyed at his disinclination to teach, the head of the Training College had his studies at Tabora Government School cut short. More stubborn than ever, Paul Bomani still refused to teach and took a job at Dr Williamson's Diamond Mines as cashier instead. He learnt accountancy by correspondence course. In 1947, when twenty-two years old, he became Secretary of the Co-operative Wholesale Society in Mwanza, which meant–among other things–that he had to purchase supplies, which not merely taught him costing, but also acquainted him with the sharp methods by which Asian traders took advantage of African farmers.

Three years later, Paul Bomani felt ready to organise a cotton co-operative, cotton being the main crop of the Lake Province. He had to stamp out three Asian malpractices: tampering with weights and thus paying far less for cotton than it was worth; deducting arbitrary sums from the price owing to alleged poor quality, and bribing agricultural inspectors (appointed in good faith by the administration) who then shut both eyes to the cheating going on under their noses.

Within two years, Paul Bomani had built up and registered the Lake Province Cotton Co-operative. He had done it by inducing every village to buy scales so that the farmers should know, before going to market, what their cotton weighed. To pay for the scales, he collected money by subscription and organised several villages into 'unions'. Then he convinced farmers that if all of them stood up to the Asian buyers, these could no longer penalise the few brave men who first dared to question weights and prices. By 1955, Bomani's organisation was registered under the Co-operative Ordinance as the Victoria Federation of Co-operative Unions, with himself as general manager. Finally, he persuaded the farmers to pay one cent per pound of cotton sold into a central fund, the purpose of which was to gain control of the Asian owned ginneries.[3] Eventually, with the help of a considerable loan, he bought up eight ginneries at a cost of £900,000. At the moment of writing, only three ginneries remain in Asian hands, and that will not be for long. The Victorian Federation of Co-operative Unions is the largest marketing co-operative in Africa.

As soon as Paul Bomani started work among the cotton growers, his organising ability was the talk of every home in the Lake Province and beyond. In 1952 he was elected Provincial Chairman of T.A.A. and his branches had lively discussions which covered not only local political subjects, but also demands for independence for Tanganyika. In July, 1954, they turned themselves into Tanu branches. But by then Bomani had gone to Britain to study. Under his successor, Bokhe Munanka, irresponsible statements on Tanu's behalf led to public disorder and the British administration banned all these Tanu branches for four years, that is until September, 1958.

Bomani's tribe, the Sukuma, had been so enthusiastic about his activities that they offered to put up the money for a new secondary school; it has however still to be built. It was most important, as it then seemed, to find the right principal; and as this plan coincided with Julius Nyerere's return from Edinburgh in September, 1952, Bomani went to Musoma to invite him to accept this position. Nyerere had to refuse as he had just accepted his job as teacher at St Francis' College, Pugu. But that meeting laid the foundations of their future friendship; and as a result of it when in December, 1954, Twining offered to appoint Bomani a member of the Legislative Council, he consulted Nyerere whether or not to accept. Nyerere told him emphatically to agree, so that he could put the Tanu point of view in Legco. From then on until September, 1957, Bomani was Nyerere's only mouthpiece in Legco.

In the same eventful September of 1954, another remarkable

---

[3] A variant of gin-house, where cotton is ginned. The word gin is derived from engine.

African was also to return to Dar-es-Salaam: Rashidi Kawawa. His destiny was to be closely linked with Julius Nyerere's, Oscar Kambona's and Paul Bomani's. As a person, he is the most typical son of the Tanganyikan soil; his career is the most romantic of all the men around Julius Nyerere.

All Rashidi Kawawa's forebears have been elephant hunters, although the British, when they employed his father, called him a game scout. He belonged to the Ngoni tribe. Rashidi, eldest of eight children, was born in Songea in 1930. He is small, five foot two, with a broad chest and short sturdy legs. He has the health and strength of the Tanganyikan peasant, whose aspirations he so well understands.

I've never had a political ideology [he has told the author]. Socialism, Communism, any kind of 'ism' means just a theory to me. My first thinking was not of politics, but of service to my people. When I was thirteen, I read about the literacy campaign in China and the co-operative movement in England. Four years later, when in Tenth Form in Dar-es-Salaam, I organised the boys for a literacy campaign among the adults we knew. I also told them that we had to work for the political, social and economic advancement of our country. I did not mention freedom, as freedom was a concept to which I had never given thought.

We had a hundred pupils; I made up a roster of the boy teachers and we charged our pupils 1/– a month. We collected quite a fund this way. Then we organised drama classes and a class for singing and reciting. We thought that, when we left school, we would go on with this work.

But the headmaster wrote to his father to say that Rashidi had passed the entrance examination to Tabora Government School, and he went there to finish his education. He was a contemporary of Oscar Kambona and Job Lusinde and of several other boys who now hold leading positions in the Tanganyika administration – under him.

Rashidi Kawawa also has high praise for John Blumer:

He had a great share in shaping my character. He broadened my mind; he gave me a desire for a full life. I was fairly good at studies, at games and at social activities. Blumer made me realise that all three mattered. He wanted me to go to Makerere, but I refused as my father had no money to pay for me and he had seven more children to educate.

Kawawa's heart was in social service, but being too young for a job in that field, he became a Public Works Department clerk.

Then his father died, and responsibility for his younger brothers and sisters fell on him. They joined him in Dar-es-Salaam; on his modest salary they all ate, but not much. He joined T.A.G.S.A., then a staff association, almost a trade union, and started to organise its members, many of whom had no idea that they were entitled to annual leave, or to a pension after retiring from work. In 1950, he was elected to the T.A.G.S.A. Executive; in 1952 he became Assistant General Secretary and in 1954 President.

But this was still three years away. In 1951 Rashidi Kawawa found employment as a social worker and quite accidentally became attached to a mobile film unit, used in an official literacy campaign. The Government then decided to make entertainment films and for this engaged a South African film company. Its talent scouts eventually discovered that the most talented African film actor was right there, in their office – Rashidi Kawawa.

He became the only Tanganyikan male star who played the lead in three popular films. He also proved himself as a producer and a script writer, but owing to excessive expense, the film venture had to close down, and Kawawa's film career came to an abrupt end.

In 1953 he was sent to Urambo, where the hard core Kikuyu Mau Mau suspects were interned, to organise their welfare.

It was the greatest challenge of my life [he has said]. First the Kikuyu thought that I was a spy, or at least a Government stooge. I pondered a lot how to approach them, eventually deciding that my best chance was to care for their needs. I got permission for them to write and receive letters, to obtain books, to buy cigarettes. I persuaded the Camp C.O. to let me set up a Camp Committee and the Kikuyu to choose their own leaders, who would be responsible for keeping the camp clean. After a month, they were all working and they trusted me.

He was equally successful at Tamota, near Handeni in Tanga Province, where 'grey' Kikuyu were merely restricted. (See also Chapter 15). Here he organised games, mainly football, and kept the detainees happy.

At this time the Governor, Sir Edward Twining, who had been interested in Rashidi Kawawa since his film star days, said that he was to be brought back to Dar-es-Salaam and given some job in which he could develop his talents. He had been a member of T.A.A. and had participated in meetings whenever an important issue was being discussed. 'But,' Kawawa says, 'my heart was in

T.A.G.S.A., which provided a better means for African workers to express themselves.'

When he arrived in Dar-es-Salaam, Tanu had been formed, with his old friend Oscar Kambona as Organising Secretary. Being a civil servant, Kawawa could not join, but there were ways in which he could help the movement. He had met Julius Nyerere in Tabora, when he came over from St Mary's College to debate at the Government school. Now, however, he got to know him well and their friendship began.

Nyerere, Kambona, Bomani and Kawawa, four future pillars of the nationalist struggle, had met in Dar-es-Salaam. All four were to be there again in February, 1955, at the next Legco meeting.

The Governor, Sir Edward Twining, thought he could dismiss Tanu as no more than the effervescence of brash politicians and would-be politicians; he believed that his policy of multi-racialism was accepted by the overwhelming mass of the people of Tanganyika. (*Tanganyika Standard*, October 11, 1954.) From Twining's point of view, Julius Nyerere and his helpers were clever agitators, who would have to be either won over or broken.

Yet the promptitude and sense of reality that Nyerere now displayed in connection with the registration of Tanu should have given the Government cause to think carefully. When he submitted the second application personally to the Registrar General, he was told that certain clauses in Tanu's constitution would have to be changed because, if given their literal meaning, they might be regarded as incitement to conduct incompatible with the maintenance of peace and order.

Nyerere at once called a meeting of the Tanu Executive and the constitution was altered. The Mwanza branch secretary, Bhoke Munanka, whose registration application had, in the meantime, been turned down because of his wild behaviour, was not invited to this Executive meeting.

Julius Nyerere then supplied a full and accurate list of the Dar-es-Salaam office-bearers, with all the required data: names, addresses, occupations, tribes, and an equally complete list of the membership. The Dar-es-Salaam Tanu branch, headquarters for the whole of Tanganyika, was duly registered in October, 1954. Six branches, Tabora, Dodoma, Tarime, Ifakara, Iringa and Tanga followed suit soon after.

As the best way of handling young Nyerere, Sir Edward Twin-

ing had wisely appointed him on May 12, 1954, a Temporary
Member of Legco to replace David Makwaia, who was serving on
the Royal Commission for Land and Population Problems. The
Governor knew little of the animosity between these two men, or
of the opposing poles they represented in African affairs. He
thought that Legco would give Nyerere an opportunity to learn
how to bear responsibility; perhaps also to develop a taste for
power, in which case the Government would have a chance to
mould him to their pattern. It never occurred to anyone on the
Government side that 'the little man with a walking stick' would
not only go his own way, but revolutionise the entire concept of
Unofficial Members.

In the years after 1946, when the Tanganyika Constitution was
first modernised, the Governor had appointed a slowly increasing
number of Europeans, Africans and Asians to Legco. They were
to sit opposite the Government benches and exercise the right of
criticism within carefully defined limits. These tame precursors of
an opposition called themselves 'unofficial members', or just 'unofficials'. In 1946 they formed themselves into the Unofficial
Members Organisation, with Sir Charles Phillips as chairman.
Phillips was a successful business man and Chairman of Tanganyika Packers Ltd. He was a staunch supporter of the official
British attitude, but many other Europeans spoke up more, and
more often, than he did on behalf of the Africans. John Baker,
Captain Jack Bennett and Dr Hannah displayed tactics which, on
occasion, considerably annoyed the civil servant members of the
Council, who had to defend their respective departments.

As an avowed nationalist, Julius Nyerere's one complaint
against the European 'unofficials' was that they would not back
him right across the board. Instead, they judged every subject on
its merits and treated it accordingly. But once they adopted a line,
they stood by it with courage.

The most outstanding Asian was V. M. Nazerali, O.B.E. He
and his colleagues helped the nationalists on political problems,
but on economic matters they were motivated by their own
interests.

The African 'unofficials' were a bitter disappointment to the
nationalists. Chiefs Abdiel Shangali, David Makwaia and Harun
Lugusha, and Yustino Mponda, a commoner, were well liked,
however, by the Governor. They had at their disposal the old

I

Chiefs' Quarters in Bagamoyo Road. Here they could stay, eat, discuss their problems and see their friends. What they would not do was to work with Nyerere; and they would not put forward Tanu ideas, or stand up to obdurate civil servants. For this Nyerere had to rely on European and Asian 'unofficials'.

The 1954 Legislative Council of Tanganyika was an artificial political creation, designed by the British authorities as a step in the gradual evolution towards African self-government. It was well intentioned and, without the advantage of hindsight, the Governor undoubtedly had sound administrative reasons for the caution which he displayed; yet the weakness of the Legislative Council as a political concept was shown up when, as a result of the controversial Mason Sears Report, Julius Nyerere and Sir Charles Phillips appeared before the Trusteeship Council in New York.

CHAPTER 23

Julius Nyerere Before the Trusteeship Council

IN August, 1954, the third U.N. Visiting Mission arrived in Tanganyika. Coming from Ruanda-Urundi, it entered the Territory by way of Bukoba, and its American member, Mason Sears, let it be known immediately that he wished to talk to Africans, to elicit African views and African hopes. Kirillo Japhet rushed forward to oblige, stating loudly that the 1951 Mission had done nothing to redress the Meru grievances. Spokesmen of the Meru, and the Arusha and the Chagga, of District Councils and Native Authorities, of Tanu branches and individual nationalists, followed close in his footsteps, all anxious to tell their tales. Complaints against the Administering Authority, in most cases inaccurate as well as exaggerated, poured into the Mission's ears.

There had been excitement over the report of the first U.N. Visiting Mission in 1948. Some of its comments on economic, educational and social matters had been inaccurate or misleading, and raised a storm of protest in Britain. The British Government were extremely sensitive about international intervention in the administration of Tanganyika, especially when weak spots were touched. The Mission report, however, was the first encouragement thinking Africans had received from abroad.

The 1951 Mission issued an optimistic report, as at that time thanks to the Korean War Tanganyikan exports were booming. From the British administration's point of view, a critical account of the Meru case was the sole fly in the ointment. To the 1951 report, made available to the public only in 1952, there was hardly any reaction either in Britain or in Tanganyika.

The members of the 1954 U.N. Mission not only held strong political views, but also hotly disagreed with each other. The American member, Mason Sears, was imbued with a keen but indiscriminating sympathy for Africans and was determined to help them obtain independence from their colonial masters in the shortest possible time. Rikhi Jaipal, the Indian representative, agreed and co-operated with Mr Sears. The Chairman, John S. Reid, of New Zealand, sympathised with the British administration's point of view, and clashed so strongly with his American

239

colleague that he eventually refused to sign the report. Rafael Equizabel, of El Salvador, tried to remain neutral, but by inclination sided with Mr Reid.

The British Administering Authority helped the Mission in every possible way. Although they had practically no contact with European settlers or business men, thanks to Mr Reid the Mission was able to confer extensively with British civil servants. The Governor, Sir Edward Twining, with his knowledge of the Territory, was well qualified to balance their African weighted information. Only on one point did Twining overstate his case: he said that the Africans had no representative organisation. This cut Nyerere to the quick and he reacted by drafting a memorandum setting out the part played by Africans and suggesting that Tanganyika should obtain independence in twenty-five years.

Nyerere had to think out all these problems alone. He was inexperienced and had no one to ask for advice. Necessarily he tripped up sometimes by being ignorant of facts and of administrative problems, although he always saw his goal clearly. Father Walsh suggested that he should find a reliable lawyer who would advise him so that he would not unnecessarily antagonise Government House.

The decisive moment in the U.N. Mission's visit came when its members reached Dar-es-Salaam and met Julius Nyerere. His intelligence and moderation were characteristics they had not encountered in an African nationalist before. They found his sense of humour most engaging.

Mason Sears was all the more indignant that a man like Nyerere could not be served liquor in a public place. He would hardly listen to an explanation of the Ordinance: that Britain was party to the Congo Basin Treaties of the nineteenth century, which forbade the supply of any European intoxicant to natives. This pledge Britain had had to renew in 1919 when she accepted the Mandate over the former German East Africa. Nor would Sears take in the fact that from 1945 onwards, D.C.s and D.O.s had issued drink permits[1] to Africans, thus overcoming the publicans' difficulty in differentiating between responsible Africans and natives living under primitive conditions. If Julius Nyerere had no drink permit,

---

[1] On April 14, 1954, it was stated in Legco that between July 29, 1952 (when a record of the drink permits issued was started) and August, 1953, sixty-four Africans had applied for drink permits and sixty-three had been granted one.

the reason could only be that he had never applied for one. Besides, at that time a sub-committee of the Executive Committee was considering a report on intoxicating liquor giving sympathetic consideration to the position of the Africans. (*Tanganyika Hansard*, April 14, 1954.)

The American Consul in Dar-es-Salaam, Robert McKinnon, and his wife were of Mr Sears' political persuasion. It may have seemed natural to Mason Sears to accept the facilities provided by his compatriot and to write a good part of the U.N. Report at his house, but the British authorities felt very differently. Mr McKinnon was recalled to Washington and appointed to the African Desk of the State Department. The Governor made no secret of it that he had asked the Foreign Office to make a *démarche* in Washington, which was the cause of Mr and Mrs McKinnon's departure from Tanganyika.

Most unfortunate of all, the Mason Sears Report (as it came to be known) was handed to the Press *before* the British Government had completed its observations on it, and before the Trusteeship Council had seen it. The Press published highlights taken out of context, much more damning to the Administering Authority than had ever been intended in the Report. Not surprisingly, the British Government rejected its main recommendations, and these were not endorsed by the Trusteeship Council either. (Even if they had been, the resolution would not have been binding on Britain.)

This controversial document contained, all jumbled together, true statements and ill-advised criticism, straightforward accounts and inaccurate, slanted information. The demand which caused the greatest sensation was that a date should be set immediately for Tanganyika's independence, or at least 'a time table (be worked out) of the steps to be taken, in consultation with the people, towards self-government'. The Report maintained that the Tanganyika Africans were unusually adaptable to modern conditions. It was scathing about Britain's slow and gradual progress towards self-government, beginning with the introduction of district, urban and county councils into local government. It waved aside as unimportant the fact that, between 1946 and 1955, in nine years, an entirely European Legislative Council was being transformed into one consisting of ten Europeans, ten Asians and ten Africans, appointed on a territorial basis, one member of each race representing each one of the nine provinces and the tenth the capital, Dar-es-Salaam.

The Report treated with scepticism British efforts to create a multi-racial society, demanding that the parity principle between eight million Africans, two hundred thousand Asians and twenty thousand Europeans should be ended in the Territory; against this it was unanswerably true that, as the Report put it, 'The political life of the Territory, like its economic and social life, functions in separate racial compartments, which outside the "multi-racial" official organs, do not overlap.'

The Meru case was presented entirely from the African point of view; colour distinction in education, hospitals, hotels and employment, was strongly criticised, the wildly biased conclusion being reached that, 'The African is at the bottom of the ladder because the British gave him no opportunity to learn.'

The Report supported Tanu's complaint about banning civil servants from political activities and about the inadequacies of education and training. It ignored British achievements in road building, a key operation for opening up the Territory economically; in legislation for workers' care, in medical research and in women's education. Most important of all, it backed the Tanu demand that Tanganyika be granted independence in twenty-five years.

British official circles and Europeans in general were indignant. Their natural reaction was to reject all the recommendations of the Report, without having read its full text. Tanu's rejoinder was to call a meeting in New Street which decided to petition the Trusteeship Council that the African point of view be put before it. Some forty-five people attended, among them Paul Bomani, Oscar Kambona, Denis Phombeah, Abbas Sykes, Patrick Kunambi and Michael Kamaliza; none of whom had read the report either.

'We nominated Julius to go to the U.N.,' Kamaliza, now Minister of Labour, recalls. 'At the time I wondered how a handful of people could nominate someone on behalf of the whole of Tanganyika. I was told that the Party's Central Committee had this power.'

On February 10, 1955, in the midst of this hubbub, the Legislative Council session opened.

Early in the morning, the African 'unofficials' met at the Chief's Quarters in Bagamoyo Road. Suddenly Oscar Kambona, Tanu's

Organising Secretary, arrived waving a copy of the *Tanganyika Standard* which carried a report that Julius Nyerere was going to New York to speak at the U.N. about the Mason Sears Report. Kambona appealed to the Africans to help to raise money for Nyerere's trip.

An hour later, the Finance Standing Committee, formed by all unofficial members, seven Europeans, four Africans and three Asians, met to review matters due to come up during the Session. The Chief Secretary, R. de S. Stapledon, and other official Members joined them. All were very earnest. Nyerere's petition to the Trusteeship Council was the first subject they discussed. The Committee promptly decided to send three 'substantial, honourable and reliable citizens', representing the three races, to put Tanganyika's case at the U.N. and to challenge any 'erroneous statements' Nyerere was likely to make.

The general opinion was that Nyerere did not represent the majority of Tanganyikans. Three suitable citizens were quickly selected: Sir Charles Phillips as the European, Yustino Mponda as the African and I. C. Chopra as the Asian. Phillips was to be the sole spokesman of the multi-racial delegation.

Then someone raised the question: How would Tanu find the money to send Nyerere. One of the civil servants replied that they could not do it in such a short time. The Chief Secretary asked Legco members not to tell Nyerere, or any Tanu member, that three substantial citizens were flying to New York. If Nyerere could not leave soon, so the Government side reasoned, he would lose the opportunity of being heard by the Trusteeship Council.

Paul Bomani protested in some agitation that it was unfair not to tell Nyerere. He received black looks from all directions and was overruled. Undaunted, he decided that Nyerere and Tanu and the Tanganyika Africans should not miss such a chance. If necessary, he would resign and in any event he would tip off Nyerere, who was no longer a Member of Legco.

Twining had appointed the Tanu leader, as related earlier, on May 12, 1954, as an Alternate Member for David Makwaia. It was typical of Nyerere that during that Season he listened and observed, but never spoke. Only during the following Session, in July, 1954, did he make his maiden speech, in which he strongly attacked Ivor Bayldon's suggestion that expenditure on education should be cut. After that, Nyerere was careful to make reasoned, factual speeches; he also learnt to appreciate the Government's problems and difficulties. Then, unfortunately, the Lidbury awards were made public.

Sir David Lidbury presided over the commission investigating civil service salaries in East Africa. His commission achieved one important point: it introduced the principles of equality of opportunity and advancement by ability for the indigenous community in the public service. This removed the racial principle, first put down in black and white by the Holmes Report in 1947.[2]

Sir David's commission, however, also produced a second change, the raising of salaries, especially those of the Junior Service, the Subordinate Service and of the police and prison staffs. The total, including the contribution to the High Commission (£100,000) and the increased house allowance (£60,000) amounted to £960,000 per annum, a sum Nyerere believed to be far too high for Tanganyikan resources. Here, in his own words, is what happened:

When I was first appointed, I was a Temporary Member. I was stupid enough to let it be known that I would oppose the Lidbury Report, so Twining brought back Makwaia from London. As he took up his seat in Legco, I could not go in. I told Makwaia our problem, that the wages and salaries fixed by the Lidbury Commission were too high and begged him to say what I thought needed saying. He did not do it. It was the Unofficial Europeans who stated our case.

I knew that if the Africans were solid, the Asians would follow suit. Because of Makwaia's behaviour, the Africans were not solid. We could not have changed the decision, but it would have made a difference if we had voted *en bloc* with the Europeans and Asians, every single Unofficial against the Government line. This is what Makwaia and Shangali rendered impossible.

Nyerere's avowed intention to criticise the Lidbury awards was not the only reason why Twining removed him from Legco. At Tanu's first National Executive meeting the members, hopelessly untutored, had passed a resolution refusing to acknowledge the Queen's sovereignty over Tanganyika. Nyerere did not realise the implications of the resolution, and underrated the importance the Governor would attach to its being passed. It was on the unchallengeable ground that its members must take an oath of allegiance

---

[2] The commission, chaired by Sir Maurice Holmes, which enquired into civil service salaries in Kenya, Uganda, Tanganyika and Zanzibar.

to the Queen before they could sit on the Council that Twining really decided to throw him out of Legco.

When European friends had explained to Nyerere the enormity in British eyes of the Tanu resolution, he wrote to the Governor assuring him that it would be withdrawn and explaining quite truthfully that he never thought that it would even come to the Governor's notice. Moreover, he wanted to avoid extremism and felt that only by being a Legco member could he objectively assess the Government's problems.

Twining treated this letter with complete lack of understanding. He refused to accede to Nyerere's appeal and failed to detect the honest contrition of the man who would have responded to a gesture of generosity. Thus he reinforced Nyerere's (and Tanu's) determination to build up the nationalist movement and to struggle for independence.

On February 10, 1955, Paul Bomani was driving with two of his African Legco colleagues to the chiefs' quarters, his thoughts full of the impending meeting of the Trusteeship Council. On the way, he saw Nyerere walking in the same direction. He suggested to his companions that they should give him a lift. They could not see why they should. Bomani replied that Nyerere had no transport and it was a long walk. His friends retorted that Nyerere was surely used to walking. As Bomani insisted, they gave in and Nyerere was invited to drive with them.

When they arrived at the chiefs' quarters, they talked for a while and Bomani felt desperate because the minutes were ticking away and he could not exchange a word with Nyerere alone. At last he got up, saying that he had a lunch appointment and had to go. He smuggled Nyerere out through the back-door and they went to eat in a small place in town. There Bomani broke the news of the Legco 'unofficials' meeting and its decisions. This time Nyerere understood the implications all too well.

And yet he told Father Walsh that he would be glad, for the sake of his pupils, if another suitable Tanu representative could be found.

Soon after, some half-a-dozen Tanu leaders called on Father Walsh begging him to allow Nyerere to accept the Trusteeship Council invitation, since they had no one else to send. Father Walsh was at this time the Executive of the Bishops' Conference in Educational Affairs of inter-territorial schools, which belonged

*

to the hierarchy and not to individual bishops. He was therefore also responsible for the staffing of St Francis' School. He told the Tanu delegation that, as they had no one else to send to the U.N., he would allow Nyerere to go, and would so inform the headmaster of St Francis'. The latter agreed, but quite naturally complained that Nyerere would probably he absent for over a month and in the meantime there would be no history teacher.

The permission of the Department of Education, which paid the grants of the Voluntary Agency Schools, also had to be obtained. Its head did not think the request reasonable, and advised Father Walsh to see the Governor. Twining said that it did not make sense that the administration should pay Nyerere's salary for the month he would spend in New York, attempting to knock the ground from under his administration.

Father Walsh had to take a chance, and let Nyerere go to New York not knowing where the money for his one month salary would come from. He prayed that in the last resort the bishops would permit him to find the money elsewhere.

For some time the Government had tried to persuade the missions, both Protestant and Catholic, to forbid their teachers to enter politics, meaning by that to join Tanu and, *a fortiori*, to become Tanu office bearers. The Catholic Bishops refused and their representative had to explain to the Governor and various committees that by this tactic the Government would deprive a growing and powerful political movement among Africans of just those educated men and women who were the only people capable of acting responsibly and whose influence could be relied upon to support moderate policies. But the Government persisted in its policy, and one Lutheran Church in the north did in fact forbid its teachers to join Tanu. No Catholic bishop ever did.

Now the Chief Secretary called in Father Walsh and asked him to refuse to give Nyerere permission to go to New York, since he represented a subversive movement. Father Walsh retorted that the Government had recently passed a new law enabling them to deal with subversive people; if Tanu was a subversive movement, he could not understand why they had not arrested Nyerere. In any case, it was a shabby trick to ask a Christian mission to pass judgment and to take steps which only the Government was entitled to take as the sole authority responsible for law and order.

Next day Father Walsh was informed that the Governor had

agreed, but had added sarcastically that he took a dim view of any Government which provided money for the employment of a teacher like Nyerere.

As far as Tanu was concerned, the only question was how and where to find the money for Nyerere's air passage. With Bomani's and Kambona's help, they mobilised all Tanu members in town. Each one went round asking for donations from all conceivable sources, African, European and Asian, in some cases not even saying what the money was wanted for. Rashidi Kawawa, not a Tanu member because he was a civil servant, helped his friends by setting an example to T.A.G.S.A. members to give all they could, and some £600 was collected. In those weeks of money raising, Julius Nyerere, Paul Bomani, Oscar Kambona and Rashidi Kawawa worked together for the first time as a team. Had they but known it, it was a dress rehearsal of the future.

At the end of February, 1955, Nyerere took off for New York. The Administration made no difficulties about his passport, nor did they take steps against Paul Bomani, although they must have known that he had informed Nyerere and set in motion the Tanu action. It was Bomani's impression that the Governor turned down the suggestion that he should be kicked out of Legco. Twining was too big a man for such a petty revenge.

Meanwhile in New York the Trusteeship Council meeting on the third U.N. Visiting Mission's Report on Tanganyika started in a tense atmosphere. Its members were sharply divided in sympathies. Mason Sears led the attack on behalf of the Africans, ably supported by the Soviet delegate, who had the good sense to let the American do the talking. Arthur J. Grattan-Bellew, Q.C., Attorney-General and Member for Legal Affairs, acting as Tanganyika's Special Representative, was invited to sit at the Council table. His self-control and well informed answers lowered the temperature by several degrees. He stated that setting a date for independence would undermine existing political institutions, cause insecurity and disorders. It would stop the influx of capital needed for economic development and the maintenance of the revenue upon which the social services depended. The civil service would collapse as no Africans were fit to take over.

Grattan-Bellew denied that Tanganyika Africans were unusually adaptable; they were keen on the development of their country, he said, but preferred to proceed 'in their own way and at their own time'. Before the Government had decided on parity, the Constitutional Committee had travelled all over the country to question associations and individuals. Only the Tanganyika European Council had at first opposed the principle, but after further consideration its members had also supported it. He agreed that parity would have to be dropped, but only after a long time.

This perfectly stated the British case and was warmly applauded by half of the Trusteeship Council, who were representatives of colonial powers. The rest, the non-colonials, looked down their noses, muttering uncomplimentary remarks.

On March, 6, 1955, the three substantial citizens, representing the Tanganyika Unofficial Members organisation, were summoned but only Sir Charles Phillips was invited to sit at the Council table. He had dark hair and dark eyes, and handsome regular features. Meticulously dressed, everything about him indicated a systematic mind.

The first question fired at him by Mason Sears was: 'Do you regard Tanganyika as an African country, or does the Government regard it as African only because of its geographical situation?'

Phillips replied that the Territory was being developed for the benefit of all its inhabitants, with special emphasis on raising the African standard of living. Eventually the voters, among whom the Africans would be in a vast majority, would decide. He was then attacked on the ground that he was not a genuine representative of the Tanganyikan people, as he had been appointed by the Governor. There was no gainsaying this, although Phillips tried to explain that the unofficial members were independent people, who took no orders from the Government.

For the better part of one day, Sir Charles was harried and provoked. Most Council members seemed little impressed by his arguments, or indeed by Sir Charles himself, whom they regarded as a typical colonialist.

The atmosphere changed completely on March 7, 1955, when Julius Nyerere came as a petitioner before the Council. His youthful appearance, more like that of a student than of a political leader, caused surprise. He was self-possessed, completely at ease and modest. His first statment was: 'The main object of my presence here is to prove the falsity of European Press reports that the Tanganyikan population is opposed to the recommendations of the Visiting Mission.'

He made his point without vilifying the Administering Authority. People sitting in the packed gallery looked up in surprise. This was not the usual tactic of petitioners from Trust Territories.

In answer to questions, Nyerere explained that Tanu aimed at preparing the people for self-government and independence. As a first step towards this goal, it wanted the elective principle to be established and the Africans to secure a majority in all representative public bodies. It had accepted the principle of parity on the understanding that it was a transitional stage towards a democratic form of representation.

Indeed it is desired that individual non-Africans should participate increasingly as leaders of the people [Nyerere said], side by side with educated Africans. The Tanganyika Africans desire a categorical statement from the Trusteeship Council and the Administering Authority that the future Government will be primarily African; only when they have that assurance, will parity representation cease to inspire false hopes in the non-Africans and false fears in the Africans.

The Members of the Trusteeship Council indicated their approval of words which no European democrat could have bettered. Nyerere won further sympathy by saying that Tanu was asking for very little–only that three of the thirty unofficial members of the Legislature should be elected, representing Dar-es-Salaam, and that the Governor should nominate the other twenty-seven provincial representatives from a panel of names supplied by the three races.

Then came Nyerere's most unexpected statement: 'Tanu's policy is one not of discrimination but of brotherhood. I believe this also to be essentially the policy of the Administering Authority.'

The Soviet representative turned away in disgust. This was not what he had expected from the much advertised critic of the British colonial power. All Nyerere did by way of censure was to say that he wished immigration and alienation of land to stop; trade unions and the co-operative movement to be built up; education and technical training to be greatly expanded, adding: 'As the Government seeks the same objectives, the members of Tanu co-operate with it and it is our greatest friend.'

This was in line with his tactics towards Twining. In New York as in London, Nyerere kept up the fiction that Twining approved of the independence demanded by Tanu on behalf of all three races in Tanganyika. No one at the Trusteeship Council understood what he was driving at. If the members thought the above statement less than candid, they did not say so.

In answer to further questions, Nyerere described Tanu's political structure and how its petition to the Trusteeship Council had been drafted. He did not claim that it represented the whole African population, only that it was the strongest, in fact the only African political organisation.

In conclusion, he hoped the day would come when all the inhabitants of the Territory had become a community which, though racially heterogeneous, was nationally homogeneous. However, should self-government be attained before that stage had been reached, guarantees would be provided to protect minority rights. 'We will ensure that Asians and Europeans will not be swamped by an African majority.'

When Julius Nyerere left the Council table, the gallery emptied and public interest in the proceedings evaporated – for ever. All that happened during the Fifteenth Session of the Trusteeship Council has long been forgotten. The Mason Sears Report, the British resolve not to be dislodged from their chosen course, the baiting of Sir Charles Phillips, all these are only of academic interest to the historian. But the impression created by Julius Nyerere when he first stepped on to the world stage, without experience in public life or even advice from someone with such experience, has laid the foundations of his career.

It is sad to relate that on this occasion the British authorities stooped to an unworthy tactic. They appealed to the State Department to restrict Nyerere's movements during his New York visit to an eight block radius from the U.N. building and his stay to within twenty-four hours of his appearance before the Trusteeship Council. This not only rendered it impossible for him to make propaganda speeches, but even to see his friends. The Maryknoll Fathers read about his performance at the U.N. in the Press; when Father Albert J. Nevins, who had known Julius Nyerere well during the years he spent at the Nyegina mission near Musoma, tried to get in touch with him, he had already been put on a plane to return to Tanganyika.

The timidity and excessive caution with which the British authorities, on the advice of Sir Edward Twining, handled this incident were an unfortunate lapse. It almost seemed as though the greatest colonial power in the world, when first challenged in public by an unknown young African, had lost its sense of proportion. After the tremendous gestures of granting independence to India, to Burma, to Palestine, to Ceylon, the British had apparently suffered a *crise de nerfs*. It was to last three years, until Sir Edward Twining's retirement.

PART IV
THE NATIONALIST TRIUMPH

CHAPTER 24

Initial Hopes are Dashed

IT was natural that the prestige which Julius Nyerere acquired by his statesmanlike appearance before the Trusteeship Council should have raised the hope among Africans that their aspirations had come nearer to fulfilment. The experience of the next three years was to show that any such hope was premature.

On his return from New York, Nyerere had to face the problem of his personal future. Since October, 1952, he had been history master at St Francis' School, the territorial secondary school the Tanganyika Roman Catholic Bishops' Conference had built in Pugu. The Holy Ghost Fathers, in charge of St Francis' School, may not have fully understood Nyerere's political activities, yet without their sympathy he would have had difficulties much sooner than the spring of 1955. Both the headmaster and Nyerere were aware that from now on he could not devote himself to politics as well as to teaching.

As the Executive of the Bishops' Conference in Educational Affairs, Father Walsh–who had originally appointed Nyerere to the post at Pugu–now went to see the Director of Education, L. P. A. Attenborough, and proposed that Nyerere should be given three months' retirement leave with salary. This was eventually agreed to, but the Government understandably insisted either that he should not be paid a salary for the month he had been in New York, or that this month should be counted as part of his retirement leave.

In his official capacity Father Walsh then wrote a letter to Nyerere. In it he stated that, in the spirit of the 1953 Pastoral, *Africans and the Christian Way of Life*, the Church was most anxious for Africans to advance towards full development. Therefore it would never forbid teachers (except priests) to join Tanu, or to become Tanu office bearers. On the other hand, since teachers in their schools were preparing future African leaders, they had to make sure that their classes were properly taught and that politics did not interfere with education. For the same reason, no teacher must ever use his class as a political platform for any kind of party politics. As for Nyerere himself, the Bishops'

Conference had always found him an excellent teacher, efficient, loyal, hard-working. If he were now to decide that he could no longer afford to be both teacher and leader of a nationalist movement, the Conference would see him go with regret and would like him to know of their grateful appreciation of his services.

Father Walsh sent a copy of this letter to the Director of Education, who made no secret of his displeasure over the Catholic attitude, which he regarded as contrary to Government policy because it allowed teachers to play with politics.

Nyerere's reaction was one of gratitude and generosity. On March 22, 1955, he resigned his position as history master, and was left facing penury. This was one of the most impressive gestures he made in the service of his fellow Africans.

The present headmaster of St Francis' School, Father L. O'Connor, has explained Nyerere's resignation to the author as follows:

My predecessor did not order Mr Nyerere to resign because of his political work. The time had come when his extra-curricular activities were taking up so much time that classes must suffer. No man can do two full time jobs with success. If the political work was to go on someone else must be put to class work. This was put up to Mr Nyerere and he saw that it was reasonable and that the Headmaster's first duty was to the pupils of the school. Mr Nyerere decided freely to enter the field of politics and we parted company on good terms. (April 20, 1963.)

When Nyerere handed in his letter of resignation, word went round Dar-es-Salaam that he had been sacked because the headmaster objected to his politics. The *Tanganyika Standard* asked to interview him on this question, and Tanu prepared to stage a protest meeting for next evening. The interview duly took place and next morning the *Standard* reported that Nyerere had flatly denied that he had been sacked. He had said unequivocally that he left of his own accord. Nyerere also saw to it that there was no Tanu protest meeting.

As Nyerere had no worldly possessions of any kind, his friends wondered how he would maintain his family; not only his wife and three children, but also his mother and brother Joseph. Tanu offered him £25 a month, but they knew as well as Nyerere that there were no funds. The Maryknoll Fathers had invited him to go to America to give some lectures. If the invitation was confirmed, there was the hope that he might earn some money in the U.S.

Father Walsh tried to get Nyerere a job with the Shell Oil Co., which offered him a post as salesman with a graduate salary of £600 a year. Tanu officials would not let him take the job on the ground that it might well mean a post up-country or even in Kenya.

Then an attempt was made to secure for him the editorship of *Kiongozi*, the newly established Catholic territorial newspaper. Nyerere felt that his political obligations would not leave him enough time to develop it properly. In April, 1955, he went with his family back to Musoma and tried to grow cashew nuts with his eldest half-brother, Chief Wanzagi, but this venture failed.

Finally the Maryknoll Fathers, who since 1950 had been in charge of Nyegina mission, found a way of helping him. As they were planning to set up a mission in Zanakiland, they commissioned him to translate the catechism and the Gospel into Ki-Zanaki and to write a Ki-Zanaki grammar. Moreover, as a mission could only be run effectively by a father who spoke the vernacular, he was to teach Father Arthur Wille Ki-Zanaki.

Nyerere carried out these assignments with enthusiasm.

At the end of the daily five hour lesson [Father Wille has told the author], I was exhausted, while Julius seemed as fresh as a daisy, and in the evening he went off to build a house for his family. He told me that he was certain that Twining would have him imprisoned when he returned from America, where he had been invited by my Order. 'If he doesn't, I don't think I'll ever become Prime Minister,' he said, 'I must go to prison, but I don't want Maria and the children to remain roofless.' Julius was most anxious that there should be no bloodshed. He told me that he prayed every day it should not come to violence.

By the autumn of 1955, the translation and the Ki-Zanaki grammar were ready and I spoke the language reasonably well. Only the roof was missing from the house. Julius borrowed the money from me to have it put on.

Having completed his temporary job for the Maryknoll Fathers, Nyerere felt the urge to be nearer the centre of political events, so he returned to Dar-es-Salaam to develop Tanu.

Still he was faced with the nagging problem of how to earn a livelihood for his family. He obtained a tiny house and it was his wife who shouldered the immediate burden of making ends meet. Maria Nyerere opened a little shop, a *duka*, selling mainly flour, paraffin, oil and soap. Very often customers did not pay up and she was almost constantly in debt. Being an excellent knitter, she also took orders for knitting jumpers, pullovers and cardigans. She was knitting day and night, sitting up until all hours by the light of an oil lamp. Sometimes she got no more than two hours sleep at night. With the money she made by her knitting, she dressed her children.

As far as the British administration were concerned, Nyerere could not have chosen a more inauspicious moment to try to revitalise the African nationalist cause. A month after he had resigned his teaching post, Sir Edward Twining opened the new Legislative Council for the first time, with all pomp, in Karimjee Hall in Dar-es-Salaam.

The reconstituted Legislative Council consisted of the Speaker, thirty-one *ex officio* and nominated members and thirty representative members. The Government's strength of thirty-one had been made up by adding fourteen unofficials (including six members of the Executive Council) to seventeen experienced senior officials. The Representative Members were the ten Africans, ten Asians and ten Europeans, appointed on the basis of the controversial one–one–one formula, selected from names put forward by a variety of interests to represent particular areas. For the first time, the Governor had appointed 'lady members', whom he entreated to show impartiality and to speak up on behalf of family interests.

In his address, Twining said of the principle of parity:

Although I do not consider this by any means to be perfect, I do think it suits the conditions of Tanganyika at this stage of its progress, and is likely to continue to be the best arrangement for a long time to come. It ensures equal representation of all three races and diminishes the possibility of domination of any one race. (April 20, 1955).

Twining never mentioned Julius Nyerere by name, only referring to him obliquely when he said:

There are some, a minority I believe, of people in the Territory who are disappointed that elections have not yet been introduced. Towards the end of last year Government set up an *ad hoc* committee to examine the question of the introduction of elections to local government bodies. Their report has been received and is being examined.

For the rest, he made it clear that the new constitution was to last for a long period. (He would have scoffed at any prediction that in three years' time Nyerere's demand for elections would be granted.)

The Council's 1955 Constitution was indeed rudimentary compared to that of the Mother of Parliaments. And yet, the new Legco did represent a great advance for Tanganyika. No one realised this more clearly than Nyerere, who wanted Tanu to take as much advantage as possible of the chance to have its point of view aired in the Chamber. Not being an unofficial member gave him freedom of movement and there was one issue upon which he was particularly well qualified to challenge Twining.

When dealing with education, the Governor had stated that in 1954, 880 students had reached Standard X to XII, as against 730 in 1953; that in 1954 98 African candidates had been successful in the School Certificate Examination as against 86 in 1953, and that there were 64 new entrants accepted into Makerere College as against 41 in 1953.

Nyerere was scornful of these paltry figures from eight million Africans. He was even more indignant over the allocation of the funds yielded by enemy properties confiscated in 1939 and 1940, which Britain had ceded to Tanganyika as a gift. The sum of £3,618,555 was to be spent as follows:

Tanganyika High Education Trust Fund (set aside for a future university)	£711,111
St Michael's and St George's School	£711,111
Indian Education	£711,111
African Education	£711,111
Township Development	£711,111
Roads of access into productivity areas	£63,000
	£3,618,555 [1]

[1] Two items of this allocation of funds need elucidation.

1. The £711,111 allocated for Indian education was intended to provide schools for Indians and Sikhs. The Ismaelis and the Bahoras, being very community-minded, had from the first set up their own excellent schools.

2. Before the war, European children were sent to Britain to be educated. During the war, this could not be done because of transport difficulties. Kenyan and Rhodesian schools took as many children as they could accommodate; for the rest a temporary school was opened at Mbeya.

After the war, the new settlers and employees (technicians, railway foremen, Public Works Department staff) demanded local secondary schools, towards which they paid a per capita annual tax of £20. The Twining administration allocated one fifth of the German reparations money to build a first class grammar

On June 1, 1955, Nyerere sent the following letter to the Chairman of the Tanganyika Unofficial Members' Organisation:

Dear Sir,

The distribution of the Custodian of Enemy Property Funds, as proposed by His Excellency the Governor in his recent speech to the Legislative Council, seems inexplicable. The need for education being what it is, Government could not have chosen a worthier cause on which to spend the money than education. But the decision to distribute the funds on a parity basis must have come to many people as a shock.

There are roughly 22,000 Europeans, 80,000 Asians and 8,000,000 Africans in the country. The decision to give £800,000[2] to each group gives, per head of population, 720s. to each European, 200s. to each Asian, and 2s. to each African. Disparity of educational expenditure per head of population in each racial group is always there, even in the ordinary budget of the country. But there is no 'parity' to aggravate it. This particular disparity is aggravated to the point of absurdity by this application of parity!

Now, even if the whole population had accepted the proposition that numbers do not matter, that quality makes members of the minority groups deserve more money per head for the education of their children, one would at least have expected the Authorities concerned to have considered NEED. For lack of education is one thing in which the African can claim undisputable superiority over the other racial groups. There is also, of course, his poverty. Here were two fairly good reasons to discourage the distribution of this fund on a parity basis. . . .

Despite much unfounded talk to the contrary, the principle of parity has *not* been accepted by the majority of the people of Tanganyika. Most people have let it pass because they could do nothing to prevent its adoption. The advocates of parity have a duty, I think, to see to it that its application does not make it look absurd and unjust; for such

[2] Nyerere gave this erroneous figure.

school (a boarding school) for their children near Iringa, called the St Michael's and St George's School. In June, 1957, before the Trusteeship Council, Tanganyika's Special Representative said that St Michael's and St George's would be a non-racial school; hence by 1960 the Board of Governors had agreed to its integration. From the first, the African pupils gave a very good account of themselves.

After independence, the Government found the annual deficit (about £40,000) previously carried by the British, a heavy burden and announced that it would close down the school. The money was eventually found to maintain it, although the standards of Mkwawa School, as it is now named, had to be lowered.

a thing would make even those who are willing to give it a chance strive for its early death.

I do not know whether a final decision has already been taken on the use of this fund. If it has not yet been taken, I would beg your Organisation to consider making the suggestion to Government that the whole fund be set aside for the provision of higher education to the country as a whole, instead of being allocated in the manner proposed.

Yours truly,
Julius K. Nyerere.

This letter infuriated Twining. This jumped up agitator would not desist from criticising his Government. What is more, he had managed to make the Government appear ridiculous. For instance, Oswald, as Musoma Assistant District Officer, was instructed to ask Julius Nyerere to report to him regularly. Nothing was easier; the Nyereres were staying with him. Africans had a good laugh at the British for not even knowing that Oswald was Julius' *ndugu*—tribal relation.

Nyerere held his first Tanu meeting in the Lake District at Ikizu, forty-five miles from Musoma, at the headquarters of Chief Mohamed Makongoro. (He, incidentally, was a man the Government viewed with some suspicion; not only was he a confirmed and daring poacher, but some of his own people alleged that his enemies had a habit of disappearing.) On the drive to Ikizu, the police car, carrying plain clothes men to report on the meeting, broke down and Nyerere gave the passengers a lift so that they could comply with their duty. This magnanimity caused great merriment among Africans.

Whatever tactical successes Nyerere might be making with Africans in the countryside, there was no denying that on the big issue of policy the advantage appeared to have been won by the Twining Administration.

The hopes which had burgeoned so freely when Nyerere made his dramatic appearance before the Trusteeship Council had been dashed.

CHAPTER 25

Nyerere Rallies His Supporters

SMALL as was the impact that Nyerere had so far been able to make upon the Government at the centre, his activities in the country at large were by no means time wasted. This was a period when he was able to quicken nationalist interest among the population generally and rally to his side Africans who were to prove invaluable assistants in the future.

In the north of Tanganyika, Nyerere made a great impression. Lucy Lameck, the first woman to become a junior Minister in Tanganyika, was present when he addressed her tribe, the Chagga.

I had met Julius in Dar-es-Salaam in 1953 [she has told the author]. Long before that I had felt that, in order to be effective in a hospital, or a school, or an office, I had to turn to politics. To obtain equal treatment was part of a much larger problem, the problem of existence under a colonial government. . . . At this time we Chagga had a Paramount Chief called Tom Marealle, an arrogant man who made life very difficult for all of us who did not approve of his politics. When Twining offered me a scholarship to England, Marealle turned it down. I would rather not tell you why. I have never cried so much in my life. By then Tanu was in existence and I pinned all my hopes on it.

In October 1954 Julius came to Moshi and held meetings. At one of them I enrolled my father, my mother, my aunt and my two sisters. Soon after that I was elected representative of the district. On his return from the Trusteeship Council meeting, Julius came north again and held two meetings: one in Machame and the other in Moshi. I went to both and witnessed the marvellous effect he had on my people. Now we Tanu enthusiasts began to campaign in earnest. We only had one car, but we managed to get to the most remote villages. . . . We told people about the need for education and how little the British had done about it. We talked about the land shortage, and the injustice of having large areas not permitted to be used. We told them that Tanganyika was our country and that we were going to run it in our way. We told them that Tanu, headed by Julius, would lead us to independence.

These were heady words, even among the sober Chagga. To the colonial administration they confirmed that Nyerere was an irresponsible agitator. This attitude was well illustrated by an incident in Njombe, in the Southern Highlands, where Austin

Shaba, now Minister of Local Government, was then medical assistant at the new hospital. One day he heard the local D.C. describe Nyerere as 'a first class hooligan'. Soon after, driving a woman patient to the hospital, he was told at the petrol filling station that Nyerere was in Njombe and that the D.C. had made him stay at the labour camp. This was a nice enough house, but devoid of furniture and inmates had to sleep on the cement floor, which was cold as well as uncomfortable, for in the Southern Highlands the nights are very chilly.

Shaba was shocked to discover Nyerere having tea at a dirty African 'hotel'. As he could not leave his patient, he wrote a note to his wife (they had no telephone) asking her to invite him to stay.

Subsequently the D.C. attacked Shaba for harbouring an 'undesirable agitator'. In self-defence, Shaba lied, saying that Nyerere had become ill at the labour camp. 'Am I not entitled to treat him as a patient because he is said to be an enemy of the British?' he retorted. 'In my oath I had to pledge myself to help any person in need of help.'

His explanation was accepted.

When Nyerere arrived in Njombe, there were only four Tanu members and they had to conceal their allegiance, for the party was illegal in this area. Although he could not obtain permission to hold a meeting, he enrolled twelve new Tanu supporters.

It was typical of the contradictions in Tanganyikan life that a few days later, on October 24, 1955, in Dar-es-Salaam Julius Nyerere as Tanu President entertained the Deputy Governor, the Mayor and senior civil servants to a sundowner. The occasion was the party's first annual conference which happened to coincide with United Nations Day. The legal ban on Africans consuming European type spirits having just been lifted by Twining, guests were offered a variety of potent drinks and a pleasant time was had by all.

On the same day, Legco passed the Incitement to Violence Bill, which made inter-communal attacks liable to the same penalty as sedition, and placed the onus of proving absence of hostile intent on the defence.

The annual conference passed a unanimous resolution against the Bill, yet Nyerere made so moderate a public speech that Tanu delegates were furious. The Government gave Nyerere no credit for his constructive approach, and Tanu for their part brought such strong pressure to bear on him that subsequently he had to harden his attitude.

At this time of political ferment, it was especially unfortunate that the British administration and the African nationalists, though in close physical proximity, lived mentally in two worlds apart. Responsibility for this situation rested primarily on Sir Edward Twining, who completely misread Julius Nyerere's character and activities. He could see neither courage nor dedication in Nyerere's giving up a promising career and material security in order to help his people to realise their national aspirations. Twining regarded the nationalist demands for immediate political rights and for a date to be set for Tanganyika's independence as utterly unreasonable. In his estimation, Tanganyika, deprived of British guidance, would lose her chance of attracting capital and investors, and without expatriate civil servants the administration would dissolve in chaos.

On the one hand Twining considered Nyerere as a dangerous man, who imagined he was to become another Nkrumah or Nehru, and who should be crushed; on the other he declared that he was just an upstart, intellectually second rate and personally ambitious.

Nyerere revealed his philosophy on one occasion when, in the presence of David Makwaia, Adam Sapi and Harun Lugusha he refuted

the stupid attitude of the Europeans who say easily that Africans have time only to think of their bellies [he said]. Look at Mau Mau of whom several hundreds have been shot or hanged recently. What did they give their lives for if not for an ideal?–although of course it is an evil ideal and the poor people don't know any better. But it is not because of the fleshpots that they are dying. When the White Fathers came to Africa seventy-five years ago, they presented Christianity in such a way that many young Africans gave themselves to be killed and tortured out of love of the cause of Christ. What has now happened is that Africans are indifferent to the Christian message and to my message as a Christian. It has lost its spark. Government thinks it can satisfy us by giving us a reinforced concrete and tarmac civilisation. But what we need is not material uplift but rather an ideology based on the best part of man's aspirations. Why do they put us, in any case, into what for us are luxurious school buildings and hospitals, only to send us back later to live in mud huts? Not even from government's mistaken policy point of view does this make sense.

Sir Charles Arden-Clarke in Ghana and Sir Andrew Cohen in Uganda proved that a man of different temperament and more modern cast of mind than Twining could have reached early understanding with an African like Julius Nyerere.

The situation was further exacerbated by the frequent misrepresentation of Tanu and its leaders in the local and the British Press. One reason for this was the poor Swahili of the correspondents, who mistranslated much that was said. Not one of them understood Swahili slang, and therefore missed the point of most of Nyerere's jokes. Another reason, it must be admitted, was the violent and provocative nature of the speeches of some of the more remote Tanu leaders—for not all of them shared, or even understood, Nyerere's principles.

In desperation, Tanu leaders in Dar-es-Salaam began to type their version of events on sheets of paper and stick these to trees around town. As the Party grew in numbers and therefore in influence, the *Tanganyika Standard* asked for a few Tanu members to act as reporters. But there was a string attached to this offer: these reporters could have no say in the interpretation the editor placed on their contributions.

Nyerere too, who by this time had thrown himself into organisational work and was constantly touring the country, was in a dilemma. Not only had he to correct the repeated misrepresentations in the Press, but political considerations compelled him to place the worst interpretation on the best concessions of the British administration. There were the thirty unofficial members in Legco; there was the announcement of elections to be held in 1958 and 1959; there was the liberalisation of the franchise; and there were, for all to see, the economic developments carried out by the Government, which impressed the average, non-political African. Nyerere's speeches became increasingly more fiery, and his audience reached the conclusion that he wanted an all-black Tanganyika. They cheered him for his radical views.

It was a report of one of Nyerere's angry speeches in the *Tanganyika Standard* that provoked a young Englishman, Derek Bryceson, to write a letter to the Editor attacking him for his racialist attitude. Bryceson had served in the R.A.F., was shot down over the western desert and survived almost by a miracle. Complications set in around his shattered pelvis and he became crippled for life. Eventually he went to East Africa and settled on a farm on Mount Kilimanjaro. There one of his neighbours, Robin Johnston,[1] interested him in Capricorn, the Society founded by David Stirling with the object of bringing the races in East and Central Africa together. Johnston flew him around Tanganyika for ten days to meet leading Africans. As a result of this, Bryceson became preoccupied with the need to put relations with Africans on a completely new basis.

Nyerere did not answer the attack, although in the *Kenya Weekly News* of March 1, 1957, Bryceson had described his speech as 'a masterpiece of studied inaccuracy'. But when he next came to Arusha, Bryceson invited him to luncheon and began by accusing him. Nyerere denied ever having been a racialist, and in his turn attacked Bryceson for all the sins of the colonialists.

The Englishman was deeply impressed by Nyerere's logic and his political philosophy. Their discussion lasted three days, and by the end of it, they had cleared up many misunderstandings. A mutual trust had been established which was to have a great effect on their lives, particularly on Bryceson's.

While, at this period, Nyerere was doing valuable work in increasing the number of Tanu supporters, a more significant measure of his achievement was the improvement in the quality of his support. Like all nationalist movements, Tanu attracted the worst as well as the best among the Tanganyika people. Its ranks were swelled not only by political idealists and solid citizens, but also by what in the west is called the lunatic fringe: spivs, cranks, extremists, racialists and plain greedy men, who saw Tanu as a means to achieve political or economic power. This was what Europeans who sympathised with African aspirations had feared would happen, and there can be no doubt that many of the Tanu rank and file were talking the most arrant nonsense. On July 26, 1957, the *Kenya Weekly News* wrote: 'No-one supposes that Mr Nyerere supports or approves the hotheads or rowdies among his followers, but some pretty severe disciplining is going to be necessary in Tanu if the whole movement is not to become dubbed as irresponsible and dangerous and a threat to the peaceful development of Tanganyika towards independence.'

Julius Nyerere was aware of all this. His answer was honest and logical:

[1] See also Chapter 26.

Tanu has no money, no clerical staff, no provincial organisers, no means of advertising, none of the essentials of a normal political party. We must admit anyone who wants to join, and if he talks rubbish, but enrols new members, we cannot reject him. Once we are established all over the country, such nonsensical ideas as confiscations, expulsions, archaic and brutal punishments will soon be forgotten.[2]

In January, 1958, at the Tabora Conference, Nyerere lived up to his promise and proved his statesmanship.

In 1955, however, he was faced with yet another difficulty: the British administration was trying to break up Tanu by offering scholarships to his most reliable assistants. On the Governor's instructions, Oscar Kambona, Nyerere's right hand man, was offered a scholarship to study in England. Kambona hesitated because it meant four years' absence from Tanganyika. Nyerere's advice was that Tanganyika would not have independence for a long time, maybe not for twenty-five years. Kambona should therefore go; four years would soon pass. That Kambona should acquire a really good education was the main consideration.

Kambona left for England; so did Bomani, and many other Tanu stalwarts. It was one of the mistakes of the British that they allowed these ambitious young men to become either teachers or social workers, and made no resolute attempt to compel them to take up the more exacting disciplines of science or engineering. The administration did however select some men of strong personality and good character to train them for administrative work. Later Sir Richard Turnbull speeded up the process and increased the numbers. After independence, all of them became D.C.s; some had as much as ten years training.

Nyerere appointed Steven Mhando, one of Dr Kyaruzi's promising helpers at the time he took over T.A.A., to replace Kambona as Tanu's new Organising Secretary. Mhando held extremist views; Government House knew this, but did not realise that Nyerere was much more moderate, or that Mhando never had a chance against him. In the event, ambition soon drove Mhando to overreach himself. At the end of 1956 he went to India to secure scholarships for Tanganyika students. He continued his journey to Burma, where he spent so much money that Tanu had to sack him, much though Nyerere disliked breaking with an able

---

[2] Told to the author by Miss Mary Hancock, former headmistress of Tabora Girls' School, Mbeya Girls' School and Inspector of Education.

colleague. After his return to Dar-es-Salaam, he took up journalism then for some years taught Swahili in East Germany. At the moment of writing he is back in Tanzania and is a member of the staff of the University College of Dar-es-Salaam.

A specially valuable aspect of Nyerere's work touring up and down the country was the opportunity it afforded him for rallying and encouraging the most intelligent and most talented Africans on whom the future of Tanu really depended.

In January, 1956, he went on a political *safari* with two dynamic personalities, Bibi Titi Mohamed and Elias Kisenge, both of whom have left their mark on Tanganyikan developments.

Oscar Kambona had enrolled Bibi Titi in 1954 and she was the first woman to have obtained a Tanu card. The daughter of a small trader, happily married and mother of several children, she was barely literate. Yet at this time she was running a musical group called *Bomba*. There were two more such female music groups in Dar-es-Salaam; Kambona induced all three to give a joint concert, its proceeds going to Tanu.

Back in 1950, Dr Kyaruzi had invited Haya and Asian women friends to organise sewing classes in T.A.A.'s little house in New Street, and under this domestic guise, to implant political ideas in the women's minds. Bibi Titi developed these sewing parties into indoctrination classes, and sent her trainees to various parts of Dar-es-Salaam and the Eastern Province to awaken the women. After John Hatch, the Labour Party's Commonwealth Officer, had commented during his visit in June, 1955, on the lack of women members in the movement, she used her ferocious energy to organise her fellow Muslim women. By the time of the first Tanu conference in October, 1955, the Women's Section had five thousand members, with their own leaders. It was the only such body at the time in East Africa. And by the end of the year, thanks to Bibi Titi's activities, Tanu had more women than men members.

In January, 1956, Nyerere saw with his own eyes how successful she had been. He went with her and Elias Kisenge to Tanga Province, where they had good receptions except in a few places where the chiefs would not allow them to speak. One such place was Lushoto, a town close to the Governor's summer residence.[3]

[3] Twining had agreed to serve a third term in 1955 on two conditions: that he could spend six months of the year at Lushoto and that Arthur Grattan-Bellew would become his Chief Secretary.

Nyerere and his friends were convinced that Twining had put the local chief up to this. As it was, some chiefs, *jumbes* and witch doctors were hostile to Tanu because it advocated progress, meaning new organisations, new ideas and new leaders. This boded ill for the old African 'establishment'. Frightened men can do unreasonable things.

Then the unexpected happened. The men kept away from the Tanu meetings, but not the women. In Korogwe not only did they attend, but they told their husbands that unless they plucked up courage to join them, they would not cook dinner. Not quite as drastic as Lysistrata's threat, but it worked. As soon as Elias Kisenge heard of the affair, he sent a lorry to fetch the Korogwe women to another meeting, organised on the spur of the moment as a repeat performance. The husbands had to leg it, arriving conspicuously late and shamefaced.

News of this spread fast. The Africans adore gossip and the bush grapevine is faster than lightning. Moreover here was proof that the chiefs could do nothing if their anti-Tanu orders were defied, a sensational revelation to Africans.

Later Bibi Titi learnt English at British expense, so as to enable her to become a Legco Member. She is now head of Tanu's Women's Section, as forceful and independent as ever, capable of swaying the largest crowd by her dramatic oratory. Her husband left her because she was too much absent from home, which grieved her greatly. In 1963 she re-married and once more enjoys a family life. Her husband is Micky Ndoe, head of the Tanganyika Broadcasting Corporation.

Nyerere's second companion, Elias Kisenge, was a man with many of the attributes of an American party boss: bonhomie, resourcefulness, backslapping good-fellowship and organising ability. Born a Pare, member of a proud tribe even more resentful of colonial administration than most Africans, he became aware of discrimination against Africans at Tabora Government School, when he learnt how much better were the food and conditions in Asian and European schools. After Tabora, he entered Government service, and from 1938 to 1948 worked for the provincial administration in various towns of the Northern Province. He also became Provincial Secretary of T.A.G.S.A. and a keen member of T.A.A., Cameron's organisation in which so many Africans won their political spurs.

K

In 1948 he was transferred to Same, the capital of Pareland, as chief clerk of the *boma*, when he also became secretary of the Pare Tribal Association, which taught him how to organise. At this time the Pare had refused to pay graduated tax and the Government meant to take strong measures. Pare passive resistance was led by an octogenarian called Paulo Mashambo, who headed a demonstration of some fifteen thousand people to the *boma*. He is still alive, now about a hundred years old.

At the end of 1948, Kisenge was transferred to the Treasury at Dar-es-Salaam. A year later he became T.A.G.S.A.'s organising secretary. He had a hard time, for Government kept a close watch on civil servants who dabbled with politics. Yet he managed to get a hearing on behalf of the Government Servants before the Lidbury Commission, and demanded that Africans should receive the same salaries as Asians. If they did not receive at least a rise in pay, they would go on strike. As soon as the word strike was heard in public places, Kisenge was sent for by the Chief Secretary, R. de S. Stapledon, who wanted to know what T.A.G.S.A. meant by advocating strike action.

Kisenge fibbed that he knew nothing about this. The Chief Secretary would have none of it, as he knew there had been strike talk. Kisenge then said that if there had been strike talk, maybe it was because people were dissatisfied with conditions. When the Chief Secretary retorted that if people were dissatisfied, they should come to him instead of talking about striking, Kisenge remarked wistfully: 'It is not easy to come to you, Mr Chief Secretary. . . .'

Mr Stapledon assured him that he would always be available to hear a legitimate complaint.

As far as Kisenge was concerned, the immediate result of the strike talk was his transfer to the Southern Province, which seemed to him a punishment posting. He managed to get back to Dar-es-Salaam and then to Same, where he helped to revive T.A.A. In the summer of 1954 he resigned from both the Pare Council and the Association, and became District Secretary of Tanu without a salary. He kept himself by setting up the Churchill Bar, which paid quite well. He walked all over the Pare area, holding meetings and talking to fellow tribesmen on these lines: Why should we be ruled by foreigners in our own country? God has created the world, and he gave this piece of it to us. Why should we put up with discrimination, not be allowed to enter a European hotel, nor be served even a glass of beer at a bar?' (He conveniently omitted mentioning that Africans could obtain drink permits.) 'Why are we treated as nobodies in our own country?'

In three months he enrolled two thousand members. In October, 1955, he came to Dar-es-Salaam for the Tanu annual conference, and was kept there to check the party's accounts, a job which he completed by December.

After his political *safari* in Tanga Province with Nyerere and Bibi Titi in January, 1956, Kisenge remained in Same. In April he moved to Tanga, having been elected Tanu Provincial Secretary. He had nothing in Tanga, not even an office. Meetings could only be held in private houses. To raise funds, he sold party cards. As Tanu had not yet been registered in the Tanga area, this was illegal.

Now Kisenge showed his quality as a party boss. He organised each area, saw to it that each branch was registered, formed committees, and set up the Youth League, calling it the Tanu Volunteer Corps.

When he summoned his first meeting in Tanga, he had managed to rent an office, but he had no money to buy furniture or equipment. He told the boys that chairs, tables, stationery, a clock, a pitcher and glasses, ashtrays were needed and asked whether they could produce them. Within half an hour everything was there. Some parents gave furniture, some gave other necessary things, and some gave cash. A fortnight later Kisenge began to send money to Dar-es-Salaam, sometimes as much as thirty thousand shillings (£150) a week.

In October, 1956, Nyerere appointed Elias Kisenge Deputy Organising Secretary of Tanu, Oscar Kambona retaining, despite his absence, his original title. Kisenge still holds the position, only now he is called Deputy-Secretary-General. Kambona is Secretary-General, as well as Minister of External Affairs.

That Nyerere had been able to rally to his side Africans of the dynamic qualities of Bibi Titi and Elias Kisenge—and they were by no means the only ones—boded well for the future development of Tanu. The recruitment of faithful and reliable lieutenants enabled Nyerere to seize the chance which was soon to be offered of projecting himself on to a larger political stage. He was going to visit America for a second time.

The invitation came from the Maryknoll Fathers; it included a return ticket from London and covered expenses in the U.S.A. He had, however, to get to London under his own steam. His friends set to work to raise money for this. The Dar-es-Salaam taxi drivers, who had a lively, politically alert and, most important, financially sound union, contributed a round sum. So did T.A.G.S.A. So did some Indians. The rest Nyerere borrowed from Father Walsh.

At the end of October 1956, he flew to London and from there set sail for New York.

CHAPTER 26

Multi-Racialism is No Alternative

MENTION must now be made of a political concept which, during the early 1950s, was put forward as a workable alternative to crude African nationalism. It was a fine concept, inspired by noble ideals, which has left a lasting mark for good on the African continent. For Nyerere, however, this new concept could only be regarded as a further hindrance to be circumvented if the aims of Tanu were to be achieved.

By the end of 1955, Sir Edward Twining must have realised that his struggle against Tanu was narrowing down to a duel between himself and Nyerere For he appears to have persuaded himself, that once Nyerere was broken, Tanu would collapse. At the same time he was aware that a major weakness in his own position, as was to be demonstrated sixteen months later, was the absence of an alternative organisation, which could be pitted against the nationalists.

After the war, the Labour Government had initiated a policy of multi-racialism in Britain's East and Central African territories. Labour and Conservative leaders stated that all three races, Europeans, Africans and Asians, should participate in the economic and political life of the countries in which they lived together. True, of the 26 million inhabitants of this vast area only 250,000 were Europeans and 400,000 Asians, but the minorities had made an infinitely greater contribution than the immense African majority.

In Tanganyika the Trusteeship Agreement imposed on Britain the task of preparing the Tanganyika Africans for self-rule and independence. Multi-racialism was to have been a stage on the road to independence, and Britain hoped that it would be a long stage. And yet no one, either at the Colonial Office or in Tanganyika, had seen the need for creating any kind of multi-racial organisation, let alone a political one. It was left to a remarkable private individual, Colonel David Stirling, to draw attention to worsening race relations in Africa and to declare that, unless these improved, the development of the African continent would be gravely jeopardised.

He was one of the legendary Stirling brothers who, during the war, had formed the Special Air Services Regiment (S.A.S.) in North Africa, and spent long periods deep behind enemy lines. They destroyed airfields, shipping and supply dumps; David Stirling was credited with a tally of two hundred German planes blown up on the ground. In 1943 he was made a prisoner by the Germans; and it was during his captivity that he reached the conclusion that Africa was the continent of the future. If only he had known it, at the same time, young Africans were awakening to the same realisation at Makerere and Tabora and in the ranks of the K.A.R.

In 1946 he went to live in Southern Rhodesia and formed a business partnership with his brother, Bill, who headed the construction engineering firm of Stirling-Astaldi. This company built some of the best roads in Tanganyika.

David Stirling was deeply perturbed by the conduct of the white settlers in the Rhodesias, and by the implications of the theory of *apartheid* which Dr Malan, in the Union of South Africa, began to put into effect in 1947. He set about organising a movement 'to demolish the colour bar', and after two years of preparation he founded the Capricorn Africa Society. He chose the name as a sign that he wanted his anti-racialist ideas to apply in all British territories between the Equator and the Tropic of Capricorn.

Magnificently persuasive, he made converts not only among liberally minded public men, but among the most reactionary settlers. His basic conviction was that a policy for the salvation of Africa could only come from within Africa, that it had to recognise that all men were born equal and that differences between them, whether of creed or colour, were honourable differences.

His Capricorn Declarations started by saying: 'The colonies of Southern Rhodesia and Kenya, the Protectorates of Uganda, Nyasaland and Northern Rhodesia and the Territory of Tanganyika should be bound in a single self-governing federation under the British Crown.' The duty of the Europeans was to develop the African continent jointly with the Africans and to give them 'both incentive and opportunity to achieve a higher standard of life, and so make possible a true partnership between the races'. In the meantime, European guidance and leadership in federal and territorial government was needed; to quicken Africa's development, increased western immigration and technological skill had to be combined 'with the latent capacity of the African and other races'. In the African reserves no European was to own land; in areas to be developed, no African was to own land, only houses in urban centres.

Stirling stressed the need for a policy of race relations 'flexible enough to meet the special requirements of each territory, and broad enough to face with confidence the scrutiny of enlightened opinion throughout the world'. Africans who had attained the necessary social and educational standard must be accorded the responsibility of franchise.

Despite outdated proposals such as white leadership in Government and industry, increased white immigration and a qualified franchise, Capricorn was the first attempt in Central and East Africa to form a multi-racial organisation and the first invitation by a white settler group to Africans for *joint* development of their continent. At the time, this was a sensational departure.

That is why the Capricorn Declarations received such wide publicity in the British Press. On December 8, 1952, every London daily and most of the provincial papers devoted extensive space to a sympathetic discussion of their significance. The Liberal *News Chronicle* said editorially:

Apartheid reared its ugly syllables five years ago and we have waited ever since for some more inspiring and creative credo to emerge. The Capricorn Declarations issued by Colonel David Stirling are the first sign from within Africa of a coherent alternative to Dr Malan's barren policy. . . . The dream of a great federation extending from Ethiopia to the Limpopo may be visionary, but is none the worse for that. (December 9, 1952.)

The British reaction indicated relief that someone had at last made an imaginatively constructive move in Africa It was as though writers and politicians, who had watched paralysed the unhappy drift towards racial strife, were all too glad to give an accolade to the war hero now waving the banner of an idealistic programme.

The reception in Africa, both on the European and the African side, was far different. Most Europeans regarded the Capricorn Declarations as an attack on their birthright; their letters in the English-language papers in Africa voiced angry protests against the demand (as they saw it) that they should abdicate their position. But those who had attached themselves to David Stirling remained staunchly loyal. One of them was Colonel Laurens van der Post, whose descriptions of Africa have the deep sensitivity of a poet; another was Dr J. H. Oldham,[1] the veteran missionary with fifty-five years experience of Africa; a third was the South African writer, Alan Paton; a fourth was Sir Archibald MacIndoe, the famous plastic surgeon.

In 1952 there was no African Press, so spontaneous African views cannot be quoted. But thoughtful Africans were suspicious from the moment they heard about the qualified vote, the white leadership and the large areas in which they could not own land. They interpreted the Capricorn Declarations as a cunning effort to block the nationalist struggle for independence in East and Central Africa.

Undaunted, Stirling went on with his efforts in the knowledge that, under the Capricorn system, the African majority would soon occupy a dominating position. He wanted to have his ideas thrashed out urgently by representatives of the three communities, but like so many before him, he had to learn that Africa cannot be hurried. The 1953 convention, to be held in Mbeya, Tanganyika, had to be cancelled. Then Stirling tried to set up citizenship committees to consider the forms of human relations which must govern the life of the inter-racial society, and the ways in which they could best be given constitutional expression. After 1956, Capricorn came to regard multi-racial as a derogatory term, the object of its philosophy being to set up 'a nationalism of the human race'.

In 1955 Dr J. H. Oldham, by then eighty-one years of age, published a book on the Capricorn Africa Society called *New Hope in Africa*. In his view many of East and Central Africa's major problems were caused by wrong human relations, which could be solved by a new habit of mind, a new kind of fellow feeling, a new way of executing the responsibilities of office. All educational agencies in Africa had to be so reorganised that they should communicate to their pupils a spirit of dedication, self-help and community service. In this Dr Oldham was appealing for the wider application of those ideals which had always inspired Tabora Government School since its foundation in the days of Sir Donald Cameron.

About the rising tide of African nationalism, he expressed the deeply held belief of Capricorn:

[1] See also Chapter 9.

It is a force that cannot be stayed. Those who wish to live creatively in Africa must work with the tide and not against it. . . . The acid test of the idea of partnership as a basis for policy is whether it is accepted by the Africans. At present it is viewed by most Africans with the utmost mistrust and suspicion.

Events were moving with alarming rapidity, Dr Oldham declared. International Communism was actively at work to worsen deteriorating race relations. A revolution was bound to come. Would it lead to ruin and conflict, or would it be constructive through a fundamental change in men's ways of thinking and feeling? Dr Oldham's book ended with the hope that Capricorn would provide this constructive force.

Unfortunately it did not. At the Salima Convention, held in June, 1956, in Nyasaland, the delegates from thirty-five citizenship committees passed the Capricorn Contract. This document accepted the vote as a responsibility, not as a right; it laid down a qualified franchise with a maximum of six votes for persons meeting certain educational and property qualifications; it stressed the need to eliminate racial injustices. Among the delegates there were a few genuine African nationalists; David Stirling was proud that no African racialist had joined Capricorn as he had no use for them, but it disappointed him that Tanganyika could only muster a token delegation. Because of Julius Nyerere's opposition, the society never took root there.

The aspect of Capricorn which was fraught with danger for the nationalists in Tanganyika was that from 1950 onwards David Stirling had been a welcome visitor at Government House and Sir Edward Twining was impressed by his ideas. He introduced Stirling to Robin Johnston, former D.C. at Kongwa, who was now farming on Mount Kilimanjaro. Johnston became Capricorn representative in Tanganyika.

Only a handful of idealistic Europeans, who had for some time wanted to break down the race barriers surrounding Africans, were prepared to accept the Capricorn ideas. Among early members were Derek Bryceson and Michael and Susan Wood. Wood is a famous plastic surgeon with headquarters in Nairobi, always willing to give his services free to poor Africans. As Tanganyika citizens, the Woods are now striving to promote a medical research foundation which they created in their adopted country with the help of the late Sir Archibald MacIndoe.

*

The reasons for European rejection of Capricorn could be grouped under three headings. The first, that of the reactionaries, was represented by the woman who told Johnston: 'I don't understand what you mean by saying that we must improve race relations. We were born to rule.'

The second category, that of the average Tanganyika white settler, was not so articulate. He was simply immersed in the business of earning a living, and was not interested in improving race relations. Regardless of whether he grew sisal, cotton, coffee or pyrethrum, the only thing that mattered was that his African labour should work properly and that his land should yield a decent return.

The third reason for rejecting Capricorn had genuine substance. Stirling had calmly included Tanganyika among the territories of the new Dominion-to-be, without consulting any Tanganyikan. The Europeans wanted no part in such a high-handed arrangement even though it was proposed by a fellow white man, and were reluctant to accept formal links with either Kenya or Rhodesia.

The key to Capricorn's success or failure in Tanganyika, as in other parts of Africa, was the African attitude. Few joined. One of them was David Makwaia, but he was no nationalist, and he had no organised following.

In October, 1952, Father Richard Walsh introduced David Stirling to Julius Nyerere. They had a long talk, in the course of which they developed a liking and high regard for each other. It is Stirling's belief that Nyerere understood his ultimate aim of a world free of racial prejudice, and realised that if Capricorn were to succeed, it would present a real alternative to the nationalist movement. Therefore, in Stirling's view, Nyerere decided early on that, from a purely political point of view, he had to destroy Capricorn. He agreed with Stirling on the need for racial co-operation, but not as a generous gesture on the part of the Europeans. He felt that it was the Africans who should make the gesture once the nationalists had achieved power. After the successful foundation of Tanu, Nyerere could see the way to achieving his conception.

The Governor for his part had merely considered Capricorn as a potential weapon in his attempts to keep the nationalists in check. In 1955, he no longer believed that it could be used against Tanu, because the Europeans regarded Capricorn as too negrophile, while the Africans mistrusted it because its offers were far less attractive than those of the nationalists. Twining therefore decided to encourage the formation of an alternative multi-racial party by men close to Government House.

Stirling and Johnston were worried by this. According to gossip emanating from Europeans, Capricorn drew not only its ideas but also its funds from across the borders. Johnston hoped that an entirely local and autonomous organisation, to be called the Tanganyika National Society (T.N.S.), would make the ideas and ideals of Capricorn more acceptable to Tanganyikans. After long discussions with Stirling, he decided to publish the T.N.S. programme, partly to make it known, partly to avoid the danger of the Governor's men using some Capricorn ideas in their impending party declaration while omitting the sterner stuff of principle.

On December 5, 1955, the T.N.S. Manifesto appeared in the *Tanganyika Standard*; the following day the paper commented that it was the first multi-racial society to be formed in the country. 'Its formation is most welcome particularly as an association of this kind is essential if the purely racial nationalism of Tanu is to be successfully combated.' (December 6, 1955.)

Meanwhile in Lushoto, at the Governor's residence, Ivor Bayldon and a few friends had decided that their new party should be called the United Tanganyika Party, (U.T.P.), and that its inaugural meeting should be held on December 10, 1955, at Dodoma. Knowingly or otherwise, they did exactly what Stirling and Johnston had feared; they incorporated into their programme Capricorn concepts, without incorporating the Capricorn philosophy.

With the publication of the T.N.S. manifesto, it became impossible for the U.T.P. to use this programme. The inaugural meeting had to be given over to a discussion of what the U.T.P. was to stand for. Only two months later, on February 17, 1956, did a U.T.P. manifesto see print, signed by twelve Europeans, twelve Asians, eight Africans and a descendant of the Sultans of Zanzibar. David Makwaia and Chief Haron M. Lugusha, two of the signatories, were well known personalities, but neither carried weight among young Africans.

Of the ten articles of belief laid down by U.T.P., No. 2 was a clear paraphrase of the Capricorn precept on racial equality and read: 'All men are born with certain inalienable rights as human beings and are equal in the love of God and in the dignity which

He gave to man. Differences in race, colour and creed do not constitute any inequality in human dignity and in those inalienable rights.' No. 4 read: 'All races of Tanganyika are completely dependent upon one another for their peace and happiness and prosperity, and for their upward progress towards nationhood.' And No. 10: 'The party formally declares its abhorrence of the attitude of mind known as the "colour bar" and its manifestation in the form of racial discrimination.'

The aims of the party were said to uphold the principles of the manifesto: to respect the established Government, to expose all attempts at unconstitutional or seditious changes in the constitution, to raise the standard of living and of education, to promote the utilisation of natural resources, free enterprise and co-operative effort, and so on.[2]

Nyerere's reaction was characteristically quick and to the point. In a circular to Tanu he said that the formation of the U.T.P. had created a new situation, which demanded a new Tanu policy. Hence he asked that Legco be dissolved, as its members, nominated by the Governor, had formed themselves into a rival party, which he later nicknamed, 'The Governor's Favourite Party'. As U.T.P. members now attacked Tanu for its racialism, on the ground that it admitted only Africans, the 1956 Tanu conference made a small concession by agreeing that persons of mixed African and other blood be admitted.

The Capricorn Contract, accepted at the Salima Convention, confirmed Nyerere's expectation as well as providing him with the opportunity for a knock-out blow against Stirling's multiracialism. He published his attack two months later in a duplicated pamphlet, *Contra Capricorn*.

He quoted the American Declaration of Independence and the Universal Declaration of Human Rights to demolish the Capricorn Precept that 'the vote is not a natural right but a responsibility'. He pointed to India, where a predominantly illiterate electorate had just participated in a one man, one vote election.

About the multiple vote and the conditions on which one person could obtain as many as six votes, he wrote: 'A few thousand

[2] The Europeans and Asians who founded the U.T.P., set about it in the wrong way because at the back of their minds they wanted to maintain European supremacy. They had not understood the writing on the wall that in East and Central Africa the period of white rule was over.

European residents would have no difficulty in the Legislative Council in perpetuating for a long time their domination of 8,000,000 Tanganyikans.'

Not surprisingly, he interpreted the statement, 'in the special circumstances of East and Central Africa, universal suffrage would give rise to the danger of irresponsible politicians being elected to the legislature' as referring to the Tanu leaders. He poured scorn on the presumption that it would take a very long time before Africans could reach a civilised level which would entitle them to political rights. 'It is a dangerous thing to tell people tired of being treated as less than human that they must go slow in their demand for dignified and civilised treatment.'

Nyerere's pamphlet was a highly skilled weapon of political warfare. He was able to say: 'The Capricorn literature of the Tanganyika National Society says it would remove the colour bar—but not too fast.' (Point 3. of the T.N.S. programme read: 'The abolition of all elements of racial discrimination with retention of civilised standards and values.')

Since we do not have that kind of bar [continued Nyerere], in its place T.N.S. has arranged to provide us with a money bar plus a special Capricorn political bar. . . . In the Capricorn Contract we see the same idealistic drapery covering concrete legislative proposals which would, if ever adopted, put over in Tanganyika and the rest of East Africa the same old perpetuation of minority domination and special privilege which Africans everywhere find increasingly intolerable.

In view of the overwhelming African majority, the last point was as false as his arguments about the multiple vote, as even on the least favourable showing, African representatives would have greatly outnumbered the Europeans. Yet as far as Tanganyika was concerned, Nyerere's broadside finished Capricorn.

David Stirling had stated that either Capricorn could work with African nationalism, or it had no future. The answer was—it could not. In 1955 no multi-racial organisation, even with genuine African backing, could have stood up against an African nationalist organisation. The nationalists were winning, and they offered power, not concessions. Multi-racialism could not compete with that.

The U.T.P. never had a hope. It had no philosophy and no ideals, except what it borrowed from Capricorn.

Capricorn was said by some observers to have been born too late. Actually, it was born at the optimum psychological moment, when Europeans were becoming aware that their privileged position could not last, and when African nationalists were beginning to realise that they would need European and Asian help even after achieving independence. Earlier, during the war, African students and soldiers would, admittedly, have been responsive, but Europeans would have turned down partnership with Africans out of hand. Later, in the mid-1950s, nothing short of full power would have satisfied Africans.

However forlorn Capricorn's failure may seem to be, it must be viewed against other multi-racial situations, if it is to be judged fairly. It remains to be seen whether in Alabama or in South Africa a compromise solution will be found. Or, looked at from the opposite side of the fence, whether the new African states will be able to provide a satisfactory permanent and indigenous system of European and Asian participation, instead of co-operation by short-term contract expatriates. The policy of Julius Nyerere in Tanganyika is generous; Jomo Kenyatta in Kenya is also holding out an olive branch. But only the future will show whether they will succeed in East Africa, and whether their ideas will be acceptable in Central Africa. We may yet be driven to the sad conclusion that, in the second half of the twentieth century, multi-racialism is not a workable form of government.

Many liberal European men and women have in the past made individual efforts to break through the colour bar. David Stirling was not the first in this field. His outstanding contribution is that he worked out a programme and consolidated it into a political platform from which the Europeans would offer to work on a basis of equality with the Africans in whose country they had made their homes. For this David Stirling has deservedly earned a place in the history of East Africa.

CHAPTER 27

Abroad and at Home the Struggle
Gains Momentum

WITH trusted lieutenants ably holding the fort at home, Nyerere's second visit to the U.S.A. was an occasion for spiritual refreshment and new inspiration. Two Maryknoll Fathers met him when his boat docked in New York in 1956. They drove him to their beautiful mother house on the Hudson river, looking its best in October as the leaves were turning red, gold and purple.

Fathers Albert J. Nevins and William Collins, who had spent many years in Musoma, gave Nyerere a particularly warm welcome. They have told the author: 'It seemed as though Julius had always been here. He just fitted in. He lectured to our students and shared our fare. On this visit neither the British, nor the American authorities took any notice of him.'

The Maryknoll Fathers had organised a lecture tour for Nyerere to acquaint himself with the American educational system, and to introduce him to colleges where he could secure scholarships for Tanganyikans. Both aims were achieved during the five weeks he spent lecturing in Washington, Chicago, Boston and New York. He also appeared on the Mike Wallace Television show; with his fee he repaid the money Father Wille and Father Walsh had lent him.

Nyerere could not but notice the advantages American Negroes enjoyed compared to his own people in colonial Africa. They had material comforts in their homes; their children obtained general education; talented youngsters could train as doctors, lawyers, architects, or enter other professions. Many times he was asked whether he would like to live in the States. Invariably Nyerere replied that Tanganyika was his country and that was where he wanted to live and work and serve.

In New York he stayed with Maida Springer, at that time a district organiser of the Ladies Garment Workers' Union, who was becoming very interested in African affairs. A few months later, the AFL–CIO sent her with their mission to Kenya and Tanganyika, where she took an active part in organising the African trade unions. She shared her deep insight into the realities of Negro life with Nyerere. What he learnt from Maida Springer and others

283

about the work that still had to be done for the U.S.A. to become an integrated country, further strengthened his resolve to fight for his peoples' rights and eventual independence.

On December 20, 1956, Julius Nyerere appeared before the Fourth Committee of the U.N. This is a large body, with eighty members, which is well accustomed to fire-eating petitioners. Nyerere caused disappointment because he did not play it that way. Quietly and soberly (as during his appearance before the Trusteeship Council) he outlined Tanganyika's historical background, saying that all British Governors with the one exception of Sir Donald Cameron, had administered the country as if it were a colony and exploited the fear instilled into people by the Germans. He accused the Tanganyika settler (Sir Charles Phillips), who had participated in the discussions which led to the Trusteeship Agreement, with seeing to it that the paramountcy of native interests should not even be a specific principle of the Trusteeship Agreement. He described the multi-racial situation in Tanganyika, where twenty thousand Europeans (of whom only three thousand were settlers) dominated the Executive and the Legislative Councils. He argued that representative members should be elected not only by common roll, but by universal suffrage. By fulfilling these moderate Tanu demands, Nyerere said, the administration would demonstrate to the people that they could realise their legitimate aspirations through democratic means.

During the following day's discussions he outlined Tanu's origin and membership. He quoted from the memorandum of the Asian Association which also opposed a system of voting which would give virtually universal suffrage to the minority of the inhabitants, without giving it to the majority. The memorandum had said that this would jeopardise the Territory's harmonious development.

Nyerere insisted that there was no conflict between Africans and Europeans. Tanu was not opposed to them, only to British policy. On the vital issue of independence, he tried to avoid giving a date. When asked point blank by the Philippine representative, he replied: 'It is difficult to specify a date in such cases, but I think Tanganyika should be independent in about ten years' time.'

Nyerere's technique may have disappointed those who liked theatrical performances, but it impressed men of discerning judgment. One of these, Jay Lovestone, Director of the Department of

International Affairs of the AFL–CIO, told the author on February 10, 1962:

Julius was quiet and solid, there was nothing flamboyant about him, no Emperor Jones touch. His address to the U.N. was precise in presentation and responsible in conclusions. Unlike many other Africans, Julius was receptive; he absorbed all he saw and examined the persons he talked to. With him I didn't have to worry that he would interpret an opinion as a commitment. I've seen him every time he has been over here since then, and he is the only African who has never asked my organisation for money. I regard him as the ablest African politician of our day.

As to contemporaneous developments in Tanganyika, Nyerere was well justified in his confidence that the home front was being looked after during his absence in America. By the autumn of 1956, Tanu claimed a paid up membership of a hundred thousand and some thirty branches. Nyerere was recognised as its national leader, not only because Tanu was his creation, but because his appearance before the Trusteeship Council had given him exceptional prestige. Followers of his ideas were coming forward in all parts of the country, particularly in the north and the centre, where the best educated and most progressive tribes lived. Later several local leaders became Legco members, thus gaining national standing.

In the Tanu campaign a notable part was played by Rashidi Kawawa, who has told the author:

In July, 1955 I first met Tom Mboya when he came to Dar-es-Salaam as representative of the I.C.F.T.U.,[1] which had guided him in the formation of the Kenya Labour Unions. At that time in Tanganyika only T.A.G.S.A., of which I was President, and the Railway African Association were national in character. All other unions were local craft unions; for instance the Tanga dock workers had no dealings with the Dar-es-Salaam dock workers. We learnt for the first time that trade unions could be organised on a territorial basis, with a national centre affiliated to an international organisation like the I.C.F.T.U. After Tom's departure I, with Maynard Mpangala[2] and Michael Kamaliza organised a trade union and staff conference, and we worked out a constitution for a national centre, the Tanganyika Federation of Labour, which was formed on October 7. I was elected its first Secretary-General. The

---

[1] International Confederation of Free Trade Unions.
[2] M. B. Mpangala is now Industrial Relations Officer for the East African Railways.

Government was opposed to it at once, and tried to win us over by organising trade union courses. At first we attended them, but when we discovered that they were teaching us how to keep accounts and how to compromise, but not how to bargain with the employers, we boycotted them.

On February 6, 1956, I resigned from the civil service and then began my real career: I joined Tanu. In July, 1956, the quarry workers of Konduchi went on strike. This was the first time that Tanganyikan workers struck officially and won. On December 6, after Princess Margaret's visit, the domestic workers also struck because their outstanding wage demands were ignored, and no Statutory Wages Council was set up. Government advised the employers to sack all workers who intended to strike; this brought out the Building, Commercial and Industrial Workers Union in sympathy, and the number of strikers in Dar-es-Salaam rose to 10,000. At the end of the month I went to Brussels at the I.C.F.T.U.'s invitation, then to Britain at the T.U.C.'s invitation, then to Accra and returned with an I.C.F.T.U. and a T.U.C. representative to help settle the long-drawn out strike. The men gained little, although a Wages Council was set up, but I learnt an awful lot. As soon as the settlement had been agreed, I began to organise the sisal workers.

In September, 1957, Kawawa was to become a Member of the Legislative Council.

Another young African who helped in the renewed struggle on the home front was George Kahama, a member of the Haya tribe, born in Bukoba on November 30, 1929. At Tabora Government School he had been a contemporary of Rashidi Kawawa, Oscar Kambona and Job Lusinde. Being a Roman Catholic, he attended mass at St Mary's College, Tabora, where he first saw Julius Nyerere, but he did not actually meet him until 1951, at East Africa House in London. By then Kahama was studying at Loughborough College on a British scholarship. He and Nyerere became good friends, yet Nyerere did not tell him about his political plans.

George Kahama returned from England in December 1954. On leaving school he had become the first secretary of the Bukoba Coffee Co-operative; now he was promoted to be its first General Manager. Naturally, he joined Tanu and was soon elected to its Provincial Executive Committee, subsequently renamed Working Executive Committee. When the Governor was looking for outstanding Africans to appoint to Legco, the Bahaya Council put up the names of possible candidates, among whom Kahama received more than half of the total votes. He was to be appointed a Member in December, 1957.

In the all-important sphere of publicity, especially useful work was done by Edward Barongo, a former policeman who met Nyerere in 1954. Having become an enthusiastic Tanu supporter, he returned to his native Bukoba and transformed its flourishing T.A.A. (which had seven thousand members) into a Tanu branch. First as its District Secretary, then as its Provincial Secretary, he stumped Bukoba with a wealthy Haya friend, S. K. L. Luangiza (the present Commissioner of the West Lake District), enrolling Tanu members. He quoted freely from a Swahili pamphlet called *Tanu Katika UNO* (Tanu in the U.N.), which contained Nyerere's 1955 address to the Trusteeship Council. Barongo kept records of all meetings, sent hand-outs to the vernacular Press and provided his helpers with speakers' notes. At the time he was the only provincial Tanu official to do this. His articles were published not only in the Swahili papers, but also in the English-language daily *Tanganyika Standard*. Within Legco itself, Paul Bomani continued doggedly to work for Tanu's objectives. From September, 1954, to September, 1957, he alone represented the Tanu point of view at this central point. During these years he got most support not from fellow Africans like Chiefs Harun Lugusha and John Maruma, nor from David Makwaia, but from Europeans like Captain J. Bennett and John Baker. Bennett in particular harried the Government over the Five Year Education Plan, which, having been grandly published, was suddenly postponed owing to lack of funds. To the Governor's annoyance, Bennett created such an atmosphere that not only liberal Europeans, but even normally submissive Africans backed him. The administration was forced to implement the Five Year Education Plan early in 1957.

The increasing nationalist pressure at home was sufficient by itself to lead the British administration to view Nyerere's visit to America with anything but enthusiasm. His success upon his second appearance before the U.N. gave rise to visible distaste and concern on the part of the authorities.

The members of the administration were particularly disturbed by his increased demands. In March, 1955, he had asked merely for three Dar-es-Salaam Legco Members to be elected; he now wanted all Representative Members to be elected by universal adult suffrage. In 1955, he had wanted more African members, but now he demanded that half of the members of the Executive and Legislative Councils should be Africans. The tumultuous welcome he received on his return added to the administration's alarm. Although reports to the Colonial Office still described him as an irresponsible agitator without serious following, Sir Edward Twining decided to take two strong measures to check his growing popularity. He instructed the Secretariat to correct the misrepresentations in Nyerere's speech to the Fourth Committee, and to place a ban on his open-air meetings because of the inflammatory statements he was making.

It took three months to prepare the pamphlet; it was finally printed in April, 1957, under the title: *Some Comments on Mr Nyerere's speech at the Fourth Committee of the United Nations.*

This pamphlet scored some points. It stated, for instance, that Nyerere had omitted to refer to the unselfish efforts of many hundreds of individuals, both officials and non-officials; that he had mentioned neither the Order-in-Council for the new Constitution, nor the one authorising elections, the former having been published before Tanu had even come into existence; that he spoke several times of the Asian Association suggesting that it represented the Asian Community which was hardly in tune with the fact that even the Association itself claimed only one thousand members out of a total Asian population of eighty thousand; that in commenting on the educational situation he had omitted to mention that the administration paid a hundred per cent of the African teachers' salaries, or to refer to the enormous advance in education and other social services in one generation.

But what makes the *Comments* on Nyerere's speech such embarrassing reading is the spirit informing them. They harped on 'the careful and deliberate omissions' directed at 'the self-glorification of Mr Nyerere and the denigration of all that has been done for the people of Tanganyika within the space of a single generation', on 'the irresponsible generalisations in referring to the British record', on the 'jealousy which has presumably inspired his slur on the U.T.P., an association which at least seems to be making an attempt to build itself into a genuine party rather than a racial cabal', on 'a tendency to exaggeration as well as conceit wherever Mr Nyerere touches anything concerning his own personal position'.

Members of the Secretariat had not met Julius Nyerere and were not encouraged by the Governor to do so. Those who compiled the *Comments* were writing about a man of whose character they knew nothing. Had they consulted a European like Father Richard Walsh, or David Stirling, or Fraser Murray, they would have been told that Julius Nyerere was the very reverse of conceited, that he worried lest he had put himself too much to the fore, and that he considered politics in terms of principle, not of personal advancement. As for jealousy of the U.T.P., the Secretariat only showed its ignorance of African public opinion by imagining it could conceivably provide any serious competition for Tanu.

Nyerere did indeed omit facts favourable to the British administration. But then he was not delivering an academic lecture, he was making a political speech intended to further Tanganyika's chances for independence. Were anyone to dissect political speeches in Britain or in the U.S.A. in the same legalistic manner as the Secretariat in Dar-es-Salaam dissected Julius Nyerere's speech before the Fourth Committee, all British and American politicians could be accused of similar or worse distortions.

The effect of the pamphlet was unexpected. Few Europeans and practically no Africans read it. But the Africans interpreted the fact that the Governor had written pages about Nyerere as proof that the Tanu leader was even more important then they had hitherto thought.

In the course of his statement to the Fourth Committee, Nyerere had said: 'When I go back to Tanganyika, the entire adult population of Dar-es-Salaam, amounting to 60,000 people, will assemble in the open air to hear the message I am carrying back to them.' Events proved this a pretty good prediction. Thousands of Africans thronged the airport, cheering him enthusiastically. A week later, the largest crowd ever seen in Tanganyika assembled in Msimbazi Fields to hear him speak. Whether it consisted of fifteen thousand people, as the Government maintained, or of thirty-five thousand as the general public believed, it was a most impressive turn-out.

The official reason the administration gave for imposing a ban on Nyerere's public speeches was that he had made inflammatory statements at this mass-meeting and had repeated them, despite official warning, in Moshi. Nyerere was in possession of a tape recording of his Dar-es-Salaam speech, which he first offered to submit to the authorities to prove that he had said nothing to endanger law and order. Later, it was said, he changed his mind because a British official who heard the tape pointed out eleven inflammatory statements. The true facts of this affair were only to emerge at the Trusteeship Council meeting in New York in June, 1957.

Maida Springer and Lucy Lameck recall the circumstances under which the ban was imposed.

Mrs Springer has told the author:

In January, 1957, in Tanga, Mr Nyerere was scheduled to report on his mission to the United Nations. I was scheduled to address a meeting of the trade unionists. On arrival in Tanga we learned that Mr Nyerere's meeting was banned for the reason that it was construed to be against the public's good. This ban was only one in a series during the period. In addition to banning public meetings, the Government had banned about ten of Tanu's local branches.

Lucy Lameck has told the author:

In 1956 Julius came to Moshi and there were some 2,000 people at the meeting. In 1957, when he returned from his visit to the U.S.A., there were 20,000 people to hear him! We counted some two hundred motorised policemen, and there were many C.I.D. men taking notes. Anyhow Julius repeated the speech he had made in Dar-es-Salaam, and this apparently made the British authorities furious, for his next meeting, to be held in Tanga, was cancelled, the police having withdrawn permission to hold it. Tanu officials drove all the way from Tanga with a letter informing Julius that he had been banned from public speaking for four months. When we heard about the ban, we vowed, each one of us, to work harder than ever to build up Tanu and to enrol into it every African in Tanganyika.

And so the campaign went on, with redoubled effort. Nyerere also continued with his political *safaris*, concentrating his efforts on the *wazee*, the elders. Age being venerated among Africans, they, as much as the chiefs, sub-chiefs or headmen, determined public opinion. Nyerere knew that if he could get the *wazee* on his side, he had gained the villages. As he could make no public speeches, he talked to them inside grass huts, answering their questions, putting at rest their doubts. Many told him that his efforts were hopeless; the British were far too strong to be defeated by the Africans.

'You remember the mighty *Wadachi*?' the *wazee* would say. 'We thought them invincible. Look at this picture,' and they would produce a photograph of a tree on which the Germans had hung Africans. 'You know what they did to us? And the British defeated these powerful, ruthless *Wadachi*. Now you are trying to tell us that you can defeat the British, who have proved themselves more powerful than the *Wadachi*?'

Nyerere would patiently explain why he thought that together they could do just this, how the present situation differed from that in 1918, what Trusteeship meant, what allies Tanganyika had in the United Nations. He did not mind answering the same question over and over again, until he had convinced his elderly audience.

The four months Nyerere spent going from village to village, talking mainly to the elders, proved of inestimable value to Tanu. Also, to keep in touch with the party, he started a small duplicated publication, *Sauti Ya Tanu* (The Voice of Tanu), which appeared at irregular intervals. Nyerere wrote most of its four pages; this was a blessing in disguise as it forced him to express himself in terms intelligible to popular as well as to sophisticated readers, and he had to learn many tricks of the journalist's trade. Later on, when his articles appeared in the world Press, this proved a most valuable training.

Early in 1957, Joan E. Wicken, travelling as a Research Fellow from Somerville College, Oxford, came out to Tanganyika to gather material about Tanu and its organisation. Both before and after this trip, she was Assistant Commonwealth Officer of the Labour Party, and had first met Nyerere when he called at her London office in 1956. From the end of 1958 to April, 1960, she was Secretary to the Africa Educational Trust, of which Sir Alexander Carr-Saunders was the Chairman. Then she came to the Tanganyika Education Trust and Kivukoni College.[3] Now she is Personal Assistant to President Nyerere.

In 1957, Nyerere invited her to accompany him on a political *safari* to the Southern Highlands.

In every village people rushed out to see him [Joan Wicken has told the author]. They crowded around him, they tried to touch him, they wanted to hear his voice. They could not understand why he could not speak to them, except in suffocatingly hot mud huts. I remember two incidents, both in Mbeya. In the first, we arrived at about 9 o'clock at the Tanu office, and as the cars drew up, people poured from the

[3] See also Chapter 29.

surrounding houses in order to see Julius. We went into the office, which was just a local house, and the people poured in after us. There was no room to hold everyone and the crush was getting dangerous. It was agreed that everyone should go outside again and two chairs were taken out on which Julius and I stood and an oil lamp was lifted so that people could see us. By this time the police had appeared, and held the crowds back from the chairs. This was a good idea because otherwise we may have been pushed off by the enthusiasm of those at the back. It was obviously impossible just to stand there and say nothing, but as Julius opened his mouth to speak, one of the policemen (all were African) took a step forward and lifted up his truncheon. Julius just thanked the people for coming and said he would see them next morning and asked them to go home quietly. The policeman then took his step backwards. That is when I felt that the atmosphere was charged: had that policeman made one wrong move, the people would have torn him to pieces.

The other incident occurred the same evening, but later when we went to a Trade Union Office for a tea-party. We were just sitting chatting when the European Superintendent of Police knocked on the door and came in. Everyone else looked a bit startled, but Julius just got up from his chair and invited the man to come in for tea. He did so, and Julius talked to him; having drunk his tea, the man left. Although the situation felt awkward because of the previous incident, there was no question of interfering with a meeting, because one was not taking place.

During the same trip, one evening we arrived in a village hungry, tired and dusty. An Englishwoman had a small hotel there. We knocked on her door, and when she opened it, Julius tried to explain in English, very politely, how much we needed some food and shelter. She answered in Swahili, as though he were not fit to be spoken to in English, and told him that she did not cater for Africans. Then, as she noticed me, she said with disgust in her voice that it was far too late to cook any food.

Julius tried, once more, in English, to explain that I at least needed some food. She replied furiously that I could have some sandwiches, but he could not come in. Naturally, I would not accept anything from her. We went to an African hotel a little further down the road where we were given food and I was treated with the utmost courtesy. The only reason I did not eat was because I was so upset about the incident at the roadhouse. All the people there were worried by my reaction and went out of their way to make me feel at home and to show me that they did not hold me responsible for this.

I have never felt more ashamed than on that occasion. The British trained policeman and the British hotelkeeper displayed the worst features of colonialism.

The Twining Administration was unaware of the effect of the ban, just as it had been unaware of the effect of the *Comments* on Nyerere's speech. No publicity could have whipped up so many Tanu members as the humiliation inflicted on their leader by a foreign ruler.

Shrewd observers felt certain that Sir Edward Twining's unrealistic attitude towards Julius Nyerere and Tanu could not last much longer. Ghana's independence, obtained on March 8,1957, was proof that the African dream could come true. Kwame Nkrumah's message: 'Ghana's independence will be meaningless unless it is accompanied by the total liberation of Africa,' had the effect of a clarion call. Nyerere and his followers reacted as forcefully as other Africans.

CHAPTER 28

Nyerere Forges Ahead

IN June, 1957, the Trusteeship Council was to discuss the Administering Authority's report on Tanganyika. When Sir Edward Twining heard that Julius Nyerere would once more appear as a petitioner, he decided that another African should put a point of view friendly to the administration. His choice fell on Tom Marealle, paramount chief of the Chagga. With two Europeans, Sir Andrew Cohen and John (now Sir John) Fletcher-Cooke, there was now completed an ill-matched foursome representing four different attitudes to Tanganyikan affairs. The two Europeans had not met Nyerere before.

In 1957, the Trusteeship Council had fourteen members; seven of these were colonial powers: Australia, Belgium, France, Italy, New Zealand, Britain and the U.S.A.; and seven were non-colonial nations (some definitely anti-colonial): Burma, Nationalist China, Guatemala, Haiti, India, Syria and the U.S.S.R. The British aim was to obtain a majority, which meant winning over at least one non-colonial vote. In the event, Nationalist China accepted the reasoning of the British Representative on the Trusteeship Council, Sir Andrew Cohen.

It was Cohen's first appearance in this capacity. He had just ended his term of office as Governor of Uganda, and he arrived with the reputation of a convinced liberal who had eliminated the need for a Tanu-like party in Uganda by his acceptance of African nationalism as a natural and proper development.

Sir Andrew Cohen's brief on June 10, 1957, was not to his liking. Twining's treatment of Nyerere and Tanu was anathema to liberals who understood the situation. Unfortunately their number was very small; Cohen was one of the few who knew the facts. Yet as an Englishman and as a British civil servant, he put up a spirited defence of Britain's efforts to prepare Tanganyika for independence.

Details had to be filled in by Tanganyika's Special Representative, John Fletcher-Cooke, Minister for Constitutional Affairs since December, 1956. Tanganyika was the only Territory within the British Colonial Empire with a Minister whose sole function was to deal with constitutional problems.

A month's tour all over Tanganyika with Twining had kept Fletcher-Cooke away from Dar-es-Salaam when Julius Nyerere held his first mass meeting at Msimbazi. He has told the author that he had no direct knowledge of the reasons for which Nyerere was banned from public speaking, nor was he concerned with the final draft of the *Comments* on Nyerere's speech before the Fourth Committee, which had been delivered before he went to Tanganyika. He had met none of the nationalists, certainly not Nyerere, before going to New York to defend Twining's policy.

Fletcher-Cooke had as distinguished a record as Cohen: after a rapid rise in the Colonial Service, he became British Representative on the Trusteeship Council at thirty-seven, and was now a key minister in Tanganyika. In the first round he did well by contrasting conditions under the Twining administration with those before 1939. He enumerated achievements like new schools, new hospitals, consumer co-operatives, two new councils, the Tanganyika Broadcasting Corporation, an Election Bill with liberal franchise qualifications, and the appointment, due to come into effect on July 1, 1957, of six Assistant Ministers four of whom were to be Africans. These achievements were indeed substantial.

He said that there were only two territorial political organisations, Tanu and U.T.P. The latter he praised for its multi-racial policy, while Tanu was only open to Africans, many of whom wanted to remove or expel all immigrant communities. Membership figures had never been published, but there were forty-eight branches. Some of these—Lushoto, Korogwe, Kondoa-Irangi, Handeni, Pangani—had to be closed because the local leaders opposed such essential measures as soil conservation or famine reserve rules, or pretended that Tanu was the Government and summoned people before its tribunals. Tanu officials responsible for such misdeeds had been sentenced by proper courts. As for Nyerere, he had been banned from holding public meetings because of inflammatory statements at a Dar-es-Salaam meeting which, despite official warning, he had repeated verbatim at a Moshi meeting. At his most urbane, Fletcher-Cooke said the Government had been most reluctant to take action against Nyerere and Tanu, and they were now considering on what conditions they could lift the ban without endangering law and order, or prejudicing the raising of foreign capital.

The third speaker was Tom Marealle, paramount chief of the

Chagga, whom the non-colonial members of the Council regarded either as a British stooge or, in the words of Maida Springer, 'as a study in contrast to Mr Nyerere, Mr Marealle being the able administrator who recognised the progress made under the colonial system as the only means by which responsible government could gradually be achieved'.

Marealle did not figure as a member of the British delegation, but as a petitioner in his own right. It was none the less taken for granted that he had been coached by Twining. To the great surprise of the Council, he voiced the African point of view and asked for independence in fifteen years.

The fourth person to address the Council was Julius Nyerere, for whom a small but respectful following had been waiting. While Marealle, who represented the views of the conservative chiefs, was treated with the courtesy due to a prominent celebrity, little attention was paid to Nyerere, the champion of the common men of Tanganyika. Maida Springer, who was there, has told the author:

The U.K. delegation came prepared to report not only on their Trusteeship of the Territory and their preparation of the Tanganyika people for self-government, but to prove that Mr Nyerere was an irresponsible agitator. Mr Nyerere's performance of restrained, factual presentation and clear exposure of inaccurate statements by the U.K. experts were his weapons.

Nyerere welcomed the fact that, for the first time, he was not alone before the U.N. to express Tanganyikan feelings. Courteously he commended the Council for accepting Marealle's views about African fears and hopes, only he asked for independence in twelve instead of in fifteen years.

He made short shrift of Fletcher-Cooke's statement about Tanu and himself. He proved that his organisation was not racial, as its leaders had repeatedly declared that they had no intention of applying discrimination against any other race in reverse. He demanded that Africans, who formed ninety-eight per cent of the population, be given fifty per cent of the unofficial seats in Legco, instead of the ten to which they were restricted, while two per cent of the population, the Europeans and the Asians, had twenty seats. As the so-called liberal franchise qualifications were grossly unfair to the overwhelming majority of Africans, he wished for adult suffrage as well as a common roll.

Then he related the tape-recorder incident. When he heard official complaints about his speech of January 27 in Dar-es-Salaam, he offered to hand over the tape of his speech if the Chief Secretary's office gave him a written account of his alleged inflammatory statements. The authorities knew he had never made these statements. As no list was forthcoming, he did not hand over the tape. The point Nyerere stressed was that if he, in Dar-es-Salaam, could be accused of having said things which thirty-five thousand people could bear witness he had not said, how much easier was it to accuse provincial Tanu leaders and ban their organisations on the basis of equally untrue allegations. He quoted a letter of apology he had received from the Chief Secretary, who admitted that the accusations against the Morogoro branch had been untrue, yet the ban on it remained. . . .

Nyerere described the U.T.P. as a small organisation, without any future in Tanganyika, yet the Government had appointed five of its members to the Franchise Committee, against one from Tanu. He predicted that Tanu would win any election in which it participated. His arguments, backed up by Marealle, forced Fletcher-Cooke to deny that U.T.P. was the Governor's party. This was lucky in view of the debacle the U.T.P. was to suffer in the 1958-9 elections. Equally significant, in view of the coming Tanu Conference at Tabora, was Nyerere's statement that Tanu wished to participate in the elections.

The four protagonists were able to avert an open break by agreeing on the importance of the Post Elections Committee, which was to prepare the ground for further constitutional development, especially the expansion of the ministerial system.

After the Trusteeship meeting, the scene shifted back to Tanganyika. Two participants disappeared: Sir Andrew Cohen remained in New York and Tom Marealle was soon to be forced out of public life.[1] John Fletcher-Cooke, representing the old imperial traditions, and Julius Nyerere, representing those of the new African nationalism, were to face each other in many battles in and outside the Tanganyika Legislative Council. But at least they knew each other and there was personal contact between them.

Unprecedented scenes took place at Dar-es-Salaam airport when Nyerere returned from his third U.N. appearance. They were reported in the *Tanganyika Standard* as well as in the

[1] Marealle is now a U.N. official in Rawalpindi.

vernacular Press. Vast crowds, wild with excitement, milled around as far as the eye could see and all along the seven mile road into the city, waving palm leaves and green branches. Any dispassionate person could sense that Julius Nyerere was regarded by the ordinary Tanganyikan as a Messiah, who would wipe out the humiliations of the past and lead them to an independence in which they would find dignity, happiness and well being. He would have been less than human had he tried at that moment to tell them (what he well knew) that no man can offer the millennium to people unprepared to work hard for it.

Henceforth the British administration could not have maintained the ban on Nyerere's public meetings short of using force. In any case Twining would never have resorted to that, for in 1957, with Ghana's independence an accomplished fact, the British public would not have stood for it. Whatever Twining's misgivings, not only was Nyerere free to speak when and where he liked (and his audiences grew vastly) but he was appointed a Member of Legco.

He was also offered an Assistant Ministership.[2] Before replying, he went to Nairobi to seek the advice of a remarkable man by the name of Sir Ernest Vasey, at that time Minister of Finance in the Kenya Government. Vasey had risen from a humble background, had tried many careers, including the stage, before landing in Kenya, where he went into local politics and twice became Mayor of Nairobi. His ability earned him the respect, but not always the love, of the white settlers, for he had the courage to tell them in the Press and over the radio that Kenya was an African country which one day would be run by Africans. 'Negrophile' was the kindest epithet attached to him.

To Nyerere's query Vasey answered tartly: 'Accept for Tanu, but do not go in yourself until you have a majority in Legco. Any man who accepts office without power is committing political suicide.'

Nyerere heeded the advice and three years later showed his appreciation. In February 1960, with his approval, the then Gover-

---

[2] It was not specified which one; had he accepted such an appointment, the expectation was that he would have chosen education. Although Nyerere refused to join the Government because he felt he could serve Tanganyika better as leader of the unofficials, consultations did take place between the Governor and Nyerere. At this stage, in the recollection of Sir John Fletcher-Cooke, Sir Edward Twining would not have appointed any person to whom Nyerere objected.

nor, Sir Richard Turnbull, invited Vasey to work out a plan for Tanganyikan finances as Head of the Treasury. Vasey jumped at the chance, hoping to achieve good results in a country where his sympathies for Africans would not cause him difficulties. His Three Year Plan became the basis of Tanganyika's financial development, but unfortunately Vasey himself was too intelligent and too prone to lecture inexperienced colleagues to gain popularity. In January, 1962, he resigned as Minister of Finance, and is now advisor to the World Bank with his headquarters in Rawalpindi, Pakistan.

On July 1, 1957, Nyerere's only close friend among the six Assistant Ministers was Derek Bryceson. The four Africans were four chiefs: Harun Lugusha, Humbi Ziota II., David Makwaia and John Maruma, not one of whom supported Tanu. The sixth, the Indian Amir Karimjee,[3] hardly knew Nyerere. In Legco the Tanu leader first had two staunch friends, Paul Bomani and Rashidi Kawawa, to whom in December was added George Kahama. It was a small group nevertheless.

At the opening meeting it became clear that the Government had no intention of making any concessions to Tanu demands. The course was set by Twining, who said in his address:

The constitutional progress of Tanganyika is an organic growth ... of a very healthy plant. ... The need above all else today is for political stability and economic development. With these the speed of our progress can not only be maintained, but probably enhanced. Secretaries of State of both political parties in the United Kingdom have solemnly stated that the aim of the Administering Power is to grant Tanganyika self-government when she is ready for it. ... But the intermediate target must be responsible government, by which I mean an unofficial majority with an unofficial Ministerial system and reserved powers over certain important subjects. ... Many conditions must be fulfilled before responsible government can be achieved on a lasting basis. In particular the economy of the territory must be sufficiently viable to produce the revenue to provide the services needed. Furthermore sufficient local personnel must be educated and trained up to man the posts in the Government, Local Government, commerce and industry.

And as though this were not clear enough, Twining reminded Legco that in a recent debate in the House of Commons two

[3] Amir Karimjee is the half-brother of Abdulkarim Karimjee, from 1959 to 1962 Speaker of the Legislative Council, later the Parliament of Tanganyika.

Labour M.P.s had rejected universal suffrage as unsuitable for East African territories at the present time. Then he announced that non-racial district councils would be set up, which meant European participation. He added that it would be necessary to establish 'a body consisting of chiefs and their advisers to regulate matters of custom and customary law not suitable for regulation by the district council'.

Twining's intention to use the chiefs in his struggle against Tanu had been indicated earlier when, in June, 1956, he called a Territorial Convention of Chiefs, and let it be known that it might be developed into a Second Chamber of Chiefs. To prepare them for this constitutional role, they were to meet at regular intervals to discuss problems of common concern to them.

From the opening of Legco, Nyerere was frustrated at every turn. He was put on no important committee, and all his suggestions, during both the September and December meetings, were rejected. By December 13, 1957, his cup was full and he resigned. In No. 18 of *The Voice of Tanu*, an English edition of his duplicated publication, *Sauti Ya Tanu*, he explained the reasons for this action.

When I was offered a seat as nominated member on the Legislative Council I believed that Government's offer was an indication of a change of heart. . . . During the last four months I have made a series of compromises to enable Government to demonstrate my understanding of the spirit of give and take in the development of a democratic process.

Firstly, my acceptance of a nominated seat on the Council was a compromise since I am opposed to the continuation of nomination. Secondly, opposed as I am to Government's system of elections on the 1–1–1 basis I suggested, first through the press, and later in our memorandum to the Colonial Secretary, that half the number of representative members could be elected on Government's plan of 1–1–1 and the other half from single member constituencies. I was trying to meet the Government half-way.

Thirdly, I suggested that if Government cannot change the Constitution now at least a Constitutional Committee could be appointed now to study the Constitution and make recommendations concerning both the Constitution and the franchise. This would have meant in effect that the present Constitution would have gone on. It is understood that the committee would have taken some time to produce its own report. Then too Government itself would have taken time to study and make its own observations on this report. The present Constitution, therefore, would have continued for a longer period than was originally acceptable to my Organization.

Fourthly, I moved a motion in Legislative Council asking for the removal of the compulsory tripartite voting system (a small thing to ask for) and for the elections to take place throughout the country next year. I had purposely left out the question of Parity. This was a compromise on my second compromise. In fact it was not a compromise but a complete surrender. I was now willing to agree to elections on the basis of the Government's plan of 1–1–1, not for half the representative members, but for the whole membership, i.e. in *all* the Constituencies.

Fifthly, during the debate on my motion an amendment was moved leaving out the second part of my motion. The motion was now asking that the compulsory tripartite voting system should be removed. I purposely acquiesced in this amendment. Here was an opportunity for Government to invite the confidence of the people by removing this irritation which, it was a public secret, Government was only a few months ago willing to remove. Government's opposition to the amended motion was a typical example of its attitude of opposition for the sake of opposition carried to its logical but absurd conclusion.

Sixthly, if my motion as amended had been carried it would have meant that after September, 1958, the Legislative Council would have had 15 elected members, and since my own Constituency is not scheduled for elections next year, I would probably be sitting on that Council with 16 other nominated members as a nominated member. A most compromising compromise!

The Government had refused to show any good-will in connection with the Local Government (Amendment) Bill, although he, the so-called agitator and racialist, had suggested ways for developing the multi-racial councils without irritating chiefs and people.

Nyerere's conclusion was bitter:

The Government has consistently, and for the most unconvincing reasons, rejected every proposal that I have made in the Legislative Council. Most of the proposals which I have made have been compromises on the proposals originally made by my Organization. If I could believe that my function on the Legislative Council was always to give and never to receive, I would still resign: I have given everything that it was in my power to give, and what I have given has been rejected. I came to the Council expecting a little of the spirit of give and take. That spirit is not there. I would feel that I am cheating the people and cheating my own Organization if I remained on the Council, receiving allowances and attending sundowners as an Honourable Member, giving the impression that I was still of some service on that

L

Council, when in fact I know that I am useless. I had, therefore, no alternative but to tender my resignation, and to ask that it take effect from Friday, December 13, 1957, the day my last compromise was rejected by the Government.

The unbending attitude of the Twining administration lost the opportunity of transferring the battle with Tanu into the Legislative Council. With hindsight it seems incredible that a man of the Governor's intellect should not have seen that in the public forum only Nyerere could win, and win much more quickly than inside the Chamber.

CHAPTER 29

The Tabora Conference

IT was not only Julius Nyerere personally who faced a crisis at the end of 1957. Tanu had also reached a crossroads: it could either participate in the first general elections and follow the path of constitutional development; or it could boycott the elections, stage a general strike and drift into violence. The future, in fact the existence of the movement (for Tanu was still a movement), depended on the answer to this issue. It had to be given promptly, clearly and irrevocably. The occasion for taking this fateful decision was the Annual Delegates Conference, to be held in January, 1958, at Tabora.

The locale was appropriate, as Tabora is in the very middle of Tanganyika. In the nineteenth century, the east–west and the south–north slave routes crossed here; in the twentieth century it became a commercial entrepôt, whose importance was greatly enhanced by the German-built Central Railway. Later still, under the British, Tabora developed into an educational centre, with five excellent schools, including the famous Tabora Government School. On January 19, 1958, Tanu delegates from all parts of the country poured into Tabora.

They represented the three sections of the party: the women, the young men and the elders. Bibi Titi had built up the Women's Section, still the most important women's organisation in the African political scene. The Youth Section, known as the Tanu Youth League, whose members ranged from eighteen to thirty-five years of age, had been nationally organised by Rashidi Kawawa. He was also Secretary-General of the T.F.L., and this combination reflected the close connection between the party and the trade unions.

The Elders' Section indicated the great respect shown to age in African society. A place had been created for the *wazee* so that their traditional authority could be used within the party. Their first leader was Sheik Sulemani Takadir; it was he who, nine months later, criticised at an elders' meeting the absence of Muslim candidates from the Tanu election list. It is revealing of both Nyerere's resentment of religious (and racial) partisanship, and of

one of his rare dictatorial flashes that he promptly expelled the
Sheik from the party. To this day Takadir complains, rightly, that
this action was unconstitutional as only the elders could have
dismissed him.

The atmosphere in Tabora was charged with excitement for a
number of reasons. Nyerere had just resigned from Legco, but had
instructed his Tanu colleagues to stay in and continue the fight.
On this most people supported him, but not on the attitude to
independent candidates, or on the role of the trade unions. At the
end of December, a trade union secretary had been sacked because
he wanted to support an independent in a constituency where
Tanu planned to put up a candidate. Nyerere refused to heed his
appeal that: 'It is all one national movement and Labour is to
Tanu as a son is to a father.' At this time Nyerere considered that
trade unions must have an independent existence because in areas
in which Tanu had been banned, as in some of the Lake Districts,
in the Geita area and Tanga Province, the Labour Unions carried
out holding operations for the party. (Later, when Tanu became
the Government, he was to change his mind on this subject.)

The main issue exercising delegates to the Tabora Conference,
however, was none of these. It was the issue whether or not Tanu
should participate in the elections. The overwhelming majority
wanted to boycott them because of the resented system of tripartite
voting and the fear that Europeans and Asians would not sign
their petitions as candidates. Feeling was running so high that
many Tanu members advocated a policy of *kugoma*, a general
strike. Rashidi Kawawa, by then on both the General and the
National Executive Committees has told the author: 'In 1958,
the situation became very tense. The Tabora Conference passed a
resolution demanding responsible government, as otherwise the
whole country would be called on to strike against the colonial
government. The T.F.L. declared its support for this stand.'

Edward Barongo, who was present, has given the author a description of the setting for this historic occasion:

The 1958 Tanu delegates' conference was held in the parish hall of
Tabora, a small, low room; the hundred or so delegates could barely
squeeze into it. The place was surrounded by people, who were shouting
and screaming, demanding a boycott of the coming elections. There
were many journalists and also many policemen about. The latter were
partly trying to keep order, but mainly to see who was there. Every-

one wanted to know whether or not Tanu would participate in the elections.

In that boiling hot hall, the Conference was presided over by Mwalim Kihere, subsequently M.P. for Tanga. On his right sat Julius Nyerere, Tanu's President, and on his left Elias Kisenge, Organising Secretary-General, who made history by laying on the table an agenda with sixty-eight items to be discussed by the Conference. The most interesting items were: the participation of Tanu in the first general elections of Tanganyika; responsible government; the raising of funds to build a university of Tanganyika.

The first speaker on the all-important elections issue was Abdulla Rashidi, a Tanga delegate, who made a courageous speech recommending participation. The reaction was stormy: members shouted him down and jeered at him. Kihere, as Chairman, appealed to them not to interfere with a speaker who was giving his views to the conference, but his appeals had little effect. Then Bokhe Munanka, the big voiced delegate from the Lake Province, who is now National Treasurer of Tanu, rose and began his passionate speech by saying: 'You must pray that God shall curse Abdulla Rashidi . . .' At this the wretched man was nearly chased out of the hall and Kihere suspended the meeting for the lunch break.

Julius Nyerere witnessed the scene uneasily. He had known that he would meet with opposition over the issue of participating in the elections, but it was[1] a novel experience to find himself with only a handful of supporters. He who normally had the power of controlling vast crowds and of quieting people roused to fever pitch by other speakers, now wondered how his followers would behave to him.

In the afternoon [Edward Barongo has said], Julius spoke in Abdulla's support. He said in effect: 'Let us come to a decision about participating. Having done that, we will go to the British Government and demand that it give us our rights. And we will ask: "Are you prepared to

---

[1] Before going to Tabora, Nyerere had discussed participation with Paul Bomani, who agreed with him that the battle for independence had to be fought out by constitutional means. Nyerere sent Bomani to Nairobi to discuss this with Tom Mboya. 'Tom told me that this was the sensible thing to do,' Bomani has told the author. 'I then went to Mwanza and raised the issue there with the result that the town was divided between Bokhe Munanka and myself. Bokhe was violently against participation, supported by the local Tanu secretary Abdu Kandoro. I could not go to Tabora myself because of urgent business in the Victoria Cotton Federation but my supporters played an important part. Although silent at first in the Conference hall, outside they helped to prepare the atmosphere in Julius' favour, and I led the cheering when the Conference eventually backed him.'

face the consequences of what will happen if you refuse?'' We are not going to spell out what we mean by that, but by the way we put it, we will worry the British. We will go to the Queen and appeal to her over the heads of her ministers. The British will not like that either.'

The C.I.D. men were indeed worried, but the delegates were not impressed. When Nyerere sat down, there were mutterings, but no cheers. One after another, they got up to speak against Tanu's participation in the elections. The debate went on for four days.

During these crucial four days, Elias Kisenge, Rashidi Kawawa, Edward Barongo and other trusted Tanu colleagues threw themselves into action and gradually more and more voices were raised in support of Nyerere's reasoned policy. But the anti-participationists had by no means given up. On the afternoon of the fourth day, Mwalim Kihere as Chairman gave Bokhe Munanka and Julius Nyerere the floor to sum up for the two opposite points of view.

It was Elias Kisenge who gave the author an eye-witness account of the last scene.

Bokhe spoke first, talking for about one hour, demanding that Tanu should boycott the elections. His appeal was passionate, but he said nothing we had not heard before. Then Julius spoke for forty-five minutes, reasonably, logically and sensibly. He said: 'Imagine that you have a *shamba* and that in front of it there is a pond, with a lot of mud around it. If you want to harvest your crops and carry them out of the *shamba* you must step into the mud and dirty your feet. What would you prefer? To lose your crops and keep your feet clean? Or to harvest your crops and dirty your feet? Now think about what we want. We want that house in which Twining is now living. In order to get into it, we must dirty our feet by walking through the mud of an unfair election. What would you rather do? Keep your feet clean and not get the Twining house, or dirty your feet and get the Twining house?'

The delegates shouted that they were prepared to walk through the mud in order to reach that house.

But what impressed me most [said Elias Kisenge], was his conclusion: 'If we do not achieve our aim by this method, then we can only turn to God . . .'

Julius won hands down. We cheered for all we were worth. When Kihere put the matter to the conference, it was carried overwhelmingly that Tanu should participate in the first general elections of Tanganyika. That was the moment when Tanganyika as a nation was born.

It was Julius Nyerere's most important victory, for it made it possible for the independence struggle to be waged in the constitutional field. This is why he is rightly called the architect of the new Tanganyika.

In the evening, after his great triumph, he had to face one more show-down—with his younger brother, Joseph Nyerere, whom he had brought up and who was very close to him. At that time Joseph was Tanu Youth Leader for Dar-es-Salaam and in charge of Tanu schools. Wanting the Tabora Conference to be an historic event, he trained a choir and hired a bus to take twenty-five Youth League members to Tabora. But he had no funds to pay for their keep; they had to maintain themselves as best they could and missed the historic meeting because of a fund-raising expedition.

These young people were violently opposed to participation in the elections and had been openly canvassing against Julius Nyerere's policy. When they learnt that the conference had decided after all to carry out this policy, they became very angry. They tore into Julius Nyerere's room, where Joseph called his brother a dictator.

What followed, Joseph has told the author:

Julius received us courteously and asked us all to sit down. Then he began to explain what was on his mind. 'If we do not participate in the elections this year, the U.T.P. will put up all the candidates,' my brother said. 'They will then obtain all the positions. When this has happened, what is Tanu going to do? The first thing we will do is to send a memorandum to the Colonial Office. There it will be studied and when the officials have convinced themselves that we have a case, they will appoint a commission and send it here to test the feeling of the country. This will take not less than a year. The Commission will stay here for some time, travelling about Tanganyika. Then it will draft a report for the Colonial Office. Again the officials will take their time to study it, perhaps another year will pass. By then it will be 1960. We may be able to hold our first proper elections in 1961–62. With the U.T.P. running them after three years in power, it will not be easy for us to do well, yet we will win. Then our team will get office. We may then be able to convince the Colonial Office to give us responsible Government in 1963. Then there will be a fight for a new Constitution; by the time we get it, it will be 1965. After that, we are likely to get independence by 1970.

'But if we do participate in the coming elections, the situation will be entirely different.' By now my brother was speaking as serenely as though he were lecturing in a classroom. 'We have European and Asian friends, whom we will support during the elections, and we are likely to get them all in. I believe that all the elected seats will be held either by Tanu members, or by Tanu friends. As soon as I am in Parliament, I shall build these people into a group, and we will have a real opposition. The first thing we will do is to ask for a new Constitution. Our Ministers will sit on the Executive Council; they will fight in Exco while we fight in Legco. We will have a new Constitution in 1959. Then we will fight for responsible government. As soon as we have that, we start to fight for full independence, which we will obtain in 1961.

'This is how I see it. Joseph, have I convinced you?' my brother asked. 'Do you feel happier about the situation?'

'Yes,' I replied, feeling very small.

'And this is what you called my dictatorship . . .' Julius laughed. It was as though I had been put into a frig., my anger cooled down at once. My friends reacted in the same way and they were willing to do anything for Julius. . . .

Nyerere did not tell Joseph that at the Trusteeship Council he had committed himself to Tanu participating in the elections. Nor did he mention it in his speech to conference, although it must have been much on his mind. Had Tanu boycotted the elections, not only H.M.G. but many of Nyerere's supporters in the non-colonial world would, not unnaturally, have regarded him as guilty of a gross breach of faith.

And yet Tabora was not an unalloyed victory. It resulted in the first breakaway from Tanu. Zuberi Mtemwu, one-time Acting Organising Secretary-General of Tanu, who failed in that job as he failed in many lesser ones, resigned from Tanu on a matter of principle over the participation in the elections. The principle was probably a different one, as he formed a racialist party, the Tanganyika African National Congress, with a policy of Africa for the Africans only and self-government for indigenous Africans only. He dreamt of taking with him a large part of the Tanu membership; he deluded himself that he was imitating Kwame Nkrumah, who was followed by the majority of the people when he broke with the United Gold Coast Convention in 1949. Mtemwu achieved nothing of the kind; in fact one third of the list of a thousand members he published denied ever having joined his Congress.

Unfortunately, yet perhaps understandably, black racialism

attracted some followers. One of them was Christopher Tumbo, an intelligent but somewhat over-intense young man, who at the age of twenty-one was elected Secretary-General of the Miners Union. Later on, in the T.F.L., Michael Kamaliza, as Minister of Labour, was to have great trouble with Tumbo's black racialism and its supporters.

At the moment of writing, Zuberi Mtemwu is back in the Tanu fold; when Tanganyika became a one-party state in 1963, he gave up his ridiculously unsuccessful efforts to oppose Nyerere. Tumbo, on the other hand, went to live in self-imposed exile in Mombasa, Kenya, from where he was extradited in the aftermath of the 1964 mutinies. But this is looking ahead six years.

The immediate way in which the small, violent racialist group affected Nyerere was by providing a brake against him. Dissatisfied Tanu members could have defected to the racialist group. This deterred Nyerere from throwing the Tanu ranks open to European and Asian sympathisers until 1963, much longer than he would have liked.

Although the Tabora Conference will always be remembered for its historic decision on Tanu's election participation, a number of other decisions were also taken. The most important concerned responsible government.

It recaptures the mood of the values of 1958 to quote what Julius Nyerere had to say about this in No. 19 of *Sauti Ya Tanu* (*The Voice of Tanu*), dated February 13, 1958:

After a hot debate on the advisability or otherwise of pressing the Administering Authority to announce a target for the country's Independence, it was agreed that . . . it is now up to the people of Tanganyika to announce it, and no purpose can be served by pressing those who have proved that they intend to govern us as long as they please. . . . The Conference therefore decided to press for:

a) Elected majority in the Legco next year.

b) A majority of ministerial positions in the Government next year.

In other words, 1959 is the target date, not for independence but for what, in the constitutional development of the British Colonial World is called 'Responsible Government.' This was the most important policy decision taken at the Conference. It was not taken blindly. The Conference was fully aware of the opposition that is certain to come from the Government and other reactionary circles. But Tanu is prepared to face such opposition.

*

Another important decision concerned education. When Tanu was formed, the first general meeting announced that the party would run schools to combat illiteracy. By mid-1956, several night schools were in existence; in December, 1956, the Vice-President, John Rupia, laid the foundation stone of the first Tanu primary school in the Lushoto District, but its completion was delayed by the closure of the local Tanu branch. Then in the Southern Province, the enthusiastic Lawi Sijoana planned to open a Tanu night school at Masani.

The Tabora Conference accepted Nyerere's idea of building a college modelled on Fircroft College, Birmingham, or Ruskin College, Oxford. It passed a resolution setting up the Tanganyika Education Trust, consisting of six Tanu and six non-African members, with Nyerere as chairman. It met for the first time in December, 1959. Two years later, a total of £80,000 had been collected. The most generous donors were A. Y. A. Karimjee who gave £60,000 and George Arnautoglu and the Tanganyika Sisal Growers Association, who each gave £5,000. Smaller sums were donated by Clayton Robson on behalf of the Tanganyika Association, by Mahmud Rattansey on behalf of the Asian Association, by the Coffee Board and by the Lint and Seed Marketing Board. The most moving contribution was that of Joan Wicken, who came out from England to tour the country and collected, literally from pennies and half-pennies donated by African peasants, £4,500. On one occasion, somewhere in the bush, a poor old woman gave her one egg, which Miss Wicken was to sell for the cause of that college . . . Eventually a hotel on the shore of Dar-es-Salaam harbour, which had run into financial trouble, was purchased for Kivukoni College which is regarded with great pride by all Tanganyikans.

A third important Tabora decision concerned relations with the trade unions. Because of the services the labour organisations could render in areas where Tanu was banned, it suited the party to keep the two movements separate. Yet in fact the link between them was very close and had to be so, as there were not enough experienced Africans separately to man important positions in both organisations. To obtain the best of both worlds, the Tabora Conference passed a resolution giving two seats on the National Executive to the T.F.L. But as it also resolved that no Tanu official could be office-bearer in a union, Rashidi Kawawa, as Secretary-General of the T.F.L., had to resign the leadership of the Tanu Youth League. From then on the Youth League fell increasingly under Oscar Kambona's more radical influence.

When the delegates dispersed from Tabora the days of wild talk were over. The decision to participate in the elections, and to fight the battle for independence in the constitutional arena, had assured eventual victory without bloodshed. Nyerere had proved his statesmanship, his political skill and his faith in principle. He had reached his zenith as a leader who could induce an emotional crowd to renounce a policy which suited its temperament and its pride, for an alternative which seemed like a surrender, almost a betrayal of the New Jerusalem he had promised. Yet they followed him and there was no turning back.

In spite of its contentious opening and the bitterness that resulted, Tabora ended as a turning point in African history. The Tabora decisions have had repercussions in all neighbouring countries. The more is the pity that the Western Press did not report, let alone appreciate, this dramatic event. Nor did Government House do much better, for on the eve of his retirement Sir Edward Twining made one more effort to wipe out 'the irresponsible agitator'.

CHAPTER 30

The Chiefs Back Tanu too Late

WHILE Tanu's main fight was with the colonial authorities, there was another battle that also had to be fought out. Implicit in nationalist aspirations was the assumption that within African society itself there had to be a revolution from the old order based on tribal chiefdoms to a democratic system more closely related to the western pattern. The chiefs still stood in Julius Nyerere's way. Not the least important consequence of the Tabora Conference was that it provided the occasion for resolving this problem once and for all: the chiefs had to come into the open for or against Tanu.

Up to that time they had tried to remain neutral, on the principle that they had to be above politics, the traditional rulers watching over their peoples' interests. The more intelligent chiefs realised that the new and revolutionary African society might have no place for them. Their position, already cracking, had been further weakened by Sir Edward Twining's attempts to involve them in his struggle against Tanu. To retain the respect of their people, the chiefs had to prove their patriotism.

The impending break-up of the chiefly system was a symptom of the convulsion that was already seizing African society at all levels. In a political history of Tanganyika, a detailed account of this system over the centuries would be out of place. A brief sketch, however, is essential to any portrayal of the great changes that were taking place in the late 1950s.

Although laws and customs in Tanganyika differed from tribe to tribe, the usual position of the chiefs was roughly similar to that of medieval princes and barons. Before the Europeans came, the chiefs of the more warlike tribes had held power of life and death; they were the supreme commanders in wars which they had themselves declared; they had complete executive and judicial powers. From the tribesmen they received large dues which enabled them to live well, by African standards, and to provide the lavish hospitality that custom demanded they should offer to their tribespeople.

Chiefs of lesser tribes could best be compared to feudal barons

312

except that no African chief was a personal landowner. They enclosed land in the name of the tribe: as individuals they had no legal ownership, only usufruct. They sat in judgment over criminals and offenders against custom, but their *barazas* might be attended by the entire tribe and each of its members had the right to speak. As in medieval Europe, so until recently in African society, everyone knew his or her prescribed status and understood the rules by which the chief or his deputy meted out justice or administered affairs.

The chiefs directed communal work and tribal hunting; in all emergencies they set an example which the tribe automatically followed. They headed ceremonies and dances, the only distractions in the monotony of the African peasant's harsh life.

In the practice of religion the African chiefs had power far greater than a medieval ruler. They led (or offered) the sacrifice to the deity; many of them were witch doctors and rainmakers, while others delegated these functions to assistants. In whatever form they exercised their supernatural powers, these gave them a tremendous hold over their people.

The more advanced a tribe, the more carefully regulated was the chief's succession; in the more backward tribes there might be no rules about it at all. In most cases the deceased chief's son had to be chosen; in a few the eldest son automatically inherited his father's mantle; in some the new chief was selected by the witch doctors; in yet others any tribesman could put himself forward. Elaborate ceremonies attended a new chief's election which was decided either by voice vote, or by the number of tribesmen walking towards the most popular candidate, or by 'a movement of the magic wand' held by the witch doctor.

Ancestry was of immense importance and carried great prestige. Chief's children had to memorise many generations of forebears; the oldest ancestor and the deity of the tribe was usually synonymous. One evening, in the garden of Karimjee Hall in Dar-es-Salaam, the author was talking to Chief Abdulla Fundikira III., Sultan of the Nyamwezi, at that time Minister for Legal Affairs. In answer to a question, Chief Fundikira asked for a piece of paper and a pen, and then wrote out without hesitation his genealogy for thirteen generations. He said he could have gone much further back. Abdulla Fundikira is a graduate of Makerere and he learnt his excellent English at Caius College, Cambridge, but this part of his erudition lay deep in the history of his people. It is the pride of all aristocracies.

The African chiefs were not supposed to marry outside their caste. They protected each other's dignity and position, sealing their pacts by dynastic marriages. In fact, the family histories of the chiefs make up the history of pre-Colonial Africa.

African aristocracy consisted of three tiers: at the top were the paramount chiefs, sultans and chiefs; councillors, among whom witch doctors and medicine men ranked high, stood on the middle steps of the ladder, while headmen crowded the lower rungs. Below them thronged the masses of ordinary Africans, with few rights and fewer possessions.

Because of the immense respect Africans have for age, the elders held a special position in all tribes. They could bring influence to bear on any chief, for on their advice tribesmen could impose what would nowadays be called economic sanctions against a chief by refusing to pay such dues as the tithe of their crops, their cattle, sheep, goats and fowls, of everything they grew or bred. Similarly the tribesmen might be induced to withhold their labour from the chief. The elders were the only people who could keep in check the dictatorial tendencies of the chiefs, and this was the strongest democratic influence in African society, for, although no question of elections could arise, it fairly reflected public opinion. Democratic, in the original Greek sense of the word, were the *barazas*, the meetings under the big tree, when chief and elders discussed problems of interest to the tribe until everyone present was convinced. If there were any who were not satisfied, they had no alternative but to conform. Julius Nyerere and other African leaders have repeatedly declared that they aim at establishing an African democracy, based on the ancient principle of arguing out differences until every member of the tribe (or the nation) is convinced. From this ancient concept it results that there is no place for an official opposition in modern Tanganyika, at least not in the present stage of development.

The first change in the traditional position of the chiefs took place soon after the arrival of the British in Tanganyika in 1916. Chief Harun M. Lugusha, who has made a special study of this subject, has told the author:

In those early days, the British had neither the staff, nor the means of administering the vast territory that is our country. So they had to fall back on Indirect Rule, which meant using the chiefs to run the country for them. They gave them specific powers for maintaining law and order, and for carrying out local government known as Native Authority. The British did not interfere with the traditional power of the chiefs; but Sir Donald Cameron gave them a regular salary in place of their dues from the tribesmen.

As time passed, it became clear that local government could not be left in the hands of one man. Therefore, in the early 1940s, in the Tabora District the Nyamwezi Chiefs and in the Shinyanga District the Sukuma Chiefs formed a Chiefs' Council, which was similar to a District Council. This example was followed in other parts of the country by other chiefs who also formed councils to advise them in the administration of their chiefdoms.

These Chiefs' Councils decided on policy and on specific subjects of joint interest, naturally under the guidance of the local D.C. His ability to steer the Chiefs' Council depended on his personality. Some were popular and gave a constructive lead. Others were disliked and were of little use.

Chief Lugusha did not mention that, already before the Second World War, certain Africans had made a good deal of money. There were rich 'coffee men' and 'tea men', who were indignant because powerful chiefs forced them to part with some of their new wealth. Like all traditional rulers, African chiefs were always short of money.

A natural consequence of the successful African's changed outlook was that he learnt to ask why anyone should lord it over him and found out that there were other systems, under which commoners were protected by law against arbitrary orders. For personal reasons such as these, wealthy Africans backed British efforts to democratise the Native Authorities. Some wanted to go further and to get rid of the chiefs altogether. A few years before, no one could have expressed such an idea without terrible retribution from the chief. Now ordinary Africans discovered that they could voice discontent with impunity.

In other words, the chiefs were powerless against the politicians. They were protected by custom and by law from many kinds of things, but they had no armour against Tanu, nor for that matter would they have had any against U.T.P. or A.N.C.

Chief Lugusha has described another change:

In the early stages, only chiefs were members of the Chiefs' Council. In the 1950s, however, the chiefs also nominated subchiefs and *jumbes*, then elders of the tribe, then men of substance, who in Europe would have been called 'The New Rich'. Thus almost overnight, non-chiefly families also obtained power. Some chiefs had an inkling that this might greatly affect their position, but most of them regarded it merely as a convenience.

In 1953 the Governor, Sir Edward Twining, issued a Local Government Ordinance with the intention of creating a multi-racial local government system. This was an excellent idea which was fully developed in 1956 with the Amending Ordinance 333. This laid down that in rural areas outstanding local people, whether Africans, Europeans or Asians, whether peasants, settlers, traders or missionaries, were eligible for election. No numbers were fixed, which meant that the people could elect as many persons of each race or occupation as they liked. I was Assistant Minister for Local Government at this time; hence I can state categorically that this scheme failed merely because it came from Government House. Even today the spirit of Ordinance 333 is still alive, but very few non-Africans are now being elected.

In 1954 the foundation of Tanu by Julius Nyerere gave a lead to the new generation of nationalists. Most of them were young, enthusiastic and brash. Their revolutionary teaching about new leaders and new forms of social organisation was a direct challenge to the old African establishment: to chiefs, witch doctors and *jumbes*. As Tanu was also challenging the colonial administration, the chiefs and the British authorities now had a mutual interest. As related earlier, in some districts the chiefs would not let Tanu organisers operate, and this the nationalists, not surprisingly, interpreted as collusion between the chiefs and the colonial administration.

Chief Lugusha has further described how matters developed:

As time went on, the chiefs realised that the people wanted the members of their councils to be elected. Elections were, therefore, organised and the majority of members returned were, perhaps not unnaturally, Tanu men. But the chiefs were still chairmen of the councils.

By June, 1956, Twining was aware of the strength of Tanu and of the negligible impact made by the U.T.P. At this point he first thought of using the chiefs in his struggle against the nationalists. He set about it tactfully, sounding them out on whether or not they would like to meet at regular intervals to discuss common problems. When he found that the idea appealed to them, he suggested that the Ministry of Local Government should organise a meeting at Mzumbe School in Morogoro, and that one chief from each of the fifty-six districts should be invited.

On May 14, 1957, Sir Edward Twining, attended by senior members of his Government, addressed the assembled chiefs. He told them that, in his view, they formed a reservoir of political and administrative talent hitherto not sufficiently tapped; he suggested that the Chiefs' organisation should be called the Chiefs' Convention, for which they had to work out a constitution; eventually, the Chiefs' Convention might be elevated into a second chamber, where the traditional rulers could make a special contribution to Tanganyika's advance to self-government.

After many long speeches, the chiefs got down to business. The main problem facing them was the election of a president. In Chief Lugusha's words:

This proved difficult because of rivalry between Abdulla Fundikira, Tom Marealle and Adam Sapi, respectively the Nyamwezi, the Chagga and the Hehe Paramount Chief. To save themselves from dangerous internal discord, the other chiefs elected Mwami Theresa, Chieftainess of Kasulo, a beautiful young woman of twenty-five, as their President. Thus they put a 'neutral' compromise candidate into the foremost position, and Adam Sapi was elected Chairman.

From then until 1961, the Chiefs' Convention met two or three times a year.

Actually, the first meeting proved unmanageable because of the vast difference in ability among the delegates. Some were of first class education and strong character; others were little more than illiterate peasants. Under British influence, the chiefs approved a constitution on a provincial basis, which allowed for the selection of fewer but more capable men.

In November, 1957, at Iringa, the chiefs first discussed what attitude to adopt towards Tanu. Some took the view that they alone represented the people and that their position in the future Constitution of Tanganyika must be clearly defined. Others warned against the great humiliation which would result from taking part in elections if one of their number failed to be elected to Legco.

One chief, and a very important one, decided to take the risk. Abdulla Fundikira was not only a friend of Nyerere, but he was certain that all Nyamwezi voters would vote for him. Nyerere and

Tanu also knew this and did not put up a Tanu candidate against him. When Nyerere formed his first Responsible Government, he appointed Fundikira Minister for Land, Surveys and Water.

With Tanu strengthening its hold at every turn, the chiefs had to make up their minds at their next meeting, in March, 1958, on their relationship with Tanu. The nationalist leaders knew that the chiefs were in a cleft stick. If they backed Tanu, they sanctioned the forces bent on replacing them with new leaders, which in effect meant that they were going down without a fight. If they stood aloof from Tanu, or condemned it for wanting to uproot the traditional organisation of the tribes, they ranged themselves with the British colonialists, and had an open fight on their hands which they were bound to lose. Both alternatives implied the end of chiefly rule; the only issue was which would be more dignified. Only the shrewdest among the chiefs saw the alternatives as starkly as stated here.

In the ensuing arguments some chiefs took the line that, whether or not they approved of all Tanu methods, they had to support the movement which was fighting for independence; others insisted that their position had to be clarified before they openly backed Tanu.

Both sides agreed that their position could not be underwritten by the colonial Government, and that they could not align themselves with the U.T.P. Therefore, the only possible course was to negotiate with Tanu. But while the enlightened chiefs felt that this had to be done at once, and that the best preliminary move was fully to support Tanu, the others believed that their popular support was a strong bargaining counter, which they should use to obtain recognition before giving open backing to the nationalists.

For three days they argued, backwards and forwards, and the meeting broke up without a clear-cut decision. One thing, however, did emerge, and even the least politically minded chiefs saw it: Twining's efforts to use them against what he called the politicians, meaning obviously the Tanu leaders, had involved them in the raging political battle of the day–on the wrong side. As they were irretrievably drawn into it, they had to make a choice. The meeting did not itself resolve their dilemma, but a rapid and drastic solution was now inevitable.

The chiefs went so far as to set up a committee to study Twining's suggestion that they should transform their Convention into an Upper Chamber which, they felt, would give them a chance of making a real contribution to the country's development. None the less they also realised that this solution would not be popular with the people, who suspected that the chiefly Upper Chamber would be in league with the British, so this proposal was never seriously pursued.

The next Chiefs' Convention met on December 18, 1958, at Moshi, three months after Tanu's overwhelming success in the September elections. All Tanu's European and Asian friends as well as its African candidates had been returned; the U.T.P. did not get in a single candidate, and the February elections seemed set for a similar pattern.

Sir Richard Turnbull, who in July had succeeded Sir Edward Twining as Governor, addressed the assembled chiefs very frankly about their problems. He said that at times the Government and Tanu appeared to be in opposition; this was not so, at least not as far as Tanu's ultimate constitutional aims were concerned, for the Tanganyika Government as well as the British Government were in duty bound to prepare the territory as soon as possible for self-government. Nyerere had said that Tanu aimed at responsible government, then self-government, and that they intended to obey the laws of the country, to avoid breaches of the peace and to respect the rights of inhabitants of all races. The only difference between the objects of the Government and those of Tanu lay in speed and timing.

Unhappily the constitutional ambitions of Tanu, which Turnbull called Part A, represented only half of what they were doing. The other part, Part B, was manifested in the wild talk and behaviour of minor Tanu leaders and speakers who 'constantly deceive the people and inflame their minds, who encourage them to defy authority and do harm to the peace and good order of the countryside'. Further, they made ridiculous promises about the ease and wealth that self-government would bring, when inconvenient laws need no longer be obeyed, nor taxes paid, Nyerere himself had described these dangerous and nonsensical utterances as 'porojo'.

Because of threats and intimidation, sensible, law-abiding men had not attempted to deny this wild talk. This was the most vicious and the most dangerous aspect of Part B.

Turnbull said that many chiefs worried lest their allegiance to the Government would bring them into hopeless conflict with Tanu, and those of their people who had joined Tanu, or were filled with Tanu ideas. There was no need for this feeling, he claimed, provided the Government, the chiefs and responsible Tanu leaders joined together in stopping 'the dangerous and lawless sabotage of the territory's economy'.

These were strong words, yet even now some chiefs did not see the necessity of backing Tanu in the right way for they still did not know what their position would be under any new constitution that might be evolved. To this question they were to get an answer only in September, 1961, from Julius Nyerere in person.

After the February, 1959, elections, in which Tanu again swept the board, there was no more room for prevarication. The chiefs next met, symbolically, at Tabora. Tanu, by now preparing to get into the saddle, and no longer in need of their support, was ready to give them a lesson. They were invited to a tea party, held in a mud shack. It was a sign of the times that they all went, and C. I. Meek, as Secretary of the Chiefs' Convention, went with them.

At this gathering, Saidi Maswanya of Maswa addressed them on Tanu's behalf. In a fiery speech he blackguarded the colonialists and the imperialists and advised the chiefs in no uncertain terms to jump on the Tanu bandwaggon while the going was still good. His audience clapped politely, although some of its members still had serious misgivings about underwriting unconditionally the nationalist movement.

Next day at their own meeting, there was little argument. Even the backwoodsmen knew the inevitable. One chief said sarcastically that this was tantamount to unconditional surrender. A few months later he found out that he had stated a plain fact.

This is how Chief Lugusha has described the last phase:

From 1960 onwards, all members of the District Councils were elected, but the chiefs were still *ex officio* chairmen. Early in 1961 it became apparent that they could not retain even this position. Through Tanu the people were demanding that the chairmen should also be elected. There was a tendency to elect new men, but the chiefs were still ex officio members of the District Councils. Events were now moving so fast that urgent considerations had to be given to their position. Julius was brave enough to deal with it personally.

He invited twelve Chiefs 'as a Committee' from their Convention held in Dar-es-Salaam from September 25 to 27, 1961. The twelve were: Chief Amri Dodo of Babati; three Chagga chiefs: John Maruma of the Rondo, Petro Marealle of the Vundjo and Abdiel Shangali of the Hai Division, Moshi; two Nyamwezi chiefs: Abdulla Fundikira of Unyanyembe and Harun M. Lugusha of Itetemia, Tabora; Chief Patrick Kunambi of Morogoro; Chief Michael S. Lukumbuzya of Ukerewe Island; Chief Kimweri Mputa Magogo of Usambara; Mwami Theresa Ntare of Kasulo; Chief Adam Sapi of Kalenga, Iringa; Chief Humbi Ziota of Nzega. C. I. Meek was present in his double capacity as Principal Private Secretary to the Prime Minister and Secretary to the Cabinet.

The twelve chiefs sat down expecting to discuss how to reconcile their traditional office with the elected bodies of the new democracy. Instead, as courteously as ever, Nyerere told them that, while he bore no ill-feeling to the chiefs, he could not see a place for them in modern local government. The twelve were stunned, although, with the self-control typical of their kind, they did not show it. They put forward a number of counter-suggestions, but these made little impression on Nyerere. The meeting ended on the understanding that the chiefs were to abdicate their positions of their own free will, although they might retain their courtesy titles.

One chief has commented in the author's presence:

These twelve chiefs had no mandate to take vastly important decisions about our future. They had not been elected; they had not even been sent by their fellow-chiefs; they yielded to Nyerere's demand in order to avoid a head-on collision with the politicians. They fought back for a time, but Julius was adamant. They held out on one point only: they refused to issue a communique about their decision to abdicate. The Government had to issue it, and did so stating that the decision had been 'voluntary' and 'unanimous'.

In Chief Lugusha's words, the end of the matter came about as follows:

We came to a mutual agreement in view of the changed circumstances. We realised the necessity to withdraw from our administrative responsibilities in favour of the elected District Councils. By July 1, 1962, we had to hand over all our powers and close our offices. But we did agree that the real, traditional chiefs should be permitted to carry on as titular clan leaders. In effect, we have withdrawn from our administrative offices of our free will.

Abdication, even if the ruler abdicates genuinely of his free will, is still abdication. The African chiefs of Tanganyika resigned their administrative responsibilities because they had no alternative but to do so. In the manner of their acquiescing to the inevitable, the traditional rulers of Africa behaved with a dignity that worthily marked the end of their role over some thousands of years of history.

One more blow was to shatter the little that was left of the chiefs' traditional position. It fell when they discovered that, not only was there no place for them in modern local government, but as from July 1, 1962, there were no more salaries for them. These were the salaries, established by Sir Donald Cameron in lieu of tribal dues, which they had been drawing as heads of the Native Authority. When they appealed against this harsh measure to Nyerere, they were wholly unable to move him.

With the abrupt end of their allowances, some chiefs were left in dire poverty, depending on the charity of their former subjects. Others, who had been very popular and who still had a great position, found that a brother (or another relative) was elected as district magistrate. For instance, the Hehe elected Daudi Sapi Mkwawa, Chief Adam's brother; the Nyamwezi elected the brother of Chief Abdulla Fundikira. But in the summer of 1963, the Government decided to move district magistrates from one place to another, to give them more experience. When district magistrates from chiefly families were transferred to other tribal areas, one of the last ties between the ruling families and their former subjects was snapped.

As always with Nyerere, there was a constructive side to his revolutionary measures. He did what Twining had talked about: he used 'the political and administrative talent of the chiefs hitherto not sufficiently tapped' by appointing gifted individuals to a variety of positions. Adam Sapi became Speaker of the Tanganyika Parliament; Michael Lukumbuzya became Tanganyika's High Commissioner to New Delhi; Harun M. Lugusha[1] became Chairman of the Tanganyika Agricultural Corporation, to mention but three. Provided they are loyal to Tanu and do not intrigue to restore the past, educated and capable chiefs are being given opportunities to carve out new careers for themselves in Tanganyika.

[1] In January, 1964, Lugusha was removed from this position and sent into enforced exile. His successor is H. R. Msefya.

CHAPTER 31

Julius Nyerere Tried for Criminal Libel

ORDINARY Africans could have had no conception of the significance of the Tabora Conference. All they knew was that Nyerere had advocated something no one had at first wanted, but in the end had won unanimous support. For this they admired him immensely, and his political *safaris* took on the character of royal tours.

And yet Nyerere still faced great difficulties. For one, Tanu subscriptions were not being paid regularly. It was much easier for the party to raise funds for specific objectives, such as Nyerere's visit to New York, than to collect routine monthly dues, however tiny. Even for Kivukoni College the Asians contributed most of the money; as for the new Tanu headquarters, it was not Tanu that paid for it. When it was taken over for the Law Faculty of the East Africa University, the builders were paid with British money.

Another difficulty was that Nyerere found it impossible to impose a national policy. From the first, Tanu branches had a high degree of local autonomy; each one assumed that it had the right to act on its own ideas. In the words of one observer: 'Party self-government soon meant a number of quite incompatible utopias.'[1]

Tanu had given the people a new awareness, but it was not a disciplined force and the danger of uncontrolled enthusiasm was aggravated by poor or non-existent communications. During the rainy season, several parts of the country were completely cut off. Not even letters reached them; and very few individuals owned radios. The Southern Province had no through roads at all. For months on end isolated areas heard neither about decisions taken in the capital, nor even about world events.

Nyerere himself experienced this in the spring of 1958. Back from a political *safari*, he ordered some beer. He opened the bottle and had just begun to drink when Elias Kisenge warned him that the Tanganyika General Workers Union, T.G.W.U., had proclaimed a beer boycott. Nyerere poured the contents on the earth,

---

[1] 'An Outline History of Tanu', by George Bennett, in No. 7 of *Makerere*, *1962*.

flung the bottle away and admitted that this was the first he knew about it. Kisenge explained that T.G.W.U. had called a strike over wages and that the employers had retaliated by using non-union labour. Whereupon T.G.W.U. imposed a beer boycott. When the employers went on paying Asian and Somali strike breakers 25s. a day while the strikers only asked for 5s. a day, the boycott was extended to all types of European liquor.

Then and there Nyerere decided that Tanu should back the boycott. The co-operation between Tanu and the labour unions paralysed the bars and African Clubs throughout Tanganyika. Coupled with the prevailing nationalist agitation, the boycott created a dangerously tense atmosphere.

While Dar-es-Salaam was in the throes of the brewery strike, different trouble was mounting in the provinces. Several D.C.s and D.O.s reacted peremptorily to nationalist badgering. Their patience had been severely tried by the cumulative irritation of unfair political pinpricks. One of the worst affected areas was the Lake District. In and around Geita, the nationalists clashed with the police, who on one occasion were compelled to disperse with baton charges and tear gas a gathering of six thousand people. In Musoma trouble centred around the two figures of F. B. Weeks, the D.C., and Mohamed Makongoro, Chief of the Ikuzu, a small tribe living next door to the Zanaki.

Weeks was a forthright, down-to-earth personality, who had an outstanding war record; he was incidentally one of the British expatriates who stayed on to serve Tanganyika after independence. But by his enemies he was secretly nicknamed 'The *Gauleiter*'.

Chief Makongoro was sixty-five years old and had been chief for thirty-two years. He had established a reputation as the most daring poacher of the north and it was rumoured that he had amassed great wealth by the most dubious of means and that he did not stop at murder when he wanted to settle a score.

In May, 1957, Makongoro fell out with Weeks. The D.C. had sent him, as senior chief of Musoma District, to the first Chiefs' Convention at Morogoro; and Makongoro's version of the instructions given to him by Weeks was well calculated to create an inflammatory situation. He alleged that Weeks had told him to tell the Convention, untruthfully, that the Musoma chiefs wanted a multi-racial District Council, and had said that on his return he was to report, again untruthfully, that the Convention had commended multi-racial District Councils for the whole of Tanganyika. Makongoro complained that because he would not be party to such lies, Weeks had unscrupulously turned against him. The story sounded highly improbable. Makongoro was already in trouble and he knew it. His accusations against Weeks were just an attempt to get his story in before his many chiefly malpractices were brought home to him. In any case, Makongoro was shortly after sent for trial by the D.C. on charges of poaching, embezzlement and corruption. The chief was found guilty and was sentenced on January 11, 1958, to fines and six months' imprisonment.

When Makongoro announced that he would appeal, Weeks–so Makongoro further alleged–declared: 'Even if you do get off, I'll never allow you to return here.'

The case caused much excitement in the Lake Districts. After the Tabora Conference, Nyerere, who knew the chief from his childhood as a friend of his late father's, went to Musoma to find out what had happened. Friends and relations told him of the allegations Makongoro had put about and Nyerere seems to have accepted them at their face value, without informing himself of the precise facts. It was then common knowledge that Makongoro was in deep water; indeed a formal enquiry had recently been held under the provisions of the Chiefs' Ordinance into the manner in which he was administering his chieftaincy.[2]

Makongoro won his appeal, but only on a technicality. In view of the Ministry's findings on his general record, the Government refused to allow him to return to his chiefdom. On the face of it, this decision lent some colour to Nyerere's impetuous indignation against Weeks. It was thus doubly unfortunate that he had not acquainted himself with all the facts.

Nyerere also had news that feeling was running high in the Songea District, where G. T. L. Scott was D.C. A conscientious civil servant, he had perhaps been excessively meticulous in insisting that the nationalists should observe every single letter of the law. The result was increased tension in the south.

It was against this background of disquiet that Legislative Council met on May 6, 1958. Sir Edward Twining, about to retire at the end of his third term as Governor, addressed it for the

[2] The civil servant who carried out the enquiry also stayed in independent Tanganyika to serve until he could hand over to an African.

last time. Having reviewed Tanganyika's chances of achieving responsible government, he made a thinly-veiled threat:

If, however, African leaders should prefer to pursue policies which neither the Tanganyika Government, nor H.M. Government in the U.K. as the Administering Authority could accept, then they will retard the progress which, given favourable circumstances, could be made, and will put back the hope of attaining self-government for very many years to come.

This could only mean that, either the nationalists conformed, which they clearly could not do, or they would get nowhere for a long time to come. Nyerere was incensed, especially as Twining had not acknowledged the Tabora decision to participate in the elections. He felt that he was being put into a position in which he could not avoid being labelled as an irresponsible agitator.

In this mood, Nyerere wrote a bitter and ill-advised article in his broadsheet, *Sauti ya Tanu*. Its 29th issue, dated May 27, 1958, said that F. B. Weeks was D.C. in Geita 'when trouble began there. . . . He succeeded [in causing it] in Geita and hopes to succeed in Musoma.' The article alleged that the senior chief had been taken to court in Musoma for 'cooked up reasons' and the D.C. (Weeks) refused to let him go back to his people.

Nyerere had also written concerning Scott:

At one time trouble was reported in Mahenge. On inquiry I learnt that the D.C. had already closed down a Tanu branch before being posted to Mahenge. . . . This evening I am interviewing an elderly gentleman from the same district. He says our branch is in danger of being closed. I am not surprised. The D.C. is the good gentleman who, had he stayed longer at Mahenge, would have closed down our branch there and is bound to close down this other branch. He has already dismissed a subchief who refused to give false evidence in court against Tanu.

Mahenge is in the south, and everyone knew that the D.C. referred to was G. T. L. Scott.

Finally, Nyerere wrote: 'These same officials would have people committing perjury in court if only to vilify Tanu. These same people who intimidate and punish innocence, cajole and reward crookery, have the temerity to invoke law and order.'

These statements were blatantly libellous and highly inflammatory. They greatly upset civil servants in Dar-es-Salaam, who for the last two years had had to swallow nationalist accusations of incompetence, arrogance and trickery, without a word of recognition for the conscientious work they had been doing.

The British administration had to make a difficult decision. In the prevailing tense atmosphere, were they to take action against Nyerere, or were they to ignore a cyclostyled publication which had a circulation of only two hundred? Perhaps Weeks had been somewhat high-handed, and Scott too strict in dealing with the nationalists. Even the Governor must have had misgivings, for he brought the matter, as he has told the author, before the Executive Council. In Twining's recollection, it was the Attorney-General, J. S. R. Cole, who, against Twining's own wishes, insisted on a prosecution for criminal libel.

All Africans believed that Twining, who had actually left Tanganyika by the time the trial began, wanted to use the libels to put Nyerere behind bars. Some Europeans, including the late L. A. Davies, the magistrate who was to try Nyerere, were also under the impression that Twining wanted Nyerere locked up in the naïve hope that Tanu, deprived of its leader, would collapse.

The case opened in Dar-es-Salaam on July 9, 1958, before L. A. Davies, sitting as Senior Resident Magistrate. The prosecution was led by the acting Solicitor-General, John Summerfield, assisted by N. M. Dennison. Nyerere pleaded 'not guilty' to the three charges of criminal libel against F. B. Weeks, D.C. of Musoma, and G. T. L. Scott, D.C. of Songea. His defence was led by D. N. Pritt, Q.C., whom he had engaged on Fraser Murray's advice. Pritt had frequently appeared in colonial trials; his left-wing views were common knowledge, as was his deep sympathy for his coloured clients. His juniors were M. N. Rattansey and K. L. Jhaveri, two Asian lawyers. Rattansey, a personal friend of Nyerere's, also nursed political ambitions.

For the first five days, the trial unfolded according to the expected pattern. It was established that some two hundred copies of No. 29 of *Sauti Ya Tanu* had been cyclostyled and dispatched to readers, some outside Tanganyika. Nyerere took full responsibility for the article about the two D.C.s and said: 'In writing this issue of *Sauti Ya Tanu*, my motive was to draw the Government's attention to the discontent and to get it remedied. I did not write it to court a prosecution. I published it in the English language which the Government could understand.' But he touched on the heart of the matter when he said: 'I wrote nothing until I was provoked by the Government action which purported to close down my branch in Geita.'

Pritt took the expected line that the British administration, rather than Nyerere, was in the dock, for the manner in which it had treated the Tanganyikan people. He was extremely indignant when the prosecution would not put the two libelled D.C.s into the witness box. Stung by Pritt's vehement protests, Summerfield promised to produce them 'at the right moment'.

Hassani Ngunyunka of Songea was the 'elderly gentleman' of Nyerere's article, who had informed him about conditions in the south. Under cross-examination he made a poor showing.

Then Chief Mohamed Makongoro was called for the defence. Under Pritt's examination-in-chief, he related his version of the clash with Weeks. It tallied completely with Nyerere's article. This too was to be expected.

On the sixth day of the trial, something happened that was not merely unexpected, but unprecedented in British legal history. The Attorney-General of Tanganyika committed contempt of court.

On the morning of July 14, 1958, the magistrate, L. A. Davies, was about to leave his house when a copy of the *Tanganyika Standard* was dropped before his door. On an impulse he turned back to pick it up and read, spread in banner headlines across the front page, an official statement that Chief Makongoro, who was still being cross-examined, had been dismissed as chief and exiled from his chiefdom. Mr Davies was enraged.

Had the magistrate not seen the paper – and it often arrived after he had left – D. N. Pritt would have sprung the news on him as a surprise. As it was, when Pritt got up to say that he had an important but unpleasant task to perform, the magistrate interrupted to say that he proposed to read a news item from the *Tanganyika Standard* dealing with the dismissal and exile of Mohamed Makongoro, a material witness who was giving evidence. Having read out the item, he ordered the Acting Solicitor-General to bring before the court the next day both the officer who had the order served on Chief Makongoro and the editor of the *Tanganyika Standard*.

(Bill Otterwill, who had become editor only the previous week, has told the author of his alarm and distress at this development. He had received an official release and had been assured that the

Attorney-General had approved it. He had had no choice but to print it.)

Then Pritt pressed the point home. He related that the previous day, while Makongoro had been giving evidence, the order of dismissal and exile had been served on him. Also, a Government spokesman—'and I use the word in quotes' Counsel added—had made a number of detrimental statements about Makongoro to the Press with the knowledge that they would be published while he was still giving evidence. It seemed clear that the Officer Administering the Government, the spokesman, and the newspaper had all rendered themselves liable to prosecution for contempt of court.

The Acting Solicitor-General had no option but to ask for a twenty-four hour adjournment to get further instructions.

Next morning, on July 15, the Attorney-General personally appeared before the Court to answer for his contempt. In a hushed courtroom J. S. R. Cole said that he felt that the directions of the magistrate were of such importance that he had come to court himself; he added that both the officer responsible for serving the order on Mohamed Makongoro and the editor of the *Tanganyika Standard* were in court and that he had made inquiries himself. He stated he was probably the only person at that time who was fully acquainted with the facts leading to the Press release.

He wanted to make clear that the *Tanganyika Standard* could not be held responsible for its publication. The paper had not sought information, and not asked any questions; it had been handed a Press release from Public Relations in the normal way, which it had printed without comment 'in all good faith as it has done in the past and, I hope, will continue to do in the future. . . . We take responsibility for whatever was printed in this matter.'

As for Mohamed Makongoro, the Attorney-General said that the orders of dismissal and removal to another district had been made on July 9, the day on which the hearing of the case against Nyerere began. It would have been inhuman to serve them that day because Makongoro was at that time so ill that it was not known whether he would live or die. By July 12, after he had been brought to Dar-es-Salaam and examined by specialists, 'his health had improved so much that there is no point in disguising the fact that the Government were in a dilemma. We could have held the orders further but not for the reason that had obtained.'

Government considered that if the orders were served, Makongoro would have nothing to hope for and nothing to fear. Whereas if they had not been served until after he had given evidence, it might have been maintained that they were being held over his head in the hope of influencing his testimony. In answer to an objection by Pritt, Cole said that publication of the dismissal of the former chief could not have intimidated Makongoro and other witnesses as there was nothing wrongful in the service of the orders. The reason for releasing the statement was to make clear that the orders and their service on Makongoro had no connection with the case that was going on. He was not attempting to defend the release, but it had been drafted and issued without the knowledge of what Makongoro had said in evidence.

The contempt was not a calculated one and was not obvious to the public, who were concerned with the case against Nyerere, said the Attorney-General. It had not defamed the accused or insulted the court. 'This release refers to a witness for the defence. I am not trying to minimise it at all, but it might have been a lot worse. I have come to apologise on behalf of the Government and in view of the Press release I have come to purge, in whatever way I can, whatever contempt there is,' the Attorney-General concluded.

The Attorney-General then entered a *nolle prosequi* on the first count against Nyerere, concerned with the alleged libel against F. B. Weeks, the D.C. of Musoma. He also applied for the third count, which he described as a 'joint count' against F. B. Weeks and G. T. L. Scott, D.C. of Songea, to be amended so that Weeks' name be removed from it.

After several submissions by Pritt, the Magistrate said that in view of the explanation given by the Attorney-General, he would take no further action in the matter of contempt, and he was satisfied that no discourtesy had been intended on the part of the editor of the *Tanganyika Standard*. Finally he ruled that the case should continue on count two and the amended count three, both of which alleged libel only against G. T. L. Scott.

Thereafter the case lasted only forty-eight hours and the hearing ended on July 18. The closing speeches of the prosecution and the defence took less than two hours; the magistrate reserved judgment until August 11.

Long before eight a.m., on August 11, when the court opened, large crowds gathered outside it. There was a rush for seats inside; every square inch of standing place was also filled. As at the opening of the case, when Nyerere arrived in grey flannel trousers and a green shirt worn outside them, his friends tried to get up and cheer. He silenced them with a wave of the hand.

The magistrate took his place and started reading his judgment. He recapitulated the events of the case. Originally there had been three counts of criminal libel, but 'certain circumstances had supervened' which led to the withdrawal of the first count and the modification of the third. Neither of the libelled D.C.s had been called to give evidence; the defence closed its case without calling any more witnesses after Mohamed Makongoro. The magistrate had refused the prosecution's application to call Scott after that.

Hassani Ngunyunka, the only witness produced by the defence concerning Scott, the magistrate described as 'shifty, mendacious and unreliable'.

The court accepted that Nyerere, as a leader of a nationalist movement, had a legitimate interest in that he wanted to draw the attention of Government to certain alleged acts of maladministration in the Southern Province. But the magistrate did not agree that the extent of the publication had been reasonable to the occasion. Copies of *Sauti Ya Tanu* had been sent to people outside the Territory and to individuals within the Territory who were not concerned in the matters alleged.

Although the defence had maintained that Nyerere published the matter in good faith, the magistrate said that Nyerere could not be vouchsafed any protection under that heading. He had not been under any legal, moral or social obligation in publishing the defamatory matter.

I have had no evidence before me that the accused had undertaken any serious investigation into the matters concerning Mr Scott. The accused said in evidence that he knew that Mr Scott had not closed down the Tanu branch and had acted within the law in not having it registered. He was not acting in good faith, but from motives best known to himself. He cannot satisfy me that what he wrote was true or that it was privileged.

Passing sentence, Mr Davies said he had formed the opinion that Nyerere was an extremely intelligent man and a responsible and reasonable public figure. It was not customary to impose a prison sentence in such cases and he was not going to depart from that, although it was a grave and mischievous indiscretion. He fined Julius Nyerere £50 on the first count against him and £100 on the second. Both fines were accompanied by an alternative of six months' imprisonment in default of payment. Nyerere was given forty-eight hours in which to pay.

As for the political implications of the case, everyone in Tanganyika knew that this was the final show-down between the Twining Administration and the nationalists. Even without the surprising lapse by the Attorney-General, which eliminated the more serious charges, Nyerere could not help but win politically. The harsher the legal sentence, the more advantageous the effect for Tanu and the nationalists. A small incident illustrates African feeling. When Nyerere was leaving the court room, protected by the ushers against his over-excited followers, some of the African women who had not understood a word of the proceedings thought that he was being taken to prison. They were about to attack the ushers when Nyerere reassured them.

It was indeed the talk of all Dar-es-Salaam that two men had been moved so as to prepare a cell for Nyerere. One of these two men has confirmed to the author that this was so.

Elias Kisenge[3] has told the author: 'On the last day of the case, without my knowledge, women and boys separately planned to organise a procession. They intended to start to *ukonga* from the ferry, dancing right to the prison, and then break in and rescue Julius.'

Certain members of the British administration expected and possibly wanted Nyerere to be imprisoned, although not the new Governor, Sir Richard Turnbull. He had called in Nyerere for a conversation eighteen days before sentence was passed and this first meeting with the Tanu leader changed the political climate. The British *crise de nerfs* was over; from now on a generous and broadminded policy was the order of the day.

The final outcome of the trial shows once more the statesmanlike qualities of Nyerere.[4] The fines were promptly paid from funds supplied by Tanu. Had he chosen to go to prison instead of paying them, the colonial administration would have broken down. There

[3] Had Nyerere gone to prison as originally he intended to do, Kisenge would have stood in his constituency.

[4] See Nyerere's letter to Turnbull, Appendix I.

4 (*a*) Lord Twining

4 (*b*) Independence conference, Dar-es-Salaam, 1961
Front row: Sir Ernest Vasey, Minister of Finance; Mr J. Fletcher-Cooke,
Deputy Governor; Sir Richard Turnbull, Governor; Mr Iain Macleod,
Secretary of State for the Colonies; Mr A. Z. N. Swai, Minister for Commerce
and Industry; and Mr Julius Nyerere, Chief Minister

5 (*a*) Demonstration by Dar-es-Salaam taxi-drivers, 1961

5 (*b*) Self-help: digging a road in the Pare Mts., Tanga Region

would have been a campaign of *kugoma*, passive resistance; as essential services have to be maintained, the military and the police would have had to be called out and from then on resistance would no longer have been passive. Nyerere, who during the twenty-four days between the end of the trial and the passing of sentence had carried on with his normal activities, showed amazingly cool nerves. On August 10 his wife was in great distress. Before friends who tried to cheer her she wept bitterly for fear that Julius might be imprisoned for a long time. When told that she was not alone, she replied with a cry from the heart: 'I know, I know–he is married not to me, he is married to Tanganyika. . . .'

On that same day Nyerere attended a Bank dinner in Dar-es-Salaam, sitting next to the Minister for Constitutional Affairs, John Fletcher-Cooke. In great good humour, at one point he told the minister: 'I must enjoy this excellent meal, who knows where I'll have supper tomorrow. . . .'

By his responsible act in rejecting the martyrdom of a term in prison, Nyerere allowed the case to drop out of mind, and a new chapter to begin in British–Tanganyikan relations.

With hindsight, it is clear that Nyerere had lost his temper and had libelled the two D.C.s. In view of the Twining administration's rigid refusal to concede even Tanu's most modest demands, this may be understandable, but in view of Nyerere's character it came as a surprise. He erred, but by paying the fines, he demonstrated both his good sense and his trust in the new Governor, Sir Richard Turnbull.

M

CHAPTER 32

The Last Pro-Consul: Sir Richard Turnbull

ON July 15, 1958, there were huge crowds in two parts of Dar-es-Salaam. African nationalists thronged around the Court House in which Julius Nyerere was standing trial on charges of criminal libel. They had camped out for three days, and were going to wait until their hero's fate had been determined. Europeans, Asians and other Africans gathered at Government House where Sir Richard Turnbull was going to take the oath.

The new Governor had two immediate surprises in store for Tanganyikans. As he came from Kenya, they expected him to be harder on the nationalists than even Sir Edward Twining had been; instead his inaugural address contained words of encouragement; what is more, he was the first Governor to speak not only in English but in Swahili, the Tanganyikans' own language.

First reactions differed. The Africans and their friends felt relief that the new Governor showed no signs of Kenya white settler mentality; some Europeans and Asians were alarmed that he might give in to those they regarded as hooligans. As Turnbull was known to have cleaned up the Mau Mau in Nairobi, he must be a strong man. Yet the sentiments of his speech sounded like an olive branch to Tanu.

Then on July 24 he invited Julius Nyerere to Government House. This caused a furore. Judgment had not yet been pronounced in the Nyerere trial and yet the new Governor was willing to talk to the accused.

For Turnbull's critics the next reports of this meeting were even more astonishing. As the Tanu leader walked into the Governor's study, the Governor greeted him with the words: 'Well Mr Nyerere, you and I working together have got to solve some very big problems in Tanganyika.'[1]

What the Governor said and the way he said it impressed Nyerere immensely. The conduct of the man from Kenya, whom Nyerere had feared so much, indicated that Turnbull took it for granted that they were going to work together. This was a stagger-

[1] Compare with President Nyerere's version, Appendix I.

334

ing change from Sir Edward Twining's attitude during the previous three years.

Nyerere spontaneously responded by saying that it was not in the future interest of Tanganyika that Tanu should go on fighting the Government. There was bound to be conflict in the political sphere at the centre, but he was anxious that neither the administration nor the handling of development projects should be interfered with. Then he stated on his own and on Tanu's behalf the need that responsible self-government should come at an early date. Surely it was time that there should be an elected majority in the Executive Council and in the Legislative Council. 'This majority will include Europeans and Asians,' he said. 'I am determined that their interests should receive all the consideration they need.'

Turnbull could not, however, take Nyerere fully into his confidence. Not only had he no authority from the Secretary of State, but he had no timetable, for he knew that he would have to be guided by events and the climate of feeling. Nor could he guess what would be the findings of the proposed Post-Elections Committee, within whose terms of reference it was, at that time, intended to include advice on constitutional change.

All the Governor could do was to speak in generalities about development in other territories, for instance in Ghana, where from a purely colonial régime the country had progressed to responsible self-government, then to full internal self-government and finally to independence. He went into some detail about the introduction of the ministerial system, which meant a majority of elected members in the Legislative Council, the Government majority being created by a number of unofficials crossing the floor and joining the Government side. The Executive Council would, from then on, become the Council of Ministers. Ministers had to bear three kinds of responsibility: responsibility for the direction of their ministry, common responsibility to the Government and to their colleagues in the Government, and responsibility towards the electorate.

Nyerere listened fascinated to this lucid exposition of British constitutional practice, spoken in a friendly, simple way. Despite his years in Edinburgh, he was surprised to hear that a minister might have to subordinate the policy of his ministry to fit in with the over-all policy of the Government, and that an unofficial majority in Legco and in the Council of Ministers did not necessarily mean self-government. That would only come when Colonial Office control had been removed from all save a few specified fields.

In later years Nyerere had occasion to remember the Governor's statement that 'the appointment of Ministers is a good deal easier than the Africanisation of the civil service'; also his explanation about the functions of a civil service in providing the minister with information and advice as a basis for decisions of policy. In Ghana self-government had come easily and quickly because the civil service organisation had been ready and waiting for ministers.

Julius Nyerere talked about the problems foremost in his mind: the District Councils and the lack of consultation with the people. In many districts, he said, there was suspicion because the D.C.s were in such a hurry to set up their councils that they neglected to acquaint the people with what they were doing. They placed too much emphasis on the councils' multi-racial character. The chiefs also were mistrustful, but they did not like to tell Europeans.

Turnbull replied that he would look into this problem. Meanwhile he could assure Nyerere that multi-racialism did not mean that there should always be a division of power and responsibility on a one–one–one basis, but only that no one should be ineligible for any position either in the Government or out of it merely on account of the colour of his skin.

Then they discussed with complete ease the desirability and the practicability of speeding up the coming elections. Again, Turnbull could not, without the Secretary of State's sanction, tell Nyerere that he, personally, hoped to hold the second batch of elections not in September of the following year but much earlier – in February.

Sir Richard Turnbull's comment on this conversation is: 'I clearly could not form an alliance with Julius Nyerere to put pressure on the Secretary of State. My purpose was to enlist his support and to let him know that, on the way to independence, certain stages just had to be passed through.'

For his part, Nyerere instinctively realised that he was dealing with a friend and the whole situation suddenly seemed different. He recognised that perhaps imprisonment and martyrdom were no longer necessary to achieve his aim. Here was a real sign that the

British might co-operate after all with him, on terms acceptable to African dignity in order to achieve independence without bloodshed.

Nyerere left Government House in a thoughtful mood. He and his Tanu colleagues, and their European and Asian friends, would have to rethink their situation and re-plan their campaign. Before going any further, they would also have to find out a lot more about the new Governor.

In a short time the people of Dar-es-Salaam witnessed the unusual spectacle of His Excellency the Governor going for a bicycle ride at six a.m. every morning, sometimes without even an A.D.C. accompanying him. He talked to everyone in perfect Swahili; he collected plants and rocks and it was said he intended to climb every mountain in Tanganyika. It took the nationalists time to take the measure of those novel traits; they wanted to make sure how far they could trust him and how far he could influence British policy.

*   *   *

The new Governor's career had begun, as it was to end, unusually. Sir Richard Turnbull was a Scotsman, a borderer, whose family had been scattered after the '45. His forebears had gone to Jamaica, and started growing sugar in the casual and unbusinesslike way that characterised West Indian plantations at that time. In 1859 his grandfather came back to be educated in England. A year later German beet sugar undercut cane sugar and the Turnbull plantations no longer yielded a revenue. So he stayed on in London and went into the City. One of his six sons was trained as a chartered accountant and was to be Sir Richard Turnbull's father.

Young Turnbull was educated at University College School and then at University College, London, as a physical chemist. He took his degree in 1929, at the time of the Depression. Nobody seemed in need of physical chemists, and the future appeared anything but bright. One day he was walking down Whitehall towards the Abbey to hear a Bach Chorale that the choir was singing as an anthem. On his way he passed Richmond Terrace and saw a notice advertising jobs in the colonial service. He went for an interview, was accepted, and was sent for a one year colonial course at Cambridge.

His first appointment, as a cadet, was to Tanganyika. All his luggage was labelled Dar-es-Salaam. Then a D.O. in Kenya was unexpectedly transferred to Tanganyika, creating a vacancy in Kenya, and Richard Turnbull was switched over there. His spell of service in Kenya lasted from August, 1931, to April, 1958, nearly twenty-seven years.

In January, 1936, he was sent to the Northern Frontier District, an inhospitable, arid and desolate area. There was not enough money to provide for transport or communications on one tenth of the scale that is today regarded as essential. Police and soldiers were thin upon the ground. But Turnbull remarks: 'As George Robey said—"what was there was good".'

In those days a young D.O. or policeman seldom had more than a dozen men with him on patrol. He had no communications with his District Headquarters, which might be as much as two hundred miles away. He had to weigh up for himself any situation that might arise and do the best he could with the resources at his command. If he did the wrong thing, he not only disgraced himself, but might stir up trouble on an international scale. (A badly interpreted piece of intelligence in 1935 nearly resulted in a major international incident.)

At Isiolo, Turnbull witnessed a striking example of African psychology. A quarrel had been raging among the local Somali for years. It seemed insoluble. His predecessors had done their best to resolve it, but had achieved nothing. The whole thing, laced with local intrigues and personal hatreds, made no sense at all. Then one day, in a lighthearted mood, Turnbull assembled all the characters concerned and said to them mysteriously: 'When the elephant walks in knee-high maize, no birds will fly in the sky.'

The Somali looked at each other, clapped their hands and declared ecstatically that this explained everything. He never heard another word about the big quarrel.

His real education was at the hand of the Ethiopians. They were a touchy, difficult and suspicious people, of whom the Africans were terrified because of their reputation for utter ruthlessness. Yet they were a sovereign nation, as independent as Great Britain, who had succeeded in keeping out the Europeans, and they had to be accorded the same consideration and respect that one would give to the representatives of, say, France or America.

When the Italians were advancing in Southern Ethiopia,

several thousand Ethiopians fled towards the Omo river, which flows into the northern end of Lake Rudolf. The party, numbering more than eight thousand, moved southwards through the desert country on the eastern shore of Lake Rudolf; and despite the skill and devoted work of the Kenya police and the army and of the British doctors who met them and cared for them, something like a quarter perished on the way. The remainder, racked by exhaustion and hunger, and suffering from the ravages of smallpox and dysentery, were settled at Isiolo by Turnbull and looked after there by him. Here an immense town was made with acacia boughs and thatch and in it were housed the great army of Ethiopians, men, women and children, noble families, priests and soldiers, free men, feudal tenants and slaves. In the camp were built a hospital in which the sick were restored to full health; schools in which the host of children were educated, and Coptic churches in which the Ethiopians could worship. Those who could profit from such teaching were trained as spinners, weavers and smiths, and in a variety of other crafts. Some returned to Ethiopia in 1939, the majority in 1941, after the Emperor's reinstatement.

In the Northern Frontier District Turnbull says he learnt three lessons. The most important was that policy must be determined by the strength that authority could exercise. The tribesmen could be seen counting the weapons on both sides, and figuring out who would acquit themselves the better if it came to the test.

The second lesson Turnbull learnt when dealing with Ethiopians was the paramount importance of patience and courtesy. When a D.C. crossed the frontier, he often had to eat humble pie. Patience and courtesy were the only resources he could fall back on. Yet, if the Ethiopians could defeat him in any contest–drinking, horsemanship, shooting–they were so pleased that they were willing to make almost any concession. Turnbull says that in spite of all the frustrations endured in dealing with them, they commanded his admiration and respect.

The third and hardest lesson of all was the recognition of the limitations of one man's knowledge and abilities; it was salutary for him to have to admit that the Ethiopians might, on occasion, be more accurately informed than he was.

In 1941, he was appointed to the Secretariat in Nairobi. Eighteen months later he was back at the Frontier, but on the other side of Lake Rudolf. At the end of 1944, he was summoned again to the Secretariat, this time to reorganise frontier affairs. In 1947 he was lent to the army as liaison officer to help to sort out some of the problems arising from the move to the Canal Zone.

From 1948 to 1953 he was P.C. in control of both sides of Lake Rudolf, spending five more years on the frontier. In May, 1953, he was appointed Minister of Education and in 1954 he was transferred to the Ministry of Defence and put in charge of Operation Anvil, to break Mau Mau in Nairobi. His partners in responsibility were the Commissioner of Police and a Brigadier of the military forces. It was said at the time that Turnbull was running that show single-handed, guided by only two principles: to keep within the law and to act with an eye on the future. The situation in Nairobi at that time was very bad. In 1953 over a hundred murders had been committed in the city, in every case African murdering African, yet not a single prosecution could be effected as no witness would go into court. Guns were passed from hand to hand.

It took nine weeks to prepare Operation Anvil, during which time a camp for 30,000 Mau Mau suspects was being built. Turnbull was afraid lest the Kikuyu should get wind of this and run away from Nairobi, but none did.

In 1955 he became Chief Secretary to the Kenya Government. He held this position until his appointment as Governor of Tanganyika in April, 1958.

Nyerere recognised at once that he was dealing with a friend and a top British civil servant who had a mind and will of his own. But the task confronting Turnbull was far more complex than merely fostering friendship and mutual trust with the nationalist leader.

Quite apart from what was happening in Tanganyika, a change was taking place in the attitude of Whitehall towards all native Africa. The task and the personal aim of the new Governor were to make sure that the ground was carefully prepared to receive the tender plant of independence, and no one saw more clearly than Turnbull that this process of preparation would require great firmness. At first sight the need for firmness might seem incompatible with the friendship which he wished to extend to Nyerere, but the Governor had far-sighted plans.

In the coming weeks he remained Nyerere's staunch friend but was compelled to take a much tougher line with the Africans in general. The reason for this was that Turnbull saw that Nyerere was unable to control Tanu activities at any distance from Dar-es-Salaam. Whenever he went to a place he asserted his authority, but his good influence did not last long after his departure.

A typical incident occurred in Mwanza at the end of July, 1958, when Tanu followers swarmed on to the football ground and refused to go away. They seated women and children in the front row. They flouted authority and created insanitary conditions. Eventually the police dealt with them, but it was an unpleasant and unnecessary affair.

On a wider front, the years 1958–9 were the time when in all parts of Tanganyika Tanu followers were talking about *kugoma*, which is the Swahili word meaning 'to strike'. In the sense in which it was then used it meant either passive resistance in imitation of Mahatma Gandhi's tactics or, a more sinister interpretation, positive action.

Unlike some of his advisers, Turnbull took this threat very seriously. Not because he believed that the Africans would carry it out efficiently. On the contrary, he was convinced that it would have been an incompetent and ineffective venture. But it would have strengthened the growing tendency to regard idleness, obstruction and defiance, even of African officers, as a civic duty.

Turnbull had the prescience and the courage to recognise that if this development went unchecked it would be disastrous to all the aspirations which he and Nyerere shared. If Africans became used to regarding all authority as an enemy this ingrained habit would eventually make Nyerere's task infinitely more difficult. Turnbull was determined to stamp out 'romantic lawlessness'.

That the policy Turnbull carried out differed greatly from the one applied by Sir Edward Twining had little to do with their respective personalities, but it was Tanganyika's and Nyerere's good fortune to have a Governor of Turnbull's outlook at the time when world events were to begin to shape Tanganyika's future.

By 1958 the Wind of Change had begun to blow as a result of the independence gained by India, Pakistan, Ceylon, Burma, Ghana and the Sudan. It was given increased strength by the French defeat of Dien-Bien-Ph, where foreigners were beaten by natives on equal terms and driven out of the country. The British withdrawal from Suez had a tremendous impact on Britain, for it meant that the British Government had to give way to American pressure; on the Africans it had much less effect than Dien-Bien-Phu.

From 1959 onwards British policy was reshaped to give independence to all colonial possessions as fast as possible. The cost of maintaining these overseas dependencies on the basis laid down in 1946 by the Labour Colonial Secretary, Arthur Creech Jones, had become prohibitive to an impoverished Britain and the decision to liquidate the British Empire gained momentum.

In such circumstances in Tanganyika it fell to Sir Richard Turnbull to carry out the policy which was to lead to independence at a much earlier date than even Julius Nyerere had really believed practicable. Thanks to his vision and firmness, and his personal affection for Nyerere, it was realised not only without bloodshed, but on a basis of close co-operation between the British Governor and the African nationalist leader.

CHAPTER 33

The First Elections

AFTER his talk with Sir Richard Turnbull, Nyerere knew that the British Government were at last prepared to accept Tanu as a negotiating partner. Now it was up to Tanu to demonstrate that the country stood solidly behind the nationalists. In the elections, all of Tanu's candidates had to be returned with overwhelming majorities, not only the African candidates, but also the Europeans and Asians who were standing with Tanu support.

Tanu also had to take into account Twining's pledge that after the elections a committee would be appointed to report on possible constitutional changes. To impress this committee, it was doubly important that every Tanu supporter should go to the polls.

Nyerere realised that after Tanu's vociferous propaganda against the 'one–one–one' system, it would be difficult to induce every African with a right to vote to do so. The Asian Association would help to select Asians friendly to Tanu; but only a handful of Europeans sympathised with the nationalists, and even they had no personal contact with Nyerere. The three races still lived in strictly separated compartments.

Turnbull was very conscious of the cold war that Tanu had been waging against the British Administration for the last two years. His main purpose was to stop the habit of non-co-operation and of the nationalists' blaming their own deficiencies on the fact that they had not yet got *uhuru*. He wanted to placate and to advance, but at a rate within the capacity of the available leaders; and there was none with more than a few weeks of parliamentary experience, and none who really understood the relationship which should properly exist between the legislature and the executive. Even the Assistant Ministers had had little notion of how government worked, and how grave the Territory's financial situation was. None the less, Turnbull tried to get Tanu to accept the limited changes which he on behalf of the Government was prepared to make.

His first concession was to change the date of the elections. After consultation with the Colonial Office, he announced in his first broadcast that the second half of the elections would be held in

February, instead of September, 1959. This was the second time that the Governor addressed the people in Swahili. The effect was very great. Speeding up the elections was taken as further proof that the new Governor was a friend who could be trusted.

The elections were to be conducted under the parity system to which the nationalists were basically opposed. There was a common electoral roll but each voter was compelled to vote for one candidate of each of the three main races; if he did not cast the three votes, his ballot paper became invalid.

It was not, however, Nyerere's intention to provoke controversy over the electoral machine. With singleness of mind, he saw clearly that all problems of subsidiary importance must be subordinated to the supreme aim of achieving *uhuru*. To this end he was ready to accept any temporary limitation–such as that imposed by the parity principle–as long as it could be used to bring about an orderly advance to responsible government, then internal self-government and finally to independence.

Thus Nyerere was aware that slogans like 'One Man, One Vote', 'Responsible Government in 1959', were bound to create the impression that, with the elections won, the millennium would be round the corner. And he was prudent enough to realise that for the sake of Tanganyika no less than for his party, premature and thoughtless enthusiasms would be damaging. In presenting Tanu's policy to the electorate, he had to explain every issue in the most simple terms for all to understand, but he had to do so in a way which would not provoke controversy or raise false hopes.

Despite these difficulties of presentation, Nyerere was successful in driving his arguments home. First among educated Africans, and then more gradually throughout the electorate, it came to be realised that the non-Africans who had settled in Tanganyika were there to stay, and should be encouraged, provided they were prepared to do so without imposing conditions. Despite the apparent unfairness of the parity principle, it was soon recognised that Asian and European candidates were in a position in which they would have to depend on the goodwill of the overwhelming African majority of the electorate. Once the ordinary African grasped the extent of his power, he would fulfil his electoral duties with pride.

One of Tanu's particular difficulties was in the choice of the Asian and European candidates whom it would support. The Asian

Association, with its small band of thinking individuals, could only exercise moral influence. Its two leading figures, Amir Jamal and Mahmoud Rattansey, were close friends of Nyerere's (although not of each other). He could rely on them to pick the right persons. What no one could guarantee was that Asians in different parts of Tanganyika would abide by their decisions.

In her charming book, *The Tanganyika Way*, Sophia Mustafa has given a graphic description of how she was asked to stand as the Asian candidate in the Northern Province. Six Asians proposed to stand and they were quarrelling hard with each other. The local Tanu leaders did not like any one of the six, so they invited her. Having obtained her husband's agreement, she secured twenty-five signatures for her nomination, and drew up her election manifesto. At a mass meeting in Moshi she met Nyerere for the first time, as well as the other Tanu-supported candidates, Solomon Eliufoo and Derek Bryceson.

Mrs Mustafa admits that it was a European nurse, who refused to look after her because of her brown skin, that made her realise that Tanu was speaking for the people. It took all Nyerere's influence to force the six Asians to stand down, and to persuade some of the Chagga to vote for a woman. He told the Africans that if they wanted *uhuru*, they had to back the Tanu chosen candidate. Mrs Mustafa was returned with a handsome majority.

It was even more difficult to find Europeans upon whom Tanu could rely. Derek Bryceson alone had befriended Nyerere and backed Tanu throughout, fighting its battles from behind the scenes as Assistant Minister of Labour. He resigned his ministerial position in order to stand in the elections, but he had other worries, for his farm on Kilimanjaro was not yet paying. Shortly before nomination day he suggested to his neighbour, Robin Johnston (the Capricorn representative who had formed the Tanganyika National Society) that he should stand in his place, provided the Africans accepted him. They did not; twenty-four hours later Bryceson was compelled to change his mind. He stood after all.

About a week before polling day, September 8, 1959, he had a bad car smash, in which he broke his polio-weakened leg, and several ribs. He was unconscious for many hours, and spent the election in hospital. Although the European community, infuriated by Bryceson's pro-African attitude, voted solidly against him, Tanu votes enabled him to eliminate his U.T.P. opponent, John Hunter, a successful coffee grower.

One of the most interesting contests took place in the Southern Highlands, where Marion Lady Chesham opposed Ivor Bayldon, U.T.P.'s president.

Lord Chesham had died in 1952. He had inculcated his love of Africa into his American wife. In her maiden speech in Legco, she was to state:

I have always had faith and confidence in Tanganyika. This faith was given me by my late husband over twenty-five years ago. He believed and taught me to believe that Tanganyika could and would be a great country; that it could and would lead Africa, that it could and would be a shining example to the rest of the world. He said that it would happen only when we all became Tanganyikans. I never heard him mention the word 'race' or 'racial' in this connection. He never thought that way. I have tried to carry on as he would want me to. When I took the oath, I became fully Tanganyikan.

Lady Chesham knew a good deal about the political scene in Tanganyika. After her husband's death she stayed on in Rungemba, the house he had built for her, and was a frequent visitor at Government House in Dar-es-Salaam. As a friend of Robin Johnston and of Derek Bryceson, she became interested in Capricorn, but did not go on with it. She rejected the U.T.P. because she felt that the Africans had to come into their own.[1] She decided to help them build their country and stood as an independent candidate.

She had started campaigning vigorously when, one evening, she heard on the radio the names of candidates to be backed by Tanu. Her name was among them. The following Sunday, Nyerere came to Iringa to address a meeting and she sat in the back of the large circle surrounding him. Nyerere spoke in Swahili, and her knowledge of the language was limited. Suddenly she heard him say her name and saw him look towards her. She understood him to say that the people of the Southern Highlands were to vote for her because Tanu trusted her.

After the meeting she thanked him and they shook hands warmly. They had a long political discussion. Her European neighbours were shocked by her fraternising with an African. Today, Lady Chesham is one of Nyerere's European political

[1] Although for a short time both Lady Chesham and Derek Bryceson had belonged to U.T.P.

confidantes. Through the Community Development Trust Fund which she founded, and with the generous help of American friends, she has brought large sums of money into Tanganyika.

Nyerere considered it politically necessary to oppose U.T.P. everywhere. Unlike the European Press and European observers, he knew that U.T.P. had no footing in the country. Voters in Government service or in the Native Administration might back it, but their number was negligible. U.T.P. had changed its programme, now demanding most of the things Tanu was fighting for. Nyerere wanted to show that this was not a change of heart, but political tactics. In the event, all U.T.P. candidates, including its president, Ivor Bayldon, were heavily defeated, he by Lady Chesham at the rate of three and a half votes to one, the same number as Nyerere obtained against his opponent, Patrick Kunambi, Sultan of the Luguru.

Zuberi Mtemwu's racialist African Nationalist Congress did even worse than the U.T.P.; Mtemwu himself polled only fifty-three votes. And yet Nyerere took this much more seriously than the U.T.P. The A.N.C. indicated danger ahead: dissidents or dissatisfied elements could go over to it. According to Amir Jamal: 'The A.N.C. appears to receive support from forces outside Tanganyika who are probably anxious to impede the present incipient stage for their own, selfish motives.' (*Venture*, Nov. 1958.)

For the opening of Legco, the fifteen elected members assembled in Dar-es-Salaam. They founded T.E.M.O.: the Tanganyika Elected Members Organisation, and elected Julius Nyerere as their leader. The other fifteen Representative Members were still those that had been appointed over the years by the Governor. They agreed to take the T.E.M.O. whip and proved completely loyal; at the February elections, the Tanu members among them, Rashidi Kawawa, Paul Bomani, George Kahama, stood for election and were naturally returned.

As Nyerere had predicted, in February Tanu repeated their September success, only three of the fifteen seats being opposed. The most interesting newcomer was Barbro Johansson, a Swedish Lutheran missionary, whose Tanu sympathies had been known for some time. She had been visiting her family in Sweden when she received a telegram from a Mwanza Tanu organiser asking her to stand for the West Lake Province.

Of all the European women in Tanganyika, Barbro Johansson

has done most to help Africans. With money provided by her family, friends and the Swedish Government, she had financed community development courses, library services, women's clubs, sewing classes, and so on. She had taken education to places never before visited either by Christian or by Moslem missionaries.

Sir Richard Turnbull addressed Legco both after the first and after the second elections. In his address of October 14, 1958, he guardedly and unobtrusively set up the first milestone on the road to independence; he said:

In terms of population the Africans are and will be an overwhelming majority in Tanganyika; and, as the country progresses, it is right and proper, as indeed it is natural and inevitable, that African participation both in the Legislature and in the Executive should steadily increase. It is not intended, and never has been intended, that parity should be a permanent feature of the Tanganyika scene. On the other hand it is intended, and always had been intended, that the fact that when self-government is eventually attained both the Legislature and the Government are likely to be predominantly African should in no way affect the security of the rights and interests of those minority communities who have made their homes in Tanganyika. I am glad to note that the responsible leaders of major political parties in the Territory are in complete agreement on this important matter; and that there is therefore a good prospect that in due course there will exist in Tanganyika a government to which H.M. Government will be able to devolve their trust as being a government under which responsible people of all races will feel secure.

Turnbull also said that in districts in which non-African interests were limited, purely African district councils could be established. (This meant that there was to be no doctrinaire enforcement of multi-racialism.) But he insisted that the chiefs had to occupy a very special position. A working party, consisting of some members of the Chiefs' Convention, and of some of his own advisers, was to consider the desirability of setting up some form of Territorial Council. He ended with a warning that Tanganyika, especially an independent Tanganyika, had to stand on its own feet financially. Unless it produced what the world market needed and at a price it was prepared to pay, the country would not have the money to meet the cost of the progress that was so ardently desired.

On March 17, 1959, Turnbull was faced with a completely

different situation. He had had a first warning in February, when Randal Sadleir[2] met Nyerere once more at the Cosy Cafe, and stood him a cup of tea. Over it, Sadleir has told the author, Nyerere said: 'You know Mr Sadleir, you'd better tell your bosses that if they won't grant us responsible government, the colonial administration will break down. We will see to that, we can do it. I mean it.'

When Sadleir presented his report to the Chief Secretary, Arthur Grattan-Bellew commented: 'Another of Mr Sadleir's remarkable conversations with Mr Nyerere in a teashop. . . .' Next day, in a changed mood, Grattan-Bellew sent for Sadleir as the Governor wanted to see him and to find out some more.

Nyerere came to see Turnbull on a number of occasions in February and March of that year, ultimately insisting that he had to have an unofficial majority in the Executive Government. Nyerere was clearly in difficulties because of his own ambitious promises to Tanu. At the Tabora Conference held in January, 1958, he had launched the policy of self-government in 1959 'or else . . .'. By the middle of 1958, he began to realise that there was not the slightest chance of his getting self-government in 1959; he therefore began to demand responsible government in 1959 'or else . . .'. There probably was not a man among his followers who knew the difference between responsible government and self-government. At this stage his demands were:

(a) A majority of unofficial ministers in the Executive Government.

(b) A majority of elected members in the Legislature.

(c) The abolition of the tripartite vote.

(d) Universal franchise.

All of these must, he said, be brought about before the end of 1959.

At the meeting between them on March 12, Turnbull explained with great patience and courtesy, and with an obvious liking for Nyerere, that he could not possibly give him a majority of unofficial ministers in the Executive Government, or a majority of elected members in Legco. Nor could he do anything about the tripartite vote or about the franchise; for these were clearly matters that would have to await the deliberations of the promised

2 See also Chapter 21, pp. 220–221.

Post-Elections Committee. And then he revealed that he had a serious offer to make: namely four unofficial ministers, whom he wanted to be elected men, although he would have to reserve the right to nominate them if necessary. (Turnbull knew perfectly well that he had little chance of nominating an African, for the power of Tanu was so strong that none would have dared to accept a ministry without Nyerere's specific approval.)

Nyerere was fully aware that this was a substantial step forward; it would mark the change from a purely official civil service Government to a Government in which the representatives of the people had a say. Turnbull carefully pointed out to Nyerere that they would have not only executive responsibilities in their ministries, but would have a share in every decision made by the Executive Government on any matter whatsoever.

Turnbull also promised that, provided law and order were maintained, a statement would be made when the outcome of the Post-Elections Committee's recommendations was known, indicating further constitutional steps. He referred specifically to the possibility of the introduction of unofficial majorities in the Council of Ministers and in Legco. Finally, he reminded Nyerere that, when drawing up this statement on future constitutional changes, he would have among his advisers the four unofficial ministers.

This was solid advance, an advance Turnbull was not certain the country was ready for. But he was quite certain that it had to be taken, if only for Nyerere's sake.

Nyerere appreciated Turnbull's goodwill and understanding. He admitted to him that the constitutional changes which were to be announced on March 17 (the opening date of Legco) were fair and reasonable, he even said that they were generous. His fear was that he would be unable to explain them to his followers, and that the country would suffer widespread and serious disorders. The point was that he was reluctant to admit to his followers that he had failed so badly in what he had promised.

Nyerere was tense, and Turnbull admits that he too was 'tolerably anxious'. Nyerere felt that the loss of his hold over Tanu might well be the end of his career; it seemed to him that it would be opening the door to a less far-seeing man who would be likely to lead the nationalists on the wrong lines; or to a bunch of small men, who might shatter the unity he had striven so hard to maintain. Anxiety made him seem jumpy and irresolute.

He did not realise how worried Turnbull was. Of all the people concerned, Turnbull alone knew what an Emergency meant. He had recently been through one in Kenya, and he realised the suffering it inflicted, especially on the weak, on women, children, old people of both sides. If he was forced into declaring an Emergency, Richard Turnbull had every intention of seeing it through, and hitting the nationalists as hard as was necessary. He had the bedrooms of the north wing at Government House stripped and prepared for the reception of those departments of the Government that would be primarily concerned so that he could co-ordinate their functions from there. The military were not mobilised, but that was a matter of an order. The police were constantly on the alert. Turnbull knew the moves all too well. His one desire was to avoid having to go through with them. Apart from the human suffering entailed, what kind of impression would an Emergency in a Trust Territory make? The U.N., the world Press, the Communist powers, they would all send their representatives and try to interfere, and with incomplete knowledge or sheer malice distort the course of events. This was what caused Turnbull anxious hours. Somehow he had to persuade Nyerere to accept his offer.

On March 13, a Friday, Lady Chesham arrived in Dar-es-Salaam from Rungemba. Without giving her time to take off her hat, Nyerere and Jamal called on her and asked her, as she had the entrée to Government House, to act as their 'aristocratic messenger' and to repeat to Turnbull the demands Nyerere had made in person to him on the previous day, explaining the dire consequence if they were not fulfilled.

Turnbull had heard them many times before, and it sounded to him like a gramophone record. Nothing less than a majority in Executive Government would satisfy the millions of Tanu followers. Turnbull explained to Lady Chesham, as he had to others, that this was impossible. Even if he were prepared to recommend it to the Secretary of State (which he was not prepared to do), and even if the Secretary of State were prepared to consider it (which seemed unlikely, to say the least of it), it would still need a decision of the entire Cabinet. At that time the British Government's policy was still geared to slow and unspectacular advance with a tentative timetable for independence in 1970, which meant responsible government in 1963-4.

To Lady Chesham's warning that his negative attitude would lead to very serious trouble, Turnbull answered that he had a substantial proposal to make, and hoped that she would advise her friends to accept it.

Finally Lady Chesham informed him that Nyerere and his colleagues wanted John Fletcher-Cooke to become Chief Secretary. Turnbull looked at her, then without saying a word, got up and went to the window. After a few seconds he turned round and said: 'So that's what they want. All right, I expect I can meet them on that one.'

He understood Nyerere's thinking perfectly. Fletcher-Cooke was the most intelligent and, therefore, the most dangerous opponent of the nationalists. Tanu wanted him out in front, publicly responsible for his actions. What Turnbull could not tell Lady Chesham was that he had already asked the Secretary of State that Fletcher-Cooke might be his Chief Secretary. With his experience of the U.N., where he had been Deputy Leader of the British Delegation, with his knowledge of the law, with his acute intelligence and energy, he was the man Turnbull wanted as his second-in-command. Here was at least one point on which the two sides could agree, although for very different reasons.

Only once during these difficult days did Turnbull lose his temper. It was when Derek Bryceson came to see him alone. It was a strange conversation between an experienced British civil servant, and a young idealist, who in the heat of argument muddled up the functions of the Executive Government and of Legco. This was more than Turnbull could stand from a man, however well meaning, who had been Assistant Minister for nearly eighteen months. Bryceson capped his mistake by making a glib statement about *kugoma*.

'I hope you will remember this talk when you have to help to pull out the bodies of women and children from charred houses,' the Governor, deeply worried about the possibility of an Emergency, snapped at him.

On March 14 the pressure on Turnbull mounted. In the morning Nyerere, flanked by Jamal and Bryceson, called at Government House. Jamal did most of the talking, trying to convince the Governor that unless the British gave in, there would be *kugoma*. Turnbull could but repeat what he had said so often before, and promised to carry out his offer faithfully—four unofficial ministers

with far-reaching responsibility, and a pledge of a further statement on constitutional advance, on which the four unofficial
ministers could advise him.

At six in the evening, Nyerere, Jamal and Bryceson returned.
In this conversation the Chief Secretary also participated. For
Turnbull this interview represented the first ray of hope. His
visitors admitted that an unofficial majority in the Council of
Ministers was just not a practical possibility. They said that they
were prepared to sell this line to the Africans, but since the rank
and file had been promised that they would get Responsible
Government in 1959, the job would not be an easy one. They asked
if they might have an additional unofficial minister, who would be
an African; they felt that the introduction of five unofficial ministers, of whom three would be Africans, would be sufficient to take
the edge off African disappointment and to prevent disorderly
demonstrations. If the changes included the appointment of five
unofficial ministers, Tanu would give its whole-hearted support to
the new Government.

Turnbull promised to do what he could and was pretty confident
that he could move the Secretary of State to agree to a fifth
minister. When he had the cabled answer to his own urgent cable,
on Sunday, March 15, he rang up the government printer to
change 'four ministers' to 'five ministers' in the text of his Legco
speech. It was duly done.

That Sunday was a desperate day both for Turnbull and for
Nyerere. The question was whether Tanu would honour Nyerere's
pledge and support the new Government. Or would the non-
cooperation and cold war against the British Administration
continue, and not under Nyerere's leadership? If they proved intransigent, Turnbull was prepared to go through with an Emergency, and Nyerere knew it. He also knew that even an ungracious
and qualified acceptance of the Governor's proposal, which
meant real constitutional advance, would lose him a certain
number of his followers. Would it do worse than that, and cause a
split in the party?

Turnbull spent what remained of that Sunday by the seaside
somewhat ill at ease, but confident that he had done all he could.
Nyerere, with his closest friends, planned the moves to make
Tanu accept the Governor's proposal, and to safeguard his own
position in Tanu. Fortunately Lady Chesham had invited him to

spend a fortnight at her house, Rungemba, immediately after the
end of the Legco session; this was where he always recuperated
when desperately tired and needing to regain his nervous energy.

On Monday afternoon, March 16, Julius Nyerere made a
personal call on the Governor. It was one of those gestures which
make him so beloved of his friends. All he said was: 'I just wanted
you to know that everything will be all right. . . .'

The situation on the morning of March 17 was described to the
author by Rashidi Kawawa, who said:

On March 17, 1959, we hoped to get responsible government. The
day before, the Party called a special National Executive meeting. Its
decision was: 'All members are to go back to their areas. Tell the people
to do nothing until they receive instructions.' The Labour Unions
backed Tanu fully. The country was tense, the colonial government
thought there would be civil disobedience. But the country obeyed
Julius Nyerere's call for calm.

On this day the Governor drove to Legco through streets alive
with police and security men. The only good wishes he had were
from the children of the European primary school, who gave him
a cheer when he passed by. For the rest, there was a hostile
silence.

Turnbull started his address by saying that, for the first time in
history, each member of the ten constituencies had been returned
by the electorate. This was an important step in the direction of
responsible government. Then he announced the appointment of
the Post-Elections Committee, and its terms of reference. It
would report on what changes, if any, should be effected in the
provisions for representation, i.e. number of elected members,
number of constituencies and their boundaries, etc.; what changes
should be made in the qualifications of the voters; whether a
territorial council composed of representatives of the chiefs and
others should be established.

And then he made the offer which took Legco completely by
surprise: five unofficial members, three Africans, one Asian and
one European would become ministers. A Council of Ministers
would assume the functions hitherto exercised by the Executive
Council, which would co-exist with it only until the Post-Elections
Committee had presented its report.

How soon responsible government would be achieved, Turnbull then said, depended on two things: 'On our ability to operate in a workmanlike manner the substantial executive changes today outlined ... on the maintenance of law and order in the Territory.' And then Turnbull gave a solemn warning:

During the past eighteen months there have come into prominence in various parts of the Territory persons who, by threat or specious promises, have brought about a climate of disrespect for law and of contempt for established authority. I do not refer to the advocacy of political doctrines with which the Government may not agree, nor have I in mind the problem presented by the ordinary law breaker ... I am thinking of what appear to be deliberate campaigns to damage the dignity and integrity of the Courts, to hamper and obstruct the Police in the execution of their duty of bringing offenders to justice, and to encourage disrespect for lawfully established authority.

The kind of incidents which exemplify the conduct I have in mind are noisy demonstrations outside Law Courts, conducted with the intention of causing the authorities to set free persons who have been placed in lawful custody; attempts, sometimes successful, to hold unlawful courts and to impose unlawful fines; and the intimidation of those who refuse to take part in these lawless occasions.

These attempts to undermine the rule of law strike at the greatest of all the fundamental principles upon which depends the liberty of the ordinary man. . . . Let it be understood that our forward progress . . . must depend upon there being no further organised defiance of the law; for if such defiance does manifest itself, the Government will have no alternative but to put aside constitutional matters and devote all its resources to keeping the peace and maintaining the authority of the Courts. I trust that Hon. Members will not be tempted to take this matter lightly.

This was the voice of the man who had cleaned up Mau Mau in Nairobi. Now, as then, he had his eye on the future: unless he could stamp out lawlessness, Nyerere and the nationalists would inherit a terrible legacy when they took over.

Tanu and T.E.M.O. disliked the speech. It took two days to decide whether or not to accept what they regarded as Turnbull's 'half measures'. Nyerere showed his skill and wisdom by the manner in which he handled both his followers and his British opponents.

At the first T.E.M.O. meeting, on the afternoon of March 17, when tempers were flying high, he quietly said that what mattered more than any acceptance or rejection of Turnbull's proposals was that the elected members should maintain their unity and organisation. He asked them to think about three problems: should they accept or reject the five ministers; if they accepted, should Nyerere himself be one of the ministers who would cross the floor; what should be said in reply to the address and what points should Tanu bring out in the debate.

By next afternoon, when reason was again in the ascendancy, Nyerere answered most of the points members had criticised. He told them that he would not be one of the five ministers; he would remain leader of the opposition until he could cross the floor as prime minister of an elected Government. He did not think that the electorate could hold it against members that they had not obtained responsible government at once. They had only promised 'to fight for the thing'; they could not pledge a date as only a Government in office could do that.

Then he explained that agreement had been reached with the Government that, should five ministers cross the floor, the number of Government nominated members would be reduced, so as not to give the Government side too large a majority. If five unofficial ministers crossed the floor, and if the Government strength was thus cut down, there would be a small majority of elected members in the Council. He reassured T.E.M.O. that if the elected ministers could not dissuade their colleagues from a measure objectionable to Tanu, they would resign. Derek Bryceson reminded them that under collective responsibility, no measure could be put into effect to which any minister objected.

Finally, Nyerere told T.E.M.O. of the Attorney-General's assurance that, before the year was out, there might be another Government statement. In making up their minds on Turnbull's proposals, they should consider whether their decision would help or hinder this second Government statement.

By now all resistance had vanished and T.E.M.O. accepted in principle the proposals contained in the Governor's address.

In opening the debate, Derek Bryceson promised wholehearted co-operation, but expressed regret that the Governor had found it necessary to say what racial proportion there should be among the five ministers. His Excellency, said Bryceson, had served many years in Kenya; he would have to learn that Tanganyika was a different country. He also demanded that there should be another Government statement before the end of the year, and a date set for the Post-Elections Committee Report. (The Governor's astringent remarks still rankled with Bryceson.)

In the debate, the elected members brought out many points, revealing strong resentment over the Governor's warning on the maintenance of law and order. Still, the point had gone home.

Nyerere wound up the debate. He voiced the regret of his party and of the people of Tanganyika that the British would not give them at least semi-responsible government. They could not understand why. Yet he and his friends had said:

Let us ask for certain clarifications, and if they are made, we will accept the proposals. . . . The clarifications were made and we are accepting these proposals as a challenge to the people of Tanganyika. . . . But, I think, Sir, it is a challenge to the British people too. . . . I am telling now my friends the British people: if they insist that we, the people of Tanganyika, try this in the form in which it has been presented to us, we will try it. We are not a people to shirk responsibility. . . . But I am saying to the British people . . . give us full responsibility when you come to endorse these demands. . . . There is some idea, and this is the last point I want to make, that when we say that we do not want a government of civil servants, we mean we do not want civil servants in this country. . . . That is not true because there cannot be any government without civil servants. . . . We shall need civil servants; in my mind we will need the expatriate civil servants even more than we need them at present.

Nyerere was cheered from both sides of Legco.

Thus another turning point had been negotiated by interplay between Turnbull and Nyerere. Elections had been fought and won without any disorder; Tanu demands had only partially been met, yet public opinion had been calmed. The scene was set for the next stage, to be reached by constitutional methods.

Tanganyika had again set an example to her neighbours.

CHAPTER 34

T.A.N.U. in Opposition

DESPITE his enthusiastic following, Julius Nyerere had enemies. Among Africans there were those who envied his position of leadership; others were impatient of his respect for constitutional practices. Some Europeans could not forget his earlier, radical speeches, and were predicting that Legco debates would show up the true nature of Tanu and its leader. The first clash between the Government and the opposition, the elected members, occurred over the budget during the session of May, 1959. It was not a happy occasion, but Nyerere confounded his critics by the aptness with which he turned to advantage the mistakes that T.E.M.O. made.

The budget was a colonial one, drafted in consideration of Tanganyika's limited resources. As the Governor had pointed out in his speech of March 17, money he would have preferred to use for educational or health purposes had to be spent on the police. 'If law goes, only anarchy remains,' Turnbull had concluded.

Still irked by the Governor's stern warning, T.E.M.O. members decided to move a motion of no confidence in the Government. This was unprecedented in a colonial country. Yet it was not done lightheartedly. John Baker, a Canadian mining engineer, European member for the Western Province, suggested it, knowing full well that it could not succeed, but believing that it would give a much needed jolt to the Dar-es-Salaam administration. To be certain of his ground regarding the Standing Orders, he went, late at night, accompanied by Amir Jamal, to call on the Speaker. Routed out of bed, Abdulkarim Karimjee at once looked up the legal authorities, and being satisfied as to British precedent, advised Baker and Jamal that their planned tactics were entirely constitutional.

On May 26 John Baker opened the budget debate by saying that he did not wish to belittle the tremendous good that the British administration had done for Tanganyika. But he certainly deplored some things which had been done in the economic field. Expenditure had been lavished on wrong purposes, such as impressive buildings, offices and staff, when the need was for communications, water supplies and other productive developments. He criticised the East Africa High Commission for favouring Kenya at Tanganyika's expense; the mineral concession holders who had done little if any prospecting; the timber concession holders who had pocketed unjustifiably large profits. He complained that the views of the elected representatives had not received due attention when the budget estimates had been drawn up.

'Be it resolved,' he concluded, 'that this Council do not go into Committee of Supply to consider estimates of expenditure for 1959–60 until more appropriate estimates have been presented.' And then he moved his motion of no confidence in the Government.

The Government front bench was appalled. Only a European could have mounted so audacious an attack. But the matter was not to end there. During the debate, which lasted six days, some African T.E.M.O. Members made grossly unfair attacks, especially on expatriate civil servants. Not a single acknowledgment was made of the conscientious work that was being done by administrative and professional officers, and that in the face of obstruction and insult by over-ardent nationalists, or of the skill and farsightedness with which exiguous resources had been stretched to hearten the economy and to strengthen the social services.

Nyerere made a compelling speech. 'I want to address myself today not only to this Chamber, but to the people of Tanganyika,' he said. He felt he had to do this because the members of the Government with their permanent majority might not even listen to his arguments. Secondly, he had to address himself to the people of Tanganyika

because I have been quarrelling with my own people, Sir. I have been asking the Wasukuma, the Wachagga, the Wahaya, the Wagogo and all the others, how long shall we continue to live in mud huts? How long shall we go on living in mud huts when we can build better houses? How long?

We go round the country and we see our people ill fed. Malnutrition is so common that it is taken for granted. . . . We see little kids with fronts like this. [He made a graphic gesture with his hands.] Those are the lucky ones. Others have died. Why? Either because of malnutrition or because of lack of a simple thing like a dispensary which provides quinine. . . . Only forty per cent of our schoolchildren of primary school age can go to school; sixty per cent are born, grow up and die without seeing the inside of a classroom. This is in the year 1959, not in the year 1859, when one could have taken it for granted. How long, how long will the people of Tanganyika put up with this? (From *Tanganyika Hansard*, May 27, 1959.)

None who heard him could doubt that this was the authentic voice of the new Africa. The East African Press splashed the budget debate in several stirring articles.

A significant aspect of the situation was the sympathy shown by several nominated members for the opposition. They went as far as canvassing the idea of a free vote. Nyerere and his friends knew well that the Government could not possibly agree and risk having the budget thrown out. None the less, this kind of talk was good publicity.

On June 1 the Chief Secretary, Fletcher-Cooke, summed up for the Government, He started by giving Legco Members a lecture on irresponsibility. He could not accept that nine million people in Tanganyika had lost confidence in the Government.

From messages I have received from various parts of the Territory during the course of this debate, I venture to suggest that some at least of the confidence which the Hon. Members enjoyed at the beginning of this debate has in fact evaporated. . . . I am much more concerned with the measure of confidence which . . . the outside world may have in Tanganyika today. . . . The opposition have said that they have no confidence in the Government. But they cannot expect H.M. Government to give a progressive and orderly transfer of power into Unofficial hands unless the Secretary of State has complete confidence in their sense of responsibility.

In Fletcher-Cooke's view the opposition, who were shortly to join the Government in shaping ministerial responsibility could have contained themselves until then, without bringing a motion before the House hardly likely to increase their reputation for responsibility. Mr Nyerere, he commented, had used the fallacious argument that sovereignty was the sovereign remedy against all the ills of poverty, ignorance and disease, but he doubted whether Mr Nyerere and his colleagues could make a better show of wrestling with this intractable problem.

Until this point, Nyerere had indeed been concerned over the extreme statements a few of his followers had made. But the Chief Secretary's glib distortion of his own deeply-felt presentation of the plight of Africa roused his anger. Since their first meeting in New York, Nyerere and Fletcher-Cooke had often met socially and appreciated each other's excellent minds, but Nyerere was now coming to regard the Chief Secretary as his most dangerous opponent.

On a motion for the adjournment he returned to the attack.

Mr Speaker, Sir [he said], I have only one reason for rising to speak. We have listened with great interest to the speech of the Chief Secretary. We have not liked the tone of the speech. We have not liked some of the implications of irresponsibility on our part. I want to put on record, and the Chief Secretary himself has just said it, we want to conduct our debates in this House as debates. A reference like the expression of hope that the Colonial Secretary may still have the same belief in the sense of responsibility as he had about our side of the House, is not calculated to make the 1st of July[1] what we, on our side, would like to make it. A statement that sounds like intimidation we cannot accept on this side of the House. Sir, I thought I should make those remarks on behalf of the side which I have the honour to lead. (From the *Tanganyika Hansard*.)

Never before had an African answered a leader of Government business in this vein – icily polite, plain-spoken and proud. In his indignation, Nyerere wanted to cap his rebuke by walking out of Legco, followed by the entire opposition. Derek Bryceson, with admirable judgment, dissuaded him from staging an open break. In the event, members of both Government and opposition left Karimjee Hall keeping strictly away from each other. It seemed that the cut and thrust of this particular debate might lead to lasting enmity.

This was counting without Nyerere's common sense. When his anger eventually subsided, he gave much thought to the whole question of parliamentary tactics. Before the October session, whips were appointed. Al-Noor Kassum was elected Chief Whip, Rashidi Kawawa Assistant Whip, John Baker Deputy Leader. With the help of the whips and more thorough T.E.M.O. preparations, both general policy and the order of speeches was planned in detail, the intention being to eliminate, as far as possible, personal demarches and those temperamental outbursts that seem to be psychologically necessary to young African politicians.

Fletcher-Cooke was never again to adopt the condescending attitude which had provoked Nyerere's scathing rejoinder. This

[1] The day on which the five unofficial ministers were to cross the floor.

was noted when the next clash occurred with the opposition three months later. Nyerere wanted to retain the counsel of the five un-official ministers, which meant that they had to remain T.E.M.O. members. The Chief Secretary held the view that they could not have a foot in both camps. When invited to T.E.M.O. for a dis-cussion, he at first refused to go, but then thought better of it, and a compromise was worked out. Later that day, Nyerere received a letter from the Governor, indicating that Turnbull was gratified to learn that T.E.M.O. had decided to elect new office bearers who were not ministers, and was content that the ministers should continue to be full members of T.E.M.O. and to attend all meet-ings of the organisation, subject to prior claims of public business.

Soon after the budget debate, Nyerere also advanced his plans in that he clarified his attitude to the Asian community. Tan-ganyika had, at this time, about 80,000 Asians, who were pre-dominantly merchants and business men. Sophia Mustafa, herself an Asian, summed up their problems on April 11, 1959:

Asians in Tanganyika have based and are basing their economic life mainly on commercial and petty trading activities. In the past these activities have been instrumental in opening up this country and thus bringing it into the stream of world events. Now however the situation requires readjustment.... The Asians must readjust their ... economic life to a wider and broader basis than mere commerce and petty trading. They will have to take part in agriculture, in farming, in industrial development, in the opening out and pioneering of new fields of mineral and energy supplies, in taking part in animal husbandry, engineering in all its aspects and in the professions. They must alter their traditional mode of making a living and take a more direct, varied and active part in the life of Tanganyika.

Mrs Mustafa in fact demanded that Asians should adopt a com-pletely new way of life. With the best will in the world this could not be done overnight, but the Africans, as their eyes were opened, increasingly resented Asian methods and Asian prosperity. Very few Asians played a part in political life, and their organisation, the Asian Association, claimed less than a thousand members in Dar-es-Salaam. True, among these thousands were the most forward-looking Asians, yet even they did little, although they spoke and wrote the right things.

'I found them useful at times,' Nyerere told the author in October, 1962, 'because they were the only voice of the Asians.

They were – and are – armchair politicians, whom in the early days I used in building the situation I wanted.'

The two leading Asians, Amir Jamal and Mahmoud Rattansey, had long been at loggerheads with each other. This worried Nyerere a good deal, but ultimately it provided the occasion for his establishing his own ascendancy over the whole Asian group.

For a number of years, Rattansey had been President of the Asian Association. He was a lawyer with a good practice and had been one of D. N. Pritt's juniors in Nyerere's trial. He had considerable social gifts, but his ability and intelligence did not compare with Amir Jamal's, who although not a gregarious person, had a first class brain. Jamal had been a devoted and loyal friend of Nyerere's and Tanu's since 1954.[2] When the five unofficial ministries were established in 1959, Turnbull, who of course had completely unfettered discretion as to the appointments, had the courtesy (and, as he himself would be the first to admit, the good sense) to consult Nyerere. Nyerere recommended to the Governor that Jamal should be appointed.

Rattansey and his friends within the Asian Association were furious and decided to unseat Jamal. They initiated a virulent intrigue and did not stop at a smear campaign alleging that Nyerere had been influenced in his choice of Jamal because of his own little house which had been built by Jamal's company.

At the meeting of the Tanu National Executive, which was called to hear Nyerere's proposals concerning the recommendations he should make in respect of the five ministers, there was an open rebellion against Jamal. Nyerere had hitherto not intervened in the power struggle between Rattansey and Jamal: now he decided that the moment had come to grasp the nettle. He told the meeting exactly what had happened. One by one the members present confessed how they had been approached – some even bribed – by Rattansey's clique. Not only was the selection of Jamal confirmed, but the Asian Association was left in no doubt as to Nyerere's views on their part in the intrigue. The Association offered abject apologies and Rattansey resigned its presidency. Never again did the Asians attempt to interfere with Tanu policies. They had learnt that Nyerere would not tolerate dictation from any minority group.

[2] See also Chapter 21, pp. 219 and 220.

On June 2, 1959, the names of the five unofficial ministers were published: Solomon Eliufoo – Health; Chief Abdullah Fundikira – Lands and Surveys; George Kahama – Social and Co-operative Development; Derek Bryceson – Mines and Commerce; Amir Jamal – Urban Local Government and Works. When they entered upon their new duties, Tanganyika had taken the first and most important step towards responsible government; those which were to follow might catch the public imagination more vigorously, but there was none as fundamental or as profound as this one. Nyerere and his friends had hoped and prayed for this for so long that it seemed almost unreal when it happened so quietly.

The Council of Ministers was sworn in on July 1, and the Governor said:

Today's ceremony marks the introduction of as fundamental a change as any that has been brought about in the fast-moving constitutional progress of the Territory; for it signifies the termination of a long period of wholly official executive government, and the setting up of a different kind of government – the kind of government in which Elected Members of the legislature will share in the formulation of government policies.

The importance of this step is that it denotes the introduction of the principle upon which the pattern of the future will be founded; it denotes the achievement of a stage upon which subsequent constitutional developments towards the final target of self-government can logically be based – for they will take the form of steady increases in the part played by Unofficials in drawing up policy, and in supervising the translation of policy into practice.

The government we are establishing today is designed to bridge the gap between – on the one hand – the old form of colonial government in which the Executive Council, consisting of government officers plus a number of Nominated Unofficials, worked to a largely nominated legislature, and – on the other – what is known as 'responsible government' in which the Executive will contain a majority of unofficial ministers and will work to a legislature of which the majority of the members will be elected. Transitional governments of this sort are by repute the most difficult of all to operate; and I have no doubt that we shall meet with our full share of complications and perplexities. But I am confident of our ability to overcome them.

The tasks that lie before you are primarily these: to accustom yourselves to the acceptance of collective responsibility, even though such acceptance may involve the temporary subordination of some of your political aspirations; to acquire the skill to devise policies which are within the bounds of financial and social circumstances, which are

6 (*a*) Julius and Maria Nyerere with five of their children

6 (*b*) Paul Bomani, Minister of Finance from 1962, with wife and child

6 (*c*) Oscar Kambona, Foreign Minister from 1962, with wife and (left) Mr J. Lusinde, Home Minister, and the Nigerian High Commissioner

7 (*a*) Julius Nyerere addressing a meeting

7 (*b*) Julius Nyerere with Oscar Kambona (left) and Rashidi Kawawa (right) at the African People's Solidarity Conference at Moshi, 1963

administratively practicable, and which will not conflict with the aims being pursued by your colleagues; and to maintain a close and sympathetic relation between public opinion and the processes of government.

Tanganyika is emerging from her period of tutelage; amongst your number today is the first generation of those of this country who, stage by stage, will take over full responsibility for the government of the Territory. I pray that God will prosper you all in the arduous duties that lie ahead.

By then the Post-Elections Committee, under the chairmanship of Sir Richard Ramage, had been touring the country for three weeks. With fourteen members—seven Africans, five Europeans and two Asians—it was to travel all over Tanganyika, collecting evidence about the wishes of the population regarding the electoral system and the setting up of a Territorial Council.

Opinion was almost unanimous that compulsory multiple voting and parity should be abolished, but the common roll and special electoral arrangements for minority communities maintained. The Ramage Committee recommended ten 'reserved' seats for the Europeans and eleven for the Asians, in addition to fifty open seats which by sheer weight of numbers would inevitably be occupied by Africans; in all, seventy-one seats. It proposed the abolition of members for special interests, although the Governor would have the right to appoint up to ten members.

The minimum age both for voting and for standing was to be twenty-one; linked with either three years' residence in Tanganyika, or a receipt for Personal Tax for the immediately preceding year, or an exemption certificate for the same period. Women could vote or stand if they owned a house or a homestead, paid any form of direct tax or rate, or held a licence or any office, including membership of a village council. The number of voters required to nominate a candidate for a reserved seat was raised from twenty-five to thirty-five, of whom twenty-five had to belong to the candidate's community. There was no support at all for a Territorial Council made up mainly of chiefs, or indeed of any composition.

Only one group disagreed with this general view: the European settlers in the Northern Province. They maintained that the members elected in the last elections were not the true representatives of their various communities, and demanded, in all

N

seriousness, that there should be a political standstill for ten years, and communal representation for the minorities.

Sir Richard Ramage dealt splendidly with these eccentrics; just as he had a way of shutting up the anti-Asian views voiced by many Africans. Once only was he on the point of losing his temper. This was at the Committee's last meeting in Dar-es-Salaam, when final touches were being put to the report. Mahmoud Rattansey once tried to cause trouble by cantankerous objections to points accepted by everyone else. When complaints from all the T.E.M.O. members about this unreasonable behaviour reached Nyerere, he finally made up his mind to withdraw Tanu backing from Rattansey in the next elections. Without Tanu no Asian had a chance of being elected. Mahmoud Rattansey has been out of public life ever since.

These elections were to take place much sooner than Nyerere had dared to hope. Because of the British elections in October, 1959, the Legco meeting was postponed from October 6 to October 20. Nyerere and his friends waited anxiously for the promised statement about further constitutional changes. They heard that a new Colonial Secretary had been appointed in England, whose name was Iain Macleod. They knew nothing about him; in fact they had never heard his name. No one in Tanganyika had any idea what he stood for, let alone what vast changes would be introduced in British colonial policy and how these would affect Tanganyika.

On October 20 Sir Richard Turnbull opened the thirty-fifth Session of the Legislative Council with the usual ceremony. He was far from happy about his speech, as he had nothing positive to offer. During the last months of his term of office, Alan Lennox-Boyd would for obvious reasons, take no major decisions and the promised statement about further constitutional advances could not be made. Turnbull temporised by stating that the new ministers had performed their duties with energy and vision and that the Ramage Report had been submitted to the new Secretary of State.

In the meantime in accordance with my undertaking of last March [he said], I have been considering with ministers of the government and with the Secretary of State the question of further advances in the constitutional field. . . .

Hon. Members will, I am certain, recognise that the timing of my promised announcement may well have been affected by the preoccupation of Ministers in the U.K. with the recent General Election. The present position is that the new Secretary of State has not yet had an opportunity of examining the Ramage Report; and, in these circumstances, it may not be possible for us to adhere to the timetable which we had tentatively set ourselves. The Secretary of State has, however . . . authorised me to give an assurance that these matters will be treated with all possible dispatch. Indeed, it has already been agreed by the Secretary of State that the life of this Council should be brought to an end by dissolution, not in 1962 as would normally be the case, but at the conclusion of this present Session.

I am accordingly authorised to say that a general election will be held in the Territory in September 1960. . . .

This was greeted with loud cheers. Julius Nyerere, who wound up the debate on the Address, said that the people of Tanganyika had chosen to proceed by constitutional methods because the attainment of independence was inevitably a slow process. Also

we are anxious that this process . . . should not create enmity between the people of this country and the people of Britain. . . . We in Tanganyika want to demonstrate to the people of Britain by the very methods we are adopting to reach our independence that we want nothing but lasting friendship between our two peoples. We are not doing this out of weakness. . . . We are doing it from a sincere desire to avoid the addition of bitterness to a world which already has too much bitterness.

I have said before elsewhere that we, the people of Tanganyika, would like to light a candle and put it on top of Mount Kilimanjaro which would shine beyond our borders giving hope where there was despair, love where there was hate, and dignity where there was only humiliation. We pray that the people of Britain . . . and our neighbours of all races should look upon us . . . and what we are trying to do not as an embarrassment but as a ray of hope.

CHAPTER 35

Responsible Government

DECEMBER 15, 1959, was exceptionally hot and humid in Dar-es-Salaam. Thousands of Africans, many wearing Tanu green, stood quietly from day-break onwards behind crush barriers in the garden of Karimjee Hall. Tanu members lined the length of Acacia Avenue; private cars and taxis were bedecked with flowers and foliage.

At the entrance to Karimjee Hall, over fifty journalists and cameramen, the largest conglomeration of newsmen ever seen in Tanganyika, waited for ministers and leading elected members. Green shirted members of the Tanu Youth League escorted visitors with tickets to the gallery, which was soon packed. There was difficulty in accommodating the foreign correspondents.

At nine a.m. some formal business was briefly transacted; then the Speaker adjourned in order to receive the Governor. Turnbull had gone to London in November and put his plea for the Tanganyikans before the new Secretary of State. Having appreciated Tanganyika's problems as outlined by Turnbull, he agreed to a date being set for responsible government, and to coming out himself to have a look at the situation.

The ancient Rolls Royce drew up majestically, Sir Richard Turnbull walked in slowly and began reading his speech from the throne. There was applause when he announced that the coming elections would be held on the basis of the Ramage Report; and that there would be a majority of elected members. There was more applause when he paid warm tribute to Sir Richard Ramage and members of his committee, whose report the Secretary of State had accepted with one change: qualifications for all voters were to be alike–ability to read English or Swahili, or an income of £75 a year, or being (or having been) the holder of a prescribed office.

And then came the announcement everyone had been waiting for: after the general election, Tanganyika was to have responsible Government. Cheers nearly drowned the Governor's last words, which he quoted from the Secretary of State's despatch:

I take this opportunity of congratulating the Government and the people of Tanganyika on the great advances which have been made in the constitutional field during the past few years. H.M. Government are particularly glad to note that this progress has been achieved in an orderly fashion and in a spirit of harmony and goodwill.

Julius Nyerere's answer was in two parts. First he thanked the Governor for his announcement.

I take it that unlike the present government . . . which is responsible to the Governor and, through the Governor to the Secretary of State for the Colonies, the new Government will be responsible to this Council and, through it, to the people of Tanganyika. The new Government will not be able to carry out any measure unless it has the support of the majority of the people of this country; their support or their criticism will be expressed by their representatives in this Council. It will be a Government which will be bound to resign if it fails to gain the support of the majority of those representatives in any matter of major policy. We, on this side of the Council, would like to fulfil the promise we made in October. We accept His Excellency's announcement, and we ask the country to accept it in the spirit in which, I know, it has been made, a spirit of confidence in, and goodwill to, the people of Tanganyika. . . .

Then Nyerere voiced his disappointment over the limited franchise.

I am extremely disappointed to hear that Tanganyika's general election next year is planned on a franchise based on literacy and income. I would still urge my friends on the other side of the House to re-consider this decision and go ahead on the basis of universal adult franchise.

But he ended on a happy note, thanking the Ramage Committee and the civil servants, and pledging no discrimination on the basis of colour, sex, race or religion. 'From now on our greatest task must be to win the war against the three chief enemies of our people: disease, poverty and ignorance. Let us face this task together as a united people.'

When the Governor left Karimjee Hall, the people outside were so quiet that the whirring of film cameras could be heard. But when Julius Nyerere, followed by the elected members, appeared at the head of the steps, the thousands of Africans outside Karimjee Hall started singing and waving green Tanu cards. Suddenly they surged forward, pushed aside the barriers and carried Nyerere shoulder-high to a jeep decorated with flowers and foliage. Sitting high and in full view, smiling and waving, Nyerere led a procession of hundreds of people, lasting three and a half hours. Elected members were tossed on top of roof racks on cars, taxis and vans, which also formed part of the procession. In the stampede, journalists and cameramen were swallowed up and had to march with the cheering, happy crowd.

Two days later, the Colonial Secretary, Iain Macleod, arrived in Dar-es-Salaam. A mixed crowd of Europeans, Africans and Asians gave him a fairly warm welcome at the airport, but the Africans lining the road to Government House, some three miles in length, chanted one and all unceasingly: 'One man, one vote.' Tanu had obtained much, but their demand for universal suffrage had not yet been satisfied. The British were to be left in no doubt as to their wishes.

Nyerere had been to London the previous month, but the Secretary of State was so busy that he could not see him personally. Iain Macleod differed from his predecessor, Alan Lennox-Boyd (now Viscount Boyd of Merton) both in philosophy and in his forward-looking vision. Now at Government House, in Sir Richard Turnbull's presence, Macleod and Nyerere met for the first time. In spite of the discourteous way in which he had been received in Dar-es-Salaam, and it must have come as a surprise after all that had been said of the good manners and generosity of the Tanganyika people, his first meeting with Nyerere convinced Macleod that in Tanganyika the desired solution could be achieved in a friendly way. In view of the criticism levelled at Britain that her colonies could only obtain independence after violence and bloodshed, Macleod was determined to prove that this was not the case. Tanganyika seemed a good place for proving it.

Macleod and Nyerere took an instant liking to each other. Their conversation lasted about an hour and a half; at the end of it they parted friends. They discussed the prospects of Tanganyika's constitutional development: the stages by which it should reach responsible government, self-government and independence. Nyerere was enchanted by Macleod's radical views. Here was a man, a Conservative at that, who could visualise the African dream.

On February 3, 1960, not only Tanganyika, but the whole world had proof of the immense change in British colonial policy. The Prime Minister, Harold Macmillan, who was visiting South Africa, made a speech in Cape Town, which was to serve as key-note for the coming era, and has ever since been known as the Wind of Change speech.

Macmillan said that the birth pangs of the nation states of Europe had been repeated all over the world. Fifteen years ago these birth pangs had spread through Asia. Many countries there, of different races and civilisations, pressed their claim to an independent national life.

Today the same thing is happening in Africa and the most striking of all the impressions I have formed since I left London a month ago is of the strength of this African national consciousness. In different places it takes different forms, but it is happening everywhere. The wind of change is blowing through this continent, and, whether we like it or not, this growth of national consciousness is a political fact. We must all accept it as a fact, and our national policies must take account of it. . . . That means, I would judge, that we must come to terms with it. I sincerely believe that if we cannot do so we may imperil the precarious balance between East and West on which the peace of the world depends.

Events were to prove that Macmillan's speech inaugurated a new era in colonial policy–the rapid and orderly dissolution of the British colonial empire. It entailed many sacrifices, but it also has contributed to the maintenance of the delicate balance between East and West, and of world peace.

In this setting, the changes that had taken place in Tanganyika aroused international interest. Julius Nyerere was invited to visit the U.S.A. as a guest of the State Department. This was five years after his first visit, when his movements had been limited to nine blocks from the U.N. building in New York. As a wag among the Maryknoll Fathers put it: 'The first time he came Julius was confined, the second time he was ignored, the third time he was an honoured guest. . . .'

From the United States on to Canada, and then to the United Kingdom. Everywhere he received considerable publicity. There were newspaper, radio and television interviews. When asked what he intended to do, his answer was: 'We are trying to weld the people living in Tanganyika into a nation.' (Characteristically he said: 'We are trying,' not 'I am trying.') His television interview on Panorama made him many new friends in Britain.

Also in January, 1960, the Secretary-General of the U.N., Dag Hammarskjöld, visited Dar-es-Salaam. Once more the airport was crowded, once more thousands of Africans and Asians lined the road to the centre of the city. Mr Hammarskjöld was much impressed by what he saw, and drove through commercial and industrial areas in convoy with reporters.

Equally impressed were the four members of the U.N. Visiting Mission which toured Tanganyika in April, 1960. Their report, which was published later, said that the most noteworthy feature of the political situation was the peaceful and harmonious atmosphere of goodwill. All the evidence indicated that the territory was progressing smoothly and rapidly towards the ultimate goal of the international trusteeship system, and that the problems which remained were, largely, of a technical and financial nature. It referred to a memorandum received from Tanu which demanded that the forthcoming election should be regarded as a plebiscite for independence: and of course it protested against the restricted suffrage. In conclusion, the U.N. Mission said: 'We would like to bear witness to the excellent relations existing between persons of various races. The ease and graciousness of social contacts is very remarkable. . . .'

What the Governor did not tell them was that during February he had been in London to guide the forward planning of the composition of responsible government. From now on responsibilities had to be clearly allocated; the processes of Government had to be streamlined, and matters so reorganised that Julius Nyerere could take over the Provincial Administration. In other words, for the first period at least, the Provincial Commissioners were to serve directly under him. This was essential if the services of the ablest men among them were to be retained.

April was a momentous month for Tanganyika for three more reasons. At one of the Legco meetings, the Chief Secretary made the following statement:

It is announced by the Governor, with the authority of the Secretary of State, that the following changes will be made in the executive government of Tanganyika with effect from October 1, 1960:

1. A post of Chief Minister will be created. The Chief Minister will be the Governor's principal adviser and leader of Government business in Legislative Council. . . .

2. The post of Chief Secretary will be abolished. A new post of Deputy-Governor will be created. The Deputy-Governor will be a member of the Council of Ministers, but not of the Legislative Council.

3. The Council of Ministers will consist of the Governor (President),

the Deputy-Governor, ten unofficial ministers and two civil service ministers.

4. An unofficial minister will be appointed as Minister for Home Affairs. His portfolio will include Police, Prisons and Immigration. Responsibility for the use and operational control of the Police Force will remain vested in the Governor himself, who, acting at his discretion, may, in the exercize of that responsibility, give directions to the Commissioner of Police as the Professional Head of the Force.

5. The Executive Council will cease to exist.

T.E.M.O. members were critical of two changes: the Governor's retention of the chairmanship of the Council of Ministers, and the creation of the post of Deputy-Governor, especially as it was to be filled by John Fletcher-Cooke, about whom they had some misgivings. What they feared most was that the Deputy-Governor would get between the Governor and the Chief Minister, and prevent the latter from assuming the full responsibilities proper to him. Needless to say, the Governor was meticulous in seeing that this did not happen.

In his reply to the Chief Secretary's statement, Nyerere voiced these misgivings.

We generally welcome that statement. . . . We feel however that the new Government will have certain features which, even within that transitional period, need not have been there. The first and the most important is the position of the Governor as President of the Council of Ministers. . . . The main function, I believe, at this stage should be to advise the new Government through the Chief Minister. In actual fact, although technically the Government is still said to advise the Governor, the respective roles of the Governor and the ministers are reversed: the Governor, in actual fact becomes the adviser of the Government through the Chief Minister, and a constitutional crisis is usually caused if the Governor insists, on an important matter, that his advice should be taken. It is for this reason, we feel, it would have been much better if the Governor did not remain on the Council of Ministers. [On this point Nyerere was to change his mind completely.]

Another point, though not of equal importance, is one concerning the new post of Deputy-Governor. We feel that, unless it is intended that the post is to be a very temporary one, there is danger of a justified misunderstanding. I think it is quite possible that people can interpret the position as keeping the Chief Secretary under a new name. . . .

But again Nyerere ended on a constructive note:
*

In spite of the causes of dissatisfaction which I have mentioned, I must express my appreciation of the attitude of the people on the other side of the table, if I may use the expression, with whom my colleagues and I have been discussing these matters. It is that attitude which makes me feel certain that the new Government, with the co-operation of the people of Tanganyika, will tackle its responsibilities with complete confidence. (*Tanganyika Hansard*, April, 1960.)

On April 27, in a speech lasting 90 minutes, Sir Ernest Vasey presented his first budget. It was a masterly survey, amounting to a plan for developing Tanganyika. He gave a warning that it would be more difficult to attain economic and financial independence than political independence. 'There are many obstacles to overcome, and many problems to solve, to ensure that economically the transition into independence improves the lot of the people.' He also gave a warning that, when the country had attained responsible government in 1960, people would wait until the Government had been in power for a year or so to ensure that it had a responsible attitude to investors. Once this reputation had been established, 'investment will come in no mean way'.

Again Nyerere was the outstanding speaker of the Budget debate. He stressed that to the war against poverty, ignorance and disease, must be added another war, war against corruption. There was corruption in Tanganyika; it must, he said, be treated with ruthlessness. If the people were to have confidence in their Government, then they must be able to have confidence in every man and woman in a position of responsibility, in local government officials as well as in political organisations. If they had not that confidence, it would be impossible for the country to get the true benefit of the independence for which they had been struggling. All civil servants, and not just expatriate civil servants, had been given assurances, Nyerere continued, and promised to respect all the contracts on which they had been employed.

The most generous tribute to this speech was paid by the Chief Secretary, John Fletcher-Cooke, who said it had been the best he had heard in all his experience in the House. 'I think Tanganyika, and indeed Africa, is fortunate in this year of destiny, 1960, to have Mr Nyerere as leader.' By a process of cool reasoning Mr Nyerere had isolated different elements in the problems facing Tanganyika in the future, and had publicly announced the inescapable conclusions he had reached, however unpalatable. 'This shows a political and moral courage of the highest order.'

In the last meeting of the Legislative Council, Nyerere paid an equally generous farewell tribute to John Fletcher-Cooke. He said:

We have had occasion more than once to exchange a few words . . . and sometimes among those words we have exchanged fairly hot ones, but every time the Hon. the Chief Secretary has stood on the other side of the House. . . . I have always felt that I would like to have him as a colleague defending policy for which I was responsible.

Two leaders, with profoundly divergent philosophies and backgrounds, took leave of each other with an elegant appreciation of their respective talents.

Finally, in April, Tanu announced their intention of sponsoring all the seventy-one seats. Candidates were to apply to district secretaries of Tanu, who were to discuss the merits of the candidates and then put the matter to the vote and send the result to the Tanu Executive in Dar-es-Salaam with their recommendations. Nine former T.E.M.O. members were chosen for the fifty 'open' African seats; seven former T.E.M.O. members for the eleven Asian reserved seats and four for the ten European reserved seats.

Three days later, on June 30, the Legislative Council was dissolved. So was T.E.M.O., which had served the purpose for which it had been formed. It was succeeded by the Tanu Parliamentary Party.

Nomination day was July 18, 1960. In the evening, it was announced that fifty-eight members were unopposed, hence already elected. In ten African and in three European constituencies there were to be contests.

The African National Congress could only field three candidates, all of whom lost their deposits; they only collected 337 votes between them. In one European and in one African constituency there was a bitter fight.

In Songea, Dr Leader Stirling, a Roman Catholic missionary, was opposed by Ivor Bayldon, former U.T.P. president. Personal as well as political antagonism divided these two men. It took all Tanu's organisation and prestige to secure a tiny majority for Dr Stirling.

In Mbulu, H. E. Sarwatt, son of the chief of the Northern Mbulu tribe, opposed the official Tanu candidate, Chief Amri Dodo, the head of the plain dwellers below the escarpment. In this constituency, tribal rivalry added to tense political competition. Sarwatt won and was promptly expelled from Tanu for not having withdrawn in favour of the official Tanu candidate. But when he arrived in Dar-es-Salaam, Nyerere accepted him into the parliamentary party organisation, thus maintaining the single party position. Although one independent would have been good publicity towards the outside world for Tanganyika, other considerations regarding Tanu members made it essential that maximum political unity should be maintained. With unsophisticated people, who hitherto had known only tribal allegiances, Nyerere regarded obedience to Tanu's central authority as both educational and vital.

Nyerere knew that Turnbull had not exaggerated when giving his strong warning against defiance of authority and contempt for law. In November, 1958, in Mwanza, he himself had told a mass audience that possession of a Tanu card did not mean that they could open shops without a licence, refuse to pay taxes or generally disobey the law; moreover, he had added, it was highly improbable that taxes would be reduced under self-government; they were likely to go up in order to provide schools and hospitals.

At the time of the Congo trouble, there was a wave of lawlessness. It was only a wave and not a tide, but it was worrying. Not only Europeans and Asians, but responsible Africans became frightened by what was euphemistically called hooliganism. The Governor and Nyerere both made speeches saying that it was absolutely ridiculous to think that Tanganyika would become another Congo. On August 5, 1960, the *Tanganyika Standard* reported:

The few hooligans in Tanganyika whose statements have created fear in some quarters that the Congo disorders will be repeated in the territory, have been warned by Mr. Julius Nyerere that intimidation in any form, and from anybody, will not be tolerated. Speaking at Mbeya, Mr. Nyerere said: 'Citizens in Tanganyika, of whatever colour, feel confident that you will not be molested.' Mr. Nyerere's answer to the question: 'Could the events of the Congo happen here in Tanganyika?' was an obvious 'No. These things cannot happen here,' he said. 'First we have a very strong organisation–Tanu. The Congo did not have that kind of organisation. The trouble in the Congo happened because the forces which Mr. Lumumba relied on to maintain law and order–the very forces of law and order–mutinied. They left Mr. Lumumba without the power to maintain law and order. Our forces of law and order are supported fully in their task by Tanu.'

There was not the slightest chance that the forces of law and order in Tanganyika would mutiny. 'I realise that a few hooligans are going around certain places speaking nonsense which is causing these jitters among sections of the immigrant communities, but I warn them that we are not going to tolerate any form of intimidation from anybody.'

Once more the Northern Province caused special concern. At the end of August, an Asian farmer was murdered near Arusha, and there were a number of robberies with violence. Alarm spread. Nyerere, accompanied by Nsilo Swai, Member for Arusha, toured the province, warning Tanu members that strong measures would be taken against them if they made irresponsible and inflammatory speeches. Action had already been taken against such people and would continue to be taken.

Changes are going to take place in this country [Nyerere said at Moshi], but there will be no change in Tanu's attitude towards law and order, except to enforce even more respect for law and order. We are pledged to ensure that this is going to continue to be an absolutely peaceful country. There will be respect for all human beings, irrespective of colour and race. We would be nothing but a bunch of hypocrites if, after all these years of fighting against discrimination, we were to turn around and allow the rights of men in this country to be based on race or colour. . . . Our reputation for peace and tranquillity can bring us millions in foreign investment, money that is needed in our fight against ignorance, poverty and disease. Do not believe that I, or Tanu, will allow ruffians to create disturbances and spoil all this.

On the threshold of responsible government, Julius Nyerere and his friends and colleagues came round to the Governor's point of view about the need to stamp out lawlessness. With a horrified world watching the Congo chaos, they knew that they had to demonstrate unequivocally that this could not happen in Tanganyika.

On September 1, Turnbull asked Nyerere to form a Government. Nyerere's proposed cabinet consisted of nine unofficial ministers and two civil servants. They were: Sir Ernest Vasey– Finance; Chief A. S. Fundikira–Lands, Surveys and Water; D. N. M. Bryceson–Health and Labour; George Kahama–Home

Affairs; Amir Jamal–Communications, Power and Works; Paul Bomani–Agriculture and Co-operative Development; Nsilo Swai–Commerce and Industry; Oscar Kambona–Education; Rashidi Kawawa–Local Government and Housing; J. S. R. Cole, Q.C.–Attorney-General and M. J. Davies–Information Services.

Two days later, at the swearing in ceremony at Government House, Turnbull said:

We have moved, in less than two years, from a government of which the executive was composed wholly of officials, to a government in which all but two of the portfolios are held, not by virtue of experience in the Civil Service, but by virtue of membership of the Legislative Council, and of the confidence reposed by the leader of the major political party, in those to whom they have been allocated. . . . We have many arduous duties ahead of us, not only in the field of domestic and East African matters, but in devising and putting into operation the legislative and policy changes which will need to be executed to enable us to take our next constitutional step forward. I pray that with God's guidance success will crown our work.

In the evening of the same day, Julius Nyerere, Tanganyika's first elected Chief Minister, broadcast to the nation in Swahili and in English. He made three points:

Tanganyika aims to achieve complete independence within the Commonwealth next year, with the co-operation of the Governor and the people of the United Kingdom. . . . Although we have reached an important stage in our struggle towards independence, we are not an independent country yet. . . . Militant nationalism has been combined with a smile and good humour. . . . The people of Tanganyika became fervent nationalists without becoming racialists. . . . This is maturity.

On September 4, 30,000 people acclaimed the non-official ministers at a mass meeting in Dar-es-Salaam. On a large platform, above which flew the green and black flag of Tanu, they stood with right arms upraised as the crowd sang 'God Bless Africa'. There were tremendous cheers as the Chief Minister, Julius Nyerere, called each of his colleagues forward to introduce him to the people.

This time the theme of Nyerere's speech was: 'The colour of a man's skin is no sin in Tanganyika'. *Uhuru* would be a mockery if the people of Tanganyika lived in hatred and without a sense of justice and respect for human beings. The example we have set is worth much more than gold, and we will continue to show the world that it is possible for people of different races to live together as one nation.

Thus had a dependent territory achieved self-government, without a shot being fired or a drop of blood being shed. Two men, Sir Richard Turnbull, the Governor, and Julius Nyerere, the nationalist leader, were responsible for an achievement which justified Iain Macleod's courageously calculated gamble.

CHAPTER 36

The Shortest Constitutional Conference

IN September, 1960, when Nyerere had formed his first responsible government, the Tanu National Executive drafted a new constitution. The party's first aim was changed from 'preparing the people for self-rule' to 'consolidating the freedom of the country and its people'. Tanu's whole future had to be reconsidered, for its original purpose had been achieved.

In the early days, Nyerere had intended to build a close-knit organisation, 'an élitist party'. After his appearance before the Trusteeship Council and the mass enrolments effected by Oscar Kambona, he had no choice but to approve Tanu's transformation into a mass movement. As already described, local branches maintained a considerable degree of autonomy, in many cases attempting to arrogate to themselves powers belonging to the administration and the police. Such local independence, especially when it took the form of compelling adherence to some parochial institution or of usurping the powers of the police in enforcing the criminal law, was an important ingredient of the atmosphere of contempt for authority that had been manifesting itself since 1957. And when Nyerere became Chief Minister, many Tanu members, especially Youth Leaguers, were under the impression that power had fallen into their laps. They proceeded in a number of instances to take the law into their own hands.

If the nationalist government was to maintain its position, this had to be stopped. Nyerere realised that he had both to check lawlessness, and to devise ways by which Tanu would become a part of the effective Government of the land, keeping its members usefully and intelligently occupied. Tanu's development had turned full circle: from an élitist group it had progressed to the ruling party of Tanganyika.

Nyerere did not mince words about excesses committed by some Tanu members. Already in early 1960, the African National Congress and other groups had complained of victimisation and of Tanu becoming a dictatorship. Tanu rowdies had threatened to beat up H. E. Sarwatt, the only Independent M.P., if he dared to hold political meetings in Mbulu. In this and similar cases, George

Kahama, Minister for Home Affairs in the new Government, intervened personally and there was at least temporary improvement.

Ministers joined Nyerere in his attack on those who seemed to think that a responsible Government would condone irresponsible behaviour. They insisted on the continuing need to obey the chiefs and to pay taxes. In November, 1960, at a Youth League meeting in Dar-es-Salaam, Kahama quoted chapter and verse of cases in which members had arrested people on suspicion, held illegal courts and drilled with imitation rifles. (See also Chapter 39.)

Two months later, Kahama warned minority political groups that they must end their disrespect for the Government, or be suppressed. He and other ministers launched strong attacks on parties based on tribal or religious affiliation. In August, 1961, the Meru Citizens' Union, formed ten years earlier to resist the colonial Government over the Engare Nanyuki evictions (see Chapter 20), was wound up because it had gone on fighting the new central government. Here was one more illustration of how well justified Turnbull had been in his warning: if defiance became a habit, it would embarrass the young nationalist administration even more than it had the seasoned British colonial Government.

Nyerere threw all his prestige into furthering the constructive side of the cure, namely the organisation of what were called 'self-help' schemes. His primary aim was to occupy young unemployed Tanu members, and to produce results welcome to villagers. In September, 1960, in Handeni, twelve hundred Youth Leaguers began building, under ministerial encouragement, three wards for the Native Authority dispensary. Others engaged themselves in road construction, and yet others in building a base camp for a group farming scheme in the Rovuma Valley, a project that resembled Tanu's earlier Kilombero Valley scheme, where Bibi Titi had planted the first rice in January, 1960.

These community development schemes, as Tanu called them, showed that the party was at last giving appropriate support to governmental functions. However, such new, quasi official activities made it unlikely that a two, or a multi-party system would evolve. The lower echelons of Tanu in particular were unwilling to share power with anyone. They defended the one-party system on the grounds that, for the sake of national unity, the country could not afford the divisions caused by an opposition.

Nyerere backed this attitude in speeches and in articles, saying that there was no room for difference or division when they were building a nation. During an emergency, western countries formed national governments; Tanganyika was faced with an emergency in the war against poverty, ignorance and disease, hence an opposition could not be allowed to divide the people. He said that, in newly independent countries, the voices heard in opposition were only those of a few irresponsible individuals. 'In such circumstances the Government must deal firmly and promptly with the trouble-makers. . . . Organised opposition is not an essential element in a democracy, provided there is freedom of discussion and the possibility of changing the Government through the ballot box.'

Another problem which exercised the nationalist Government was the relationship between Tanu leaders and trade unionists. At the Tabora Conference, Nyerere had insisted that the labour unions should be completely independent of the party and that trade union leaders should be banned from holding party office. Now the formula, stated by Michael Kamaliza, President of the T.F.L. since Rashidi Kawawa had joined the Government, was: 'A man is incomplete if he does not possess both a trade union card and a Tanu card.'

At the end of 1960 there was the first serious dispute between the T.E.L. and the Tanu leaders. Nyerere had to step in. His decision meant a complete about-face from the Tabora line. He said that the nationalist movement should be closely allied to the trade union wing, and that it was absurd for the workers to keep separate from their political party. The two were joined as two branches on the same stem. If they did not co-operate, the whole movement was bound to break up.

Behind the scenes, the battle between the labour unions and Tanu was further exacerbated by Christopher Tumbo, General-Secretary of the Railway Workers Union, and his supporters, most of whom were black racialists and wanted to capture the T.F.L. in order to promote their political ambitions.

It was against this background of dissensions among Africans that Nyerere told the Legislative Council in October, 1960, that he proposed to appoint a political head in each Province, to whom the P.C. (in future to be called the Regional Commissioner) would stand in the same relationship as a Permanent Secretary to his Minister. The kind of competition that had characterised the past was to be avoided, and the danger of two chains of command, a political and an administrative, eliminated. From now on the last word was to rest with the political centre, which was Tanu.[1]

Under Sir Richard Turnbull's guidance, Nyerere was learning fast the realities of power. Members of the Tanu Parliamentary Party were thrilled that the Governor's speech from the throne on October 11, containing the Government's aims and policies, was the policy statement of their own leaders. Technically this was true. But it was Turnbull's experienced advice which had trimmed and directed this policy. He ended by announcing that the British Government sympathised with the desire of the Tanganyikan people for self-government and independence, and would help them to achieve these aims. The Chief Minister and those of his colleagues most concerned would be invited to a constitutional conference, to be held in London, in March, 1961.

The next phase was described to the author by the then Colonial Secretary, Iain Macleod:

Between October, 1960, and February, 1961, Nyerere came to London several times to discuss the constitutional problems with me. These completely informal conversations mostly took place at my flat. No minutes were kept, no third parties were present. One evening David Stirling dined with us and we had a three-cornered discussion on Tanganyikan affairs. Suggestions and decisions were scribbled on the back of envelopes and on bits of paper, there being complete trust between me and Julius.

Only on three problems was there any argument at all. Julius wanted to become Prime Minister, avoiding the hitherto customary phase of Premier. He wanted the Constitutional Conference to be held in Dar-es-Salaam instead of in London. He insisted on Independence being granted in 1961.

On the first I did not feel very strongly. On the second also I had an open mind. On the third I was concerned because from an administrative point of view it would have been much better to wait until March 1962, giving time to deal calmly with innumerable administrative problems. I promised Julius to think over the three points.

I gave in first on the second point, since practically all major problems had been solved and I saw no reason why the Conference should not be held in Dar-es-Salaam.

[1] Also in October, 1960, on Nyerere's insistence, one Asian, Al Noor Kassum, and one European, Marion, Lady Chesham, were appointed to the Executive Committee of the Tanu Parliamentary Party. This was a small step in the direction of admitting all three races to Tanu, which Nyerere wished to do.

The Colonial Secretary, accompanied by his wife, arrived in Dar-es-Salaam on March 25, 1961. This was the occasion for unprecedented scenes of welcome. Crowds lined the route from the airport to Government House, cheering and carrying placards with the words: 'Independence 1961.'

Two days later, the Constitutional Conference opened formally at Karimjee Hall. In its centre, tables had been placed to form a square. The Secretary of State, accompanied by four senior officials of the Colonial Office and a legal adviser, faced the Chief Minister, who was flanked by his legal adviser, Roland Brown, and four Ministers, Sir Ernest Vasey, Minister of Finance, Chief A. S. Fundikira, Minister for Lands, Surveys and Water; D. N. M. Bryceson, Minister for Health and Labour, and George Kahama, Minister for Home Affairs.

To Macleod's right sat the Governor with his Deputy, John Fletcher-Cooke, the Attorney-General, J. S. R. Cole, Q.C., the Minister for Information Services, M. J. Davies, and I. H. Norton, Private Secretary. On the fourth side of the square sat the other elected Ministers: Amir Jamal, Minister for Communications, Power and Works; Paul Bomani, Minister for Agriculture and Co-operative Development; Nsilo Swai, Minister for Commerce and Industry; Oscar Kambona, Minister for Education; Rashidi Kawawa, Minister for Local Government and Housing, and five members of the Tanu Parliamentary Party who had been named earlier to attend this conference: Al Noor Kassum, Bokhe Munanka, Lawi Sijaona, T. S. Tewa and Richard S. Wambura.

Turnbull opened the proceedings with a cordial welcome to the United Kingdom Delegation, followed by a survey of the purpose of the conference and of the rapid constitutional progress made since 1949. Then he said:

I hope that you, Sir, will forgive a touch of complacency when I express the confidence of today's Government of Tanganyika that the quiet good sense which has distinguished the advances achieved by the people of the country under the guidance of their elected leaders, will be reflected in the future Government of the Territory; and that in the years ahead, as in the recent past, the strength of Tanganyika will be the determination of her people to maintain that unity of purpose and that mutual trust upon which the stability of Government so largely depends.

The Secretary of State thanked the Governor for his welcome, and stressed the need for an appropriate arrangement regarding the Public Service, both expatriate and local. Then he said:

The main purpose of this Conference is plain to us all. We are here to discuss not only internal self-government but also the great question of independence for Tanganyika. It is right, I think, that at this opening session of the Conference I should make clear H.M. Government's position in this matter. It is that we do not oppose the proposal of independence; we welcome it. We know the strength of feeling in your country that Tanganyika must soon take her place in the comity of independent nations. There is, therefore, nothing between H.M. Government and Tanganyikans on this great issue. . . .

I think that in the ordinary run of these things it would probably not be appropriate for me to mention individuals as having played a particular part in a country's affairs but this, Sir, is no ordinary man. In Mr. Julius Nyerere this country has a leader to whom not only the people of Tanganyika but many others in all parts of the world can look to with confidence to guide this emerging nation successfully through the very great tasks ahead. I have already referred to the spirit of harmony which prevails in Tanganyika. Mr Nyerere once said that the people of Tanganyika, and I quote 'would like to light a candle and put it on the top of Mount Kilimanjaro, which would shine beyond our borders, giving hope where there was despair, love where there was hate and dignity where before there was only humiliation.' These are simple but inspiring words which all who hope to see peace and harmony prevail in Africa must keep steadfastly in mind. But the time has come to replace the candle of responsible government first with the lantern of full internal self-government and then with the beacon of independence. That is what we are all here to do.

For his part, Nyerere paid tribute to the Governor and to the Secretary of State, as

two people whom we Tanganyikans regard as true and tried friends to our country. In the two-and-a-half years since one of you became our Governor and in the eighteen months since the other became Her Majesty's Secretary of State for the Colonies, my colleagues and I have seen enough of your good intentions towards us to leave us in little doubt that this Conference will have a happy outcome.

At the first formal meeting behind closed doors, Roland Brown, Nyerere's legal adviser, arrived with a collection of heavy volumes. Brown was entirely a 'Tanganyika man', yet fully familiar with conditions in Britain. He intended to prove that it was in order for

Nyerere to become Prime Minister instead of Premier. Realising how very much Nyerere's colleagues wanted this, Macleod had already decided to concede the point. When he announced that, after due consideration, he was agreeable to Nyerere's becoming Prime Minister, first there was amazement, then loud laughter, and the heavy legal tomes were carted away.

During the negotiations Macleod also announced that Independence would be granted in December, 1961, thus falling in with Nyerere's third demand.

Everything went easily and smoothly, except for one moment when, in the midst of the negotiations, Nyerere came to ask the Secretary of State that, on independence, Tanganyika should immediately become a republic. To this Macleod could not agree without referring to the Cabinet. Had Nyerere insisted, proceedings might have been held up considerably, as the immediate formation of a republic might have made the position of the British civil servants very difficult. Tanganyika needed the services of most, if not of all, of them for some time to come, and although there was no reluctance to work under an African Government, few would have felt able to accept a complete severance from the Crown and from service under it.

Fortunately Nyerere convinced his colleagues that the Secretary of State could not give in on the question of an immediate republic. As he put it to Macleod: 'I told them that, as you had given us everything we wanted, it was right that we, in turn, should give you this.' Thus the conference could be concluded as planned.

It closed on the morning of March 29 with a formal ceremony. This meant that, in effect, the working conference had lasted just twenty-four hours.

Karimjee Hall was packed and tense with excitement when Iain Macleod made his historic speech.

I am very glad to say that the conference has ended with agreement on all points. There are no notes of reservation, no minority report. . . . Of course, sometimes we differed but when we did, we argued out our differences with determination to reach agreement, and with understanding of the other point of view. So it was that we came to agreement as men of goodwill always do.

Agreement had been reached on full internal self-government in the very near future; on the public service and the police; in regard to the complex matter of the East Africa High Commission the Tanganyika Government had expressed their desire to continue participation in the Common Services provided by the Commission. Further discussion on these and other topics were to take place in London, in the second half of June.

I now come to what is obviously the feature of our discussions awaited with most attention and interest [Macleod stated in a hushed silence]. We have agreed that the date of internal self-government shall be the 1st of May 1961. We have further agreed that the date for full independence of Tanganyika shall be the 28th December, 1961. [Later changed to December 9, 1961.]

It is, I think, an open secret that, when Tanganyika becomes independent, it will also wish to become a member of the Commonwealth; I am very glad to say that H.M. Government will warmly support the application when it is made. . . .

On this unique occasion . . . H.M. Government and, I am sure, Mr. Nyerere and his colleagues will agree, the Government of Tanganyika have been deeply indebted to Sir Richard Turnbull, your Governor, who has guided the affairs of this country with such patience, wisdom and charm through its final stages as a dependent territory. From the moment of his assumption of the post of Governor, he has identified himself with the aspirations of the people in Tanganyika in a manner which has, I am sure, won widespread admiration throughout the country.

You, Mr Chief Minister, and the people of Tanganyika, now turn to the exciting vista of the years ahead. The work is not finished: indeed it has just begun. And may I–and I am proud to count myself, as Mr Nyerere said in his opening speech, as a friend of Tanganyika–wish you God speed, success and happiness on your journey.

There was tumultuous applause at several points during the Secretary of State's speech. When he announced the date of independence, his words were drowned by cheers which spread from Karimjee Hall into the garden, thronged with thousands of excited Africans. Their cheers were echoed further down Acacia Avenue, and then in the side streets, in the market place and in all the corners and alleys of Dar-es-Salaam. It was the supreme moment in Tanganyika's struggle for independence. Everything that happened afterwards, and a lot was to happen, was in some measure an anti-climax.

Julius Nyerere spoke after Macleod.

Your Excellency, Mr Secretary of State [he began], I speak to you with a full heart this morning. This is the day when all our people of

Tanganyika are made aware that they will have their independence in
1961. We can now look forward to our full independence–an independence within the Commonwealth–a Commonwealth which, in our
feeling, has recently been renewed and refurnished. We have no doubt
that we shall be happy members of that club, if that club is good enough
to take us in.

For the benefit of his people he explained that under self-
government, the Governor would no longer be Chairman of the
Council of Ministers, and the Deputy-Governor and the two civil
service ministers would no longer be members. This change was a
matter of form, because he and his colleagues had an understanding
with the Governor which was so close that the Governor's chairmanship of the Council of Ministers had never been any kind of
burden or frustration to them.

There is one matter, Sir, that has not been touched upon in our
communique [he then said], and yet it is a matter which has a vital
bearing on all the arrangements we have in mind . . . the heavy financial
burdens that are implicit in the steps that we are taking to make our
independence a real and genuine thing. I must say now, as I have said
on many occasions before, that our independence cannot be hindered by
consideration of finance and economics alone, but I am sure that it is in
the interest of all that Tanganyika should be able to stand on her own
feet financially when she becomes independent. My colleagues and I
have the greatest confidence that Her Majesty's Government will not be
ungenerous when we set out as an independent state amongst the other
nations of the world. . . .

But I must tell my people that a day's rejoicing is enough. I must
remind them that today's rejoicings do not mark the end of the road.
Rather I must tell them that in every one of the decisions that we have
agreed at our conference, there lie new challenges and new difficulties for
all our people; there is nothing soft, nothing easy ahead of us. We
Tanganyikans cannot pat ourselves on our nine million backs and think
to ourselves that all is over, since we will make nothing of Tanganyika,
and we will set no example to the world, unless it is by renewed efforts of
hard work for ourselves, and of kindness towards others. I have no
great pretensions about Tanganyika, Sir, for we all know that it is a
small country in terms of population, and a poor country in terms of
resources; but we do, Sir, most genuinely believe that we have great
lessons to teach, and most particularly in our own continent of Africa, by
virtue of tolerance and fellow-feeling that pervade our communities
here. In this field of human harmony others could imitate us, to their
advantage. . . .

Sir Richard, Mr Macleod, it is only two short days since we opened this conference, and on the occasion of that opening I expressed on behalf of all Tanganyikans, the feeling of goodwill that we bore towards you both. My colleagues and I have no doubt that it must now be apparent to all, even if it were not apparent before, why we entertained such feelings. You, Sir, have chaired our conference in masterly fashion, you have met us at every point with frankness and honesty and with willingness to help. We must tender you our profound thanks. Not thanks for our independence, our freedom, our *uhuru*, which we have always claimed to be our right. But we do give thanks, Sir, my colleagues and I, and all the people for whom we stand, to you and Her Majesty's Government for having fulfilled, in every particular, the highest hopes that we entertained. . . .

And then, putting down his prepared text, Nyerere turned towards Iain Macleod and said:

Somewhere about the 28th December, certain things may be going on in Tanganyika–something in the nature of celebrations. I am told, Sir, that the holders of your high office do not customarily attend celebrations of the sort I have in mind. If that be the case, we say in Tanganyika, we have a liking for fresh precedents, and I should tell you there is no one we would be more delighted to see with us here at Christmas and the New Year than yourself. . . .

Then he picked up his notes again:

This is the day of triumph for Tanganyika. But, because of the attitude shown by Her Majesty's Government, in your person, and because of the attitude of so many helpers of Her Majesty's in Tanganyika, I rejoice to say that it is not a day of triumph *over* anybody. It is a happy victory for a good cause in which all are winners. One and all in Tanganyika can rejoice with us in saying '*Uhuru* 1961.'

When Sir Richard Turnbull got up to close the conference, Nyerere and all the ministers rose to their feet, thumping tables, clapping hands and cheering with the entire audience. It took a long while for the applause to die down. After paying tribute to the Secretary of State and the United Kingdom staff, Turnbull said:

As the Chief Minister has told us, the triumph that has been achieved is not a triumph over anybody; but it is certainly a triumph for him. I am proud and grateful that this should be so; for I look upon it as the triumph of a colleague rather than of a political leader–a colleague with whom I, and my civil service advisers, have been able to work with as fruitfully when he was, as it were, leading the Opposition, as when he became my Chief Adviser and the senior of the ministers of the government. . . .

May I, as one who has been lucky enough in his service under the Crown, to have sat at the feet of some of the great administrators of our earlier days, say that I count it the greatest of privileges to have been so closely associated, in the past two-and-a-half years, with these present advances. I am confident that, under the wise guidance and the far-seeing direction of our Chief Minister–soon to be our Prime Minister–Tanganyika will, with God's help, fulfil the high expectations we place in her.

And so ended the shortest constitutional conference in British colonial history. When the Governor, the Chief Minister and the Secretary of State appeared at the head of the stairs of Karimjee Hall, thousands of cheering people acclaimed them. Garlands were placed round their necks and Julius Nyerere was lifted shoulder high amid a jubilant, dancing host all waving green foliage above their heads. He was, once more, seated in an open car and driven slowly in a triumphal procession through the capital. He was holding up a placard: 'Independence 1961.'

*   *   *

It had been a conference in the best tradition of British colonial policy. When trying to record the acclaim due to those who made it possible, homage must first go to Sir Donald Cameron. Without the foundations he has laid, Julius Nyerere would not have been educated in Tabora and Sir Richard Turnbull would not have been trained in the Lugard tradition. Most important of all it was in keeping with Cameron's own philosophy that Iain Macleod could say: 'It may be dangerous to give Africans independence too soon, but it is much more dangerous to give it too late. In Tanganyika I took a certain risk, and it paid handsomely, thanks to the personal outlook and contribution of Julius Nyerere.'

CHAPTER 37

Financial Crisis

JULIUS NYERERE reached his thirty-ninth birthday during the Constitutional Conference. Not one of his colleagues was as yet forty, and several were in their late twenties. They had enthusiasm and idealism but little practical experience.

When they came up against the harsh realities of their situation, it was only too easy for them to blame their difficulties on alleged administrative failures of the colonial power. Of Tanganyika's resources, agriculture was the most important. Only a fraction of the available arable land was under cultivation, mostly by primitive, traditional methods, with consistently low yields. Nyerere blamed the British for having done far too little to teach his people modern agricultural methods.

The peoples' general backwardness was, in his view, also the fault of the British. After forty years of British administration, under two international treaties, less than half of the children of school age went to school; only a small fraction of these reached matriculation standard and only a handful attended a college or a university. There was no African professional class; of Tanganyika's five dentists, for ten million people, not one was an African; of her doctors, not two dozen were Africans. Altogether, there were less than a hundred university graduates. There were hardly any African business men, administrators or senior civil servants.

Nyerere resented the lack of Africans in the higher ranks of the civil service, particularly when this deficiency forced him to agree to pay compensation to British civil servants to whom Tanganyika was offering continuity of service under the same conditions as before independence. Expatriate salaries had to be very high, he was assured, as the British civil servants would not otherwise be willing to serve outside their own country. Although most of the increase was to be made up from the British Treasury, Nyerere was irritated by the reasoning he saw behind this step: if Tanganyika did not have reliable administrators, no country or organisation would invest or lend money for her development. What it amounted to was that, unless he accepted the compensation plan worked out by the British Government for the expatriates, he would not get the money he needed for the Three-Year Development Plan, because the plan, in the British Government's view, depended on experienced administration for its success.

On becoming Prime Minister, Nyerere had moved into what had been the Chief Secretary's house, a large, comfortable villa with a lovely view over the Indian Ocean. Here, though a luxurious existence was available to him for the first time, he was made to face the many practical problems he had deliberately kept at the back of his mind during the political struggle. Every problem boiled down to the hard question of finance. Once Britain had gone, the schools, the hospitals, the dispensaries, the entire public services, would have to be paid for with Tanganyikan money. Tanganyika's income had to be raised very considerably. This meant that her people had to be made to pay more taxes and to work harder than hitherto. Nyerere, himself an African, realised how intractable these two problems were.

Sir Ernest Vasey had drawn up a Three-Year Development Plan, which entailed the expenditure of £8 million a year for three successive years. Nyerere, like Vasey, knew perfectly well that this plan was far too modest; to raise the standard of living substantially, he needed, he said, a £240 million plan. But £24 million would at least make a beginning. Expatriates had to administer the plan, and he felt that it was up to Britain to provide this sum as a dowry, one third in grants, two-thirds in interest-free loans. It was a poor dowry. Tanganyika seemed to be starting life as an independent nation far less well off than other newly independent nations.

Nyerere was also very concerned about the sudden diminution of interest shown in Tanu. A movement bound together by the drive for independence, it already appeared to have lost its sense of purpose. Although it still had 1,250,000 signed up members, subscriptions had dried up, enrolment of new members had ceased, and attendance at public meetings was shrinking. Already in February the Tanu National Executive had laid down a new policy, which in Oscar Kambona's words was to be a socialist one shaped to suit Africans. And a special council had been set up, consisting of Tanu, T.F.L. and Co-operative leaders, with the task of discussing economic developments. Nyerere had appealed to them to concentrate their thoughts on this vital problem.

With Turnbull's guidance, and Vasey's financial expertise, the immediate problems were under control. In May, Nyerere went to New York as a member of the British Delegation to the Trustee-ship Council. In June, he and half the Cabinet went to London for a conference convened to discuss the re-arrangement of the East African High Commission, which was to become the East African Common Services Organisation. This extremely complicated operation was solved with surprising speed and goodwill. Inde-pendent Tanganyika was to continue receiving the services pro-vided on a regional basis by the new organisation, which would carry on the work of the old.

Control of the new organisation was to be shared by Tangan-yika, Kenya and Uganda as equal partners; responsibility for it was to rest with the East African Common Services Authority, com-prising the principal elected ministers from each of the three territories, who were also to sit as *ex officio* members upon the Central Legislative Assembly. A Secretary-General and a Legal Secretary were to run the permanent secretariat as officials of the organisation. The Assembly was to have power to pass measures on civil aviation, customs and excise, income tax, inter-territorial research, university education, communications and public service commissions. All High Commission officers were transferred to the new organisation, and their rights to pensions or to compensa-tion for loss of career were recognised.

A very different situation faced Nyerere, and his colleagues, when the Tanganyika Financial Conference opened also in Lon-don. Its purpose was to tidy up the problems left over from the Constitutional Conference. To his shock and consternation Iain Macleod regretfully informed him that, owing to Britain's poverty, Tanganyika's dowry had to be cut by half. For an African like Nyerere, with first hand knowledge of what poverty means in a country where the average annual income was about £15 per head of the population, poverty in Britain sounded like a mockery.

Macleod explained what he meant. Selwyn Lloyd, as Chancellor of the Exchequer, was struggling to keep the pound steady under strong international pressure. To buttress it on the international market, the most stringent economy measures had to be taken at home. Selwyn Lloyd had introduced the pay pause, which meant that wages were blocked. To make this unpalatable measure acceptable to the workers, profits had also to be blocked, and all foreign aid cut by half.

Nyerere was aghast. That Britain had for the moment to economise was understandable, but it was impossible to compare her
situation with that of a really poor country like Tanganyika. In
view of their responsibility for Tanganyika, it appeared utterly
inconceivable that the British should so jeopardise the Three Year
Development Plan. This was callous neglect, not economy.
Nyerere's indignation met with ready sympathy from both Iain
Macleod and Sir Richard Turnbull, but neither of them could
move the Chancellor of the Exchequer or the Prime Minister.
The interview between Harold Macmillan and Julius Nyerere
was perhaps the most unfortunate of all.

It is only too apparent that throughout the conversation the two
men were simply not understanding each other. For Nyerere the
problem was the deeply emotional one of being able to bring his
people from their pre-feudal existence into the modern world.
For Macmillan, as head of what had once been the greatest of world
powers, to plead poverty to the leader of a genuinely poor, underdeveloped country, was highly invidious. But it was a job which
had to be done. Poles apart as they were, the distant, almost im-
personal manner of the Prime Minister did little to soften the blow.
Nyerere was left with feelings of resentment and despair he had
never before felt so personally. The only man who might possibly
have brought them together, Sir Richard Turnbull, was present at
the conference, but not at the private interview.

The Financial Conference was broken off without a communique. Nyerere flew to New York, to request of the Trusteeship
Council that before the end of the year Tanganyika might join the
U.N. as a fully fledged member. Explaining why the transition to
independence had been so smooth, he said: 'One vital fact is that
we are a Trust Territory under British Administration. I pay
tribute to my friends the British whose sensitivity to world public
opinion we have exploited more than once at the U.N. and outside.' (July 14, 1961.) Not by one word did he betray what he was
prepared to regard as the family quarrel over Tanganyika's dowry.

In Washington, President Kennedy[1] gave him a warm welcome
and showed a remarkable insight into Tanganyika's problems.
Loyal to Britain, he offered help on the understanding that it
would be co-ordinated with Britain's contribution; no terms for a

---

[1] This interview was arranged through the good offices of a British friend,
who had known Kennedy for many years.

loan were discussed, as Nyerere, Prime Minister of a not yet independent country, was not in a position to negotiate one. But on his arrival back in London Nyerere told the author: 'President Kennedy has a much better grasp of Tanganyikan problems than Premier Macmillan.' He would not elaborate, but his tone of voice was revealing.

Nyerere then went to West Germany. In Bonn, Chancellor Adenauer made it plain that help would be forthcoming if it could be shown that the Three-Year Development Plan was being efficiently administered, in other words by expatriate civil servants. So Nyerere was driven back to his galling problem.

In London, on July 20, Iain Macleod made a slightly improved but still unacceptable offer. At a Press conference next day Nyerere said:

We were absolutely shocked when throughout all the discussions H.M.G. were pleading poverty. Tanganyika's friendship with Britain does not depend on money. If Britain were really too poor to help, I would ask my people to make sacrifices and not ask for money. It seems, however, that being moderate one does less well than less moderate people. If a revolution took place in Tanganyika, Britain would spend millions. Somehow the balance of payments problem would disappear. Tanganyika's stability was used as an argument why we should not get financial help. . . . The sole justification for keeping an expensive expatriate civil service in Tanganyika is that they can help in the development of the country. If the British Government are not prepared to produce the funds that Tanganyika has been led to expect, it would be embarrassing for both the Tanganyika Government and the individual civil servants, who genuinely want to help in the country's development.

In answer to a question regarding Macleod's new offer, Nyerere said: 'Theoretically matters have improved, but in practice they have not improved, and I am going back very disappointed.' Later he explained that albeit that Britain had offered more money for 1965, 1966 and 1967, his problem was one of immediate urgency. He would approach other countries, in and outside the Commonwealth, including Russia.

The comment of *The Times* on Nyerere's attitude was: 'Throughout his Press Conference Mr Nyerere's attitude was one of sorrow rather than anger.' This changed after his return to

Dar-es-Salaam. The pressures of Africa and his own nervous system made themselves felt.

He found all his colleagues, with the single exception of Sir Ernest Vasey, in a state of fury. Even Chief Abdulla Fundikira, the most right-wing and the most pro-British of his team, was so angry that he recommended rejecting the loan and showing up the meanness of Britain. Never before had Fundikira been so fully at one with a radical Tanu proposal. The more left-wing members of the Government were quoting their hero, Sekou Touré, who had dealt so resolutely with the French and had put national pride above material advantage. The members of the Tanu National Executive were also enraged; had they made a public statement, the whole country would have been behind them.

Nyerere waited for the outcome of the debate in the House of Commons on July 25, in which James Callaghan, on behalf of Labour, attacked the Conservative Government over their treatment of Tanganyika. Callaghan said: 'Mr Nyerere has not staged a rebellion or a revolt. He is too decent. He has believed in the good name of Britain, but his reward is probably the most mean financial settlement that has ever been proposed to any territory on coming to self-government.' (*Hansard*, July 25, 1961.)

Iain Macleod, in his reply, made some pleasant remarks about Tanganyika and Mr Nyerere, whom he said he had encouraged to go ahead with the Three-Year Development Plan, but he had no further offer from H.M.G. to make.

This statement had a catastrophic effect in Dar-es-Salaam. Now Nyerere could see no further hope and with deeply felt indignation about Britain's behaviour, decided to reject the offer in order to show up Britain's meanness. He was as determined as his most radical colleagues that the British should not get away with the legend of having brought about an easy, happy transfer of power in Tanganyika, when they had failed to live up to their obligations. Nyerere knew, Turnbull knew, and several of the senior civil servants knew what Nyerere's all-out attack on the British would do. Race relations would no longer be harmonious. Resentments, smouldering very near the surface, would flare up. Expatriate civil servants would resign by the dozen; Africans would react with anti-British demonstrations, which would lead to further resignations and departures. In fact, all the delicate, carefully nursed balance and economic conceptions would go up in smoke.

What the independence celebrations would be like did not bear thinking about; and it was unlikely that Tanganyika would wish to join the Commonwealth.

On July 28 at mid-day there was a crucial Cabinet meeting in Dar-es-Salaam. Nyerere agreed with his colleagues to denounce the London offer. At one p.m he told a senior British civil servant of his intention of doing so. In the evening, at the opening of the Tanu headquarters, the Minister for Education, Oscar Kambona, invited him to tell the people about the London talks. What neither Kambona, nor anyone else (except Nyerere) knew was that Turnbull, when he realised how desperately near breaking-point the situation was, had decided to fly to London. Nyerere agreed to hold his hand until the Governor's return. He informed Turnbull of this at the Cabinet meeting of July 29, which the Governor was invited to attend.

In Tanganyika it is believed to this day that Sir Richard Turnbull threatened to resign and to tell the Press that the cause of his resignation was the shabby treatment of Tanganyika. Turnbull never threatened anything. What he did was to project to those concerned in London the consequences on the rest of East and Central Africa, not to mention the U.N. and the Communist Bloc, of Nyerere's denunciation of the British offer. It was an unpleasantly logical and compelling picture.

Turnbull's most vital interview was with Sir Edward Boyle, Financial Secretary of the Treasury. The Governor outlined to him the feelings in a young country on the verge of independence; the pride, the insecurity, the fear of affront. This was all part of a developing national consciousness. He told Boyle also of the battle Julius Nyerere had had to fight to get to *uhuru* by peaceful, constitutional means; the difficulties he had to overcome with his own extremists, his ignorant men and hysterical women.

Last, he analysed the situation from a British point of view, showing what the saving of something like £10 million would cost Britain in prestige and reputation. Much had been said about Tanganyika 'the model territory', 'the triumph of moderation', 'the perfect example of how Great Britain can do it', an illustration of constitutional advance with no emergency and not a single person detained. All these achievements, of which Britain was rightly proud, would go by the board if Nyerere denounced the British dowry. Almost as an afterthought, Turnbull mentioned

o

the statement Macleod had made in Dar-es-Salaam in March, 1961: 'You will not find us ungenerous . . .' Perhaps it was the best argument to put to Edward Boyle, a man with a sensitive conscience. It was in any event the last argument which rounded off a thoroughly disquieting exposition. Boyle promised Turnbull to do something.

Soon after, the Governor was informed that the Cabinet, having considered the matter, had decided fully to restore the cuts in grants and loans to Tanganyika. Her modest dowry would be handed over in its original condition.

On August 4, in the House of Commons, Iain Macleod, Secretary of State for the Colonies, said: 'Britain's original offer of assistance to Tanganyika for launching the territory into independence is to be increased. Mr Nyerere has expressed satisfaction with this settlement.' The new settlement provided for £8,750,000 in grants and over £13 million in loans.

In our present economic circumstances any proposal for additional overseas aid must necessarily be looked at with great care. But we recognise the quite exceptional importance of enabling Tanganyika to proceed with confidence in implementing her Three-Year Development Plan. I have therefore felt it right to increase our original offer of assistance and to redesign it to fit Tanganyika's needs.

To the Press, Nyerere said that he was completely satisfied with the new offer, which was roughly double the original. Tanganyika had not yet received specific offers from any countries other than Britain; but she had received a firm promise of financial aid for the development plan from the U.S.A. and Germany. He admitted that it was a pity that the British and the Tanganyika Government had exchanged a few 'unfortunate words' before agreement was reached, but the initial difficulty had now been amicably settled.

Only the *Manchester Guardian* referred obliquely to the role played by Sir Richard Turnbull, but anyone who happened to see the Governor arrive in Dar-es-Salaam and the reception he had from the Prime Minister knew that they had some special reason for celebrating.

There is little doubt that but for Sir Richard Turnbull the situation could not have been saved.

CHAPTER 38

Independence Without Bloodshed

DURING the final phase before independence Julius Nyerere's main task was to win understanding and support for his cause and his political philosophy in the outside world and–significantly enough–among his own people. He was soon to find out that it was much easier to apply democratic methods in dealings with foreign statesmen than with fellow Tanganyikans.

Among the nationalist leaders of other African countries, he had a great reputation because of the skill and speed with which he had led Tanganyika to independence without a shot fired, or a single person arrested. Though some criticised him for not being a 'prison graduate', or for being a British stooge, it was abundantly recognised that Nyerere had played a notable and loyal part in furthering all causes of common African interest.

Ever since he had begun to think about political issues, he had been a fervent advocate of African unity. His Pan-Africanism had a note of urgency because he was afraid that the artificial boundaries which the European partition of Africa had laid so awkwardly across the map might harden into permanence.

'We are in danger of becoming the most Balkanised continent in the world,' he has told the author. His repeated references to Balkanisation in the context of Africa may have had their origin in the history lectures he attended in Edinburgh on Balkanisation as a nineteenth-century concept. The conclusions Nyerere drew from it were entirely up-to-date.

'Federation or union of two or several African states on a democratic basis will provide useful stepping stones towards a unified Africa,' he has also told the author. He was the first East African nationalist to advocate an East African Federation. He argued, consistently, that his earlier opposition to Closer Union had been due to the fact that then it would have been a British-imposed, undemocratic development. As soon as Kenya, Uganda and Zanzibar, with Tanganyika, the natural components of an East African Federation, had governments with a mandate from their peoples, federation would become practicable and desirable. And if the wind of change should blow strongly enough,

Nyasaland, Northern Rhodesia and perhaps Ruanda-Urundi will also join.

But in deference to the wishes of the Kenya and Uganda leaders, he subsequently changed his view about the most propitious time to realise the East African Federation. In 1960, when he discussed it with Iain Macleod, he said that federation should come before each of the states concerned became independent and not afterwards, as they might then have difficulties in surrendering their sovereignty. The right stage to hold discussions, he said in 1960, would be when Kenya, Uganda and Zanzibar each had a chief minister. (He already held that position.) Then a summit meeting of chief ministers should plan the formation of a federation to coincide with the simultaneous achievement of independence by all the East African territories.

In Dar-es-Salaam, on November 4, 1960, Nyerere added at a Press conference:

It would be no use to become independent, with our own anthem, our own flag and our own seat in the U.N. and then talking about federation. To those who want to wait until the East African countries are seperately independent, I say they do not know human nature. You must rule out the question of federation after we take our seats as sovereign states in the U.N.

Jomo Kenyatta's release from detention drove it home to Nyerere that the speed of constitutional change in the three East African countries could not be altered. He had to press on with Tanganyika's independence, which the British Government had agreed should take place in December, 1961, regardless of the date of Kenya's or Uganda's. Therefore he did not refer again to his very accurate reading of human nature.

In defining Tanganyika's future foreign policy, Nyerere said in 1961 that he would try to steer a course between various power blocks in Africa and in the rest of the world.

Our desire is to be friendly to every country in the world, except South Africa, Portugal and the Federal Government of the Rhodesias and Nyasaland. We have no desire to have a friendly country choosing our enemies for us. . . . We welcome every attempt towards African unity. We do not believe either in the Casablanca or in the Monrovia group. We intend to be independent, which does not mean that we will be neutral—no country can be neutral in respect of the great issues of our time.

Nyerere was certainly not neutral in regard to South Africa. When the Commonwealth Prime Ministers met in London in March, 1961, he sent a message asking them to bear in mind how strongly

the young emergent nations of Africa feel about the South African issue. . . . It is just because we are so anxious to join the Commonwealth that it is of the first importance to us that the Commonwealth should preserve those principles of complete equality and justice for all before the law which are the finest flowering of any civilisation. The attitude which the Prime Ministers' Conference adopts towards South Africa's policies will affect the whole future of the Commonwealth. I hope that the Prime Ministers will remember that the newly independent countries of Africa and those now awaiting independence rely upon them to champion the principles of brotherhood.

This statement received world-wide publicity, and had a particularly strong impact on Canada, Australia and India. Their leaders expressed admiration for the young African who, by his outspoken appeal to principles, had risked impairing Tanganyika's independence.

Next day, the London *Observer* asked him to cable an article for its issue of March 12. Now Nyerere made his points even more explicitly:

We believe that the principles of the Commonwealth would be betrayed by an affirmative answer to South Africa's application for admission as a republic. Inevitably, therefore, we are forced to say that to vote South Africa in is to vote us out. This decision we have made reluctantly, in full knowledge of what it might mean to us, an underdeveloped country determined to overcome poverty, ignorance and disease, which now afflict many of our nine million people.

Nyerere stressed inter-racial harmony in Tanganyika, which must not be classified as a multi-racial state because

what we want is a society where the individual matters, and not the colour of his skin or the shape of his nose. The apartheid policies now being practiced in the Union of South Africa are a daily affront to this belief in individual dignity. They are also a constantly reiterated insult to our own dignity as Africans. . . . The Tanganyika Government cannot afford to have any relations with the South African Government, and it must within the bounds of international law lend support to those who struggle against the system of apartheid. . . . We believe that South African membership under present conditions makes a mockery

O 2

of the inter-racial composition of the Commonwealth. . . . We fear the evils of racialism and its consequences on the minds of majorities and minorities alike. We believe that the dignity of man is the idea which can defeat racialism; but we know that any action of ours which appears to compromise with the evil we are fighting must weaken the execution of our own politics. This means that we cannot join any 'association of friends' which includes a state deliberately and ruthlessly pursuing a racialist policy.

Iain Macleod has told the author: 'Julius' article had a tremendous effect. He swayed all those who wanted to keep South Africa in because no government or policy would last for ever, and who disliked the idea of expelling a member of the Commonwealth.'

On March 13 *The Times* summed up public opinion in the West:

Mr Nyerere's position as the leader of the most politically advanced of the East African territories, and as a man respected everywhere as an intelligent, moderate and able politician, gives to his views an importance far greater than that attributable to 'fringe' organisations, however sincere. He must be seen, also, as a leading proponent of the idea of federation of East Africa which if it came to fruition, could be a powerful force in the Continent.

On the other hand, as he himself reminds us in the article, he is writing as an outsider, not as a full member of the 'club'. Before the question of Tanganyika's admission comes up, the situation may have changed both in Tanganyika or East Africa as a whole, and in South Africa.

That, surely, is the significance of the phrase 'South African membership *under present conditions*'. But, however it is interpreted, the article must rank as a piece of powerful advocacy in this week's Lancaster House battle over South Africa.

It proved to be more than that, for as a result of it Dr Verwoerd, the South African Prime Minister, withdrew his application for his country's readmission to the Commonwealth. South African liberals were greatly heartened. One of them wrote to *The Times*:

Mr Julius Nyerere, perhaps Britain's best friend in Africa, has served notice on the Commonwealth that it must now choose between himself and Dr Verwoerd. Make no mistake. Nyerere speaks for Africa, including the coming nonracial government of South Africa. Representatives of non-whites here all call for expulsion. If their plea is heard, there might well be a post-apartheid application for readmission. If on the other hand it is ignored, the future South African non-racial government will view coldly any association which, when it had the chance of weakening the oppressor, chose rather to strengthen him.

Nyerere had reason to be satisfied with his role in bringing about the expulsion of South Africa from the Commonwealth. How many of his compatriots understood the significance of his success, or the principles upon which it was based, must remain an open question.

As regards his own people, Nyerere knew that democracy in the European sense of the word was not suited to their experience of life. In several Press, radio and television interviews he tried to explain what he meant by African democracy. In November, 1960, in the B.B.C. General Overseas and North American Services, he said that parliamentary democracy to Britons seemed impossible without one party in the Government, another party in opposition. To him this was not an essential part of democracy; to him democracy meant that Government decisions would be reached as a result of discussion. Having a Government party and an opposition party entering Parliament with the knowledge that they would disagree, was, he sometimes thought, making a mockery of parliamentary democracy. In African tribal society there was the tradition that problems at the family level were discussed in order to reach agreement and to find a solution. When this was transferred to a clan, or, beyond that, to a tribe, the whole purpose of discussion was in order to agree and Nyerere felt that in Africa they would go wrong if they tried to impose organised opposition for the sake of opposition. A government system had to suit the attitudes of the people. An official opposition would not be understood by his people because it was contrary to the basic attitude of the Africans.

Passionate non-racialism, however, remained the cornerstone of Nyerere's domestic concept, valid inside as well as outside Tanganyika. In the same week in which he broadcast his explanation narrowing the limits of parliamentary democracy within his country, he made the much quoted statement: 'A man's colour is no sin in Tanganyika.'

It was all the more embarrassing that, with the approach of full independence, a small but vocal group of his own party, Tanu, chose to begin a black racialist agitation. These men fastened their interest on the Citizenship White Paper, which recommended that

Europeans and Asians be given the same citizenship rights in Tanganyika as Africans. They demanded that Europeans and Asians should receive less favoured treatment than Africans. On October 18, 1961, in the National Assembly (as the Legislative Council was renamed after Tanganyika had reached internal self-government) five members voiced black apartheid views. Though Nyerere and his supporters scored an overwhelming parliamentary success against them,[1] they should have known better than any foreign observer how little a vote in Dar-es-Salaam meant to the African hinterland.

The black racialist agitation, political expression of jealousy of Europeans and Asians in any position or job, went on. It took increasingly serious forms inside the labour unions. The railway workers' leader, Christopher Tumbo, was the ring-leader. Other Labour leaders, who fervently believed in Nyerere's political philosophy, wrestled with Tumbo and his friends, but in the T.F.L. they could boast of no easy victory over the black racialists.

Nyerere also faced trouble on other sectors of the domestic front. The general public took the view that Tanu's sole purpose had been to achieve independence; hence there was no further need to contribute to party funds. Such ignorant critics received backing from those chiefs, headmen, witch doctors and elders, who had lost influence with the passing of the old days. These men were apprehensive of the Tanu régime under which new leaders were coming to the fore propagating ideas which meant the swift disappearance of the traditional pattern of African society. Quietly, these adversaries of Nyerere advised tribesmen either not to join Tanu, or to drop out of it. Nyerere's efforts to appoint talented chiefs to important positions helped in some areas, but many chiefs were not fit to carry modern responsibilities, and some were simply unemployable.

Dedicated Tanu supporters, for their part, criticised Nyerere's Government because they considered the Three-Year Plan in-adequate. They could not see how Tanganyika's finances would stand up after independence, when so many services, hitherto paid for by British Governments, would have to be financed with Tanganyikan money. Their fire was concentrated on Sir Ernest Vasey, who, on becoming Minister of Finance, had said that if Tanganyika had a stable régime for a year foreign capital would

[1] See also Introduction.

pour in to develop the country. Stability had been there, for all to see, for nearly two years, but there was little sign of foreign capital. What they forgot was that the British had also been there. Foreign investors were waiting to see what would happen when the Tanganyikans were on their own.

At the other end of the scale, unsophisticated tribesmen had come to believe (perhaps encouraged by people with an ulterior motive) that after *uhuru* they would have to pay no more taxes; some predicted easy jobs and high wages, others no further need to do any work at all. Nyerere tried to counteract this euphoria in several down-to-earth broadcasts, but on this subject most Africans would not believe him.

But all criticisms and disagreements were forgotten in the mounting excitement over the independence celebrations, which began on December 9, 1961. Duncan Sandys, Secretary of State for Commonwealth Relations, led the British delegation, whose members arrived two days earlier. Somehow accommodation was found for everyone–though Dar-es-Salaam is a city notoriously short of hotels–before the Duke of Edinburgh's arrival. At the beflagged airport a colourful gathering, headed by cabinet ministers, Cardinal-Archbishop Rugambwa and distinguished guests, cheered the Duke as he stepped from his red aeroplane wearing the white tropical uniform of an Admiral of the Fleet. He was received by Sir Richard Turnbull and Prime Minister Nyerere. The route to Government House was lined by Africans waving green branches of welcome. When questioned, they had no idea who Prince Philip was.

The Government had earmarked £350,000 for the celebrations, and the town was festive with flags, bunting and greenery. A few grumbled that in view of the drought and the thousands of Tutsi refugees from Ruanda to whom Tanganyika had offered a home, this was far too large a sum to be wasted on a piece of showing-off. Amidst general jubilation, such baleful voices were not heeded, nor those of the people who complained of too many white-skinned faces at the celebrations.

The State Banquet, held at the Aga Khan's Jubilee Hall, was impeccably served. A bank of flowers, reaching to the ceiling and reproducing the Tanganyika coat of arms, had been erected behind the head table, where Prince Philip acted as host, with Lady Turnbull on his right and Mrs Nyerere on his left. The youthful Aga

Khan, governors of neighbouring territories, African heads-of-state, cabinet ministers and their wives shared the places of honour. In all some three hundred guests dined at five long tables. Jomo Kenyatta, Kenneth Kaunda, Oginga Odinga and other nationalist leaders cut colourful figures in their chosen forms of national dress.

After the State Banquet, the assembled guests moved to the huge, newly built sports arena. The K.A.R. performed with precision and verve an excellent tattoo, after which a British officer handed over the regimental colours to an African officer. For British onlookers this was indeed a symbolic portrayal of the great change that was taking place before their eyes.

At midnight came the moment for which the Africans had been waiting so long. In complete silence, and very slowly, the Union Jack was hauled down in front of the Royal Box. The C.O. of the East African Forces, who sat in front of the author, could not keep the tears from his eyes. Then all the lights went out. When a spotlight suddenly lit up the flagpole the Tanganyika flag was fluttering at its head. Seventy thousand Africans, tightly packed into the onlookers' stands, jumped to their feet roaring frenetic cheers of joy. At last they were convinced that *uhuru* had come. . . .

There were further ceremonies – the handing over of the Instrument of Government, the State Ball, the Government House garden party, receptions by the Prime Minister and by the Mayor of Dar-es-Salaam, finally the opening of Parliament by the Duke of Edinburgh. All of these went off without a hitch. In the entire country, not a single untoward incident occurred. Both British and Tanganyikans felt immensely proud of celebrations which maintained the wonderful record of independence without bloodshed.

In seven years and five months Julius Nyerere had achieved his aim, a unique performance in nation-building. He had waged the nationalist struggle by constitutional means and succeeded in living up to his principles in every crisis. He had attained the highest office in his country without resort to the violence which he abhorred.

On December 11, 1961, the independence celebrations drew to their close in the same golden sunshine in which they had begun.

CHAPTER 39

Postscript I — Harsh Realities

THE independence decorations had not yet been taken down when a sense of queer malaise took possession of Dar-es-Salaam. This mood reflected the African dream more than it did the African personality. To the Tanganyikans independence had meant that overnight they would run themselves by themselves, with every African sharing in a new, prosperous, comfortable life. Now it began to be forced home to them that they would have to settle for a good deal less.

Julius Nyerere had been concerned all along that something of this kind might happen and he had been at pains to broadcast warnings against too high expectations. Yet in the course of achieving independence he himself had made promises which, although they may have seemed easy at the time, were in the changed circumstances of 1962 just not possible to keep. Now he too had to face up to unpleasant realities. For instance, the number of unemployed was increasing. With improving health and a rising birth rate, more and more young men and women had trekked to the towns. Their clamour for non-existent jobs had a disturbing echo; so had angry comments that hospitals and surgeries, schools for children and for adults anxious to learn the three 'R's', were not being built overnight. Poverty was still the general affliction, the average African family income remaining at less than £100 a year, while the average European family income was certainly more than £1,000 a year. Africans would have been superhuman had they not resented the rich, whom they could identify by the colour of their skins as much as by their way of life.

The possibility of a popular reaction against Europeans and Asians was ever present in Nyerere's mind. It ran counter to his deeply felt conviction that non-racialism was the only right basis for Tanganyika's development. Yet there was so little he could do about it. He was not in a position to divert people's attention either by political circuses, or by foreign adventures; he could not create health and educational services by a stroke of the pen, nor could he conjure up employment or increase the standard of living by merely wishing it. But, there was one thing he could do. Using the resources available to him, he could prove himself the champion of African prestige and African dignity and show for all to see that however poor he might be, the African was now indeed master in his own house. He therefore decided that the time had come to make an example of ill-mannered Europeans who continued to adopt an attitude of racial arrogance. Even in Tanganyika it is, unhappily, not difficult to uncover instances of outrageous behaviour of this sort, and in the climate of January, 1962, Africans were ready to seek out potential offenders.

Four cases of racial discrimination or behaviour in derogation of the dignity of Tanganyika were brought to the Government's notice. The persons responsible were summarily deported. In one case, such draconian treatment was justified. In all cases, a political safety valve was opened that may have prevented popular frustration from converting itself into resentment and exploding.

Yet it is difficult to condone the methods used in effecting the deportations. The persons concerned were not informed of the reason for their expulsion until they read it in the *Tanganyika Standard*. They could not defend themselves, or be defended, let alone have recourse to the courts.

Nyerere had had to weigh the pros and cons of these actions. On the one hand the conceited and the discourteous were taught a sharp lesson in social behaviour and the public was reassured; on the other, the Star Chamber technique could not but frighten potential investors and business men outside Tanganyika. If the principles underlying the rule of law could be set aside in these cases, what would happen to property, contracts, wage agreements? And the effect on the ordinary African was not conducive to social stability. Managers and foremen were suddenly meeting with truculence on the part of hitherto pleasant and conscientious workers; unofficial strikes broke out in many industries. Expatriate civil servants were becoming upset not because Africanisation was being speeded up daily—that was foreseen and acceptable—but because of an indefinable change for the worse in the happy atmosphere in which they had previously worked. *Uhuru*, Tanu's mouthpiece, carried violently anti-British editorials, which were reprinted in the vernacular Press; to cap it all, Oscar Kambona, the Minister of Education, published an attack on the Governor-General in *Nguruma*, a Swahili weekly!

Fortunately, these manifestations of frustration and suspicion did not develop into anything more than a short attack of post-independence hysteria–the national aftermath of great tensions, ambitions realised and unrestrained rejoicings. Dar-es-Salaam may have had its anxious moments but the heart of Tanganyika beat on with its accustomed kindliness and reliability.

Tanu too was facing the problem of adjustment to post-independence conditions. It seemed slowly to be losing its morale and its momentum. Explanations were not far to seek; the ablest leaders had become cabinet ministers; their substitutes lacked talent as well as experience and failed to take the people into their confidence. Although Nyerere himself was venerated, the Tanu left wing took advantage of the general malaise to criticise his moderate policies and to inspire a whispering campaign that all ills could be cured provided European stooges who advocated slow, constitutional methods, were got rid of.

In this atmosphere of disquiet and disillusion, the Tanu National Executive met in mid-January, 1962. Some of the views expressed came as a shock to Nyerere. Broadsides were ostensibly aimed at George Kahama, his loyal friend in charge of the Ministry for Home Affairs. Kahama had publicly rebuked members of the Tanu Youth League who, often with genuinely good intentions and convinced that they were serving the public weal, but without a shred of constitutional authority, had arrested, questioned and punished people. He told them that they were welcome to join the police, but they could not take the law into their own hands. (See also Chapter 36.) Now the left wing clamoured for his head.

Nyerere let his critics talk for three days, just as he had done at the Tabora Conference exactly four years earlier. Then he took the floor and made a splendid speech. He explained his moderate policies and how they had achieved independence without bloodshed; he outlined his future plans and asked for co-operation. Concluding, in a moving appeal he told the National Executive that if they did not approve of what he was doing, he would resign and dedicate himself to the reorganisation of Tanu, so as to create the unity badly needed in the difficult years ahead.

There was a storm of applause and several Tanu members cried unashamedly. But not the left wing. Those intransigent men, absolute for change, stared in front of them in silence. When it was their turn to speak, they took Nyerere at his word and for the first time in his career his offer to resign was accepted.

Not even the left wing of the National Executive wanted wholly to get rid of Nyerere. They knew that his prestige and his popularity with the masses was their greatest asset. His offer to revitalise the party suited their books as well as his own, for with a divided party their positions would not have lasted long either. But they intended to build a different Tanganyika from the non-racial and democratic country envisaged by Nyerere; they wanted the architect out of the way while the plans were being recast.

The bargaining between him and his critics can only be surmised. From the changes which took place, it appears that he had to make a number of immediate concessions, but that he also set to work immediately to restore his position and to make it immune from further discipline by any Tanu caucus.

Nyerere resigned. Rashidi Kawawa, a trusted friend and a tough, competent administrator, succeeded him as Prime Minister. Kawawa was prepared to carry out measures, some unpopular with Africans, others with Europeans, from which Nyerere had shrunk. To the outside world the Government reshuffle was to be presented as proof that Tanganyika was not a one-man country, or a Nyerere preserve, but a state well stocked with men capable of filling top posts.

Sir Ernest Vasey, the brilliant Minister of Finance, had to go, although he was retained as financial adviser both to the Treasury and to Nyerere personally. C. I. Meek, who doubled the posts of Secretary to the Cabinet and Head of the Civil Service, was given one month's notice. His successor was Dunstan Omari, at the time High Commissioner in London. Christopher Tumbo, the racialist Secretary-General of the Railway Workers Union, was dispatched to succeed Omari in this important and difficult post. The decision was typical of Nyerere, and in keeping with an explanation he had once given to the author: 'If I cannot convince a man of the error of his ways, I promote him in the hope that responsibility will steady him.' (In this instance, the theory did not work.) George Kahama had to relinquish the Ministry for Home Affairs to Oscar Kambona and rest satisfied with the less important Ministry of Commerce and Industry. That Kambona's views were to the left of Nyerere's was common knowledge; the Government included Job Lusinde and Jerry Kasimbala, his close personal and political friends.

Against this, four sound and devoted Nyerere men were kept in charge of important ministries: Paul Bomani of the Treasury; Chief Abdulla Fundikira of the Ministry of Legal Affairs; Solomon Eliofoo of the Ministry of Education and Amir Jamal of the Ministry of Communications and Power. With Rashidi Kawawa and George Kahama, they formed an excellent team. The Governor-General watched over the Government from the background.

Nyerere evinced more foresight at the time than even Turnbull credited him with. He knew that the development of a one party state was inevitable. After the many tributes he had paid the Westminster model, he could not say so in public; but he knew what the future was to bring and was determined that the Government should not lose the confidence of the party. The obvious way to achieve this was by returning to the party leadership. Back in his Tanu chair he could give the people convincing explanations of the underlying reasons for Government policy and see to it that criticism directed at the Government was helpful and constructive, and not merely malicious.

This and other preparations which Nyerere now set in hand for his return to power had an aim far more profound than a mere setting of the stage for his resumption of the highest executive office. This was a period when Nyerere's political thinking hardened in a way which was to affect fundamentally the very fabric of political life. He was to resume authority on terms quite different from those underlying the Westminster democracy which had been bequeathed to Tanganyika on independence, but which here, as in other parts of the Continent, was proving to be unsuited to present day African conditions. From now on *African* democracy and *African* socialism figured prominently as the system that was to be the pattern of government in the future.

Nyerere travelled the length and breadth of Tanganyika. This removed him from the international limelight and from the head-patting which embarrassed him and caused pangs of jealousy to some of his colleagues. During his political *safaris*, he pruned the dead-wood from Tanu's branches, recruited new local leaders, cut Communist links where he found them, and worked out tasks and targets for every region down to the smallest unit of the social framework. All the ministries were to play their parts in the new plan. Nyerere speeded up the appointment of Regional and Area

Commissioners, to replace the non-political Provincial and District Commissioners.[1] The new Commissioners were Tanu men, who had to report directly to the Tanu President, that is Nyerere. This change, more than any other, demonstrated that the party, not the elected Parliament, was becoming the source of authority.

To the people, Nyerere had little to offer besides dedication and hard work. As he told Richard Cox, the *Sunday Times* correspondent: 'We are not likely to get outside capital when we need it. During that period, the private investor is going to say: "I wait and see boys"; but I can't tell my people to wait. No country signs a cheque for another country. They promise money but they don't give money. You've got to reshape your plans to fit in with them.' (June 3, 1962.)

Reshaping meant initiating self-help projects as the means for constructing the most urgently needed roads, schools, hospitals. Every Tanganyika citizen was to work, free, one day a week on the local self-help scheme; anyone who failed to turn up was to be fined. Even the simplest tribesman understood this revival of the old tribal custom of free labour to the chief for communal purposes and set himself to work with a will. According to official Tanganyika statements, by mid-1963 for an investment of £100,000, 515 wells had been sunk and 10,400 miles of roads, 166 clinics, 368 schools, 267 village halls and 308 dams constructed.

Nyerere also announced that on December 9, 1962, on the first anniversary of independence, Tanganyika would become a republic. Iain Macleod had agreed to this during the independence negotiations, and the announcement gave great satisfaction to Tanganyikans who, without any personal ill will towards the British Governor-General, rejoiced that his replacement by an African President would cut the last of the colonial links.

As a result of Nyerere's thorough organisational work and the good ministerial teamwork in Dar-es-Salaam, the atmosphere improved considerably. And yet, by June, 1962, the national balance-sheet was by no means healthy. To mention but three main items: forty per cent of the expatriate civil servants had left; unemployment had shot up and foreign investment gone down; the crucial question—what kind of labour policy and what kind of republic—had been left unanswered. A White Paper was now published about the latter, and on June 3, 1962, Nyerere spelt out

[1] Nyerere originally suggested this in Legco on October 13, 1960.

in the *Observer* the four principles on which a new and authoritarian constitution was to be based.

First, government institutions had to be understandable to the people. 'There must be no confusing outward forms which are meaningless in the light of our experience and history. This alone requires a Republic, and one with an executive president.' Secondly, the President had to have not only responsibility for the actions of the Government, but also power to fulfil his responsibilities. Thirdly, the elected representatives had to remain sovereign, and have exclusive powers to make laws, raise taxes, and vote money. Fourthly, freedom demanded the operation of the rule of law.

Nyerere admitted that sometimes these four principles would clash. 'We have tried to prevent unnecessary conflict by making clear where the ultimate power and responsibility lie. Our President, who will be Head of State, Commander-in-Chief of the Armed Forces, and will have full executive authority, will not be bound to accept the advice of his Cabinet.'

The last point gave the Tanganyika President even more sweeping powers than those of the American President. Nyerere explained that the American system of 'checks and balances' was admirable for putting the brake on change, but Tanganyika's need was not for brakes. Lack of trained manpower and capital resources, as well as an unpredictable climate, combined to produce a brake that was all too effective. 'We need accelerators powerful enough to overcome the inertia bred of poverty and the resistance inherent in all societies.' Tanganyika could not afford 'neutral administrators', for enthusiasm was a most important national asset. 'We therefore propose giving the President power to appoint, promote, dismiss and exercise disciplinary control over civil servants and police. . . . While judges will have complete security of tenure once they are appointed, the man who appoints them will be the President.' He would even have power to give instructions to the Director of Public Prosecutions.

Two months later, Nyerere was unanimously nominated as Tanu's presidential candidate. He had only one opponent, Zuberi Mtemwu, leader of the tiny African National Congress. 1,123,535 votes were cast for Nyerere, against 21,279 for Mtemwu. This meant that 63·5 per cent of the 1,800,000 registered voters went to the polls.

On December 9, 1962, Julius Kamberage Nyerere was sworn in by the Chief Justice, Sir Ralph Windham, as the first President of the Tanganyika Republic. He received gifts of a cloak, a spear and a shield from the tribal chiefs, who also anointed him. Sir Richard Turnbull left,[2] and with his departure Nyerere lost the disinterested counsellor who had first explained to him the workings of a democratic government, and had subsequently kept him out of many pitfalls.

Not since Sir Donald Cameron's departure had such scenes of public grief been seen as when Turnbull went. It was as though instinctively people realised that this indeed meant 'Dropping The Pilot'. Now Nyerere was to experience the cold loneliness of supreme power. For seven years neither the Tanu National Executive, nor anyone else could touch him. Nyerere, as President, was above the law, and as long as no group of people felt sufficiently strongly to oust him – by violence, or he himself was not moved by illness or disillusion to quit his office, the formative years of the nation were in his hands.

On January 14, 1963, he took the next logical step in completing Tanganyika's authoritarian régime: he announced to the Tanu Annual Delegates Conference that a one-party system of government would be introduced. To roars of applause he said: 'In as much as the people of Tanganyika recognise only one party, the laws of the country must also recognise only one party.' He asked for approval to appoint a committee to examine the Constitution and to advise on the amendments necessary to put the one-party system into effect. Electoral procedure was to be revised so that more than one candidate could stand in each constituency on an individual basis. Tanu, as a national movement, would be identified with the people as a whole and membership open to every citizen. At last, Nyerere was able to turn Tanu, at least formally, into a non-racial party.

Under the multi-party system, the approved Tanu candidates had been invariably returned; now, Nyerere said, people would be able to use their right to vote for men of their choice. (They would all, of course, have to be Tanu men.) M.P.s would be able to follow their consciences in criticising the government policies and civil servants in participating in political affairs like all citizens. 'Those who cannot think of democracy without thinking of many parties,'

[2] Sir Ernest Vasey had left in November, 1962.

he concluded, 'will regard this announcement as the death of democracy in Tanganyika. But such people will not be Tanganyikans, because Tanganyikans at the moment recognise only one party.'

There were few who did not. Nevertheless, the leaders of the All-Muslim National Union and of the African National Congress declared vainly that they would not dissolve their respective organisations; and the editorial in the *Tanganyika Standard* of January 16, 1963, which asked whether it was necessary to ensure by statute that no opposition would ever arise, was widely quoted.

If major questions of policy or personality were to appear on the Tanganyika scene, what courses will be open to people who do not wish to work through Tanu, or the Tanu leadership? . . . If there is no freedom of operation for opposition parties, malcontents are liable to begin working underground by plots, intrigues–and possibly violence. The tragic assassination of President Sylvanus Olympio of Togo points the danger.

Nyerere was well aware of this. He had been shaken by sobs when he had had to tell Tanu delegates of his friend's murder. In January, 1963, he published five articles in the *Tanganyika Standard*, explaining the democratic nature of the one party state. Fear of violence ran through them like a red thread.

In relation to domestic affairs, he pleaded that party leaders should not assume that they knew best, or that it was sufficient to give inside information privately to the people's representatives. Expert opinion should be made available openly and to the people themselves and no limitation imposed either at election time or in debate. Such was the one party system's insurance against violence.

To try and import the idea of a party opposition into Africa may very likely lead to violence [he wrote], because opposition parties will tend to be regarded as traitors by the majority of our people–or, at best, it will lead to the trivial manoeuvrings of opposition groups whose time is spent inflating artificial differences into some semblance of reality 'for the sake of preserving democracy'.

Finally, he argued that change in fundamentals should be properly termed revolution; 'the existence of really fundamental differences within a society poses a civil war situation'. Under the one party system, Nyerere believed, all differences could be resolved without bloodshed.

About the labour leaders and the trade union officials, many of whom opposed his policy on the fundamental issue of racialism, he was significantly silent. How deep this opposition cut was revealed when Michael Kamaliza, the harassed Minister of Labour, demanded action against the black racialists who had brought the work of the T.F.L. to a standstill. Victor Mkello, Secretary-General of the T.F.L., was placed in preventive detention, and Christopher Tumbo only escaped this fate by fleeing to Kenya. But even the elimination of the two most obstructive black racialists did not settle the issue as to whether Tanganyika was to become an all-black country, as these labour leaders wanted it, or the non-racial democracy on which Nyerere had set his heart. Fundamentally, this was a new struggle for power.

Another facet of the same problem was the speed and extent of Africanisation. Obviously, in an African State all positions must eventually be held by Africans, and in the early stages vigorous action must be taken to insure that an acceptable proportion of senior posts is held by Africans, even at the risk of some injustice to others. All this Nyerere recognised; at the same time he had repeatedly stated: 'We must use the best man for the job', and had asked expatriate civil servants to stay until their successors had been properly trained. But the outcome was not going to be quite as he had wished it; and quite early he began to have fears of the emergence of a class of African mandarins. In April, 1962, when installed Honorary Fellow of Makerere University, he gave a warning against the dangers of educated Africans becoming a permanent privileged class in the East African countries. 'Some people recommend Africanisation merely because they want that job, that pay, or that house,' he said. 'It is tempting for the new leaders in Africa merely to step into the places of Europeans and Asians without really changing the colonial system.'

Yet for another eighteen months he had no alternative but to continue to compromise to the extent of sanctioning an Africanisation programme aimed at filling all Government jobs with Africans, however inexperienced. By early 1964, he felt that a proper balance had been struck. On January 7, in a strongly worded letter circularised to all ministries and public bodies, Nyerere said:

The nation must use the entire reservoir of skill and experience. . . . The skin in which this skill is encased is completely irrelevant. . . . This meant that discrimination in civil service employment as regards recruitment, training and promotion must be brought to an end immediately. Any necessary amendments to regulations will be signed within the next two weeks. . . . It would be wrong of us to continue to distinguish between Tanganyikan citizens on any ground other than character and ability. We cannot allow the growth of first and second class citizenship. Africanization is dead.

There spoke the essential Nyerere.

For thus trying to remain true to the principle of racial equality which had been the loadstar of his political career, he was immediately and savagely denounced by the trade union leaders who favoured an all black Tanganyika. How many sympathisers they had, one can only guess. For Africanisation had also been used as a lever by Africans jealous of the men in the highest positions whom they wanted to supplant. Indirectly, Nyerere's stand for equal opportunity also sparked off the army mutinies of 1964.[3]

Because of the many responsibilities his position now entailed, and in spite of the relentless way in which he drove himself, Nyerere could no longer keep in as close touch with public opinion as he had been able to do in the past. His time was taken up with presiding at Cabinet meetings, reading state documents and dealing with correspondence, receiving diplomatic representatives, going on state visits, and, last but not least, shaping foreign policy. Most important were questions concerning African unity. Nyerere placed Tanganyika to the fore by offering hospitality to at least three different groups training for subversive activities against *apartheid* and colonial rule. The Committee of Nine, the inter-African body planning these activities, had its headquarters in Dar-es-Salaam. In May, 1963, at Addis Ababa, Nyerere played a leading role in the setting up of the Organisation of African States. In his main speech, he echoed the call of the Algerian President, Ben Bella, who had said: 'One must die a little in order to overthrow the last fortress of colonialism.' Nyerere affirmed Tanganyika's readiness 'to die a little to remove the final humiliation of colonialism' and pledged one per cent of the Tanganyika budget to finance the African liberation movement.

At the end of long days, crowded with many complicated and some almost insoluble problems, Nyerere was staying up late in order to translate *Julius Caesar* into Swahili. This work was to realise two of his deepest ambitions: to prove that Swahili was

[3] For a chronology of events during the mutinies, see Appendix III.

sufficiently developed to convey the subtleties of a Shakespearean masterpiece, and to make a Tanganyikan contribution on the four hundredth anniversary of Shakespeare's birthday. This was the kind of work Nyerere found entirely satisfying, for it brought him nearest to the role of philosopher–historian–president he would have liked to be–a role less suitable perhaps for handling the explosive, post-liberation situation and for dealing with hot-headed and ambitious African politicians than would have been a more hard-headed approach. But it was not without a nobility of its own.

CHAPTER 40

Postscript II – The Challenge of the Future

THE outside world was not told of Julius Nyerere's difficulties. International journalists had more pressing assignments than to correct the notion that Tanganyika was a peaceful haven on a turbulent continent. It was therefore all the more shocking for Europe and America to learn on January 20, 1964, that the Tanganyika Army had mutinied and that in the ensuing looting and disorder seventeen persons had been killed. These events sadly tarnished Tanganyika's image as the model African territory where, despite the turmoil of the nationalist struggle, democratic methods had taken root, where there was an innate respect for the law, where responsible citizens could feel secure for their lives and property.

Julius Nyerere had known all along–and so had Sir Richard Turnbull and his senior British civil servants–that this image had been sentimental rather than realistic. The wild exhortations of some of Tanu's less disciplined district chairmen in 1958 and 1959 had come near to releasing the explosive force that underlay Tanganyika's deceptively calm surface; the financial crisis of 1961, if it had been allowed to develop, might have taken an ugly turn. But, generally speaking, the unease that threatens any multi-racial society had been little in evidence. This unease differs in no way from that which is dormant and from time to time manifests itself in other parts of Africa. It is resentment that the 'haves' should have so much and the 'have nots' so little, and its strength is due to the fact that the demarcation line between the two groups is racial as well as economic.

Nyerere himself has often remarked on this state of affairs, and has said that the whole of East Africa is sitting on a powder magazine. It was friends and admirers abroad who had created the impression that Tanganyika was immune to the dangers of this situation. Yet Tanganyika *was* in a way immune, or had a partial immunity that may have been temporary. The mutiny could well have resulted in an attack on the 'haves' by the 'have nots'. It did not. Arabs, it is true, were beaten up, but this was in repayment of a century old grudge. Asians were not seriously molested, although

419

their shops were looted. Europeans, other than the British officers, were handled roughly once or twice, but not more roughly than were the members of the Government who tried to intervene.

The mutiny demonstrated that any mob will pillage and loot. But it did not result in racial trouble, though it probably would have done so had it gone on. Put in the perspective of disturbances in other African countries, or in the Middle East, or in India, or in South America, the Tanganyika mutiny of January, 1964, was relatively mild. This may have been due to timidity, or to slowness of reaction; or possibly to a respect for law and order, which kept worse excesses under restraint. Or it may have been that the teachings of Julius Nyerere had been absorbed, and held in check the violent instincts of the soldiers and the corner-boys.

All the same, the old illusions can no longer be maintained. It must, unhappily, be recognised that the qualities of Julius Nyerere, which have gained him and his country such high repute both in Africa and outside, are not always effective when dealing with an internal challenge to established authority.

At the crucial stage, when power-drunk mutineers had the physical means to take over the Government, it was the resolve and audacity of Oscar Kambona that saved the day. He parleyed with the mutineers and extricated the British officers from their clutches. He admitted, three days before Nyerere could bring himself to do so, that unless British help was called upon, the mutiny could not be put down. The fire might be smothered for a time, but could not be extinguished without the intervention of a strong, disciplined force. Had Kambona had his way, the ring-leaders would have been court-martialled and the guilty executed. Such prompt retribution would have taught a salutary lesson and prevented the recurrence of similar treason for a long time to come.

It demonstrates Nyerere's prestige and the devotion felt for him personally that neither during the mutinies, nor in their aftermath, was the slightest effort made to dislodge him from the presidency or to restrict his wide powers. He was able to re-start the building of modern Tanganyika at the head of the same team that he had led before January 20, 1964. From the moment he took the reins of Government into his hands again, he acted, as he always had, in accordance with democratic principles. For instance, it was on his insistence that the mutineers were tried by the Chief Justice in the Tanganyika High Court. He was disappointed by the relatively lenient sentences passed on them. Imprisonment, even for fifteen years, did not demonstrate to every Tanganyikan that rebellion against the lawful Government was as evil a crime as it was possible to commit. Nyerere let the sentences stand, hoping that the Tanganyika public would take to heart his example of abiding by the decisions of the courts, although these decisions were potentially damaging to his administration.

Nyerere may have tended to idealise the reactions of his country-men to democratic processes, but his judgment was unerringly realistic in matters of foreign policy. He never underestimated the dangers of Communist infiltration. He knew, before the West awoke to the threat, that the Communist powers wanted to turn Zanzibar into an African Cuba. To foil their plans, he initiated the union of Tanganyika and Zanzibar. With patient resolution and without ever losing sight of his ultimate purpose, he is giving Zanzibar politicians plenty of time to adjust themselves to the new conditions. The great question mark of Tanganyika's future is whether or not Nyerere's design will work out in the manner in which he has planned it.

Although Tanganyika has shown that not even her army can be relied on to stand apart from the intrigues, the plot and counter-plot and endless suspicion that play such a frighteningly large part in African life, she still has a national *mystique*. It was evolved under German rule, compounded of shared triumphs and mise-ries, common resentments and common pride of achievement. She has a social structure based on indigenous institutions restored and revitalised by that incomparable administrator, Sir Donald Cameron, and adapted by Nyerere to fit the needs of the present day. She has a true *lingua franca* in the Swahili tongue. Facts of geography and the course of history have excluded Tanganyika from the impact of the great Hamitic and Nilotic migrations that have left such a simmering cauldron of ethnic rivalries in the other East African countries. She can call on a broad fund of sympathy and desire to help, less extensive perhaps now than it was in the early months of independence, but well capable of being restored to its earlier state.

Against these assets must be balanced the liabilities. Tanganyika has a degree of poverty, ignorance and ill-health that would daunt men of lesser character than the present leaders. And, above all, she lacks the trained and experienced manpower without which no

P

development plan, however skilfully devised and however lavishly financed, can be properly administered.

In Tanganyika, as in other African countries, it is the lack of trained men which is most bitterly resented. The British are constantly blamed for failing to train the civil and mechanical engineers, the mining experts, the geologists, the surveyors and the economists. And indeed the record is not as good as it might be. Embittered men make the wild statement that higher education had been withheld deliberately to keep Africa in subjection. This is nonsense. But there was neglect. The reason was lack of money and the reluctance of young Africans to accept the exacting discipline of science and engineering. They preferred the softer options of sociology, journalism and the law.

Africans feel that their independence is not real as long as they must rely on foreign technicians and professional men, and their own graduates must accept advice and leadership from foreigners. Would it not be better, and more dignified, they ask each other, to rely upon local resources and to accept a rate of advance that would be slower but would owe nothing to the West or to the East?

In contrast to these prejudiced patriots, Julius Nyerere understands all too well that Tanganyika cannot progress alone. Announcing the £246 million Development Plan, he gave forceful answers to African as well as European criticism.

We had to get control of both the government and the administration ourselves [he said], and we had to show both others and ourselves that we could run our country. We have shown that we can. We are now in a position where by our own decision we wish to advance much faster than we can do without experienced technical help. And we now know which are the highly political tasks for which we must have local people in order to safeguard our own control of the nation. (May 12, 1964.)

By this statement Nyerere not only gave a lead, but implied that without expert technical help, the advance to a higher standard of living—the main purpose of the Development Plan—would not be just slowed but would be reversed. And he has made it clear that this help would have to come from outside.

Tanganyika's present leaders would probably agree with the author that their country's best hope lies in a combination of its own strength—its co-operatives and its tradition of self-help—with the modern technical skill and financial support that the countries of the West are ready to give. This aid is not entirely without strings; that kind of aid does not exist and he who offers it is a fraud. But at least it will not be directed towards insinuating alien ideologies into Tanganyika.

Julius Nyerere still has to contend with one of the inevitable by-products of his campaign against the colonial régime, the unjustified conviction that Tanganyika has been robbed and exploited by the Arabs, the Indians, the Germans and the British. All the same, he shares with his people the determination that, not even for economic or political advantage shall the country ever be placed in any kind of dependent position *vis-à-vis* a great power. He feels that a close identification with either East or West could be bought at too high a price and at too great a risk of a return to the circumstances of the past. This is the cause of his reluctance to committ himself to any association that might conceivably turn out, at some future time, to be an embarrassment.

But neither Nyerere, nor any other leader, can divorce his country from the rest of the world politically, for that is what non-alignment amounts to, and yet remain attached to it by receiving financial and economic aid, whether from the East, or from the West, or from both.

In the life of a country, as in that of a man or a woman, decisions have to be taken and companionships formed. In the world of today, Tanganyika will reap the greatest benefits by remaining an active, positive member of the Commonwealth and by keeping a close relationship with Great Britain. This is the company in which Tanganyika can best meet the challenge of the future.

APPENDIX I

Letter from Julius Nyerere to Sir Richard Turnbull

TANGANYIKA PARLIAMENT

December 4th, 1962

Dear Sir Richard,

Parting with friends is always a problem. I am therefore trying to get round it by saying 'kwa heri' to you *after* you have left; for you are not likely to read this letter before all the official farewells are over.

When your appointment was announced in 1958, the immediate reaction in Tanganyika nationalist circles was that this was a Bad Thing. I was asked to protest to the Secretary of State for his 'blunder' in appointing the 'notorious' Sir Richard from Kenya to be our Governor. I did not protest; because I argued that since I was opposed to colonialism as such I could see no reason for protesting against the appointment of any particular individual to represent that colonialism in Tanganyika. I could demand self-government, but I could hardly ask for an 'acceptable' Governor; that would have been a contradiction in terms.

We had intended 1958 to be a decisive year in the political history of Tanganyika. In January we had passed the 'Responsible Government 1959' Resolution at Tabora; with the alternative of Positive Action if our demands were not met. In June the Government brought an action against me for libel. Politically, this was very good; it would speed things up. I was secretly hoping I would be found guilty and sentenced to gaol, or at least given the option of going to gaol or paying a fine. In fact I was determined to go to gaol, and thus bring matters to a head. Our first parliamentary elections were due to take place in September, but so confident was I that by that time I should be in gaol that I had Elias Kisenge standing by as my understudy for the seat I was supposed to contest–in case the 'star' should be 'prevented from appearing'.

Then you came. I expected that you would want to meet me, but I imagined you would wait until I had been sentenced. To my surprise you did not; but called me to Government House while the case was still undecided. I do not remember the exact date, but I do remember your first words to me: 'I am glad to meet you, Mr Nyerere. You and I have a great responsibility in this country.'

Then we got down to business. We had fifty-five minutes together, during which I explained our demands for Responsible Government. By that we meant a majority of Elected Members in Legco, and a majority of Elected Ministers in the Government. These, you thought, were 'reasonable' demands. So, I may say, did I. But it had not occurred to me that the Bad Sir Richard would be of the same mind.

My most serious complaint against the British has been that they never locked me up. But it is not really fair to blame them for this. It was your fault. For the magistrate did find me guilty, and gave me the sentence for which I had been hoping–a fine or prison. The only trouble was that the offer of 'Her Majesty's hospitality' came too late! In spite of my original contention that all colonial Governors were the same to me, my first meeting with you had persuaded me that *one* Governor, at least, deserved to be given a chance. My going to prison would have given you no chance at all. It would have meant certain trouble. I chose to pay the fine after all. And, although subsequent events have made it rather unlikely that I shall ever again have an opportunity of uninterrupted meditation in a prison cell, I cannot honestly say I have ever regretted my decision.

Nevertheless, if my reputation as an agitator is slightly dimmed by my inability to add the letters 'P.G.' after my name, you must accept the blame for that. For, however inappropriate the term 'reasonable' may be for an agitator, a 'reasonable' Governor is sufficiently rare a phenomenon to unsettle even the most orthodox of nationalists.

And now let me say 'Bon Voyage', with my very best wishes to you and to Lady Turnbull for a merry Christmas and every happiness in the future.

Yours very sincerely,
Julius K. Nyerere

Sir Richard Turnbull, K.C.M.G.

APPENDIX II

Sources

A HISTORY of Tanganyika over the centuries must, none the less, lay special emphasis on the developments of recent years. This involved the difficult and dangerous business of attempting to write the contemporary history of an ex-colonial country. I therefore count myself exceptionally fortunate in having been able to draw upon, as my source material, the direct evidence of the main participants in the struggle for independence. All three parties–Africans, Europeans and Asians–have been willing to talk to me at length, and have enabled me to learn at first hand their different points of view. Without this help, so kindly given, the writing of this book would not have been possible at all.

With each of the persons concerned I was granted a personal interview during which I jotted down short essential notes. While what I had heard was still fresh in my memory, I wrote a full transcript of the conversation and submitted it to my informant for correction and amendment. If extensive alterations were made to my text (this happened only twice) I redrafted and again submitted it for approval. In some cases I also submitted the whole chapter written on the basis of the information so obtained.

It was in the first place the idea of Marion, Lady Chesham, a Member of the Tanganyika Parliament, that I should write a history of Tanganyika. In 1961 she invited me to stay with her and introduced me to Julius Nyerere. He encouraged me to carry out Lady Chesham's suggestion. To my objection that I knew nothing about Tanganyika, President Nyerere rejoined that, coming out with a fresh mind, I would soon collect my material, and not being British by birth, I would have no inhibitions about interpreting it dispassionately. He promised to answer all my questions and to place at my disposal any information I needed. He kept his promise most liberally, even at the time when he was occupied with the tremendous task of welding the Tanganyikan people into one nation.

In 1961 and 1962 in Dar-es-Salaam I met all the members of the then Tanganyika Governments. Among the Africans I was most effectively helped by Rashidi Kawawa, Paul Bomani, George Kahama, Michael Kamaliza, Lucy Lameck and Edward Barongo. All of them corrected the transcript of our conversation in their own hands. So did Elias Kisenge, Deputy-Organising Secretary of Tanu, and Dr Vedast Kyaruzi, at that time Permanent Head of the Foreign Affairs Ministry. Ally Sykes, who vividly remembers the early days of Tanu, showed me documents and Press clippings which he alone has collected.

Amir Jamal, Julius Nyerere's closest friend among the Asians and one of his ablest colleagues, told me of his recollections of the independence struggle. So did Al Noor Kassum, who has also provided me with facts and figures about education.

Sir Ernest Vasey, who was Minister of Finance when I first met him, explained to me Tanganyika's financial problem; Barbro Johansson, the dedicated Swedish Lutheran missionary who is also a Member of the Tanganyika Parliament, invited me to her home in Mwanza to show me the work she was doing among her constituents.

Father Gerald Rupper, Principal of the Benedictine Fathers' Teachers' Training College at Paramiho, near Songea, has helped me to piece together the story of the *Maji-Maji* uprising; Father Michele Musso of the Consolata Fathers' mission at Tosamaganga, near Iringa, has allowed me to use as yet unpublished material which he has gathered about the Hehe tribe. Father Arthur Wille, head of the Maryknoll Fathers' Mission near Butiama, has told me about the Zanaki, Julius Nyerere's tribe, and secured for me a collection of Zanaki legends and traditions, which also has not previously been published.

I am especially indebted to Father Richard Walsh, the eminent White Father who spent some twenty years in Tanganyika and afforded special guidance to Julius Nyerere from 1946 until the time he gave up teaching for a political career. Father Walsh not only loved his African charges, but foresaw future developments and persuaded them to go into public life. Despite the heavy burden of work which he bears as the Second Assistant to the General of his Order in Rome, he has been untiring in answering my numerous verbal and written questions.

A great many British civil servants have told me of their experiences, helping me to obtain a rounded picture of developments. Barclay Leechman, who spent his entire life in Tanganyika and who, since his retirement, has been President of the Sisal Board, has filled in many gaps in my knowledge. He has an excellent memory and has been closely acquainted with Tanganyika affairs for over forty years. Lord Twining has been good enough to discuss with me in detail his three terms as Governor of Tanganyika.

I have talked to, or corresponded with, several headmasters of Tabora Government School, where a vast number of the Africans who are now taking part in Tanganyikan public life were educated. Alfred Travers Lacey, the founder of this great institution and now well over eighty years old, has written to me extensively from South Africa. Unfortunately, a few weeks before I got in touch with him, he had destroyed his records. This is a great loss for Tanganyika, as the story of Tabora Government School should one day be told in detail. Charles Whybrow, John Blumer and John Crabbe, all three former headmasters, have read and passed my chapter dealing with education. Maureen Cowan and Mary Hancock have told me about Tabora Girls' School, of which both have been headmistresses. Miss Hancock is a devoted friend of the Nyerere family; while Julius and Maria Nyerere were struggling with financial difficulties, two of their children lived with her.

Many more people have discussed with me different aspects of Tanganyika's development. Arthur Creech Jones, the former Labour Colonial Secretary, read and approved several chapters; it was sad to hear the news of his death while these lines were being typed. Iain Macleod, the former Conservative Colonial Secretary, has related to me the remarkable inner history of the independence negotiations and approved the two chapters dealing with it.

John Strachey and Sir Leslie Plummer have told me their version of the Groundnut Scheme; both died in 1963, as did John Dugdale, who had given me a written description of the incident which forced him to walk out of a party near Arusha in 1949. Colonel David Stirling and Robin Johnston have related the Capricorn story to me.

The librarian of the Colonial Office, B. Cheeseman, and J. A. Wright, the librarian of the Commonwealth Relations Office, have unearthed elusive pieces of information, saving me many hours of work. In the bibliography I have listed the books and the publications which I have studied and from some of which I have quoted. Duncan Sandys, as Secretary of State for Commonwealth Relations, could not see his way to make available to me certain confidential material, but his department was good enough to look up accounts of specially significant incidents and events when there was no other way for me to reach a reliable conclusion.

On the vital and difficult question of evaluating material and personalities, I owe an enormous debt to Sir Richard Turnbull, the last Governor and Governor-General of Tanganyika. Both in Dar-es-Salaam and in London he has been unsparing of his time in order to advise me. He has immense knowledge of East Africa and has been the key figure on what I might call the Government House side of Tanganyika's independence struggle. Without Sir Richard's guidance, the last part of the story could not have been told accurately. He has read my entire MS twice and thanks to his clear recollection of what happened, I have been able to present an authoritative account.

My warm thanks go to John Churchill, who read and edited the MS. His comments on my drafts, sometimes written in the small hours of the night, have taught me a good deal about English grammar and literary style.

John White, from 1959 to 1962 *The Times* correspondent in Africa south of the Sahara, has further edited the whole book with the specialist knowledge he gained as a witness of the last phase of Tanganyika's role as a Trust Territory.

In writing what is, I hope, an honest and dispassionate account of the birth of a modern African nation, I am deeply grateful for the help and guidance that has been so generously given me from so many sources. I alone, however, am responsible for the attitude which I have taken towards the events related or the conclusions which I have drawn from them.

*

APPENDIX III

The Army Mutinies, 1964

EVER since Independence, there had been sporadic threats of an Army mutiny. Early in January, 1964, the Minister of External Affairs and Defence, Oscar Kambona, heard there was to be trouble at Colito Barracks on January 16. He was not worried as there had been similar rumours before.

The rumours had some foundation in fact. There had been difficulties about fifteen officers who had been trained in Israel, about the type of officer put forward for training by the Government, about delayed promotions, unpublicised Africanisation and army pay.

Early in 1963, Oscar Kambona sent fifteen young men to be indoctrinated in Israel as youth leaders. While they were there, he reassigned them as officers to the army. In the past, officers had always been selected by the National Selection Board, with great care and according to strictly prescribed educational and physical standards. Each time the necessary qualifications had been published in the newspapers.

At the last Selection Board, held on January 6, 1964, the Vice-President, Rashidi Kawawa, who presided over it, turned down all the candidates nominated by the Minister of External Affairs and Defence.

On their return from Israel at the end of August, 1963, it became obvious that the fifteen young men were unsuited for military careers. African officers and N.C.O.s of the Tanganyika Rifles were quick to discover and to comment on their shortcomings, both educational and physical.

About this time, Kambona visited the battalion and walked around the barracks talking to the soldiers. No officer, African or British, was allowed to be present. One group of senior N.C.O.s Kambona told quite falsely that the only reason why they had not been made officers was that the Commander would not recommend them.

Force Headquarters did its best to train up Kambona's men for the appointments they had been given. But both at a three weeks' course organised for them in Dar-es-Salaam and at a second course at the East African Military Training School in Kenya, they showed no aptitude either for military training or for discipline.

In view of their poor showing, the Minister agreed to drop the bottom five from the Force, but at the time of the mutiny, these five men were still in the First Battalion, as no one in civilian life or in National Service was prepared to employ them.

In October, 1963, a new Commanding Officer was appointed to the

First Battalion. He found that his British officers were completely loyal to the Tanganyika Army Council, although they had not been specially selected for their jobs in Tanganyika. Lt.-Col. Mans made a special point about their learning Swahili, or improving their knowledge of it. Kambona showed little appreciation for these efforts and was not prepared to promote British trained African officers.

After President Nyerere's dramatic circular of January 7, 1964, that 'Africanisation is dead', the Minister gave way on this point. He then demanded that a plan be worked out for the removal of all British officers from the Tanganyika Rifles by the end of 1964. As it was, British officers and N.C.O.s were not being replaced when their time of secondment finished, except for certain specialists. There were then about thirty trained African officers with a further fifteen on officers' training courses in Britain. At the time of Independence in 1961, there had been only three trained African officers.

Kambona also stipulated that young, talented African officers should not be put in command positions, but should assist older men who, although less qualified, were to be promoted.

By this time the British officers were under the impression that Oscar Kambona wanted to set himself up as the Army's sole friend, and that he blamed all difficulties on them in order to undermine the authority of all officers, British as well as African. They believed that the Minister observed army rules and regulations only if and when it suited him. This had, in their view, been illustrated in March, 1963, after the mutiny of the Junior Leaders' Wing, when in flat contradiction to the Commander's recommendations and of army regulations, the ring-leaders were not court-martialled, but dismissed with the lame explanation that 'their services are not wanted'. All this destroyed the happy atmosphere that had existed in the Tanganyika Force, for which there had always been more volunteers than could possibly be accepted.

At this point the course of events in Tanganyika was to be aggravated by the alarming news that a bloody revolt had broken out in Zanzibar. On January 12, 1964, the world Press carried the news that the Sultan had been deposed and his Government overthrown with considerable loss of life. The plot was headed by the self-styled 'Field-Marshal' John Okello.

Already on January 7, 1964, a shipment of arms had arrived in Dar-es-Salaam in an Algerian ship. The Press got wind of it, and Kambona made a public statement, in which he said that the arms were a gift from Algeria to the Tanganyika Rifles. (Actually, they were paid for in coffee.) Journalists reported that no British officer or N.C.O. had been seen anywhere near the ship during the unloading, although the consignment went into the Army Store Depot; this, they added had for some days also been barred to British officers and N.C.O.s.

Gossip in Dar-es-Salaam had it that the arms *cache* had been intended for an uprising in Mozambique, which did not take place. It was also said that some marked cases were then to have gone to Zanzibar, but did not arrive in time for 'Field-Marshal' Okello's plot. Moreover, instead of 'sophisticated modern weapons', this *cache* was found to contain much travelled Second World War weapons.

Dar-es-Salaam was by now rife with rumours. Some had it that Kambona was planning to set himself up as supreme authority, retaining Nyerere merely as a figurehead. Others had it that the army was about to mutiny and that African officers and other ranks were to take over the Government.

On January 12, the day of 'Field-Marshal' Okello's coup, the First Battalion of the Tanganyika Rifles was placed on the alert and told to be ready to fly to Zanzibar at a moment's notice. Later this order was countermanded, although President Nyerere had gone to Arusha, to avoid contact with a régime apparently set up by a rival of his friend, Sheik Abeid Karume. The bloodshed, for which Nyerere rightly held Okello responsible, deeply shocked him. Yet it was plain that some members of the Tanganyika Government sympathised with Okello's take-over. A few days later, Karume and Okello made up their differences—if indeed these had ever existed—and subsequently it was Okello who was asked to leave Zanzibar and Tanganyika and declared a prohibited immigrant.

Two facts, apart from the Zanzibar events, seem to have influenced the Tanganyika mutinies. First, Nyerere's circular against excessive Africanisation annoyed many young Africans, particularly the students of the Law Faculty and of Kivukoni College, whose reaction was: 'Never mind the standards, give us the jobs and we will learn to do them.' Secondly, nauseated by the murders, Nyerere sent the Dar-es-Salaam Field Police, 300 men, to restore order in Zanzibar.

Now for the chronology of the mutinies.

At 1.50 a.m. on Monday, January 20, 1964, a general alarm and a fire alarm were sounded at Colito Barracks in Dar-es-Salaam. All officers on duty, who rushed to their stations in uniform, were arrested and locked into the guardroom. Other officers were rounded up at bayonet point from their houses, some in pyjamas. The C.O., who drove from his house to the Barracks with his British R.S.M., was forced out of his car and also taken to the guardroom. The African officers were locked up with the British officers;[1] later during the night they were called out

---

[1] Lt.-Col. Alex Nyirenda, who on Independence Night placed a torch on the summit of Mount Kilimanjaro, was not among them. A few days previously he had hurt his back playing football. As he could not stand up, the mutineers sent him home.

one by one, and at gunpoint assigned to various tasks. One British officer escaped from the mutineers; his wife was molested. Brigadier Douglas, who had unexpectedly returned from his week-end cottage to his house near the barracks, managed to get away across the hill with his wife and child to a friend's house, who drove them to Dar-es-Salaam along the road not passing Colito Barracks. He then collected members of his staff and tried to organise some resistance, but it was too late as the mutineers were in control of the town. Hence the Brigadier went to the Acting British High Commissioner's house, where he remained for four days.

In Nachingwea, where one company was stationed, the mutineers were polite, almost apologetic. Not so in Tabora. The Second Battalion also mutinied and several officers were manhandled. At Kazima Secondary School, an integrated day school, the mutineers asked the children which teachers they did not like? These they lined up against the wall under gun cover and fired a blank shot into the back of one British woman teacher. In fact, they beat up all Europeans and Asians who crossed their paths. The wife of one of the officers had had a baby the day before: she was made to get up and was driven to the airport in her nightgown. Against this, they issued the Tabora Education officer, a European, with a 'good conduct pass'.

The British officers in Colito Barracks guardroom were astonished by the efficiency with which they had been rounded up. They were even more amazed to learn that, in addition to the airport, the Tanganyika Broadcasting Corporation and the railway station, three obvious military targets, the Post Office, the Cable and Wireless Building and the Standard Bank were also placed under guard. The vaults of the Standard Bank housed the Tanganyika State money. Moreover, road blocks had been constructed at well-chosen strategic points. Joseph Nyerere, M.P. brother of the President, has told the author that an askari, who was not among the ring-leaders, had said to him: 'We planned all this for weeks and we are still surprised that the clever European officers did not find out about our preparations.'

The mutiny was organised by some twenty men, headed by a sergeant who styled himself 'Major' Hingo, but whose proper name was Ilogi. The British officers believe that 'Major' Hingo and the corporals who were his friends had outside advice. If they had, it is inexplicable why on January 20 this anonymous source of advice did not tell the mutineers to take over the Government, which was completely at their mercy.

Security men roused President Nyerere about two a.m. with the news that the mutineers were on their way to State House. They insisted, as did hastily contacted Ministers like Rashidi Kawawa and Paul Bomani, who lived within a few hundred yards of State House, that he should not risk sharing the fate of Sylvano Olympio, President of Togo, who was murdered by an Army revolt on January 13, 1963. This may have influenced Nyerere's decision to go into temporary hiding, although it is more likely that his main consideration was not personal safety, but time to think out the next move. Being of a contemplative nature, this was a physical necessity for him. Unfortunately, in a revolutionary situation bold action alone can achieve results. For the next forty-eight hours, Oscar Kambona was the only Tanganyika leader to show the resourcefulness needed in an unprecedented situation.

According to the evidence given at the mutineers' trials, (they began on April 27, 1964,) at about 2.30 a.m., twenty-five of them, headed by Sergeant Hingo Ilogi, forced their way past the sentries at State House to see the President. As they could not find him, they went to fetch Oscar Kambona. Having heard the news of the mutiny by telephone from Brigadier Douglas, the Minister was fully dressed. The mutineers told him that all the officers had been arrested and would remain in detention until he agreed to their demands for increased pay and the removal of all European officers. With two Police Commissioners and a party of mutineers, Kambona drove to Colito Barracks to try to negotiate with the men. As he could not agree to their demands without sanction from the President, the mutineers drove him back to State House. But as again they could not find Nyerere, the mutineers drove the Minister for a second time to Colito Barracks. When Kambona tried to address them, they knocked him about and threatened to shoot him.[2]

About 3.30 a.m. Job Lusinde, the Minister for Home Affairs, drove to State House and at the gate met the Acting British High Commissioner, Steven Miles, who had also heard of the mutiny from Brigadier Douglas. Both Lusinde and Miles were arrested by the mutineers and kept in confinement for two hours.

Meanwhile, at the Barracks, Kambona induced a chosen group of mutineers to negotiate after all. His first concession was that the Government would replace European officers with African officers; the second that the Government would immediately discuss matters of pay. In return, he insisted firstly on the release of the British officers who, he feared, might either be murdered or be used as hostages, and secondly on the return of the troops to barracks. Assisted by Peter A. Carter of the High Commissioner's staff, Kambona eventually succeeded in getting the British officers out of custody and drove with them to the airport. There the askaris were in a state of wild excitement, shouting incoherently, and shooting into the air. Some said sarcastically to Lt.-Col. Mans, C.O. of the First Battalion: '*Kwa heri Mwalimu*,' 'Good-

---

[2] Kambona had a black eye and a swollen face. Three more members of the Government were also beaten up. There are many eye witnesses to this.

bye teacher.' Others showed little respect even for Kambona, whose orders they ignored. The officers' families were flown to Nairobi in the evening of the same day.

Most inhabitants of Dar-es-Salaam learnt about the mutiny in the morning from their African servants, some of whom were late having been held up at road blocks. About eight a.m. a Resident Magistrate, Mr Oruhu, came to Joseph Nyerere to tell him that a mutiny had broken out and that State House was in the hands of the mutineers. He advised Joseph Nyerere to go into hiding, especially because he had criticised the Army in his speeches.

'But my mother is at State House,' Joseph Nyerere replied and jumped into his car. The mutineers stopped him at the gate and told him he could not go in adding: 'But your mother is fine, we are taking care of her.'

As the gate was open, Joseph Nyerere forced his way through and drove up to State House. There the mutineers arrested him, put him on a Land-Rover and drove him to Colito Barracks. Bokhe Munanka, Tanu's National Treasurer, was forced to drive there in his own car. Like Joseph Nyerere, he too was roughly treated; but as many askaris came from Bukoba, a district Munanka knew well, they gradually became more friendly. Munanka is a Kurya, and his tribe lives in the Tarime district.

At Colito Barracks, Joseph Nyerere and Bokhe Munanka were allowed to talk to Oscar Kambona, and learnt from him what had happened. Nyerere accompanied Kambona and the British officers to the airport. As this undignified convoy passed through the African part of the town, people realised that law and order had been suspended, especially as not a single policeman was to be seen. Soon after, looting broke out in the Arab and Asian bazaars, and caused much damage. Seventeen persons were killed, one of them an Arab refugee from Zanzibar, who had a loaded rifle with which he shot dead two askaris and two civilians. He was massacred with his entire family. Twenty persons were seriously injured, a hundred had minor injuries.

At noon on January 20, Job Lusinde appealed to Jomo Kenyatta, Prime Minister of Kenya, by telephone to send troops to help restore order. When on his return from the airport, Oscar Kambona learnt of this, he too rang Kenyatta and assured him that the situation had improved so much that help from outside was no longer necessary. By three in the afternoon, the police got on top of the looting, and it seeemd that Kambona's judgment had been correct.

In the evening Kambona broadcast to the country in Swahili. Introduced as 'your Minister of Foreign Affairs', he said in a shaken voice: 'I am speaking to you as your Minister of Foreign Affairs. There has been some misunderstanding between Africans and British troops of the First Battalion of the Tanganyika Rifles. . . . After my intervention the soldiers have now returned to barracks.' He appealed for calm, then went on: 'The Tanganyika Rifles and the police are still loyal to the Government, and law and order have been completely restored.' The uprising had been a purely military affair and not inspired by politics.

Two things impressed listeners: Kambona was announced and signed off as 'your Foreign Minister' and he repeated this twice in his address. Yet he never mentioned Nyerere and spoke throughout in the first person singular. Moreover, some of the troops instead of going back to barracks, were roaming around with their rifles.

By the evening, H.M.S. *Rhyl*, with men of the Staffordshire Regiment on board, arrived from Zanzibar in Dar-es-Salaam. The Admiralty also announced that 'the armed might of the British Commando carrier H.M.S. *Centaur*', with 600 Royal Marines and light aircraft on board, had left Aden to stand by off the East African coast.

On the morning of January 21, everyone went back to work as usual. The incidents of the previous day, when some mutineers had appropriated wallets and valuables of business men trying to get to their offices, were not repeated. There was a rumour that another looting outbreak was under way, this time in the centre of the town, whereupon all the shops on Independence Avenue closed and put their grilles up. At this stage the Indian community panicked and made the roads unsafe by driving blindly up-country. Some Europeans also lost their heads, though not many. By the afternoon, the police had everything under control. At that stage, only six policemen had shown sympathy for the mutineers.

That night the President resumed his duties at State House and his voice was heard on the radio. He spoke only for three minutes in Swahili and was introduced as the Father of the Nation. He said:

Yesterday there was some trouble in Dar-es-Salaam. You have been already told that this trouble finished the same day, and I do not propose to talk about it any more. My first purpose this evening is to ask you to remain calm.

Yesterday some people went about spreading rumours and claiming that I was no longer here and that my Ministers were no longer here and that there was no Government. Such rumours make a little trouble seem bigger then it really is.

Secondly, I want to warn you citizens not to get into a panic and spread false rumours. It is not a sign of a grown up. A grown up man is calm. Many citizens were in fact calm, but there were some Europeans, Asians and Africans who got into a panic, spread dangerous rumours and did things which might have brought harm to the country.

There are also some people in all countries who are an utter disgrace and who think – as some did in Dar-es-Salaam yesterday – that this is an opportunity to loot and to break into houses and take other peoples' property. It is possible that they believed there was no Government. But they soon learnt their lesson. It is a sad story that some people, among them two servicemen, lost their lives. On behalf of the whole country, I express my condolences to their families and pray that their souls may rest in peace.

Yesterday was a most disgraceful day. I thank all citizens who helped to minimize this disgrace and stopped it spreading further. My hope is that we shall never see such a disgrace repeated in Tanganyika.

On January 22 the President toured the city, which greatly reassured people, and calm returned once more. Meanwhile negotiations with the mutineers about pay and promotion continued. The President insisted on treating the mutiny as an industrial dispute, for the soldiers had all the strength and the Government was powerless. It was on the morning of this day, the Wednesday, that Kambona first began to face the fact that the mutineers would not abide by any agreement, and that outside help would be necessary to save the Government. Nyerere would not hear of it, for outside help could only mean British help. The Government had been informed that 650 Commandos on board H.M.S. *Centaur*, which had arrived accompanied by H.M.S. *Cambria*, were available, and if help was needed, the Government had only to ask for it in writing. They were also told that in the event of another outbreak of violence, troops would be landed to protect British and allied lives, and if necessary evacuate them.

At three in the afternoon, Nyerere, flanked by leading members of his Government, held a Press conference. He disappointed reporters by refusing either to condemn the mutineers outright, or to say whether or not they would be punished. The reason for this prevarication was the Government's utter powerlessness.

Two hours later, at Karimjee Hall, there was a meeting in honour of the late Dag Hammarskjöld. Organised by the University College of Dar-es-Salaam, an intellectual, multi-racial gathering filled the hall. The President was the speaker of the day. When he came in, looking tired and very thin in his black suit, he was given a five minute stand-up ovation. His speech lasted an hour and a half. He had written it earlier on, and it was a philosophical dissertation on Hammarskjöld's work for peace and betterment in the world. Only Nyerere's close friends realised under what strain he was, and what it cost him to deliver this lecture.

While in Dar-es-Salaam Nyerere paid tribute to Dag Hammarskjöld's memory, a very different meeting was held at Morogoro, some two hundred miles inland. A political plot, engineered by the black racialists, and headed by Victor Mkello and Christopher Tumbo (who had slipped back from his self-imposed exile in Mombasa) began to take shape. The plotters discussed what use they could make of the mutiny in order to obtain power, and having obtained it, what kind of Government they should form. Harun Lugusha, who was no black racialist, but a frustrated, ambitious politician, was also present. He declared himself ready to accept high office in a Mkello–Tumbo régime.

News of the Morogoro plot reached Kambona early on January 23. This, added to the behaviour of the mutineers, was rank treason. Yet Nyerere was so anxious to avoid bringing in British troops and to sustain a façade of unity, that he was prepared to show leniency to them.

This was of no avail. On the morning of January 24, Kambona even accepted 'elected officers' among those to be promoted, yet suddenly the mutineers became much more arrogant and turned their backs on their 'elected officers'. The cause was not far to seek: the Morogoro plotters had established contact with the mutineers and were by now planning to take over the State. At this stage the police were also on the point of mutinying.

The previous day Milton Obote, Prime Minister of Uganda, who had been faced with a somewhat similar situation, had, without consulting anyone, called in British troops, and they had already settled the mutineers of Kampala. Then it was learnt that Jomo Kenyatta had done the same in order to deal with the Kenya Rifles mutineers at Lanet Barracks.

Under the impact of all this, at last at six o'clock in the evening of January 24, Nyerere signed a letter requesting British help. Kambona took it to the Acting British High Commissioner. Later, at eight o'clock, accompanied by Paul Bomani, Kambona returned to the house where Brigadier Douglas had been hiding, and discussed the situation with him. After the two Ministers had left, the Brigadier and one Staff Officer, Major Brian Marciandi, were taken to Dar-es-Salaam; after some difficulty contact was established with *Centaur*. A boat came in and took them out to *Centaur*, which they reached about 1.30 a.m. on January 25.

The operation was complicated by the presence of so many women and children at the barracks; great precautions had to be taken to avoid loss of life. While plans were being worked out to land by helicopter close to the barracks and to accompany the landing by as much noise as possible, London's consent was transmitted to *Centaur*.

The attack went in at 6.20 a.m.; eight helicopters landed with full equipment, jeeps hanging from their bellies, and H.M.S. *Cambria* fired a terrifying sounding barrage with blank ammunition. The first company then made for the armoury and ammunition store, while the remaining companies were being flown in.

The second person to step on to the Sports Ground of Colito Barracks was the Brigadier. When it was seen that there was still firing from the guardroom and the armoury, he gave the mutineers ten minutes to surrender and near the end did the last count-down of ten seconds himself. Three askaris were killed and several wounded. All casualties were flown to *Centaur*, where two more askaris died.

After a single bomb had been lobbed on to the armoury, the mutineers surrendered in droves. No one tried to shoot it out, although they had arms and ammunition in plenty. A few ran away into the bush, one Land-Rover load went as far as Tanga, but all were soon captured.

The performance of the British troops was a superb one, and the mutiny collapsed in less than thirty minutes. Pressmen and photographers naturally went to the beach to watch and to photograph, but the Tanganyika police confiscated their cameras and exposed their films—the world was not to see a pictorial record of how African troops were being disarmed by British troops. Only the B.B.C. and the A.F.P. films were saved.

Yet the Commandos were welcomed not only by the Europeans, but also by the Africans, many of whom told them that they felt free of fear for the first time in months. Indeed, the British were asked to hold the town for a week, during which time President Nyerere carried out his great purge. He once told the author: 'I can only be ruthless when I am very angry, and it is such an effort to become very angry.' This time his anger was great, and no doubt his humiliation.

All labour leaders, some fifty policemen, a few politicians, and the mutineers were placed under lock and key. After due screening, those who could prove their innocence were released, but six labour leaders and a dozen others, in fact the Morogoro plotters and their sympathisers, will remain behind bars or in internment camps for a long time to come.

On January 25, 1964, President Nyerere wrote a letter to the Secretary of State for Commonwealth Relations in which he said:

It is with deep gratitude that I write to acknowledge the help which has been given by Britain to Tanganyika today. I do this on behalf of the whole Tanganyika people, for the disgraceful conduct of the Tanganyika Rifles has led to a situation of fear, with the possibility of much bloodshed.

The prompt agreement to my request for assistance and the magnificent way in which the operation was carried out in the early hours of this morning, leaves Tanganyika much indebted to your Government, the people of Britain, and particularly to the members of the Royal Marine Commandos and the other members of the British forces which have taken part in this activity.

May I say, further, how extremely glad we are that your help has not caused any injury, nor any loss of life, among the British soldiers and sailors involved. Please feel at liberty to inform the British Parliament of the contents of this letter if you so wish. I am anxious that the British people should be aware of our gratitude for this prompt expression of friendship for the Republic of Tanganyika.

Yours sincerely
Julius K. Nyerere.

Duncan Sandys read this letter to the House of Commons on January 28, 1964.

On the same day, at nine a.m. in Dar-es-Salaam, women from all over the capital congregated at Tanu headquarters. They had been summoned by Bibi Titi Mohamed, President of the National Council of Women (Umoja wa Wanamake wa Tanganyika), to march to State House. All and sundry came, including nuns. In their white habits they formed a strange contrast to the Moslem women, wrapped in their opague black cloaks. The marchers seemed in a hurry, for they almost ran to State House; some women lost their shoes and there was confusion galore, but everyone was in a happy mood.

President Nyerere, his wife and Vice-President Kawawa came out on the verandah of State House, to hear the loyal address read by Bibi Titi. In ringing tones she pledged the women's loyalty to the President and then they all sang *Tanu ijenze nchi* (Let Tanu build the country). Deeply moved, Nyerere thanked the women and asked them never to forget the disgraceful actions in which twenty lives had been lost.

During the following days, there were loyalty marches all over Tanganyika. The nicest one was organised by the taxi drivers of Dar-es-Salaam. They decorated their cars and filled them with friends who all seemed in extremely good voice. Last to march were the police, who have since remained true to their vows of loyalty.

On February 24, 1964, President Nyerere made the gesture of summoning to Dar-es-Salaam a meeting of the Organisation of African States to purge himself of the sin of having called in British help. In this he succeeded, although some of the other African leaders commented coldly that he could have achieved the same 'by correspondence'.

As the mutinous Tanganyika Army had been disbanded, Nigeria offered a battalion to take over from the British until a new Tanganyika Army could be trained. Nyerere turned down the British offer to train the new army, although the Nigerians were in due course flown in by British aircraft, having no means of transport of their own.

Thus ended the Tanganyika Army mutiny. With the exception of the ring-leaders, who were subsequently tried and sentenced to long terms of imprisonment, the mutineers were banished to their native villages, where they were treated with contempt. Up-country, people were in no doubt that they had given Tanganyika a bad name before the whole world.

APPENDIX IV

Bibliography

Ansorge, W. J., *Under the African Sun*, 1899
Bates, D., *A Fly-Switch from the Sultan*, 1961
Bennett, G., *An Outline History of Tanu*, No. 7 of *Makerere*, 1962
Blundell, Sir M., *So Rough a Wind–Kenya Memoirs*, 1964
Briggs, J. H., *In the East African War*, 1918
Burton, R., *Lake Regions of Central Africa* 1961 edition
Cameron, Sir D., *My Tanganyika Service and Some Nigeria*, 1939
Carnochan, F. G. and Adamson, H. C., *The Empire of the Snakes*, 1935
—— *Out of Africa*, 1937
Chevenix-Trench, C., *The Desert's Dusty Face*, 1964
Chidzero, B. T. G., *Tanganyika and International Trusteeship*, 1961
Clarke, P. H. C., *A Short History of Tanganyika*, 1960
Cohen, Sir A. B., *British Policy in Changing Africa*, 1959
Coupland, Sir R., *East Africa and its Invaders*, 1938
—— *The Exploitation of East Africa*, 1939
Dinesen, Isak, *Out of Africa*, 1937
—— *Shadows on the Grass*, 1960
Dundas, Sir C., *African Crossroads*, 1955
Friedland, W. H., 'Tanganyika's Rashidi Kawawa', *Africa Report*, VII, February, 1962
Furse, Sir R. D., *Aucuparius, Recollections of a Recruiting Officer*, 1962
Götzen, Graf von, *Durch Afrika von Ost nach West*, 1895
—— *Deutsch-Ostafrika in Aufstand*, 1905–6, 1909
Great Britain, Central Office of Information, Reference Division: *Tanganyika*, 1959
Gunther, J., *Inside Africa*, 1955
Hailey, Lord, *An African Survey*, 1938 (2nd ed. 1957)
Hempstone, S., *The New Africa*, 1961
Höhnel, Ludwig von, *Discovery of Lakes Rudolf and Stefanie: A Narrative of Count Samuel Teleki's Exploring and Hunting Expedition in Eastern Equatorial Africa, 1887–8*
Huntingford, G. N. B. and Bell, C. R. V., *East African Background*, 1950
Huxley, Elspeth, *The Sorcerer's Apprentice: A Journey Through East Africa*, 1948
—— *White Man's Country*, 1956
—— *No Easy Way*, 1958
—— *The Flame Trees of Thika*, 1959
—— *A New Earth: An Experiment in Colonialism* (Kenya), 1960
—— *The Mottled Lizard*, 1962

441

Huxley, Elspeth, *Forks and Hope*, 1964
Ingham, K., *A History of East Africa*, 1962
Kenyatta, Jomo, *Facing Mount Kenya*, 1938
Kitchen, Helen, 'Why Did Julius Nyerere Resign?', *Africa Report*, VII, February, 1962
Lettow-Vorbeck, General P. von, *Mein Leben*, 1957
—— *My Reminiscences of East Africa*, 1920
—— *East African Campaigns*, 1957
Little, Arthur D., Inc., *Tanganyika Industrial Development*, 1961
Lugard, F. J. D., *The Rise of our East African Empire*, 1893
—— 'The Dual Mandate in British Tropical Africa', *Blackwood*, 1922
Mackenzie, D. R., *The Spirit-Ridden Konde*, 1925
Mitchell, Sir P., *African Afterthoughts*, 1954
Moffett, J. P., *Handbook of Tanganyika*, 1958
—— *Tanganyika, A Review of its Resources and Development*, 1955
Mosley, L., *Haile Selassie, the Conquering Lion*, 1964
—— *Duel for Kilimanjaro*, 1964
Müller, F. F., *Deutschland–Zanzibar–Ostafrika*, 1959
Mustafa, Sophie, *The Tanganyika Way*, 1961
Nyerere, J. K., *The Race Problem in East Africa*, 1951, unpublished
—— *Contra Capricorn*, 1956 (privately circulated)
—— 'We Cannot Afford to Fail', *Africa Special Report*, 1959
—— *Uhuru*, 1961
—— *African Socialism*, 1961
—— 'One Party Government', *Spearhead*, November 1961
—— 'The Challenge of Independence', *East Africa and Rhodesia*, December 7, 1961
Oldham, Dr J. H., *New Hope in Africa*, 1955
Oliver, R. A., *The Missionary Factor in East Africa*, 1952
—— *The Dawn of African History*, 1961
Padmore, G., *Africa, Britain's Third Empire*, 1949
—— *Pan-Africanism or Communism*, 1956
Patterson, J. H., *The Man-eaters of Tsavo and Other East African Adventures*, 1947
Perham, Margery, *Lugard, The Years of Adventure*, 1956
Peters, Dr Karl, *New Light on Dark Africa*, 1891
—— *Gründung von Deutsch Ostafrika*, 1906
Prince, T. von, *Gegen Araber und Wahehe*, 1914
Roman Catholic Bishops, *Unity and Freedom in the New Tanganyika*, 1960
Sayers, G. F., *The Handbook of Tanganyika*, 1930
Schnee, A. H. H., *Deutsch–Ostafrika im Weltkriege*, 1919
Skeffington, A., *Tanganyika in Transition*, Fabian Commonwealth Bureau, 1960

Stahl, K. M., *Tanganyika, Sail in the Wilderness*, 1961
—— *History of the Chagga People of Kilimanjaro* 1964
Tanganyika: Arusha-Moshi Lands Commission Report, 1947
—— *Some Comments on Mr Nyerere's Speech at the Fourth Committee of the United Nations*, 1957
Taylor, J. C., *The Political Development of Tanganyika*, 1963
Van der Post, Laurens, *Venture to the Interior*, 1952
Waller, H., *The Last Journals of David Livingstone in Central Africa*, 1874
Waugh, E., *Tourist in Africa*, 1960
Wood, A., *The Groundnut Affair*, 1950
Wood, Susan, *A Fly in Amber*, 1964

Index

A

Abedi, Sheik A., xix
Adenauer, K., 395
African National Congress, 308–9,
 347, 375, 380, 413, 415
Aga Khan, 68
Agriculture, 9, 35, 49, 80–1, 120, 142 ff
Aimer (German trader), 39–40
Amery, L. S., 72, 110
Anderson, F. J., 125
Arden-Clarke, Sir C., 265
Arnautoglu, G., 310
Attenborough, L. P. A., 255
Aziz, D., 186, 215, 222, 226

B

Bain, T., 144
Baker, J., 237, 287, 358, 361
Baldwin, S., 115
Bana Heri, 19–20
Barghash, Sultan, 15, 17
Baring, Sir E., 161–2
Barongo, E., 287, 304–6, 426
Bates, D., 107–8
Battershill, Sir W., 125, 132, 156, 159
Baxter, Dr E. J., 145
Bayldon, I., 243, 279, 346, 347, 375
Bell, R. M., 36
Bella, Ben, 417
Bennett, G., 323
Bennett, J., 237, 287
Bevin, Ernest, 125
Bibi Titi, 268–9, 271, 303, 381, 440
Bismarck, Otto von, 14, 16, 18, 50
Blumer, J., 88, 90, 91, 93, 197, 230,
 234, 427
Bokero, 36–8, 41
Bomani, P., early life, 232; member of
 Legco, 233, 236, 287, 299; and
 Trusteeship Council petition, 242,
 243, 245, 247; and first elections,
 305, 347; Minister of Agriculture,
 378; at Constitutional Conference
 (1961), 384; Minister of Finance,
 411; as source, 426; and Army
 Mutinies, 433, 438
Boyle, Sir E., 397–8
Briggs, J. H., 145

Brown, Roland, 384, 385
Bryceson, D. N. M., friend of Lady
 Chesham and Nyerere, 120, 265–6;
 member of Capricorn, 277; Assist-
 ant Minister, 299; associate of Tanu,
 345, 352–3, 356, 361; in Nyerere
 Ministry, 364, 377, 384
Burton, Sir R., 11
Bushiri-bin-Salim-el-Harthi, 17, 18,
 19
Byatt, Sir H. A., 67–72, 74, 78, 87–8,
 101

C

Callaghan, James, 396
Cameron, Sir D., governorship of, 75–
 84; and education, 85, 88, 91, 92,
 94, 100, 102, 103, 112; and Colonial
 Office, 105; and indirect rule, 106;
 and Great White Dominion, 109;
 and T.A.A., 184, 222; tributes to,
 284, 390, 421; and chiefs, 315
Capricorn, 167, 274–82
Caprivi, L. von, 21–2
Carmichael, D. D., 200
Carr-Saunders, Sir A., 291
Carter, P. A., 434
Cavendish-Bentinck, Sir F., 115
Chaburuma, Sultan, 24, 26, 34–6,
 42–3
Chamberlain, Neville, 115, 117
Charman, Violet, 99
Chesham, Lord, 120, 346
Chesham, Marion, Lady, xvii, xviii,
 32, 120, 426; associate of Tanu,
 346–7, 351–3, 383
Cheeseman, B., 428
Chiume, Kanyame, 225, 230
Chopra, I. C., 138, 243
Churchill, John, 428
Coates, Sir E., 154
Cohen, Sir A., 166–7, 265, 294, 297
Cole, J. S. R., 166, 327, 329–30, 378,
 384
Collins, Father W., 200, 218, 283
Cooper, E., 220
Cowan, Maureen, 99, 428
Cox, Richard, 412
Crabbe, John, 93–4, 427

445